Michael Tierney is a multi-‐ ... nd writer. He is a winner of th... ...or Journalism and the Lorenzo N... ...ce been named Feature Writer o... ...e prestigious British Press Awards and is a four-time winner at the Scottish Press Awards. He was a contributing editor to the *Celtic Opus*.

As a teenager he had the opportunity to become a professional footballer. Andy Dodds, an old football coach of the author's, still swears he was the best young player he has ever seen.

THE FIRST GAME WITH MY FATHER

Michael Tierney

BLACK SWAN

TRANSWORLD PUBLISHERS
61–63 Uxbridge Road, London W5 5SA
www.transworldbooks.co.uk

Transworld is part of the Penguin Random House group of companies
whose addresses can be found at global.penguinrandomhouse.com

First published in Great Britain in 2014 by Doubleday
an imprint of Transworld Publishers
Black Swan edition published 2015

A CIP catalogue record for this book
is available from the British Library.

ISBN
9780552779630

Typeset in Adobe Garamond by Falcon Oast Graphic Art Ltd.
Printed and bound by CPI Group (UK) Ltd, Croydon, CR0 4YY

Penguin Random House is committed to a sustainable
future for our business, our readers and our planet. This book is
made from Forest Stewardship Council® certified paper.

1 3 5 7 9 10 8 6 4 2

To my father and mother
And my brothers and sisters
My wife and children too

Chapter One

The Rifle

My father shot at the boys in the quarry who used to steal from our apple trees. They were crab apple trees and the fruit from them was small, hard and bitter but it was the principle of the thing, he'd say, while I stood at his arm peering out of the loft window. But he didn't shoot for sport. More than anything he was protecting us. We were war buddies in the loft, side by side. And we always would be.

It wasn't apples they were taking, he said, it was a liberty. There were some things you couldn't take from another man. The shots were just pellets from an air rifle and they'd only sting a little, he said, even if they did hit their target. Sometimes when my father was out, I searched for the rifle and fired it too. Loaded it up with pellets. Smoothed my hand over the wood stock. Cradled it against my shoulder. Peered down the scope. Pulled on the trigger blade.

You couldn't be a boy and *not* fire a rifle if it was lying around. I fired the rifle because I wanted to. That'd teach them all to stop jumping on us when I was over the quarry with Iain and the rest of my brothers and sisters. The quarry boys were always bigger and wilder and the pellets, I figured, evened things out a little.

I never told my father. But I knew he knew. He always did.

He put his big hands around the rifle and shot at them from the skylight. It was like a turret at the top of our house.

There were wild rabbits in the quarry and in our garden and birds all around but you couldn't shoot them. There were rules you had to follow. He said he could shoot a flea off my ear if I stood beside the gooseberry bush but I said, no thanks and he should save the pellets for the man who tried to steal the old motorbike that had been hidden in the quarry undergrowth weeks earlier. My father had a motorbike of his own, a black Norton Commando. Although the one in the quarry did not belong to him, he hated the idea that someone would steal something that precious.

There were also rules about stealing. An old piece of wood lying out the back of a crumbling building, he said, was fair game. That didn't count as stealing. It was salvaging and it saved a few pounds here and there.

My father said not to worry myself that he'd shot at the thieving quarry man too and we both collapsed with laughter in the loft. He shot at the man as a warning. Stay away from us and leave us all alone. We would be fine by ourselves.

We fired the rifle way before they built the new houses over the quarry, before the new neighbours moved in who looked out sternly from their windows when we played football and tig too boisterously and shouted too loudly behind the trees that separated them from us. My father didn't like the change and he said all that new money could go and chase itself. He let the bushes and the trees at the bottom of the garden grow bigger and bigger. It felt like we'd retreated to the woods.

Deep down my father didn't really mind the boys from the quarry because deep down he was one of them too. Just a boy from Maryhill who used to play along the empty canal. He shot at them because he didn't trust strangers and he didn't want anyone coming on to our land who wasn't welcome. It was our garden, but he always called it *our land*.

And anyway, they'd stolen the garden bench he'd made for us from the old wood he'd collected, and they'd stolen the bright-orange dinghy he'd got from my uncle who was a merchant seaman and which the girls used as a paddling pool in the summer. Right out the back garden they took it, over the quarry and into Milton, he said. They wandered away like pirates and minstrels in purple and gold robes, carrying their loot. They took it in the dead of night like they always did, but he watched them peering from behind the trees in the evening.

It took a while but eventually the boys from the quarry, with their cursing and their threats and the long metal poles and wooden sticks they dragged along the ground, remembered not to go past the house with the man with the rifle and the skylight. Mostly, he shot because he could. And he didn't want anyone telling him otherwise. Protect your territory, lads. Always. Don't rest. Otherwise the quarry boys will take the eyes out your sleeping head.

My father loved his family and his house and his garden and he loved us playing football in it too. He even loved the quarry and the railway track that ran nearby where we all pootled around and hid in tunnels though we weren't supposed to. And he never gave up anything lightly. You never should, he always said.

The loft was where he went when he needed to talk.

He would come up every other night, with his cheese and toast and cup of tea, and sit on the edge of the bed and talk.

He'd built the stairs to the loft too steep but he said he'd built them that way deliberately because it made it easier for us to get into heaven and we said, that's some excuse blaming God. Besides, he said, it was none of our business and if and when we could use a saw and a hammer and a nail then we would be welcome and entitled to an opinion, but not until then.

And he smiled and drew long on his Benson & Hedges, and then bit on his bottom lip.

Even though we were both still quite young, Iain and I knew that the loft was, in some mystical way, just like my father's head. It was cramped and filled with stuff that wasn't always needed and it didn't always make sense. We knew this because we slept in the loft and we saw him there all the time, chatting and telling stories about the past. Each time my father climbed those stairs we knew that he was trying to share with us a little of the sadness that he'd kept hidden in the foothills of his memory for years.

We were only kids. But we knew.

One night, before midnight, Iain woke up while I was reading. My father always wanted us to read. He always said that we needed to get into those books and that you could never get enough knowledge. Iain rubbed his eyes.

'What did Dad want?'

I shrugged. 'He was just talking about Ireland and Granda Tierney and the war and Uncle Peter who threw his old rifle in Maryhill canal. All that stuff, nothing much. Stuff about Celtic too.'

'Right . . .'

'And stuff about St John Ogilvie and how he was tortured in Glasgow. Stuff about his people. The bold men of Ireland and all that malarkey. Irish as Paddy's pig and all that. All Dad's stuff.'

Iain sat up in his bed, his pyjama top half open. I could tell he wanted to talk so I put down my book.

'OK, what is it?'

'Mike, have you ever shot Dad's air rifle?'

I made a face and looked at him. 'Maybe. Just a couple of times. I've shot at the trees from the skylight and into Mr Brownlee's garden. I've shot at some of old Mr Mac's apple trees. Why?'

'I just wondered. Have you ever shot a bird? Or a cat?'

'Don't be daft . . .'

'Would Dad go mad if he saw you?'

'Of course. But I didn't.'

He sighed and shook his head. 'I saw some dead birds out the back.'

'Wasn't me . . .'

'Have you shot the boys from the quarry?'

I shrugged again. Something lingered in his eyes. 'Maybe just at their legs.'

Iain lay back in his bed. 'Sorry for asking. I bet the quarry boys went mental! They shouldn't steal our stuff anyway.' He dissolved into laughter. 'I'd like to have a shot.' He cocked his thumb and forefinger and aimed an invisible bullet at me. 'Mum says we're just like Dad. She says we're our father's sons and I don't know what she means.'

'It means we do what he does and we think the way he thinks. Now get some sleep.'

I'd been sharing the loft with Iain for more than two years now, although it had taken much longer than that for us to get a room of our own. It wasn't easy trying to shoehorn nine children and my parents into four bedrooms. The loft was large, painted in light green and white, and we had a single bed each. We never asked for much but it made a change from all the years of sharing downstairs in the other rooms while my father was fixing the house up. 'It's magic,' Iain used to say, 'stretching out and being able to fart on your own legs.'

His voice was wistful. We laughed in triumph. I suppose it was.

My father had partitioned off a section of the loft with a plaster-board wall and a door and he kept his own stuff in there. His books and his fine selection of tools and the air rifle and photographs of my grandfather and of *Ireland's Eye* and old Elvis Presley records and Tommy Makem and the Clancy Brothers too and other stuff about Ireland and the books on Germany left by Mrs Horgan, the old lady who used to live here before us.

We were not to go in the door and we were not to be nosy. Never stick your nose in other people's business, he'd say. And don't let them know yours. Sometimes he wouldn't even say it. You just knew. He could look at you. Or you could walk into the house on a sunny afternoon and before you'd made it into the living room or the kitchen you just knew. He was good at that. Making people know things without even opening his mouth. We used to laugh about it. Sometimes he laughed too. He said it was his talent and it was better to be good at something than nothing.

And then he would rub his curly hair.

My mother went up to the loft too.

She kept it as clean as a Sunday chicken carcass. My mother never ran out of things to clean. As well as Iain and me there was Lorraine and Maureen, the twins, and also Fiona, Mark, Catherine, Vincent and Claire. My mother said that you just got on with it because that's what God gave you and there was no use complaining

11

about the amount of children you had or the amount of washing and ironing because it wasn't them that asked to be brought here.

Iain was two years younger than me. He could sing and do impressions. He was always acting the goat and, whenever we went visiting, we tried to make him do a show so as the adults wouldn't ask the rest of us. My father asked him to sing 'Crystal Chandeliers' by Charley Pride, one of his favourites, and Iain always obliged. Like an eedjit.

Iain still wasn't asleep.

'What was in that bag you had the other day?' he said.

'What bag?'

'You had a bag. There were bullets in it. *Real* ones. Like the ones soldiers use. I was only pretending to be asleep and I saw you. They were small and fat and golden-coloured.'

I put down my book. It was *The Call of the Wild*, by Jack London, and it was about a dog shipped off to the Klondike and it had to rediscover the instincts of its wild ancestors. All that malarkey. 'Bullets? Don't talk daft. You were definitely dreaming . . .'

'I saw you. They were in a box. It said *Colt .45s*.'

'Colt what? You must have been dreaming. Get to sleep.'

'It was like a giant matchbox.'

I shook my head and gave him a weary look. The box flashed in my head. 'You've been eating too many carrots. Makes your imagination run wild.' The bullets were for a Colt Automatic pistol. They were full metal-cased bullets from the Peters Cartridge Company, Cincinnati, USA. 'Night, night.'

'Maybe it *was* a dream,' he said, wondering. 'Night, Mike.'

'See you in the morning.'

The walls of the loft were filled with promises. A Celtic team poster and one of Roddy Frame from Aztec Camera and a girl from a jeans advert with *Charlie's Angels* hair and marshmallow lips, her fingers stuck against them. My father told us to take it down because what would our mother and sisters think with that silly girl staring back at them?

We had a poster of Charlie Nicholas too and an Irish tricolour flag pinned with tacks, side by side. We called him Charlie Nick, or the Cannonball Kid, and he was the best Celtic player since King Kenny. It didn't take my father to tell me that Charlie was brilliant. He'd just scored something like fifty goals in all competitions, before winning the Scottish Footballer of the Year and Young Player of the Year awards. My father was always calling him the Cannonball *Quid*. 'Of course I meant *Kid*,' he said, when the mistake was pointed out. 'Away and don't be so daft.'

Perhaps he was right all along. Just like Kenny before him Charlie Nick and his mullet disappeared off to England, in a bemusing transfer to Arsenal, lured by the bright lights of the big city. 'That's what that English mob do,' said my father. 'They just *take*. Silver and gold gets everything.'

We had an ancient Liverpool FC poster as well after Kenny went there. They were supposed to be our English team, although I wasn't really sure I *wanted* an English team, because there was no team quite like Celtic and my father had never thought much of anything English, especially that Cromwell fella, and Maggie Thatcher, never mind any of their football clubs.

We woke each day to the sound of life.

Nine children and two parents made a lot of noise and twice as much on Saturdays.

I could hear my mother from early morning bustling around in the kitchen, beginning another round of eleven breakfasts, lunches and dinners that would be made without any apparent effort, but only because she made it seem simple. I would look at her in the kitchen, her beautiful Barra cheekbones rising as she talked, and wonder how she could do it all without stopping for air or even tea. My mother was sainted all her days. First up, last to eat. We were convinced she must enjoy it although we never thought to ask.

My father would be hammering something or pulling nails or fixing a pipe or running a malicious cable to safety. He helped her without complaint. When my mother felt like talking over a cup of tea she said that there wasn't a man born who did more for his children and her than my father. My mother was the quick-tempered one, she said, and she got that from Barra too. If my father heard he pretended not to. Can you get me a wee bit of lunch now, Cathie? Maybe a bit of ham? He looked at her like a shy-eyed deer.

There was always noise. There was never *not* noise. It sounded like someone had lifted the roof off a carnival tent. But there was never much shouting unless my father said something about Ireland and my mother tutted and shook her head and said, not in front of the children and would you stop talking all that nonsense and there are two sides to every story.

Sometimes, at night, I'd sit on the loft stairs and listen for an argument. It was only ever about money. Or the children getting older, and one day leaving home.

My mother cooked and washed till her hands turned soft and red, and my father hammered till his turned purple from the squeezing and then he'd put down his tool bag and say, OK, who wants an ice-cream, and he'd make up ice-cream wafers and we'd watch films like *Chitty Chitty Bang Bang* on video while my father said he was going to build a boat from our old VW van in the drive and we all believed him. My mother just laughed and said he was daft and away with the fairies. And he said, why are you shaking your head, do you not believe me? She said she would believe it when she saw it. He laughed and said my mother was worse than Doubting Thomas.

My father would build the boat and they would sail away together, he said, just you wait. It would be a grand boat. Just you wait. You're an awful woman for doubting.

One time, a friend of mine said we were rich and I must have laughed for days and days and then eventually he hit me on the arm and said, OK, OK, the joke's over. It was because my father had installed an internal phone system in the house that ran from the loft to the kitchen and we could call my mother directly, and my mother could ring us too. We would all put on posh voices and say things like, 'Hello Mother, we're in the north wing. May we have some supper sent up? Thank you.'

And my mother would reply, 'Get down here and get it your-selves, you wee scallywags. I'm run off my blinking feet with the lot of you. I'm going round the bend.' But her voice was laughing while she talked.

We didn't know where he got the phones from and it was none of our business, and anyway they were older than the ark so no one would miss them unless they had a time machine. The line crackled a little. It was only the spies listening in, he said. My mother rang the phone for get-up time for school or to tell us to come down for dinner and to remember to bring the dirty washing too. We ordered tea and toast every night and our life in the loft couldn't have been more perfect supposing my granny had hand-knitted it.

Most of the rooms in the house had slowly been repaired and decorated, although it had taken my father years and, he said, all the sanity he possessed on God's green earth. Sometimes, when he sat down, his feet soaking in hot water and salt in a plastic basin, he said he quite fancied spending a few days in prison just for some peace and quiet and, although the younger ones laughed, I knew he wasn't joking. He just wanted to sit down. He needed a rest. He just wanted to think about it all. And then he would just go back to his work.

The front room was the last one that needed fixing. It still had the whitewash on the windows. It still had a hole in the ceiling that I remembered from when I'd first seen the house, all covered in snow.

One day it would become the lounge, where my mother would sit around the large open coal fire and drink black tea or coffee and eat cakes with her sisters when they visited and relaxed all cross-legged and gossipy on the new couch that she'd save up for. They'd soon get rid of the rotten old brown one that my father had reupholstered himself with cheap material that he said looked like curtains from Long Kesh where Bobby Sands and Francis Hughes and Raymond McCreesh and all the rest had died on hunger strike in Ireland.

My father said it was all Margaret Thatcher's fault and not a word of a lie and that she was as brutal as a woman could get and worse than any of the men. And that was that, he said. And don't even mention that woman's name in the house again.

It was 1983.

A lovely, bug-infested spring night. We stayed out late in the garden playing football. And the light didn't fade till after ten o'clock so we all sat and *talked* about football and my father pretended to know a lot more than he did and that suited us fine.

Celtic were runners-up to Dundee United in the League. He stretched his legs and took a sip of Tennent's and said it was OK because United were originally called Dundee Hibernian, by the way, and they were just like Celtic, born to fill the needs of the Irish immigrant community in Dundee in the early 1900s.

'No shame in being beaten by a good Irish side,' he said. And then he whistled a sad Irish tune.

'Come on, Dad. They're about as Irish as the Loch Ness monster.'

He sat upright in his chair. 'Better than that other mob beating us . . .' He did a thing with his head. A twitch.

'Yeah, they're about as Irish as . . .'

He looked at me out of the side of his eyes. 'Quiet, you daftie. You're giving me a headache.'

After a long time sleeping on a fold-down couch my parents eventually got a bedroom of their own, and dispatched the rest of the children around the house. The rooms were allocated according to hierarchy of age and the ability to sleep, or not, downstairs in the room that may or may not have been haunted by the ghostly figure of an old, decrepit lady. We all believed it was. Claire, who was the youngest, claimed she saw her most days and she called her Mrs Appleby. And she pointed to the corner of the hall where she said she sat on a rocking chair and her pointing sent shivers up all our necks. We asked my father to tell her to stop because she was giving us all the heebie-jeebies.

The ghosts were everywhere, she said. You just needed to know where to look.

Apart from football in the garden the loft was where I spent most of my time, listening to records on the dilapidated radiogram which looked like a long pine coffin that had once ferried the dead from another century. I didn't really have a record collection as such. The records I played were simply an extension of my father's. Some Irish rebel songs, some Irish ballads, some country and western, and a few Elvis. My uncle Gerard on my mother's side, only a few years older than me, loaned me some Pink Floyd, The Only Ones and The Clash, and saved me from complete melancholy and a life lamenting a sweetheart in Texas or a forsaken Irish bog.

My father didn't really see the point of music unless it spoke of a man who was about to be hanged for the crime of feeding his children or losing his love beside a Galway stream. He tapped his feet to holy woodcarvers and loved Johnny Cash too and he sometimes played him until the brown ribbon got caught in the spool of the tape recorder. When Cash's 'Don't Take Your Guns to Town' was on my father sang every word with a smile so sad that it might break you in two.

But he liked to talk about Celtic. He sat on the edge of the bed. He talked about them like he was saying a prayer.

Celtic and Ireland were the same thing. If you said one it was the same as thinking the other. Everyone knew that. We were Celtic to the core, he said. Celtic and Ireland together, like a pot of old stew and two red carrots. We had Ireland and Celtic in our bones. Celtic was in our DNA, he said, though I didn't really know what that was so he added that it meant we had bits of Celtic growing inside us, like green, white and gold worms. And it was inside him too and his father, and his before that, and it would be inside our sons and daughters as well.

Celtic was a club born to help the poor, he said. It was a club founded in Glasgow, in 1888, by a right holy Irish fella named Brother Walfrid, who was a Marist priest into the bargain and that was surely no bad thing. And it was mainly for the Irish migrants who'd come to escape the poverty and hunger, because there was nothing to eat over there except grass. Brother Walfrid wanted the club to be a focal point for the Irish community. But it wasn't simply a Catholic club. He told us that over and over. Anyone and everyone was welcome. 'Not the same as the other mob,' he said, and he jabbed his thumb and we knew who he was talking about.

We were connected to Ireland by birth, he said. We were connected to Celtic, by Ireland. We had all met Brother Walfrid, he said. All over Glasgow. Poor and destitute and looking for fag ends in bins and eating old chips from discarded newspapers as the rain cut them in two. 'If you gave the fella a couple of bob, well, that was why Celtic started,' he said. 'Looking after the poor.'

His people had been suffering in Glasgow for years and years, he said. In Glasgow middens filled with the poor Irish who lived, huddled together, like dead mackerel. To the Scots, the Irish were strangers and cheap labour, and they foretold death in teacups. But they were no such things, he said. If you repeated an untruth often enough it became a fact. They were just families looking to live, he said. Just like us. So that was part of who we were. And he would stay standing all day to say it, like a man playing a reel or casting for Atlantic bass.

'These are undeniable truths,' he said.

But we were young and we didn't even know what the truth was, never mind an *undeniable* one, because when he asked us who'd taken the sweets from the tin in the cupboard we all just pointed the big finger at the wee fella or the wee girl. But we listened. I listened all the time, like it was a strange new, jug-eared hobby.

I listened to the stories that he told. Some half-baked, some made up, others embellished, some loaded with the truth, some burdened by it and some having no resemblance to the truth at all. I listened to stories that sounded like they were authored by fairies and I knew that they just had to be true and I listened to other stories that were so utterly believable that, of course, they must have been made up.

Rangers, he said, were our rivals in the city. Over there, in Ibrox.

They were the Establishment team and if there was one thing he didn't have too much time for it was the Establishment, with the doffing of caps to the big bosses in their bowler hats in the shipyards and in the factories and anywhere a man had a floor to work on.

Rangers were the red, white and blue, the colours of the Union and the Crown. They were the Church of Scotland and 'God Save the Queen' and the funny-handshake mob.

He said they squashed your knuckles with their secret wee messages, like Morse code, trying to find out if you were one of them. He said when Rangers won it was down to the Masonic conspiracy, which began with some Egyptian fella called Master General Kleber, or some such wizard, who was up to his neck in the Memphis Rite and the all-seeing eye on the US dollar bill. He said Rangers had an unfair advantage, what with the nod-and-a-wink stuff and the rolled-up-trouser-leg brigade and the tea-towel routine and the knuckle crunching, and the world didn't make sense to him because of that. That Kitchener fella from the war was in on the nudge too.

He just never really understood why any workingman could support Rangers. It baffled him. And it baffled him even more that Rangers didn't like to sign Catholics.

For most of his life, and much of mine, Rangers refused to sign people like us. In the early days one or two had sneaked in, he said, but they were the exception rather than the rule. It meant they thought we were inferior people, he said. And he jabbed at his chest. Us. *Inferior?* No matter which angle he looked at it from he could never get his head around it. He could forgive most things, he said, but that was something different altogether.

'The simple fact of the matter is this, Michael,' he said. 'They think we're second-class citizens. Me, your mother, your brothers and sisters. Your uncles, your granny and your aunts too. All of us. They'd ship us all off to an African Bantustan. They think they are *better* than us. And they've been getting away with it for years. Well, we're not. And they won't.'

He could be angry about it, but he could be decent enough about it when he had to be.

I remember my father once picked up a drunk Rangers fan at the top of our street. The man was so drunk he couldn't see a hole in a ladder. My father went through his pockets and found an address and he carried him across the quarry to Milton while the man sang 'The Sash My Father Wore' and my father started reciting ten Hail Marys for the man's benefit, but couldn't finish them all because of the laughter and the man cursing him, and Celtic, backwards and sideways.

My mother would say, stop all the nonsense about Celtic and Rangers, John, we've more to worry about than that.

Although my father always talked about Celtic I knew that he didn't really know that much about the game. The actual *football stuff*. He had other things to worry about than team sheets. He'd pick up some comments from his friend George or Frank in Quins, the local Celtic pub down the road, or he'd hear something on the radio or read about so-and-so in the newspapers and how well he was playing. George handed over his Celtic match programmes for Iain and me and we devoured them like hot bread.

I didn't doubt that my father wanted to go to matches, but money was always tight. Life was tight. And the honest truth was that he didn't believe there was much wisdom in wealth. Money didn't really count, he said. To chase it was worse than a sin. And besides, it didn't grow on the trees in the garden. And if it did the boys from the quarry would probably get there first.

My mother washed and ironed our clothes until every last drop of wear had been wrung out of them. The petrol gauge on the van always hovered just above empty.

We understood it. I think we all did.

Instead, my father contented himself with listening to the radio every Saturday as he worked around the house or in the garden. It was only ever a Celtic match or *Raidió Teilifís Éireann*, Ireland's national public service broadcaster. 'I can only listen to my own people,' he said, when I shot him a suspicious glance and appeal to change the station.

He banged the hammer down on the nail.

Even as he hammered he would tell us stories about Ireland and his people. And the few places he'd been and the places there he wanted to go. When he mumbled you knew he was talking about the other lot. They were beyond the pale, he said. When I was younger I used to think they lived in castles with big, black hinges on their doors, surrounded by moats and galloping black-hooded horses. Their lives, I thought, were as dark as coal. I never imagined they lived their lives in colour like the rest of us.

If my father ever heard over the radio the thunderous tones of the Reverend Ian Paisley, the fiery and outspoken critic of all things Catholic, Republican and Irish, he quietly raged. 'The worst person that God ever put breath into,' he said. 'Probably worse than Maggie.' He shook his head from side to side before hammering the nails into the wood just that little bit deeper.

He said that Tierney was an anglicized form of the Irish Ò Tiarnaigh and meant lord or chief. He said something about Tierney of Clones, a flint-eyed sixth-century saint (my father believed in the power of all the saints), who was baptized by St Conleth of Kildare with St Brigid as his godmother. The Tierney of Clones fella was captured by pirates and taken to a harsh old English king who placed him in the monastery of Rosnat, in the depths of England. Later, he would return to Ireland and the land of swords and crosses and become Bishop of Clogher, in County Down.

I loved his stories. He loved them more. I didn't care if they were true or not. I just loved to hear them told. While his face bore a profile you might find stamped on an ancient Italian bronze coin, his heart was peaty and Irish. He loved Ireland as sure as if he'd been born there. And in his head, maybe he had.

I remember, months later, once the dark nights had arrived, him coming up the stairs, walking slowly, taking his time. Quiet and deliberate. The loft was still.

'Hello, boys. Still awake? Course you are.' He stood for a moment, balancing his toast and tea.

'Hi, Dad,' said Iain.

'Hey, Dad,' I said. 'How's things?'

'Good. Brand new.'

I noticed that his face looked vigorous. There was something shining behind his eyes, and it wasn't the drink. He leaned on the snooker table he'd made for us, with the dip in the corner. A ball rolled into a pocket. Then he sat on the edge of Iain's bed.

'McGarvey's been pretty good this season, eh?' he said, and chomped on his cheese and toast. A piece of melted cheese rested on his chin.

'Yeah, not bad, Dad,' said Iain.

'He's been OK,' I said. My father shot me a look.

'I like big Bonner. Must be six foot five or something. Irish too.'

I could smell the oil on his jeans from earlier when he'd been changing the brake pads on the VW. The oil filled the loft.

'Who was in the pub? Michael? Frank and George?'

I liked my father's friends.

They all talked about the same things together. About Celtic. About Rangers too. About politics, religion and Ireland. They talked about the Catholic Church and the Masons who wouldn't let them into their secret society. Not that they were bothered. They would rather shove their grandmothers down a tenement close than hook up with that lot just to get a job. They talked about the Orangemen too, who were planning to march from Kenmure Church, which stood at the top of our street.

I liked the building, with its old-fashioned stonework and Welsh slates on the roof. The people came into our street and parked their cars and they also walked up the pavement with their noses a wee bit turned up and I liked watching them from the window, the men in their pressed suits and the stiff-backed ladies carrying their Bibles in white-gloved hands. The women looked like Harriet Oleson from *Little House on the Prairie*. The men looked serious and severe as if someone had stolen their joy.

My father's friends talked about Michael Collins, the Irish revolutionary leader, and James Connolly, the Edinburgh-born Irish Republican leader who was done in by the British firing-squad mob because of his role in the 1916 Easter Rising. They talked about them so often it was like they were performing community service. They talked about Wolfe Tone, a Protestant leader of the United

Irishmen, who was more than acceptable to them because he was, they said, a fine leader of Irish Republicanism.

Half the time I didn't know what they were talking about. But men needed to talk and sometimes it didn't matter what they said.

My father smiled and answered my question. 'I don't recognize the validity of this court!'

I smiled too. 'I don't recognize the validity of you keeping me awake at night!'

'Very funny . . . How's school?'

'Pretty good.'

'They teach you anything in there that's worth knowing?'

'I don't know. I suppose so.'

He paused. 'I used to like Latin and French. I loved it. I used to like *learning*.'

I raised an eyebrow. 'Granny told me you could have gone to St Mungo's Academy . . . the one founded by the Marists. She said all the children came out as doctors or lawyers. She said you had all the highest grades but you didn't want to go, because you wanted to bring money into the house after my grandfather died.'

'Ach, I don't know what Granny told you . . . that's all in the past.'

He sighed and took another bite. His mouth was full. He ran his hands through his Brylcreemed hair and told me more of his stories. Someone had been hanged from a tree, he said, when someone else was just a girl. There was another man too. Something about *Óglaigh na hÉireann*. The Gaelic, he whispered, for you-know-who? Over by, he said. Over the water. He mentioned Cork and Tyrone and Tom Barry's Flying Column. He talked about Mary Quinn – Mary Mahoney before she got married – who was my great-grandmother from Cork and as fierce as a mother bird. He mentioned a boat.

He put his finger to his nose. Keep it shtum.

Iain listened too.

That's what I recall. His narrative was sketchy. Time had erased some bits and added others. Gaps were being filled. The danger lay there also. Did I remember it all correctly? Did my father himself remember it correctly? And if we didn't, at what point did the not remembering become real?

Although he was born nearby in Maryhill over the back and up the road and round the corner from here, in his head and his heart he was from Ireland. But plenty of Irish lived where he grew up. You just had to look closely at the faces of the men and women or listen to the same-sounding poetic surnames. They ate bacon and cabbage on a Thursday too, he said. It was as good a dish as any. It sounded like an Act of Contrition but there was nothing to be sorry for. He *might* say sorry if you beat him with a shovel, though it would have to be a big shovel, but no one ever tried.

'It's got nothing to do with where you're born, Michael,' he would say. 'It's got everything to do with how you feel and who you are and where your people are from.' Mary Quinn used to say it to us too when we were younger, sitting in the soft chair at Granny Tierney's house and sipping tea. 'Just because a cat has kittens in an oven, doesn't mean you call them biscuits . . .'

It was a simple quirk of history, said my father, and of politics and the lottery of geography that had brought him here. He would sail to Ireland in his new-built boat tomorrow.

My father stared at the wall. He always had firm opinions and I admired him for that. He always had formidable hands too. But he was getting tired.

I looked at Iain and changed the subject.

'What were you saying about Celtic, Dad?'

He cleared the frog in his throat. My father believed utterly that it was not about how often you went to watch Celtic, it was about what you brought when you did. His lack of match attendance never perturbed him. In his head he was a supporter, for sure, visiting every ground in Scotland where Celtic played. He paid the entrance fee when he listened to the radio and watched Saturday-night or Sunday-afternoon highlights on *Scotsport* or *Sportscene*. It wasn't a football team he supported, he said.

It was a community and a way of life.

Iain and I talked about Celtic all the time. We could recite the

24

names of all the first-team players going back any number of seasons.

I could wire a plug at ten, put up a halfway-decent shelf at eleven, mix cement at twelve, fix a bicycle at thirteen and wallpaper a bedroom the following year. I could shoot at the quarry boys and never get caught. I loved the sound of an Irish fiddle and I knew the difference between Michael Collins and Éamon de Valera. But at fifteen years old I had never been to a Celtic match.

The words spilled out of his mouth.

'Do you fancy going along, boys?' he said, biting into another slice of toast. I knew he was smiling. 'George got a couple of tickets.'

Iain looked at me. His eyes were as big as prunes. For a few seconds I went quiet. My father mentioned the UEFA Cup, though it sounded like an afterthought. The UEFA Cup? It suited him when he smiled. You could see how handsome he was and his shyness was erased.

'Night, boys,' he said, and his voice trailed away down the loft stairs. 'See you in the morning.'

My head began to buzz.

I lay awake and pictured the lights shining across the pitch and the stadium at night and the long shadows and the noise that would crackle like thunder.

A few days later he was sitting in the television room singing softly. He was a good singer, like his father, they used to say. His father's family were all good singers. But sometimes the songs sounded like angry lullabies. They were for the land that he was stolen from. The music was supposed to put him at ease.

He sang about leaving Ireland, about how great Ireland was, about crossing the Atlantic to America, and about returning from America. He sang about patriots and flags and loss and hunger and Trevelyan's corn and how Michael was taken far, far away. And in another he sang about how beautiful her eyes were, and how they shone like diamonds.

25

He sipped his tea and thanked my mother for it. She smiled with the same diamond eyes of the lady in his song. My mother told him to enjoy the match and to look after the boys and make sure we were warm and not to let us hear any bad language. 'Of course, Cathie,' he said, with one leg crossed over the other and nodding his head and grinning, and then he pretended to pull a face when she wasn't looking.

'I saw you,' she said, and looked at us. 'If the wind blows, your face will stay like that.'

'Sorry, Cathie.'

They were flirting together.

I loved to hear him say *Cathie*.

It always reminded me that they had been young once and that they had once lived in that mythical land before parenthood where they had first names and lives of their own. When they stood on street corners in the town waiting for the other to arrive off the bus, their stomachs nervous with excitement. When they kissed each other in the rain and went to the pictures or to a café because that was all they ever did.

'And don't be singing any of *those* songs, John,' said my mother. 'You know the ones.' She raised her eyebrows.

He knew the ones. 'It's fine, Cathie.'

George was waiting outside.

My father got up and kissed my mother softly on the cheek and looked around to see if anyone had noticed and we had and the younger ones giggled. 'Best behaviour for your mum, children. OK? Come on, boys.'

Footsteps across the ground. My father shook hard George's hand. They were like two men in a fifties gangster movie. Two big-shouldered men going about their business. They shared a quiet few words and then my father laughed and nodded.

'How's it going, boys?' said George.

His voice boomed. He spoke loudly and fast. He was as Glasgow as the long, twisting river running through the city. George drove a taxi and worked at the Brothers Bar in Possil. My father always said

26

it was a tough bar and that a man stood at the door and asked you if you had a knife before you went in and if you said no then he would offer you one. He always laughed at that. They didn't get their noses in there dooking for apples either, he would say. My father drank there too. George said my father always held his own no matter what the company.

'I'm good,' I said to George in reply. I tried to sound as if going to the match was no big deal. But it was. My heart was turning over.

'Magic,' said Iain.

The van took us along Kirkintilloch Road, through Springburn and past the high flats that looked like sentries on patrol, where someone had been killed not long before. My father told us that Springburn and the areas around it were called the Rome of the North and that the surrounding hills were the only other place in Europe where there were seven of them, like in the Italian capital. He was always saying things like this. Stuff that no one else knew.

'There's Stobhill,' he said, 'round the corner from us, where the hospital is. Then there's Balgrayhill, Keppochhill, Petershill, Sighthill and Springburnhill. But what's the last one? Boys? George?'

'Ach, I can't remember, John. How do you know all that stuff?'

'Barnhill. They kept a poorhouse there. The paupers had to break rocks. Can you imagine that, boys? And bundle firewood too. Whole place was filled with the Irish, you know.'

George looked at my father.

'Terrible, John. Terrible. Liberties. They took liberties.'

My father talked while he drove.

'When the Romans came here hundreds of years ago,' he said, 'they built the Antonine Wall. It was the most northwesterly Roman outpost. They took men from Springburn, conscripted them into fighting for the Romans along the German frontiers. Flippin' murder stuff that, lads. Same as the Irish. The English took them to Australia. Off to Botany Bay for stealing a sheep or a scone.'

The van shuttled down the High Street, coughing and spluttering, and we could see the crowds gathering, moving towards Celtic Park only a few miles away. The gears crunched but we reached the

Trongate before heading along London Road. Iain sniffed the air and the smell of the chips that wafted in from the road and the mobile vans that sold burgers and sausages and hot dogs. It was a savage good smell, we all agreed.

'Not too long now,' said Iain, leaning over the passenger seat to get a better look outside.

'Place is mobbed,' said George. 'Just goes to show you, John. Even when we're two–nil down the fans will still come out. Best fans in the world, John, eh?'

He nodded. 'Aye.'

'Boys, you think we can win?'

'Yes,' said Iain. 'Easy. Skoosh it. We'll win three–nothing.'

'I think we'll win. But we need to watch out for the away goal.'

'We will that, son.'

A cold dark of winter had settled over Glasgow. The city looked big and sharp, with needles coming out of cathedrals and churches and halls. We could see crosses against the purple and black sky, moving slowly like the spars of a Viking ship off to pillage and ruin an island. It was cold enough for snow. Iain had his neck wrapped tightly in his scarf. I carried mine. It was old and tatty. My father had brought me it home one day when I was much younger. I sat in the living room and I told my mother I would be fine and that I could sew all the patches on myself. And I did. And they're still there now.

'Got the tickets OK, Dad?'

He tapped his back pocket. 'Safe and sound, Michael. Safe and sound.'

Celtic Park smelled of cheap tobacco and stale lager and the trapped air of something burning. The faces of men and boys were just like he had promised. Just like ours. The colour of wet cement.

Some men stumbled and fell in different directions, already filled to the brim with Tennent's lager and Guinness; they slipped away like steamed skin dropping off fish. Raincoat drunks, alcohol thickening their language, alongside leather-jacketed men who had just finished their day shift and boys running after their fathers as if escaping from a bad dream. Someone bumped heavily into my

28

father and he gave the man a stern look. It was a look that could turn an iron jaw into glass.

We all moved on. I looked at my father. He seemed more excited than me. He was with his people, and there were 39,000 of them tonight all warming up their lungs before the match.

Turnstiles up ahead.

George rubbed his hands together. 'Busy night, John, eh?' he said, and they talked together with their hands and their mouths, but we couldn't hear anything amid the screams and shouts of the jostling crowd. George moved towards the turnstiles on our left. A man beside us swore loudly and my father said to him to keep it down as there's boys here.

Swearing was something my father never did. Or, if he did, none of us had ever heard him. 'For flip's sake' was the worst of his language. Or 'that flippin' eedjit'. But we always knew what he meant.

He fished around for some change in his pocket and bought a match programme. It had green and white hoops across it. *UEFA Cup Second Round, Second Leg. Celtic versus Sporting Lisbon. Wednesday, 2nd November 1983. Kick-off 7.30 p.m.*

Iain read it as he walked. The Portuguese were favourites because they were already 2–0 up from the first leg. The programme cost forty pence, nearly the price of a pint of beer. The man at the turn-stiles looked stern. He'd seen a million faces before and there was no longer anything in his job to excite him. Someone said, 'Christ, he's got a face like a box of smashed crabs.' I laughed. So did my father. We waited for George to come through. He was talking to another man he knew from the Brothers.

'Boys, the first turnstiles were installed here in 1895,' said my father. 'You imagine that? That was wee Granny Quinn's time. Long time ago, eh? The first turf was brought here from Donegal. Laid by a fella called Davitt. His people were from Mayo.'

'Right, Dad. We believe you.'

He laughed. 'Not interested in your own history now, Michael? Ah, well. You'll be telling me you're a Tory next.'

'Very funny . . .'

George was beside us now. He jerked his head sideways. 'That fella might have a bit of work for you, John. I'll let you know at the weekend.'

My father nodded but said nothing. He didn't like being beholden to anyone. Besides you needed a birth certificate to get a decent job, he would say to me. 'And it shouldn't have *RC* written across it.'

The noise was unlike anything I'd ever heard before, as if a latched cage had been opened and something monstrous had been let out. There were scarves in the air and there were flags held aloft. Flags of Ireland. Flags of his people. The sky was streaked by delicate clouds. But the cold was coming. We could feel it. I'd waited a long time for this. I'd waited a long time just to see my father's face. I knew he was worried about the cost. My mother reassured him it would be fine. And anyway, she said, if they could put a man on the moon he could find a few extra pounds somewhere on earth.

Maybe I would work with my father. Maybe I would become an electrician too. And we could bring home money for my mother like he did for his when he was also a boy.

'Magic, this,' shouted Iain, above the din. I nodded. 'Dad's loving it.'

The Celtic players appeared. They were wearing their new lime-green strip. Sporting Lisbon were in their green and white hoops. *Celtic's colours!* Iain looked confused. I was too.

'They're wearing *our* hoops,' said Iain.

'There's Francis,' said George, pointing at striker Frank McGarvey. George knew him off the pitch. He called him Francis, the same name as my father's older brother who lived in England. We all called him Frank, as if we knew him too.

I had been over at Frank's house with my father and George a year earlier. I don't know why we were there but I remember Frank was cutting a piece of wood in his living room. He was a joiner by trade and my father said later that you could tell because of the way he worked the wood. Long, neat and driving thrusts with all the sawdust falling easily out of the cut. The saw went quickly through the wood. 'He used the full length of the saw,' said my father, in his serious voice. 'Not just the middle teeth like most folk. That's how the blade goes blunt. You don't need to go fast.' He mentioned nothing about Frank's football skills.

The shouts of the fans came swirling around the ground as they sang 'You'll Never Walk Alone' and we joined in with our scarves waving above our heads.

'Christ, John,' said George, when he saw Tommy Burns galloping through the midfield, as if bandits were chasing him. 'Tommy's flying.'

A wee man shouted out, 'He's got mair moves than a monkey on ten foot of grapevine!' Laughter all around.

Celtic attacked from the beginning. Tommy Burns twisted and Tommy Burns turned. That's what they sang. My father liked Tommy because he was religious and he believed in Our Lady and the intercession of all the saints. I liked him because he was a number ten, like me.

The red-headed midfield maestro, with his neatly parted hair, scored after only seventeen minutes. But I missed it going in because I was looking up at the sky and listening to all the noise around me. I knew he'd scored because the whole ground erupted and my father jumped, along with George, and then he lifted Iain up and he smiled and shouted, 'You beauty. You wee cracker.'

I could see Burns blessing himself as he ran to the fans.

The man beside me blessed himself too and a woman with a patterned Celtic sweater did a wee jig and she looked like one of the sisters from Fran and Anna in their tartan miniskirts. 'Come on the Celts,' she shouted, and she waved a fist, and you could feel her love for the team running through her and into the night air, filtering through the raw geography of this part of the city.

Two—one on aggregate. It was impossible not to be entranced by my father as he shouted at the players, and then talked to George for guidance and then shouted again. But we didn't let on when he got a few of the players' names wrong. You shouldn't really judge a man for that, unless you know his story.

Celtic scored another two just before half-time.

Davie Provan crossed and it reached Tam McAdam, who caught it on his chest as easily as if it had been with his hands, before battering it home from six yards. The goalkeeper flapped like he was waving a damp rag. 'He's buried it,' shouted my father. 'Yes! Buried. Right foot. Cracker, boys.' In the second minute of injury time Brian McClair hopped and skipped a stunning solo. Burns, the architect, fed him before McClair kept on going, racing to goal, like a man possessed, racing to local immortality. The stadium bounced on its foundations.

A man took a swig of drink from a silver flask. Then he winked at me. The first half was still not over. Three-two on aggregate.

'For Pete's sake,' said my father. 'We're ahead now, George. Can you believe it?' He rubbed Iain's head.

'Looking good, John,' said George. 'Give the boys their due. Doing well. Burns is electric the night.'

We all jumped up and down. My father lost his mince pie in the tumult. 'Flip's sake,' he shouted, but there was laughter in his voice too. Bits of mince, like an old man's precious few teeth, fell to the ground. I looked down. Shoes were covered in gobs of saliva as men and boys talked and moved. Cigarette butts and discarded matches and packets of crisps and plastic cups of tea littered the ground. I looked to my right and I could see the face of a girl in the crowd who looked like a pretty girl from school. She saw me and then looked away. Maybe it was someone else. She was smiling too.

Iain looked petrified and happy at the same time. He was scared he might get lost in the crowd. I held on to his jacket. He could be out on the Campsie moors and no one would find him. But he wasn't. He was here with our father and me. And what a thing that was.

Half-time arrived.

Big men pushed their way to the toilet, unzipping their flies as they went, and our father put his arms out to protect us. He held his shoulders wide, as if he was sheltering a sidearm. When he saw himself in the mirror each day he must have known that he was capable. It must have been a good feeling.

'OK, boys?' he said.

'Yes, Dad,' said Iain. 'Totally brilliant.'

No matter how hard it was to find work he would be fine tomorrow if the match just kept going like this. And he would finish the house for my mother and she could sit with her legs crossed in the lounge eating cakes with her sisters.

His heart was beating, his heart was singing.

My father said we were watching history.

And history was important because if you didn't have history you didn't really belong to anywhere. You were just a boat drifting against the tide. You needed to know where you'd come from in order to know where you were going.

Celtic kicked off for the second half. One goal to Sporting would change everything and 39,000 men and women and children all held their collective breath. The jaw in my father's face kept moving, willing and shouting the team on as a spot of grease rolled down his chin. Katzirz, Sporting's Hungarian goalkeeper, looked like a drunk man chasing a pigeon. It was slow hands against quick feet.

Celtic attacked again. The alarm in the Sporting defence was palpable. They were slowly sinking into the earth. They were surrounded.

McGrain, MacLeod, McGarvey. Then back to MacLeod. He had a part in it and he would finish it, ramming the ball past the keeper while the stadium erupted. 'You beauty,' shouted my father, pulling a fist from his pocket and punching the air. 'Yes, you beauty!' I hugged Iain and then George and then my father. Thirteen minutes into the second half. Everyone looked at their watch. Could Celtic really do it now, we wondered? My father patted my back and squeezed my arm.

'Have we won yet?' asked Iain. The innocent concern in his singing voice.

'Nearly. Nearly.'

The lights of the stadium seemed to glow brighter. The players, separate from the rest of us, looked fearless and happy and relaxed. My father looked relaxed now too. Sharing the glow of new things.

He laughed as he joined in with the fans singing, 'Here we go, here we go, here we go . . .'

Then it was Burns, doing all the work again, to McGarvey . . .

Frank ran to the fans with both hands in the air and he screamed. You couldn't hear him but you could see him. Katzirz lay exposed like the bloody guts of a fish on the ground, a prostrate monument to the death of his team. The last two goals in two minutes tied the match up for Celtic. 'Heaven, John,' shouted George. 'We're in bloody heaven!' He rubbed his hands together. 'Well done, Francis. Five–two, John. We're through.'

My father was forty years old.

His eyes were anchored to the pitch. He was smiling. We all smiled together, in the joyful brutality of the football arena. But I knew that he was already thinking of other things. He was thinking about work. And the house. And my mother. And his mother. And my grandfather. And how much petrol cost and how much brake pads cost and what was the price of a new exhaust and the real cost of the match programme that he'd just bought.

And he thought about nine children. And how he would get them through it all.

We came out of the stadium to the sound of singing. 'Hurry up, boys,' he said, and we all walked back towards the van. 'I'll drop you off, George.'

'Lovely, John.' George rubbed his hands together. 'We gave that mob their tea, John, eh?'

'Oh, aye. Flippin' right we did.' He walked briskly.

My father wanted to get us back to watch the highlights. *Scotsport European Special*, he said. Or maybe catch a pint in Quins. The van spluttered along London Road, through the Trongate, the main route from the East End. 'We used to visit Goldberg's nearby,' he said. The shop belonged to an old Jewish guy from Eastern Europe. 'Good at business the old Jews,' he said. 'Knew what they were about. Can't say the same for their politics though. Wee Yasser will sort them out.'

George nodded his head in agreement.

We continued up the High Street. It looked sinister and dark, what with the cathedral and the enormous gravestones of the medieval necropolis and the oldest house in Glasgow nestled at the side of the road. 'There's the Royal Infirmary,' he said, pointing. 'You wouldn't want to be going in there with toothache. They used to wheel the bodies in there on a horse and cart years ago. The fellas were never the same when they got out. Cut the poor souls to ribbons, so they did. Can't stand those hospitals.'

'Scary stuff,' said George.

'I used to run electric cables in they hospitals.'

The sky was dark blue and grey now. Red sky at night, shepherd's delight. Red sky in the morning, shepherd's warning. We continued through Springburn and Kirkintilloch Road before dropping George off on the other side of Bishopbriggs. Iain recited the names of the Celtic players as if recalling the ten-times table.

I remember them now like a faded song.

Bonner, McGrain, Sinclair, Aitken, McAdam, MacLeod, Provan, McStay, McGarvey, Burns, McClair.

We turned left at the bottom of our street. My father was singing quietly. 'The Black Velvet Band' was a song about a woman who had stolen something and then passed it to a tradesman fella who ended up in court for the crime. As punishment he was sent away to a penal colony in Van Diemen's Land.

I'd known the words for ever. We sang it together.

'Can we go to another match?' Iain asked. 'There's a Rangers game on Saturday.'

'Of course,' my father answered. 'Of course we will.'

Chapter Two

My Father's Brain

The flat still carried the harsh breath of a Scottish winter and every day we'd been waiting for spring to appear but it seemed to take for ever. My wife, Kathleen, and the children were asleep, and had been for hours, and every now and then I got up to check on them, watching through the darkness as they moved and twisted and gently stretched out across the mattress and quilt. Mahoney and Gabriel had their infant limbs tangled around their mother like the mouths of three rivers meeting. They still smelled of fresh milk.

They made me smile, even in their sleep. If a child couldn't make you smile, my father always said, you were probably dead already. I rubbed the sleep from my eyes. It was almost the end of January, 2002.

Years ago, he said that the sleep was made from sand that came from Barra, my mother's island home. He brought it back in the van in heavy plastic sacks and it would be sprinkled in our eyes every night to help us sleep. We would dream of fish and mermaids and gulls in their rookeries and all the good things in the sea. He took enough sand from Barra to cover a clutch of sea turtles laying eggs.

I thought of all the white and silver and gold sand near Tangusdale beach and of my grandmother's house, in Castlebay, and the croft going down to the shimmering Atlantic sea and the black beast she said had haunted her from her childhood. El, my grandmother, believed in ghosts too. They all did. The ghosts of fishermen and the dead men and women and children of Mingulay, where her father, Neil, was born.

My grandmother was a MacPhee and the ruins of her father's house still sat in the abandoned village on the abandoned island. They were island people to their bones and they sailed all the boisterous waters around Berneray and Pabbay and Eriskay and Vatersay, the ragged islands of her birth in the Outer Hebrides. Like many Gaels, she had old ways dressed in stories and oratory that were the fuel of her people. When my grandmother spoke it was with words that might shift stones.

I don't know if the sand helped us sleep, but I liked to think that it did because the sand was fine and it came from a place that had as strong a history as any.

Kathleen stirred and half smiled when she saw my head through the door, but said nothing before weighting down the bodies of the children with a mothering hand. She knew how to hold them, how to keep them just so. Then she fell back to sleep. The kettle boiled and I returned to the living room and to my desk and listened to the low fiddle and bodhrán of a Clancy Brothers and Tommy Makem song. They had followed me around since my childhood. We followed each other.

When we'd moved to the southside of the city, a couple of years earlier, my father brought a few CDs over and forgot to take them away. Or maybe I'd forgotten to remind him they were still there. He was always doing the same to me. New tools disappeared from my cupboard, like smoke into the air, and he laughed and gave me his word that he'd never do such a thing. Certainly not to a man's tools, and certainly not if they belonged to his eldest son.

I turned the CD player up a notch. Liam Clancy, with his astonishingly warm voice, was singing 'The Dutchman', a love song about an old couple and the man who was losing his mind. Clancy's voice was made for ballads and he made the song weep. Sometimes, when no one was looking, he made me weep too.

Would you lighten up, Liam. You're killing me here . . .

The weather wasn't shifting. Maybe it would by Saturday. Celtic were playing Hearts at home and my friend Brian wanted to go. I hadn't been to a match for months because of trying to finish a writing project but he was insisting. The project was almost done. Celtic were looking to keep hold of the Scottish Premier League title. I could do with a few hours away from the desk. Why not? I would call him when he'd be up.

My father had been there that morning, helping to rewire the older lights in the flat. Fixing and mending were his thing. He could light up the Earl of Hell's waistcoat, he said. I would help him too when I could and he said we'd have it finished soon, working fast and efficiently and without much effort. We worked together. We joked a lot. Why had he placed a bucket beside me, filled to the brim with cold water? He smiled. 'You'll need it to dip your red-hot hammer in, you'll be working so fast . . .'

I liked working with him and I think he liked working with me. Neither of us said as much. You never did with your father, did you? I had always been the apprentice, regardless of what age I was. Look at me, I'd say, I'm all the man I'll ever be and you're still telling me how to pull a nail out of a wall. I shook my head. It was the natural order of things. I stood beside him, asked what he needed. I passed tools to my father. I could have pretended to be indignant but there was no point. Pick that up, please, and pass me two of those.

He was my father. That's what we did.

Over the years he suffered mild, and sometimes not so mild, electric shocks. He liked to work with live wires, he said, because it was a bit more exciting even if it might kill you. I was never sure if he was serious or not, but whenever he received another shock he would lie down for a few hours, saying very little. My mother was asked to boil up some lemonade, or send one of us to the garage for a bottle of Lucozade. Convinced about the healing elements of both fizzy drinks, he drank it as if it was holy water sent directly from Lourdes. Boiled lemonade, for my father, was the panacea that cured all ills.

The tenor of his voice rarely changed. A please and thank you would do. It had been that way for years. I was in my thirties now.

He would be in his late fifties. You're getting on now, Da, eh? A shrug. A glare. A smile too. Birthdays no longer really mattered unless it was the birthday of the very young or the very old. I preferred it that way. We both did. I detested fuss as much as he did. Birthdays seemed such an incredible indulgence. And anything that reminded me of the passage of time was not something I wanted to celebrate.

He'd left the flat before I arrived home from work but we spoke that evening on the phone, about the upcoming match, and whether Henrik Larsson would score again. He'd scored against St Johnstone a few days earlier. There was a Scottish League Cup game coming up in a few weeks against Rangers at Hampden Park. We didn't care what Larsson did in the other games as long as he scored against Rangers.

All those years had drifted away since that Sporting Lisbon game and we still hadn't gone to another match. Nothing was ever mentioned of it really. Perhaps, that was just how some things were meant to be. So much had got in the way. But it always did. Life was a series of obstacles, he said. At least ours was. We knew he held on to that match tightly. He wrapped his fists around it and wouldn't forget it, he said. It didn't matter that we had asked him to go again, to another match. He would always say yes, and then say no. There was always something to do, something that needed fixing. Somewhere else he had to be. Maybe that match was enough. I thought about it now and again. I missed it.

'Did you see it?' he'd said on the phone, only a few hours earlier.

I knew what was coming.

We talked about a programme on the television we'd both watched. He couldn't fail to call about it. It would have been impossible. *Bloody Sunday* was a dramatization of one of the key moments of the Troubles, when soldiers of the British Army opened fire on a civil rights march in Londonderry, leading to the deaths of fourteen unarmed civil rights protestors and bystanders in Northern Ireland.

'What?'

'OK, it was a mistake. My mistake.' Of course, I hadn't meant to say Londonderry. I meant *Derry*. And he knew I meant the *north of Ireland*.

He laughed, but he was serious too. 'Don't go giving credence to it all . . . that's all I'm saying.'

'OK, OK.'

'Scoundrels, the lot of them . . .'

'Anyway, you'll need to watch what you're saying, Dad . . . you know they'll be listening.'

His favourite subject. I could feel him grinning at the other end of the line. He would have his say. The dark forces of the British government, he believed, were still listening to his calls. And to my calls too. They had been doing it for years.

'Of course they will be,' he said, his voice brimming with satisfaction and a hint of pride. 'Broadsword to Danny Boy, are you receiving?'

They'd tapped our telephone lines for years, he said. I was a journalist, after all, who'd been to the Middle East and Ireland, and he believed this was enough to warrant special attention from the British Secret Service. Laughter followed. I was of little renown or reputation but that didn't stop him believing it to be true. Sometimes *wanting* it to be true.

Some years earlier, I'd met and written about a priest in New York who'd been imprisoned in connection with an armoured car robbery. British Intelligence had once described him as 'an underground general' of the IRA and his brother was suspected of being a member of the same organization.

Then there was Libya. I'd met Colonel Gaddafi in Tripoli, in his compound. It was a Lockerbie story. The slaughtered camel and the returning Al Amin Khalifa Fhimah. Those stories always made my father smile and shake his head. 'They'll be on to you now,' he said. He meant it too. 'Mark my words . . .' Even before I became a journalist, he said, they were listening to us. They were listening to all of us. A wink. A tap on the side of the nose. Mark my words. Listening now. Always listening. Always would. Some day we would see. 'We're letting them get away with it,' he said. 'Not enough questions. No one asks enough questions. They've allowed it to happen. Right here and now, they're *letting* it happen. It doesn't happen overnight.' Collusion. Conspiracy. Buzzwords of an active, probing mind.

Much of the time he talked to my brothers and me in a kind of verbal Morse code that only we could really decipher. Clipped conversations and unfinished sentences, peppered with nods and winks and tics. He rarely mentioned anyone by name. Inference was enough. No names, no pack-drill. A glare too to underline the seriousness of the situation.

He did the same with Celtic and Rangers. This one and that one. Him and you-know-who. That mob. The scoundrels. They're involved with this one and that. And don't even ask about *that* fella. In the boardroom. Backhanders all the way . . .

'You mention so-and-so's name,' he said, 'and, boom, the recorders kick in. London, Washington, New York. Belfast too. They've got it all sewn up, I'm telling you. The Masons, the Israelis, Mossad, the CIA, the Secret Service. The lot of them. Watch what you're saying, Michael. Just be careful, is all I'm saying.'

'Behave yourself, Dad.'

'Nothing is the way it seems, mark my words. I've been around the block. I've had the polis asking me questions, you know what I mean? Questions they had no right asking.' I didn't want to believe him but much of what he said made sense. Why would they *not* be listening? 'One of these days you'll see what I mean. I'm telling you, mark my words . . . it'll all come out in the wash. It's the truth, Michael.'

Too much truth could kill a man stone dead. He said that too.

'Why are they listening to you, Dad? I mean, come on . . . are they listening to you talking about entering the All-Ireland dung-shovelling championships?'

He chortled. 'You're an eedjit,' he said. How could I *not* see it? 'You believe they're innocent? Well, I've got a nice castle to sell you. They're listening to tons of things. You just need to open your eyes.

41

They're listening to the poor complain. They're getting the *measure* of us. And by the way, Gordon Gekko, they're into your fancy mobile phones as well. At least I didn't have to worry about that in my day.'

My father believed it was his duty – our duty – to stand up for the downtrodden. It was all our duties. We were Celtic fans, so of course it was our duty. If he hadn't been so quiet he might have ended up preaching about it. But his quietness was powerful. He understood what it meant to be quiet. The spaces between sentences. He had the courage to be quiet in front of others. He didn't need to fill space with chatter.

You couldn't be giving alms to the poor on the one level and have your hands around their necks on another, throttling them. It rarely stopped. He'd been telling me for years. His people – our people – were against the naysayers. We always were, he said. And, more than anything, of course, we supported the Irish and their grievances over stolen lands and starvations. We had causes, he said. We always would have.

We'd supported the miners too and we were all against Thatcher who took the milk out of our mouths when we were young.

'And God can forgive her, because I certainly won't,' he'd say.

I stood beside him when he turned his back on the Yuill & Dodds lorries passing the street. And when he shook a fist at them on the M8 and shouted, dirty scabs the lot of you. They'd broken the miners' strike and he hated them for it. His grandfather, Francis Quinn, had been a coalminer. His great-grandfather, Patrick Quinn, had been an ironstone miner too, known to be as strong as a Flanders mare. Terrible conditions for men, he said. The miners worked in coffins. They worked in furnaces underground, close to the devil himself. His memories ran deep. And they numbered many, like weeds on a kerbside path.

'That lot killed the unions as much as Thatcher and MacGregor.'

He said what he meant and he said it quietly. If you disagreed, that was up to you, but he would say it again and again just so that you knew exactly where he was coming from. He spoke poetically

42

sometimes, of the secret scripture of the poor and how we should always speak up for those who were the least of us. We would never run out of them, he'd say. Mark my words. If you were alive you may as well have a decent opinion. 'The higher the monkey climbed the tree,' he said, 'the more you could see of its backside.'

'I know, Dad. I know,' I'd say. 'I know . . .' It never struck him for a minute that I might change.

Or that he might change too.

'Look, I'll have to go.'

We were never on the phone longer than a few minutes. Who wanted to spend their life on the phone, he said. Especially if there were things to be done. Or if people were listening.

'Ach, you're just turning into a *souper*!' He slapped me down remorselessly.

'Don't be daft. I need to go.' I laughed loudly. 'Anyway, the children are crying.'

He always got me at that. A souper, he said. They were turncoats and you might as well call a man a coward or a sell-out. Years ago, in Ireland, he said, the Protestants got the poor Catholics to renounce their faith when they fed them through their soup kitchens. They were clever, he said. Food over God. The starving relented. Hunger was a good kitchen for Bible Protestantism to flourish.

'I'll call you tomorrow.'

'Only kidding about the souper, Michael, don't worry. There's hope for you yet . . .'

'I know, Dad. Bye now.'

'OK, Michael. Bye now. Talk to you tomorrow.'

That was the last time I ever heard him speaking any more than a sentence.

I rubbed my eyes again. The project could wait. I was tired. It was black outside, slightly depressing. The streetlamps didn't stand a chance against so much black. Liam Clancy was in his stride and I sang quietly along with him. Then the phone rang. I got up quickly and went into the hall, hoping that the ringing wouldn't wake the children. I grabbed it and then dropped the receiver and made more noise than the ringing itself.

'Mike? Is that you, Mike?' The voice on the end was quivering.

'Yes. That you, Maureen? Everything OK?' I shook myself upright.

'Dad's collapsed. I don't think he's . . . I don't think he's well. I'm at Mum's.'

'What happened? Quickly, tell me what happened.'

She mentioned the bathroom. He'd fallen. It was late. He wasn't responding. There was some blood from his mouth. He'd collapsed and my mother was there. Claire was there also, and her hands were really shaking and her insides too. She'd put him in the recovery position. She knew it was serious. She was trying her best. Vincent had heard the commotion. He was there now. My mother was crying.

'Put Vincent on, please. Quickly.'

Maureen was stumbling over her words. She was also crying.

She passed the phone to Vincent. My heart was pounding. He fell? What exactly did Maureen mean? He'd probably been to Quins with Michael or George. Maybe he'd fallen on his way home. Whatever had happened it couldn't be that serious. It wouldn't be. Maybe if he'd fallen from the roof, I could understand the concern. The skylight in the loft. Or from a tree out the back. But the bathroom? He would be fine, of course he would. My father's face floated in front of me.

'Mike, you'd better get over,' said Vincent. His voice was calm and even but I could tell from the flatness of his tone that he was serious. 'You'd better hurry. He can't get up. He's been sick and he can't speak. There's nothing in him at all. He can't respond. We've called the ambulance. Meet us at the hospital.'

'OK. I'm leaving.'

It was raining now and I could hear it bouncing off the windows. Thunder wasn't far away.

For a moment I paused and leaned my head against the wall.

I closed my eyes before exhaling deeply. Kathleen was listening by the door now. I dropped the telephone and scrambled for the car keys and told her about the bathroom and my father's fall and his head and Maureen's voice and the ambulance and them telling me I *needed* to go over. 'It'll be fine,' she said, searching for the right words. 'It'll be fine.' They weren't empty words. Kathleen knew. There had been enough death in her family to shame God. She rarely talked about it but it was always there. She could see the panic in my eyes.

The children stirred. She reached out her hand. It was warm and felt secure, like a child's faith in grown-ups. 'Your face looks drained. Hurry.'

Outside now. The car took an age to start. 'Come off it, come off it . . . Jesus, what's wrong with this heap of crap?' What did they mean, he couldn't speak? The windscreen wipers weren't working properly either. The rain stuck like glue drops on the glass. I tried to think of his voice but I couldn't. It was gone. That's when I knew that he had already started to disappear, that his hand was slipping beneath the water.

Not yet, Dad. I thought about the first time we all went to Barra. It was a place where he always smiled. He told us that it was never as good as Ireland, never in a million years, but it was, and he knew it. It was somewhere real. Not imagined, or dreamed up and invented. As real as my mother in her ironed Sunday dress.

Remember the outside toilet, Dad, with the corrugated-iron roof, where we had to do our business in a bucket and then one of us had to pour it all in the burn that ran past El's house? We played Paper, Scissors, Stone to see whose turn it was to empty out all the muck.

The rain lashed the windows. The motorway seemed to stretch for miles and miles. I could see the dark waters of the River Clyde now as the hospital drew nearer. A loop of Barra rewound in my head. My father said that Barra got its name from St Finbarr, the founder of Cork, where some of his people were from. My mother just laughed and tutted and said, you'll claim that Jesus was Irish next as well, won't you? Her voice was warm, like she was fixing a stew.

Stobhill Hospital was only a few streets from where my parents lived and my mother, Maureen, Vincent and Claire were already there. With flashing blue lights it was a five-minute drive at most. He would have got there quickly and then the doctors would have told everyone not to panic, that it was a false alarm, and that the man lying there in front of them was not in any danger and we could all breathe a mighty sigh of relief.

My mother's face was like a broken porcelain plate. She had already turned as small as a fallen bird. Her eyes were black as ink. She struggled to get up from the chair. 'Michael,' she said, 'I can't live without your dad. I can't. I just can't.' She looked around the room. 'He'll be all right, won't he? He'll be fine. He's a big, strong man. Your dad's strong, isn't he?'

I hugged her. She was still dripping from the rain.

'He's the strongest, Mum.'

I looked at Vincent. He shook his head and whispered but I couldn't hear. It was his whisper that made it real.

'He'll be fine, Mum,' I said.

A nurse asked if anybody wanted tea. There was a machine for coffee but she went away and made tea for my mother. Someone else from the hospital spoke. The information came in torrents. A registrar based across the city at the Southern General Hospital, the west of Scotland's centre for anything to do with neurosurgery and neurology, had already been contacted and informed there was a patient who was likely to require surgery. Duty consultants had already been briefed and the CAT scan had been sent across the city in a taxi.

'What's a CAT scan?' asked my mother.

'It's like a photograph of the inside of Mr Tierney's head, of his brain.'

'His *brain*? Oh, no. Oh, dear.'

'Yes, his brain.'

The scan was indicating that my father had a blood clot putting pressure on his brain. The clot needed to come out. Something had exploded. But we were not to worry. The surgeons over there were the best. They would take the roof off his head and they would fix him.

'A taxi?' I said to the nurse, trying not to raise my voice. 'My father's brain scan is in a taxi?'

'Yes, that's how we do it.'

'Is there not a quicker way? By computer or something? I hope to hell the driver knows where he's going . . .'

I knew what my father would be thinking. Vincent did too. Incredulous. We tried not to laugh. *A taxi?* He would have shaken his head even if it had just exploded. His brain scan was being driven across Glasgow and he'd say the fella was probably stopping off somewhere for a fish supper before he got there. You couldn't make it up, he'd say. The bloke was probably a Rangers man. No doubt about it. He'd probably drop by Ibrox too. My father rarely took a taxi anywhere. Maybe at a wedding when he'd had too much to drink. Even then he didn't like the idea of paying extra just to go somewhere when a bus fare was fine. If he wasn't driving he would just get up and walk. To my grandmother's or to Quins.

A taxi? I've heard it all now . . . make sure he puts that meter on.

A nurse assured my mother that he was fighting and my mother just nodded automatically, and her lips moved, reciting a prayer. She wasn't really taking anything in. Her thumbs were touching her lips as she prayed. She made the Sign of the Cross and rolled the wedding and engagement rings on her finger round and round and said more prayers. She said them properly, like we'd all been taught as children. Her thumbs were at her lips again. She recited her words quietly and with great dignity and, right there, God was an inescapable fact of her existence. She never doubted His presence. Nor would she.

Our Father, who art in heaven . . .

Maureen prayed standing up.

I closed my eyes. I know that I must have prayed or said something. But not like my mother. It wasn't that I didn't believe. I just didn't know anything any more. I went to Mass when I could, but mainly for the children. A head start. A grounding. Something

47

familiar. I wished I had her faith that day. He needed it. A little help from upstairs. A *lot* of help from upstairs.

My mother was a true professional at praying and put us all to shame, but mostly the boys. She attended Mass as regularly as the priest, walking there and back in the mornings because she liked to get some fresh air too, and I always believed she went there with more conviction than the man in black in every step she took. She prayed that His will would be done. While my mother prayed I closed my eyes. I could hear my father talking again.

I'm fine, Cathie. Maybe just boil up some lemonade or Lucozade . . . forget about the taxi. Get the boys to put me in the van and take me back down the road. I'll be fine. Just a slip. Nothing to worry about. Bit of a bump . . .

The van was gone now, long gone.

They said my father had suffered a spontaneous cerebral haemorrhage, what the doctors usually classified as a stroke. We were told that even if the surgeon operated, the chances of survival were only fifty-fifty and the longer the delay for the operation to take place, the worse the potential outcome would be. His medical history was reasonable, they said, but the truth of the matter was that he never really *had* a medical history, such was his intransigence over visiting the doctor's for anything.

You don't go to the doctor unless . . . well, you just don't go to the doctor.

My mother sometimes said that I needed to *speak* to him because he was driving her demented. Demented about doctors and sore feet and sore this and my leg and my head and my back and nobody cared at all. Drove her demented, she said. And then she would raise her eyebrows. The eyebrows meant it was nothing serious. She didn't know how she put up with all his nonsense. You would need the patience of all the saints, she said, shaking her head but smiling.

'How can a doctor possibly know anything about me?' he would say, when I spoke with him. 'That's just daft. Stupid. Just plain stupid. You're all as daft as brushes. Did they speak to my mother? Did they ask *her* what was wrong? No, I didn't think so. My mother knew who I was better than any daft doctor. Did anyone bother to ask my mother how she felt? Did they ask her even once how she was since my father died in France? I doubt it. I flippin' well doubt it. Well, if they didn't bother to ask after my mother's health they can chase themselves about mine.'

And he would go into the garden or drive up to B&Q or just sit and stare at the wall until even the wall started to feel uncomfortable too.

'Christ, Vinnie, this looks serious.'

'I know, I know.'

'Did he have a drink?'

The men never called it a bar. It was just Quins. It was down the road at the Cross. In the rough-and-tumble world of men and football, Quins was the place where Celtic men assembled to discuss their lives and their problems and their hardships and their work and anything really that men talk about away from their wives: which is to say, everything else apart from their wives. Drink coursed through the place like a glorious green river.

The barmen were dour and miserable on a good day and if they told their customers to get lost it was considered a fairly amicable conversation. Good service was nothing to be particularly proud of and the men were happy with a few pints, a whisky and a conversation that touched only on football and politics and religion and work. They called it a Celtic shop. The appearance of a stranger was regarded with utmost suspicion. The interloper was either a bluenose or a policeman and frequently both. There was an occasional Irish song at the end of the night to quell the interloper rebellion, or simply just to identify the miscreant. If he didn't sing or dance, he was definitely a copper.

Quins had been there for years. An old photograph showed it in 1910, looking resplendent as it sat across the road from the Bank of Scotland. The tramlines and cobbles of the street had long since disappeared. The sons of the men who drank there in the past, but not so long ago that they'd been forgotten, frequented the pub.

We didn't know when it became a Celtic shop, but it had.

Quins had a few chairs and it sometimes smelled like a zoo and that's the way the men liked it. It was where they could go to let off some steam and happily stand around for a few hours talking about the state of the world, and the only thing that was asked in return was that they pay their money and lay off the fighting. And if they did fight, keep it inside in case the polis station across the road wakes up to all their enjoyment.

When I was sixteen or so I used to run home from my girlfriend's house, to catch my father coming out of Quins with George, or Michael, or Frank, or old Charlie, and I'd stand at the door waiting. I could see his giant shadow through the smoked glass and he would sink another beer and then another whisky and then another one just as it was time to go and the barman would never be allowed to pick up their empties and take them away until every last drop of whisky had been got from the tumbler and every last lick of beer from the glass. A pint would be sent back if there was too much froth. 'Fill it up, son,' the men would order, staring in such supreme concentration that the doors began to howl on their hinges. 'It's not a cocktail we ordered.'

The men would give me some loose change and the newspaper they had just finished reading. Back pages had already been scoured. Celtic scores appeared in the late editions. Those who'd been at the game had returned to Quins and would regale the assembled crowd with concerned tales of the incredible and frightening prejudice and outright and blatant bias that had been visited upon their mortal souls. 'You wouldn't *believe* what happened the night,' said a voice, snorting with disdain. 'Wouldn't believe it. You shouldn't even ask, because it was that unbelievable.' The referee, of course, was a Mason. Or an Orangeman. Or both. 'A Mason?' said the man. 'That guy's got more degrees than Patrick Moore.'

We would talk together about Celtic and the players I thought were playing well and I'd say Paul McStay or Peter Grant or Davie Provan. They nodded. And they asked if I was drinking yet, and I could see my father turning his head slightly and glancing over to

50

listen. And the answer was no. Because, in truth, I was going to play for Celtic.

There would be no women in my father's company. At some point, much to the disgust of the regulars, a toilet for the ladies was installed. By law, of course, and they all wondered what kind of laws they were living under in this country. The snug at the side held around six or eight people and that was where the occasional battle-hardened lady might find herself of a Saturday night. But there would be no straying into the other parts of the bar, where the men talked, cursed and drank as if it was their human right. And, in that world, it was.

He drank with all sorts of men. Occasionally a rumoured bank robber, or a getaway driver too. They were all part of the company and there was the fella who'd been to prison, but it wasn't for drinking too much wine during the Offertory Procession at Mass. There were men who were teachers, and others who worked with their hands. If they had anything in common it was that they were all ordinary. And that isn't a description to belittle them. In fact they mostly soared.

The men were just like him. Celtic was their common denominator. It was a great leveller. Some men went to matches, others didn't. But they all went to Quins. Apart from the drink, football matches and the bookies were their only form of entertainment. But my father never bet. A mug's game, he said. The only winner was the bookie. He said he'd bet on a horse just the once. It was a terrific horse, the best he'd ever seen. Such a bold, fast horse. Amazing. You should have seen it. I wished I had, Da. He put a week's wages on it, he said, and lost the lot. Every penny. The horse came last. But he still swore it was a great horse. Fast and strong. It was so good, he laughed, that it took seven other horses to beat it . . .

We said our cheerios and then I walked up Kirkintilloch Road with him, talking. He was never drunk. There were very few times in my life that I had actually seen him drunk. He just seemed to be able to weather it all regardless.

My father took long, languid strides and I could rarely keep up.

Sometimes, we stopped outside the Bishopbriggs Building Supplies, a local builders merchants on the main road, and he would point out a few pallets of stray bricks that had been unloaded or were due to be sent out in the morning. 'Couple of these will do,' he chirped, smiling. 'Good for the base of the hut. Going to build a bigger one. I'll show you how to build it. You can give me a hand.'

He passed me a couple of bricks. It would be near midnight, the moon behind a cloud, on Kirkintilloch Road, only a hundred metres or so from the local police station, and we'd each placed two bricks in our pockets or under our jackets and carried on walking. In a couple of months, give or take a few missed opportunities, we had enough bricks to build the hut's foundations and that was quite a trick, he said.

'Johnny Cash built a car this way,' he said, grinning.

'What do you mean?'

'You not heard the song "One Piece at a Time"? I've been singing it for years.' And my father started singing the Cash song as we walked up the road. It was the story of a man who worked at General Motors, in Michigan, and who started taking pieces of cars to make a vehicle of his own because he knew, deep down, he would never be able to afford a new one.

The drink wouldn't hurt my father, I thought to myself in the hospital. He wouldn't let it. He had too many responsibilities to let the drink hurt him.

'No,' said Vincent. 'It's not that.'

'Has anyone called the rest of the girls or boys yet?'

'Maybe we should wait until we know a bit more. We don't want to scare them. What do you think?'

Really, I had no idea what we should do. I shook my head. It might be a false alarm and he might just wake up from it. We just didn't know. This was a new land. A landscape of illness and injury. There were eleven of us, counting my parents, and we had all managed so far. Why would that change now? It didn't make any sense. They were getting ready to travel, to see a bit of the world with their children.

Lorraine, Fiona and Catherine were in Dubai and Abu Dhabi; Mark and Iain were in New York. The girls had already booked my father on a flight to New York for St Patrick's Day in March. He loved it there. Of course he would be fine. He had a ticket. It was upstairs in my parents' bedroom. No one bought a ticket if they thought their father was dying. You'd never buy a ticket to a Celtic match and think that you might lose.

The ticket gave us hope. It was a reminder of possibility. He would be fine for the trip. He would sit back on the plane and quietly ask for a beer, or maybe just the two, and my mother would sip a small glass of wine, but one would be enough, dear.

I thought there would have been some blood. He was naked apart from a sheet around his waist.

When they allowed us in to see him he looked fine, as if nothing much had happened. There was little sign of the impending death they had warned us about. Nothing. It was a relief and I closed my eyes. I thought his skull would have been damaged. But there was nothing to see. He looked peaceful and intact. My mother sobbed.

A doctor with an unprepossessing face was talking to us, saying something like, 'It is an invisible misfortune', but I barely heard a word. A connection had been switched off in my father's head, something to do with wiring. The internal wiring had been messed up. A marionette with its strings cut. The doctor talked. It all sounded dramatic. The theatrics of the medical profession. I wondered how many people had died or been saved under his care. I listened more intently. How little we knew of our bodies. It was a simple fact. We knew nothing of the mechanics of actually *being*, of living. We went to the shops but we didn't know how we got there. We played sport but we didn't know how we reached the net. We shouted at each other and we expected our voices just to be there every day, in support of our anger. We just got up and got on with it all hoping that, one day, we wouldn't shut down.

Or get our wires crossed.

His eyes were closed, and there was a tube in his mouth. I listened as his breath escaped in a rush from his chest and then it slowed down. My mother continued to cry. There was a soft glow from a stainless-steel standard lamp by his side as a group of doctors and nurses stood over him talking. Beside them were the machines, a labyrinth of strange wires and screens that were trying to save his life. They looked unspectacular and unrelentingly dull, the type of machines an odd-job man might fix with a soldering iron on the weekends for a fiver an hour.

We put our faith in these machines. We all did.

I worried about his naked body.

It would only embarrass him if he knew.

Someone, young and plump, his upper lip perspiring, talked to my father while a nurse ran her fingers softly through his hair. John. *John*. I heard his name called out. *John*. But no one responded. His consciousness, the thing you couldn't touch or see or feel, was elsewhere. Floating around. There was a slow beeping sound, the kind you get on quiz shows. More equipment was brought into the room. One of the nurses rushed away.

'Don't even think about it, Dad.'

What?

'You know what.'

It's just a question.

'I know . . . but it's not relevant just now.'

Everyone in Glasgow thinks it. Don't pretend otherwise. Even the blokes in the West End. Especially, the blokes in the West End . . .

'Just leave it . . . it's hardly important.'

I didn't say it was. But it would be good to know. Part of my mental insurance policy, you understand. So ask the doctors. Are they Rangers doctors or Celtic doctors? It's just a question.

'Dad, there's more to worry about.'

I didn't say there wasn't. I just think it would be good to know if the bloke that's going to cut me up has a preference. Do I keep the Rosary beads by the bed or not?

'Don't act the goat. You would keep them there regardless . . .'

True . . .

My mother, her head twisted sideways, looked at my father on the hospital trolley as she squeezed his hand. When we were children and she used to hug us, she would tell us that she wanted to squeeze us for all she was worth. Or she would squeeze the life into us. It didn't make sense to us then. But it did now.

He was mortal. Vulnerable. She would squeeze life into him. The blood ran from her fingertips. It would find a way to my father's heart and it would run to his head too and it would help him to get up and he would cut the grass soon and wash the windows and take her out for the messages and they would go to Mass as well.

'I'm scared,' she said, in a voice that was below whispering. It rumbled too: so low and sad. She took a deep breath, the type you take before you submerge yourself in the bath. It was a reflexive gesture. Love was a reflex. She knew then she would be holding her breath for the rest of her life.

The medical team stood to the side for a moment as my mother stroked his face and ran her trembling hands across his eyes. She whispered again. Her hands across my father's face were an un-expected intimacy that made me turn away. She just needed a moment. They both did. My mother's mouth opened and shut like a fish caught on dry land. We knew that she was drowning in the air. She was drifting into smallness again. She would need a map and a sure hand to guide her back.

As the minutes passed, his flesh changed. It became paler and greyer, like the washed-out colour of an old cooking pot, or a man in a trench. He was turning into the body of the nearly dead, not yet debris, and not yet memory.

'Listen, Dad,' I said, out loud, 'you *need* to get through this. You really do. Just . . . look, hold on for a bit longer . . . they'll sort you. The surgeon will sort this.' I levelled my finger at the doctors. 'That's what they do.'

I could hear him again.

Look, I'll be fine. This is just . . . temporary. He shook his head and then pointed to something unseen.

Now listen. Closely. I'll need to phone that bloke. Or write to him.

You know the one? The one who can get me my father's medals. My mother should have had them. They should have been Jane's. I would have kept them polished for her. They belonged to her. We're due them. My people are due them. Once I'm up and about we'll do that, eh? And we'll visit him again. Off to Bayeux again. Next time we'll go in summer. That was a good trip, eh?

His eyes remained shut. Even behind them there was stillness.

I was struck by how powerful he still looked. We used to take turns riding on his shoulders across the quarry and over to my grandmother's. Sometimes there were nine children walking across the quarry in a conga line, a football skipping across the ground, and then it continued in the streets past the Glen Douglas bar and then to the railway. Sometimes he let us wear our Celtic jerseys too. He would let us wear them out in the street, but only if he was with us. We rode for miles on shoulders as big as plates. It's little wonder he grew tired. His feet troubled him. And now they just lay there, stretched out beyond the end of the trolley, like a child's off the edge of a bed.

I went to say something again. But I couldn't. My throat dried up.

The nurse who had been caressing my father's hair left. Another nurse prepared a needle.

I wanted to tell him that I loved him but the words turned heavy and crusted with broken glass. Even though he might be dying, I was embarrassed to say the words. I couldn't tell him and it was because people were *listening*. They were listening to see if the dying man on the trolley had a son who could tell him he loved him. But he couldn't. Just give me a bit longer, Dad. Don't die until we're somewhere a little more private. I shook my head and put my hands to my face. I bent down and kissed him on his cold head.

My mother always said that he told us all he loved us when we were children, when we were that high, she said, but no matter how hard I tried, I just could not remember it. But I knew that he did. It was the truth. He must have. You don't spend your life with nine children, never wanting them to grow up and leave home and *not* say it. It was impossible.

Suddenly, we were ushered out and into another smaller room, with a partition. Vincent bent to kiss my father too. His brain was shutting down further.

'Oh, John. Come on, dear. Please. *Please, John.*'

He always said if he died we were to bury him at the bottom of the garden beside the apple trees that bloomed in summer and shed their bitter fruit in winter. On no account were we to waste money on a funeral. That was just plain daft, he said. You would be half mad to pay for a funeral.

There will be no funeral here, lads . . . mark my words. There's a match on Saturday. Hearts, is it? I'll get the radio on for it, no problem.

We sat in the quiet room. A clock ticked and my mind wandered. I dreamed of burying him in the garden where we would all be standing around. We were just small children, all holding hands in a row. We were each dressed for Sunday. For some reason we were saluting him too, which was strange because he didn't have much time for the military. At least that's what he always told us. But I think it intrigued him. Why did men go to fight? What did they think of when they did? Who did they fight for? And what had happened to his father?

'You can follow behind the ambulance,' said a nurse. There was more urgency to her voice. It sounded weak too, as if she was more worried than she was letting on. 'They'll be taking him over soon. The surgeons at the Southern are the best.' The nurse touched my mother's hand, now wrapped in a set of Rosary beads. 'They're the best.'

Hail Mary, full of grace, the Lord is with thee . . .

One thirty in the morning. Tick-tock.

The world narrowed with every passing minute into the shabby, low-ceilinged room where we stood. We let my mother finish her prayers in silence. Maureen's hands were clasped and her eyes were red. Vincent stared at the ceiling. 'Jesus . . .' he said, shaking his head. Claire huddled beside me. She was still too young for this. I stopped dreaming of his funeral. Instead, I tried to dream him alive.

Pass me that bandage and a pair of scissors, Cathie. And some string.

I'll sort this out myself ... Has anyone got me that Lucozade yet?

As if it had been ordained by my mother's round of prayers, a priest appeared in the corridor, a crucifix and bottle of oil in one hand, some holy water in the other. He began to talk loudly over us without a hint of self-consciousness in his voice. My mother nodded. I looked at Vincent. Father So-and-so's bag of rituals gave my mother comfort. It gave me some too. We were given Heaven and Hell as children and we would always have it in some way. The pew at St Matthew's was always filled with eleven Tierneys. It was hard to let go. And sometimes I didn't want to.

My father believed in God and goodness and decency before any-thing else. He was fierce about these things. He always carried a laminated picture and prayer of St John Ogilvie in his jacket pocket and, later, his mother's Rosary beads. The poorer the church, the poorer the people, the better the priest. Faith always existed, he said, on a different level than proof. So say your prayers. St Matthew's had more money than St Augustine's nearby and he would alternate between the two, putting brown and silver coins in the collection plate of the former and a note in the latter's. Sometimes he went to St Mungo's and then St Aloysius' when he had a notion for it.

But he found the Church's materialism unsettling and protested weekly when the old wooden plate came round. 'Too many priests are only in it for the big house and free rounds of golf.' If a priest had not gone to work at some point in his life in the missions in Africa and South America, then my father eyed him with a glare of suspicion. And woe betide any of them who got a free ticket to Celtic Park just because they were wearing a collar. If he couldn't afford it why should they get in?

The priest wanted to help. My mother nodded some more.

Father So-and-so had a curious manner but an unshakable con-fidence that my father would be fine and he told us that in a booming voice as if he was ordering us all to sing louder at Sunday Mass. The area where we stood was empty. The voice filled all the corners. 'Don't worry, Mrs Tierney. There *will* be an Intercession.' Smiling at this, I nodded glibly in his direction.

The priest had worn-out, scuffed shoes. His trousers rode up past his ankles and there were loose threads that needed stitching. His charcoal-grey sweater had seen better days. A scent of cheap aftershave covered him. He was clean-shaven but there was a nest of greying stubble under his chin that he had missed in his haste. There was dandruff on his collar. Vanity was not something that concerned him an ounce. He looked as poor as Job's turkey.

Perhaps I was wrong. He was *exactly* the type of priest my father would have liked. He sliced a Sign of the Cross into the air and we received a blessing. A deliberate provocation against something unseen. In the Name of the Father, and of the Son, and of the Holy Ghost. Amen. There was another family nearby. They were looking over. The nurse came for the priest to administer the Last Rites to my father. My mother put her hand to her mouth.

There was silence.

I looked at her. I could see my mother in the bathroom standing over my father, trying to save him. And I wanted to save him too.

The nurse explained that my father had already been intubated. The tube in his throat was basically helping to control his breathing. Once the decision had been made to operate on him it was more or less a case of getting him ready for immediate intervention rather than waiting to take him to a ward in the Southern General Hospital and then going through the same procedures and checks all over again.

His brain had been bleeding heavily.

It had been doing so for some hours.

I could have told you that . . .

A doctor apologized and said it was like an explosion inside his skull. Like a red party balloon. It was the easiest way to explain things. An actual explosion. That's how people died. The bleed was frontal and in the left basal ganglia. My father would have liked that. A frivolous smile would have crept on to his face.

Bleeding in the basal ganglia? Not bad. None of your bump-on-the-forehead rubbish, lads. None of your concussion here. The basal ganglia

. . . I think that might be Latin . . . Might even be Irish Gaelic? I'll need to consult the books . . .

'It's a bleeding brain, Dad. You need to be *careful*. Sit down for a bit, now would you.'

He'd say that he couldn't really be hurt, that he was too big and strong to be hurt by something so small and insignificant. He said he was strong as the first King of Ireland and he would throw a few imaginary punches. Thunder and lightning, he called them. 'Thunder always follows lightning. Left, right. Boom.' But deep down he would know it was a crisis, and that he couldn't just laugh it all away.

But he'd laugh again anyway, and say, don't be so daft, of course I can. He would joke it all away. He would sit at the kitchen table and laugh to himself. 'I'll tell you *exactly* what happened. Someone must have planted something in there. In my head. Go and get my camera, boys . . . this has to be recorded. We need a record of this. We need *evidence*. The mob have been at it again!'

And we would all have laughed with him.

'They'd have to get up earlier in the morning to take me out the game.'

We kept laughing. But we all knew. It was already a kind of death.

If my father had fractured his head, said another voice, due to a fall, the bleeding would typically have been just below the brain's surface. Injuries that were stroke-related were usually within the brain itself and more problematic. My father's bleeding had started within the brain tissue and then ruptured into what was called the ventricular system, the system that drained fluid from the brain in order that the brain tissue continued to work effectively. In my father's case a tiny blood vessel had burst and bled under high pressure, leaving a path of destroyed brain tissue in its wake.

All the cables in the circuit had been pulled out of the wall.

Thunder always followed lightning.

We all sat listening.

There was an extensive amount of blood inside his head and what was really happening was that the remaining brain tissue was still being compressed with all that blood, weakening my father's system. As the compression continued, and without evacuating the blood surgically – without reducing the pressure – the patient would die because the brain could not function with that amount of pressure on it.

Nonsense. I'm fine . . .

But deep down he would have known.

After years of dragging electric cables through some of Glasgow's hospitals a man got to understand the demand and supply of energy. Cut the supply and the lights didn't go on. Cut the power and nothing worked.

'It was a thud,' said my mother. 'I knew something was wrong.'

'He was just lying there,' said Claire. 'It was terrible.'

But even as he was falling he would have fought it.

He would have reached out his hands to hold himself upright against the bathroom wall and tried to shout out one last time for my mother. That's what the dying tried to do. He'd have tried to shout but the words were already gone. They existed only in his memory.

Instead, a dark pool of blood spewed from his mouth.

His face would have been filled with fear. Not of dying, but of not *living*. With all of us. The difference was vast. If you feared something, he said, well, that was almost to submit to it and encourage it. As he was falling, no matter how much the pain was, he'd have tried to survive a little longer so that the last things he saw were not white floor tiles or a toilet seat, but the face of my mother. He'd have thought of her and his children, and his dead soldier father and his mother, Jane. He'd have risen a little off his knees even though it would be impossible because the connections between his brain and these functions were actually gone.

And he shouted once more. 'Cathie. *Cathie!*'

Then his knees collapsed as the wires in his head were finally severed, as if someone had taken a sharp Stanley knife to them, like the ones he kept in the loft. But there would be good news too. My father was smart. One of the smartest. He'd also know that the wires could be repaired, like those in a house. Of course they could. He'd spent his life working with electricity and wires and cables and components and circuits, sometimes just a flick of a switch away from death, so he knew that when the mess had been untangled, the machine would work again. When you are that close to death, he said, just a switch away, you are also that close to life. He pinched his thumb and forefinger together. That close.

Just give me a little longer, son.

My mother prayed hard. She looked for guidance.

She said he'd tossed and turned on his side of the bed that night, complaining of a headache. Painkillers from my mother were refused, of course, in the way that most men would refuse to put on a dress. A few more minutes passed and he sat up rubbing the left side of his head, a dull ache growing bigger behind his left eye. Is that where it's sore? He nodded. And then he got up. She heard the sound of his voice and his body hitting the ground. 'John?' she said. 'John?' My father was leaving us. He gripped hard on to his own skull and he knew.

My mother clutched her nightdress. '*John?*'

The nurse said it was time to go.

It was such a difficult job. Saying things about the dead and the nearly dead, to the living. Trying to bring them back to life with a smile, a gesture or a touch of the hand. Already his whole body had been medically paralysed, in order that the surgeon would not have to fight against the muscle tone in my father's skull when he got down to work. His body – his head – had been prepared for cutting.

We stood up, amid utilitarian furniture and cheap coffee, while strangers loaded his body into an ambulance. The men, their faces dark and their eyes anonymous, worked quietly like meatpackers filling a huge fridge with fresh cuts.

I could still hear my father's voice.

I'll be fine. Tell Mum not to worry. Right as rain. Need to nip up to B&Q in the morning. I need to sort that door . . .

The blue light from the ambulance swirled. There was no sound except for our footsteps in the rain as we hurried to the car. We sat behind the ambulance before it pulled away. My father and his exploded brain were being ferried inside and I pictured him in there holding his own brain and looking at it and shaking his head and saying, it's nothing. It's not *that* bad. It's just a cut.

We all sat in the car. I was driving. But first I needed to talk to the driver of the ambulance. I had to tell him that my father would try to get up and it didn't matter that he was comatose. That was irrelevant. He would shake his head and say, what the flip was he doing inside their van? He would say that *his* van was just fine and that they had better not be working for the government either and where were they taking him?

I also needed to speak to the surgeon, the one who would be drilling a hole in my father's skull. I needed to tell him to watch out because my father would wake up during the operation and tell *him* what to do. He'd just wake up. No matter what drugs they'd given him. He'd be awake. You couldn't knock the man down with an engine that turned the world.

The ambulance wouldn't slow down. I followed the blue lights.

It would be fine, I thought to myself. There was the Celtic match on Saturday. I still hadn't called Brian. I would call him later. Once my father had been fixed, I would go to the match on Saturday and my father would listen to it on the radio, at home, and my mother would make him ham sandwiches and black tea and he would rub his sore head. It wasn't that bad. He would be fine.

In the loft there was a box. It was filled with all his drills. There was the expensive Bosch one and a few cheaper ones from B&Q that he bought because they were on the discounted table. He didn't need them but they were cheap and it made him feel busy. Each had the same purpose. To drill holes in metal, wood or concrete.

I wondered what kind they used for bone.

Chapter Three

Falling Snow

It was snowing the day he took me to see our new house for the first time. I was a slip of a boy with arms you could wrap your thumb and fingers around. My hand was in his and he smiled at me and then up at the large building in front of us. The smile didn't leave his face for ages and it would stay with me for years. He rubbed the grey stone with the edge of his thumb, holding the weight of the building like Atlas held the celestial sphere.

The snow fell on our faces.

I stuck out my tongue and caught the delicate, embossed wetness of each snowflake. We did it together. They were just like communion wafers at Sunday Mass, he said. No snowflakes were ever the same, he said, as he tried to catch some more in his hands to show me their distinct faces before they disappeared into his palm for ever. I rocked back on my heels and tried to catch them with my eyelashes. I caught some and they melted over me. Blinking and blinking, I could see oceans of falling white ghosts. There was always something about snow, said my father. It never failed to stop him in his tracks.

Earlier, he'd collected me from St Peter's Primary, in Partick, before driving us across to the other side of the city to Bishopbriggs where the streets and houses were large and the trees held snow on wide branches without much of a fuss. We drove in his old grey car with the sagging and cracked leather seats, as cracked as an old clay pot. I watched, mesmerized, my face pressed to the window while the white city drifted by in a blur. I drew wet faces on the glass.

'Still don't know how we got it,' he said, quietly. 'Borrowed God knows how many tenners over the past few months. Didn't think I'd a chance.' He sounded like he was talking to my mother, but she was back in the flat. It was just my father and me. I liked it that way.

He shoogled his heavy blue coat and the snow dropped from his shoulders and his arms. He tilted his head up again while I craned my neck. This was our new house. It looked like a giant, post-war ocean liner towering above us. I pressed my nose into him. He smelled of Benson & Hedges, oil and biscuits. 'What a house, my boy. What a house.' Apart from the church near Gardner Street where we still lived it was the biggest building I had ever seen close up.

Behind us a robin scratched at a tree root, searching for dead leaves and moss. 'Those wee robins will sleep anywhere,' he said. 'Under the car bonnet or in my old shoes. If you can sleep anywhere you'll be fine, eh? I tell you something, we're fine now.' He bent down in the snow-covered grass in the front garden and pushed aside the top layer with his shiny, black Sunday shoes until he could see the green that lay dormant beneath.

'See, Michael. The snow preserves it all just now. It's like a freezer looking after the food. Protects it from the top down. In summer this grass will be perfect. You'll be playing out the back with the children. I'll get you a new ball too. You can play with Iain, and Mark when he's bigger. The girls too.' He re-covered the bare patch of grass and cupped his hands before lighting up a cigarette. He talked as he smoked.

'You can play like Kenny or Jinky or Bertie,' he said.

Bertie Auld was one of his favourite Celtic players, he said. He was from Maryhill too and as tough as a rock-solid middleweight. Black-haired, good-natured and matador handsome, Auld had first joined Celtic in March 1955 from Maryhill Harp. After the signing he returned home, with his father, on the back of a coal lorry. He had received a signing-on fee of twenty pounds and the young Auld, who had three brothers and two sisters, offered the money to his mother and she promised him a huge treat as a reward.

Auld shared his single bed with the brothers.

Later that night, in desperate anticipation, he asked his mother what his treat was going to be. 'What end of the bed do ye want tae sleep on?' came the answer.

My father always laughed at that. '"What end of the bed do you want?" Brilliant. Just like you lot.' He liked Auld because he had been raised with a smile and old-time politeness by parents who would always struggle for money but not love.

'You can learn to play football out the back, like Bertie in Maryhill,' he said.

I shivered.

My father loved the winter and the snow. There was something plaintive about it, he said, but I was too young to know what he meant. I'm freezing, I said, and he just laughed before holding both my cold hands, which my mother had covered in woolly mittens, in his. Stamp your feet, son. The snow fell into the neck of my wellington boots.

'Can we go now, Dad?'

'Not yet. Won't be long.'

The snow was in his hands. Snowfall always made everything new. A mute landscape of potential. A blank white of possibility. But the snow, he also warned, could freeze a man to certain death.

There was a girl at my primary school who'd come from Australia with her parents for only a short time, and she'd never seen snow. The teachers said she was nervous but she wasn't, not for one minute. Now I remembered her face in the playground when she was allowed outside and she was so happy she almost cried. I didn't know her name and probably never would but that never really mattered. What mattered was the delight on her face when she looked up to the sky and let the snow fall on her as I had done with my father only a few moments earlier.

She had red hair and wore a grey duffel coat. A cardigan too. She had probably never known it so cold before in her life but she didn't care. The memory of the sun in Australia had gone and was replaced by the cold and the ice of Glasgow in winter. Some of the boys annoyed her by pulling and tugging her hair and she would shout back at them in her strange, exotic accent. Even then I loved everything about her.

When the snow came she stood by herself in the middle of the playground, her hands out wide catching the flakes, and then she twirled around, laughing. We never spoke, at least I don't remember speaking, but almost forty years later, I still remember her as if it was yesterday. Some things were not supposed to leave you. They could change over time. You could add new dimensions but the basic picture remained the same.

That's the way it was with my father that day.

He was as happy as a red-haired child in snow.

The house was a tall, detached stone structure built over a hundred years ago by people, he said, with more money than sense, but he was glad they had. Bishopbriggs had a bowling club, a rugby club and golf clubs. It had a big library too. A train line ran through it to a neat station. It was a far cry from the top-floor tenement where the Tierneys all lived, at that time seven siblings, and my parents, in a two-bedroomed flat. My mother wanted more space because we were growing but she worried about leaving the flat where my father had built fitted wardrobes and a fitted kitchen for her, and besides the children were settled there too.

He wanted to give us more.

Bishopbriggs was part of the historic parish of Cadder that boasted a fine history, it seemed, with lands granted by a pale King William the Lion to Jocelin, a Cistercian monk and the ruddy-cheeked Bishop of Glasgow. But these things meant nothing to my father. They were simply the names of old thieves. They must have been, he said. Behind every fortune there was a crime and don't be forgetting that now.

He would say things like, aye, they remember the names of the kings who owned the land but no one remembers the names, or the blood, of the poor men and women who worked it.

I learned later that Bishopbriggs had been bombed by the

Luftwaffe, near South Crosshill Road and near the library, and a pane of glass had shattered in Kenmure Church, but my father said that was a long, long time ago and we shouldn't worry about the old Germans now. It was the British, he said, who were for the watching. If they told you one thing you'd be better off believing the other. He said it's the moneymen you need to watch out for too and no mistake about that at all.

If you shook the hands of moneymen, you'd have to count your fingers when you let go. The moneymen could do what they wanted and the poor people could sing for their supper. If you wanted the truth, just shake on the Bible. That's where poor people kept their pound notes.

All he really wanted was a house big enough to keep his children from straying into bother. My father said some people thought we were moving upmarket and forgetting our roots but that was nonsense. We could never forget our roots even if we lived in a castle and he told us his stories every day just in case we forgot.

Some people called it Spam Valley because they said that if you lived there it was only because you could afford the house and nothing else. A big house and no food. Just Spam. You were buying the house only for show. You were showing off but you never had two bob to rub together. You were lifting your skirt to show a bit of ankle. You would be eating Spam for the rest of your days.

My father said he owned the house now.

It belonged to him and my mother. They might have to wash their faces in cold water for the next ten years but it was theirs. The bank or the building society didn't have a penny of the place. He'd paid for it with every last coin he had, and he'd to sweat hard for it, and my mother too, and people could say what they liked. Some of them thought that he'd taken on too much work but that's what God gave you two hands for. He touched the stonework again. 'It's ours. It's your mum's. I'll fix it up for her if it's the last thing I do.'

And there was nothing wrong with Spam anyway because, sure, his mother and his father and his uncles and aunties all ate it. His father probably ate it in France, he said. He would have punched open his tin can of Spam with his pocketknife, with the rest of the soldiers, while they sat in the fields or at a farmhouse table.

But he didn't talk much about him. My grandfather was a ghost. My mother said it was taboo. I didn't know what that was either, but she raised her eyebrows when she said it so it must have been something. My grandfather was long dead but my father never let him go and he kept him alive like a thousand fat candles. It was hard, said my mother, because he was only a baby at the time. He grew up without him but he kept him alive in his imagination. That's what you do with the dead. Sometimes you did it with the living as well.

And anyway, people should stop being so pass-remarkable about poor folk trying to get ahead. What if it was Spam Valley? They could all just take a run and jump. They could all jump in the Clyde. They could take a long walk off a short pier, he said. They could away and boil their heads.

We should all help each other instead of laughing at each other and then we would all be a lot better off.

I knew my grandfather was in a box in a hole in the ground, somewhere in another country. Sometimes it felt like my father was in there with him, staring at his dead father's face. Other grown-ups would get things out in the open when they were worried and say things like, well, the past is past. Or let sleeping dogs lie. Or that's about the size of it then. Time to move on. My father wouldn't even mention it, or only very rarely. That's how I knew it meant so much.

Our house sat off the main Kirkintilloch Road.

He said it meant 'fort at the end of the hillock', whatever that meant. And he laughed, and held my face. 'Do you know what a hillock is?'

I shook my head.

'It's a fancy wee word for a small hill.'

Our street was lined with privet hedges that went all the way up to the Kenmure Church of Scotland, at the top of the road. It rang a loud bell in its stone belfry on Sundays. It belonged to the

Protestants. They had a different God to our God. Theirs was a wee bit more severe. They weren't that much into smiles.

Their God didn't like you laughing much. He wouldn't let you play on the swings on Sundays and He didn't much like anyone singing my father's songs. He didn't like statues of Our Lady and He didn't like you drinking Guinness and He said that's what all the Catholics did. We ate fish on Fridays too. The Protestants called it Catholic steak. He put children in the bad fire and they couldn't get out even if they were sorry. *And* their God supported Rangers.

When my father drank his Guinness he said it was just to annoy them. He said they were nutters thinking what they did about us. Most of them were off at Plumpton.

Kenmure Church had Gothic windows that looked on to the Men's Own Quarry. The Men's Own came alive at night, said my father, with the wild boys and the ghosts of the Good Templars that used to ride around there in a right hullabaloo at all the drinking going on under their very noses.

When I first saw the new house it was already familiar, like the one I drew in class at St Peter's. I always drew it tall and wide with two upright chimneys weeping upwards with clouds of smoke and huge bay windows and a big front door with a black, circular doorknob. For all the world the house looked exactly like my father, square-shouldered and staring directly at you. Immovable too.

He didn't mind the church up the top of the road. As long as it didn't mind him. And as long as it didn't mind us either.

My father said that the house was big enough for all of us, and we could all stay there for ever. No one would need to leave even when we all had children of our own. 'We'll all live here together,' he said, and you couldn't get the smile off his face with a blowtorch or a police stick.

Jack had just discovered his beanstalk.

Alice had slipped into the rabbit hole.

My father had bought his house.

He bought it for the sunshine. He knew that it would spill through the windows in summertime, the way it couldn't in a tenement with the toilet in the close downstairs. It would come in from over the Campsies and into the garden with the trees and the gooseberry bush. It would spill over the brambles that we would squish when they were ripe and pretend it was blood. It would lap around us playing football and tig and kick-the-can and we wouldn't have to worry about a thing.

The only other family to have lived there were the Horgans who, my father secretly believed, had been German spies, on account of all the radio equipment and German–English translation books left behind in the loft. Despite the fact that the Germans had killed his father he still felt an affinity with the old lady as she came from the land of his people. She was as Irish, he said, as harvested seaweed from Harrigan's Rocks in Toormore Bay. She was certainly from some grand Irish family, he said, with a house like that. She must have had a few bob in the bank and under the bed too, and no messing around for sure.

She had an album of treasured photographs that told the story of a wealthy family, perhaps from Kilkenny, given the images of the Castle of Kilkenny and one of Derrynane O'Connell in 1875. They were kept in an album that looked like a Bible. She had three photographs relating to the Boer Wars in South Africa, with a portrait of a handsome and goateed old fella named General Christiaan de Wet, some kind of rebel leader and politician who served in the first War of 1880–81, and who took part in the Battle of Majuba Hill, wherever that was. Two other photographs, of soldiers shooting, would have been from the same time and the men also had beards.

For some years she lived alone, with the utmost caution, following the death of her brother in an accident, and much of that loneliness clung to the walls of the house for years thereafter. I would never know her age, nor did I want to, preferring instead to do as my father did and let her live in the gnarled branches of his imagination.

But I would always be thankful to her.

Mrs Horgan died, as quietly as a door being shut, allowing my father and my mother to inhabit her old existence in her old rooms and garden and make them new. They swapped their life the way some people swapped coats, and that was all that really mattered. They took seven children from one side of the city to the other and added two more while they were at it. That was *all* that mattered.

My father could not have been happier buying his home from such a capable and mysterious Irish woman. She became part of his time-travelling experience: helping to carry his Irish past much in the same way that Mrs Horgan herself had brought her secret life to Scotland in a suitcase filled with the ancient, the present and whatever lay in between.

And where are my people from, I said to the big fella, and he looked at me quizzically and said, from the same place as his people, of course, in Ireland, with the cottages and the streams and the old post offices and statues of Our Lady at the side of the roads and with all the red-haired frecklers. And what about the twins and the rest of us? We were all from the same place, of course, as Irish as two-bob cabbages.

And what about Mum's people, are they from Ireland too, I said, and he said, sort of, but not really, they were from up north in the Hebrides in Castlebay and Eoligarry and Kisimul Castle that sat in the water. I said, that's nice, maybe we should all be Scottish like Mum because we were born here same as her. And he looked at me funny and then laughed and said, 'What's all the questions about? What are you, a wee polis or something? Are you a wee skittering polis? There'll be no wee polis in our family.' He lifted me up in the air and threw me higher. My feet flew above his head.

And anyway, he said, like your wee granny used to say, if a cat has kittens in the oven, doesn't mean you call them biscuits. And I said, I don't see what biscuits and ovens have got to do with being Scottish.

When you're bigger, he said. When you're bigger.

The porch had two imposing green storm doors, berthed in front of a bushy rhododendron. The shadows cast by the delicate fingers of every branch covered the front garden and gave an extra sense of privacy, and sanctuary, to his new home.

'Ah, well, Michael, the poor old lady is dead,' he said, and I knew his heart was beating loudly at her memory. 'But that's what happens.'

And then he said something about stuff being ordained this way and that's the way it goes and this was this and that was that. And sometimes, good things come of bad so don't worry about it. He said if she was alive she would be delighted that a big family like ours was moving in, even if it set the cat amongst the pigeons with the neighbours up the road – and he did the nudge-nudge thing with his head – in the big old Presbyterian church where they cast stones at the heathens.

If I'd been older I would have said, you're as mad as a box of hair.

He took a sweet from his pocket. He always kept something there for one of us. He sucked the oose from the sweet, spat it out and gave the boiled offering to me. He sucked the snotters out of my nose once, to help me breathe. He said it tasted like a slug.

I had a packet of crisps too and a plastic bottle filled with Creamola Foam holstered in each pocket.

'Who killed her?'

'Nobody, son . . . I think she just grew tired. Maybe she missed her brother. Anyway, wee boys don't need to worry about that kind of thing, now do they?'

I held his hand and thought of Mrs Horgan in all her reduced ways staring at me from the watery, bubbled windows. Over the years I would imagine her, a respectable woman who kept her burial clothes in the top drawer of a large brown chest so that, as the long days passed, she took some comfort from knowing how she would be dressed when she departed. Even now I shuddered at her fate.

'Is she in heaven?'

'Oh, I would think so.'

'Is she there with your daddy?'

He laughed at the question, pulling a face as though he'd just eaten something bitter. 'Who told you about my father?'

'Mum said he died when you were a wee boy. Like me.'

He knelt in the snow and talked softly. 'Oh, did she now? Well, I think he might be up there right enough. He was a soldier and a good one too.'

'Do you miss him?'

'Yes, I do.'

'Does Granny miss him?'

'Oh, I think she does. But she knows where he is. She prayed for him to get into heaven quickly. She said, "I hope Michael gets to heaven half an hour before the devil knows he's dead!" But I was just a baby so I can't remember him. Anyway, let's have a look inside.'

'His name was Michael? Did you name him after me?'

My father laughed. 'Yes.'

'That's nice.'

He lifted me up.

I rubbed away a knot of dirt on the window with my mittens. With its broken cornices and holes in the ceiling, the room looked like an impeccably mannered shipwreck by the Clyde. My father blinked before uttering something silently. He was talking to the building. Then he turned away from the house and looked across the road at all the other houses in our new street. He pointed up the road and said that Kenmure Church had to give away its railings during the war. The army needed all the metal they could get for their munitions. There was a soldier from the Scots Guards, he said, who once lived in Brackenbrae Avenue, just round the corner, who was killed in France too.

The street was something out of a postcard, he said.

'Are the people here nice?'

'I don't know, Michael. We'll soon find out, won't we now. You can tell good people by how they treat children.'

'Can you lift me higher, Dad?' I said, eager to see new things.

Through the glass I could see boxes and cobwebs, a dirty carpet, some peeling Chinese-style wallpaper, a big fireplace with broken tiles, a few sticks of furniture and a pile of yellowing newspapers abandoned like an old, dead goose. There was a hole in the plaster of the ceiling, as if someone had put his large boots through it, and some of the lathe was poking down like a ragged jigsaw face.

None of it worried him. He had lots of dreams and plans. He was an idealist and a maverick. He said he wanted to dig a giant bunker out the back where we could hide from the next big war.

And he wouldn't be put off by anyone, he said, because the whole country was full of people who said you couldn't do this and you couldn't do that, and where are you from and what's your religion, and were you in the funny-handshake mob and how old was your granny, nudge, nudge. And how far have you travelled, wink, wink? But never mind them, he said. You should just get on with your own business. He said we would do our best to fit in and do our own thing and we wouldn't worry about what the others thought of us if they thought anything at all.

Sometimes, he laughed and said he didn't have a brass razoo. He didn't have two bob. He didn't have a pot to do a pee in. He said the church mice had more than us. But that was fine. We had the house.

We didn't need money.

He said money didn't buy happiness.

My mother joked that he didn't know where to shop.

He believed in the corrupting and dishonest influence of money. Instead, he would fix the house for sure, no matter how long it took. He would plant vegetables out the back, carrots and potatoes and leeks and peas and tomatoes. He would be happy there with all of us, amongst so much grass and so much stone. But he would never have any money. That was his belief. As natural as a leaf falling.

And we would all be happy.

I wasn't sure what to believe.

He also told me if I swallowed seeds a giant watermelon would grow inside me. He said if I made a funny face the wind would make it stay like that. He told me if I kissed a girl all my teeth would fall out . . .

The name of the house was *Belisle*.

'Imagine having a house with its own name,' he said. If I recall anything it was how alive and at ease his eyes were. 'It's French. It means beautiful island.'

'Like Barra?'

He shook his head. 'Is your mum putting you up to this, you wee scoundrel? It's from Brittany. Somewhere in France, near where my father is buried.' He said the last bit slowly, like my grandfather might have died the previous week. But the deadness stayed in the air. Then he took a deep breath. 'Funny that, Michael. Our big new house is related to France. Not bad, eh? A chateau. But I'll put our own name on the door.'

There were dots in his life everywhere. He just needed to join them up.

He was so proud of his name, my mother would say. Proud of who he was and where he came from. 'He wouldn't let go of Ireland for all the world,' she said. 'For all the tea in China. That was just your father's way.'

Our feet crunched on the snow as we walked over to the long, narrow passageway where the red-brick wall began and ran into the large garden. 'A lot of work ahead, my boy.' He whistled and lit up another cigarette. A swirl of blue-grey smoke drifted into the cold air. He peered over the wall into next door's.

'I think there's an old man and lady lives there. Need to watch the ball doesn't go in the garden too much, eh?'

He blew another swirl in the air. There was no one else about.

'Like a big, Irish castle,' he said, excitedly. 'Like Cuhullin's.'

It was 1974 or 1975, I can't remember exactly. That was when I first started to hear about Celtic and Ireland and his tales and myths and songs. They were his paper and glue.

But sometimes the Irish stuff didn't make him so happy.

Harland and Wolff, and the B-Specials, and the Black and Tans, and Oliver Cromwell. He called them all a right shower. A shower of dirty scoundrels. They would disgrace a nation of savages, the lot of them. But I wouldn't know any of them from a can of paint. Sometimes you could close your ears and not hear adults talk. Other times you opened up your ears and you sang along too. The singing was good. Even though I was just a boy I loved the songs my father sang and whistled.

'Sing "Whistling Gypsy Rover" Dad . . .'

And he did.

He rubbed my head while he sang and my head turtled into its own cold and slender neck. He bent down and fixed the top buttons on my jacket, singing through the cigarette that dangled from his lips. He liked to smoke. It calmed him. And I liked to watch. 'The Irish say tobacco is really just a vegetable,' he said, when I asked him why he smoked.

Then he began to whistle another. 'The Black Hills of Dakota'. He sang the song when he was happy and when he was working and when there was a smoke between his powerful fingers and when we played out the back and when my mother put a hot meal of stew or liver or chicken and vegetables in front of him and when he waved away the steam with his hands and said, thanks, Cathie.

The variable nature of memory is a curious thing. I'm not sure if all these details are correct but I know it *felt* like this. They might not have happened exactly this way, but it is the way I always want it to be.

I was picked up from school. I was driven in the grey car, but I can't remember if we went to the tenement flat first to see my mother and brothers and sisters. I can't remember all of it. Did my father wear a blue coat? I remember him wearing a blue coat, but I don't know for sure if it was on *that* occasion when I saw the house for the first time. It was snowing, for sure, but was it really so heavy that it changed the world around us?

But I did it again, over and over. I closed my eyes tightly, trading memories like football cards.

I could see my father, a stub of his cigarette between the grooming and middle finger, red ash burning his skin but he paid it no heed, taking me by the hand and walking us round the side of the house, the snow melting on my face, to the big old garden that went on for ever. He flicked the butt and it died in the snow.

The garden, covered by a veil of white, was one of the first things that I could ever recall in my life, apart from my mother, that was truly beautiful, and its vastness wrapped itself around me. I'd never really seen a real garden before, apart from the small, communal one all the families who lived in our tenement shared. We played in the grass of the Botanic Gardens but my father said we were only loaned it on Saturdays and Sundays.

My mother had said they couldn't afford the house. She said that there was too much work and there was. She said she would support him but it was so much to take on and could he manage it all by himself? He said, of course he could. He could afford it *because* it needed so much work and that was the way it had been ordained. We shouldn't really have been in that street. It was made possible only by old Mrs Horgan's dying off and all that stuff and the sheer Victorian state that she'd left the place in.

But our new garden didn't need a lick.

It was a vast field. Just like a football field. It had a feeling of distance and weight. It was the best football field we'd ever seen, an altar of green. It was as big as Celtic Park, he said, where Hay and Connelly and Davidson and Macari and Dalglish and Gorman and McGrain and McCluskey and Quinn all played. We were Quinns too. On my father's side. Celtic was in us, he said.

Our own pitch, he said. Imagine having your own football pitch? Where you could play three-and-in, shots-in, best-shot's-the-winner or just keepy-uppy till the sky grew dark and your feet and knees ached. My father would go in goal and he'd say, you can be Kenny and I was, and it would be impossible to score against my father because he was so big, but now and again he'd let one in because he knew it was driving you mad, what with all those goals that were saved. He saw us in a huff. So one would roll through his legs. And we'd shout, you let that one in. And he'd shout, no I didn't, it was a great shot. And we'd shout back, that's it, I'm not playing.

And that was what it would become for my brothers and for me. Our own pitch. Our own stadium. Celtic Park. My father said we nearly had enough players for our *own* team. A few more and we could field eleven Tierneys out the back. The girls could join in a game as well if they wanted, or maybe just use it as a place to run around laughing in their bare feet and their red cotton shorts. They could still just *play* . . .

He pointed to one of the large crab apple trees, bereft now of its fruit. The gooseberry bush beside it was covered in a sparkling, icy-white dress that looked like a gang of swans at rest. He had a broken branch in his hand and he was whittling it down with a small penknife.

'Hey, *look* at those, Michael,' he said, his voice filled with surprise. 'Perfect for climbing. Go on, climb to the top.'

'They look scary.'

'You know what can't climb trees?'

'What?'

'All your worries . . . You just need to be careful. I'll hold you. You don't need to go *all* the way to the very top.'

'Nah . . .'

I threw snowballs at him and he was mock-amazed when one landed on his coat, acting like he'd been all shot to bits and blown up by the Germans or the Japs. Then he came back to life and fired one back. We rolled snow and slowly it gathered more snow, getting bigger and bigger like a pale horse rising from its knees until we could no longer push at all.

The snowman had no face, no carrot nose or coal-black eyes. The snowman looked empty and alone. It knew it would only be there for a short while. I looked at my father, eagerly packing snow with his cold, powerful red hands on to the body of the snowman without a face. He took out his camera, a Zenit. It was Russian. He laughed and said it was pure rubbish. He took a photo anyway.

I didn't even know what age he was. It was always hard to tell with him. He was in his early thirties, I think. The years had already passed like a steam train, he said, what with half a dozen children and more on the way. He was handsome and smart with curling hair that my mother loved. He was tall. His arms were like pistons and his legs were as long as the Liffey.

The snow fell heavier on the two of us.

'Do you like it?' he asked, still throwing snow in my direction, knowing my answer already. 'What you think, son?'

I nodded. It was ours now.

'Your mum will love all the space. Just wait till I fix it. We'll bring a load of good stuff to it.'

He could be infuriating, said my mother occasionally, drive a person to distraction with all the rubbish he talked sometimes, but he always made her feel safe and warm.

The swirls of snow were still stuttering down. We sat down in it at the bottom of the garden, where the red bricks from the old outhouse lay by the back gate, which led to the quarry. There was no one and nothing in the quarry apart from all that white. There was so much white it was blinding. The house peered back at me. There were loose slates hanging off at the gutters. One of the clay chimney pots wobbled. It had a crack down the middle. The skylight and roof looked like an old man staring out of one eye.

My father said it would be summer soon. We would go to the hills for the views. We would look back from the Campsies and see the house in all its glory.

Chapter Four

Colonel Gaddafi's Green Book

The wild rabbits from the quarry sat perched like stones before dashing to the trees for cover. He caught a grey-brown baby rabbit for us once, and put it in a makeshift pen but it died a few days later. He was angry and upset at the unnecessary death. We had fed it raw carrots and celery but it was a wild rabbit and we had only made things worse. We made a mistake. It got sick. My father sat us down and said that the rabbit was a small, weak thing and that we must learn to look after things like that better.

We buried it in the garden and the children stood around the hole and we said our prayers and hoped that God would keep the baby rabbit safe in baby-rabbit heaven. My father promised it would go straight there overnight on the rabbit express. The following morning the earth had been dug up. At first we thought that God had come down and dug the hole and carried the wee piddling rabbit up to heaven. But it wasn't God. It was a hungry fox.

The younger ones cried for weeks. That's when I began to wonder a wee bit about God.

In the waiting room, my mother was praying again. I wondered about Him again too. I just couldn't fathom why He would do this to my father. There were so many more people out there much more deserving of a deadly stroke than my father. You just had to look around a bit and you could see them. There was a list as long as my arm. I knew some of them too. I could have thrown a stone from the hospital entrance and it would have landed on the heads of at least two of them.

The nurse stuck her face round the door.

'Mrs Tierney?'

'Yes . . .' She took a deep breath.

'I just wanted you to know that Mr Tierney is in surgery now. The operation is underway. He's in good hands.'

'Thank you, nurse.' She made another Sign of the Cross. She hunched down.

It would be a simple contest now, I thought.

Steel versus flesh.

Vincent was sitting beside me.

'I hope to God the surgeon's got a steady hand,' I said.

He shook his head and sighed, before rubbing his hands across his face as if he was drying it off after a long shower. You could feel Vincent's presence in the room. He had that same quietness my father possessed. Quiet and undemonstrative. He sighed deeply. 'He needs to play the game here, Mike, you know what I mean? He'll be in there fighting against every drop of medication they give him. Trying to prove to them that it doesn't work.'

Knock me out? Don't be so daft . . .

We shook our heads and tried our best not to laugh.

'You actually believe this?'

'It had to come to this, Mike,' he said. 'It was on the cards.'

My father said you would need four hands to count the cause of things. I pictured the house. The chimney stacks had cracked and the skylight was rusting and difficult to open now and there were loose tiles falling from the roof. The loft had been leaking badly over these past few winters and he always said he'd fix it come spring. But there was always something else. Too much work needing to be done elsewhere. A few buckets and pans in the loft would make do for now, he said. One of these days he'd deal with the rain properly. He'd do it when the weather picked up. But the rain kept falling.

*

My father's head was placed in a supine position on the operating table and it was shaved backwards from his hairline. He still had good hair, strong and curly, and he kept a silver comb in the back pocket of his trousers and usually combed it twice daily. Once in the morning after he'd got up and then at night, usually before he went to Quins. He didn't like you to catch him combing it as it was too much of a vanity and if you *did* catch him he muttered something as an excuse and told you to get on with what you were doing and to go and help your mother.

Lately, he'd been bothering less with the comb. He just rubbed the top of his head and that was that. It would do for now.

His body was covered in a warming blanket because the temperature in the theatre was low and his paralysed body could not generate any heat. The warming blanket protected it from a too-rapid decrease. Cooling was good for the brain, a surgeon said later. It protected it. If the patient was cooled down the cells switched off and didn't need as much energy to keep going because he was doing very little. And you couldn't do any less really than lie on an operating table with your brain exposed.

'Oh, and by the way, Dad.'

What?

'I checked.'

Checked what?

'The doctors. Every one of them supports Partick Thistle . . . They're Liberal Democrats too.'

Very funny.

It was all a matter of trust now. If the surgeon trusted his eyes, he would see that everything was ready for cutting and if he trusted the beat of his heart, he would know that it was time to take up the scalpel and begin the cold-knife incision into my father's skin. It was like slicing a good piece of ham.

Although my father's brain had detached itself from the mechanics of his body, I still believed that his mind was floating around like a sheet in the wind. And I knew that he would happily offer a few, unsolicited opinions to the surgeon . . .

Are you sure that scalpel's sharp, son? Give me it here, please. Sharpen it up on a water stone . . . make sure and soak the stone for ten minutes. Thirty strokes. It'll feel brand new. I'll be fine. Just take your time. Be as careful as you can. This is my brain we're dealing with here.

The incision cut through the myocutaneous flap and down to the bone. Because the scalp was very vascular, which meant there were a lot of fluid-carrying vessels, clips were put in. These were called Rainey scalp clips and they pinched the edges of the skin where the surgeon had made his cut to stop the bleeding. If the skin here died there wouldn't be enough material to re-cover the hole that had been made in my father's skull and he wouldn't thank them for that at all. Especially during a Glasgow winter. He'd not like that one tiny bit, walking around Sauchiehall Street with a great, big hole in his head.

I hope he's not using an old tin opener . . .

Once the cut had been made, the area was sealed and the muscle was lifted off the bone before they drilled burr holes, using a high-speed air drill. Much to my father's consternation it was a much better one than those he kept in the loft.

High torque. Nice and compact. Wouldn't mind one of them.

'What on earth would you need a surgeon's drill for?'

That's not the question, Michael. The question is, 'Why would I not have one?' If it's good enough for him then it's good enough for me. Now, tell me, why are you writing this down?

'Well, if you get through this, though it seems very unlikely, you'll want to know what happened to you. You know what you're like. It's all just evidence, Dad. I wouldn't want you saying that none of this happened and blaming it on the government or something.'

True. The medical mob will probably deny any of this took place . . . what with all the drilling and cutting business. Can't be too careful. Keep writing.

'The truth is, you should be dead already. We thought we'd lost you hours ago in the ambulance . . .'

Onwards and upwards, Michael. I've never been given a burden I couldn't bear, so I'll see you once all this business is finished . . .

The surgeon drilled the holes in the bone and placed an elevator through the holes to free the underlying dura. Then it was more drilling, before lifting the bone off my father's skull. It was like a brick being removed from a garden wall. Now there was a trapdoor into my father's head. There was nothing metaphorical about it. It was a hole, the size of a child's fist.

Meanwhile, phone calls were being made to the rest of the family and flights were being booked. Iain couldn't get home just now. He'd been working in America without proper documents and he didn't have a work visa, and if he left now he wouldn't get back in to be with his girlfriend, Natalie, and his son, Quinn, who was born in New York. Wait for now, we said. Mark would be over soon. He was married to an American. He had all the right papers. Gerard and Donald, my mother's brothers, who lived in Glasgow, would be over straight away.

I dialled the number for my father's brother, Francis, who lived in England.

The phone was ringing.

It had been some years since I'd seen or spoken with him. Francis and Anne, my aunt, used to live in the tenement flat below us in Partick when we were much younger. But that was a long time ago. I hadn't seen my cousins, Declan, Fergal, Maeve and Niall, for a good while either. Perhaps when my grandmother was last down in Horsham to visit them, but I couldn't quite recall.

My father used to drive her down to Sussex and she would stay there with Francis for a few weeks in summer. It was a change from the house in Ruchill with all her memories and empty rooms and old clothes and furniture. She would be enthralled by the journey south, along the rolling motorway and past service stations where they stopped for bacon and baked beans and tea and toast and jam, and she asked a thousand questions of my father. They took their time on the journey down, in no rush to get anywhere, and you would think she'd taken a cruise ship to Europe such was the excitement on her face when she was with my father in the van.

She sat in the front seat with her hair newly curled. My father wore his aviators and he had his arm out of the window and RTÉ was on the radio until the signal disappeared and he put on Irish tapes.

'Are you enjoying the journey, Ma?'

'It's great, John. It really is. Not as far as I thought.'

My father stopped regularly to let her stretch her legs and see what England looked like, the place where her husband had signed up for the war in France decades earlier. She always said England looked lovely and she meant it. I had never once heard bitterness in her voice. She was happy in my father's van. She knew it almost as well as he did. Although she got tired of the long hours it was magic, she said, going on her wee holidays. *Magic*, she said. Her voice was always sweet and true.

But we rarely saw Francis and the cousins now that my grandmother was dead.

My father kept some photographs hidden upstairs of the two brothers as boys. They were playing together in Maryhill and Ruchill. In one picture they had their arms around each other. Wearing short trousers, 1950s elasticated snake-belts and their cotton T-shirts, they looked uncommonly happy together. If they had been American they would have been something from a Norman Rockwell painting, two boys waiting to bat in a Little League baseball game.

The long shadows they cast hinted at summer and a warm, dry day. They stood on neat grass that might have been Ruchill Park, or perhaps they had wandered further away from home to the Botanic Gardens we used to visit when we were the same age. But that was an awful long time ago.

Francis picked up the receiver.

He was surprised to hear my voice. He sounded tired. Anne had passed away a couple of years earlier. I imagined it was still difficult. I told him what had happened and that my father was in surgery. We thought he might be dying. The conversation went by in a blur. I would phone again when I heard more. He would get up there as soon as he could. The phone clicked. I couldn't think straight. The only thing that was clear was the image of the surgeon peering inside my father's head. It must have been quite a sight.

The surgeon needed to make sure that he'd got the trap in the correct place, as being even an inch out would make a difference to what could, or couldn't, be done. He wanted to be where the clot was closest to the surface because that meant going through as little of the brain as possible before hitting blood. And that would minimize the amount of damage he would have to inflict on the brain.

Tell him I just want a rough job. So he's to do his best . . . that'll be rough enough.

'Behave. This is really serious.'

Behave? You're not the one with a big hole in his head.

The bone flap was removed. The surgeon incised the dura, and exposed the fissure. My father's brain was now utterly laid bare. His whole life lay there, all condensed into what looked like a bloody cauliflower or walnut.

The surgeon's hands went in. There was blood everywhere, so to stop the bleeding he cauterized the surface of the brain with an electric current that generated heat to make the blood coagulate. The surgeon used a Coagulation Diathermy, a pair of tweezers with a little current running between them.

I'll have one of those too . . .

The surface of his brain was just like a steak with blood seeping out. Once this was exposed to heat and seared the blood stopped. The same principle applied here.

Despite the surface of my father's brain being intact, it was not actually working in any proper sense because all its wiring had been disrupted. It was like having a telephone that's not plugged in: you could not phone in or out. In that sense, even though the area of the surface of the brain that the surgeon would burn and cut through may still have been alive, its connections were not intact.

A suction device was used to remove the clot, washing and sucking at the same time. By now the blood was no longer liquid, it was clotted and solid. Most of it would have been like a thick jelly. Some of the clot had gone into the fluid cavity of the brain but that was not the real problem, as that would get replenished all the time. The problem was that as the surgeon was coming towards the end of the operation, he might inadvertently start sucking brain matter from around the cavity.

What? No one explained to me about all that brain-sucking nonsense . . .

While most of that material was probably dead, the deeper the surgeon went, the more damage he might cause. The cavity was washed with a solution to make sure that what came out was clear and this told him that there was no further active bleeding. If he was happy with that, and once the brain had decompressed, then the process of closing things up would begin. The operation would simply go into reverse.

In my father's case, because the brain was very swollen the bone flap was not replaced. Not then. Not ever. Given that the head was a closed box he would need extra space while things settled down. The clot had been successfully removed.

It took me a while to really understand what had just happened.

My father had had a stroke.

But it was much more than that. Another man had cut open my father's head and placed his own hands *inside* the pulsing and bloody surrounds.

There was still a real possibility that he might die.

We knew it. And somewhere, as my father's consciousness floated around, he knew it too. The next seventy-two hours would be crucial. When we were allowed to see him he was lying, as flat as a board, on a bed. There were drainage bags everywhere, including one that seemed to be coming directly out of his skull. Monitors beeped, slowly and regularly. 'The Last Post' for the dead. A melody for the dying. 'The Green Fields of France'.

We needed something more upbeat. What about 'The Celtic Song'?

For it's a grand old team to play for, for it's a grand old team to see, and if you know the history . . .

The medical team called it a deep coma and he was locked into it. Already, he had a serious chest infection that might kill him too.

My mother touched his face. 'Oh, my dear goodness,' she said. Suddenly, she became very sad. His head appeared to have been cleaved with an axe. His eyes were shut and his mouth remained open, as if searching for his last few breaths of air. Blood had been removed from his brain, leaving room for the oxygen and glucose that would nourish him back to life. He looked peaceful. I hadn't seen him this rested for years. But he didn't move. He couldn't move. His right side was frozen. And that's the way it would stay.

The things I remembered made little sense now.

A male nurse came on duty smelling of coffee and aftershave. It was Fahrenheit, by Dior. I had some at home. *Fragrance for men*, the advert said when it first came out. I remembered it now. It was like a Duran Duran video without the music. A male model walked from a beach along a wooden bridge that led into the ocean. A voice said *fifty-five*. The bridge looked like it was made from large railway sleepers. And then the weather turned to rain and he was still walking into the ocean, but then the scene was transformed and the end of the bridge was facing the other way round and he walked on to the beach again.

It was striking and eerie. I didn't know what it meant, but it seemed like the man was going towards the light, the end of his life, perhaps, before having a sudden change of mind, or having it changed for him. And he stayed on shore. It probably meant nothing of the sort. In fact, I'm quite sure it didn't.

But whenever I smell it now I see my father lying in his hospital bed trying his best to survive. That was a better advert than any.

My father was *very* seriously ill, said the nurse calmly, before pausing briefly and trying to offer the comfort of a smile. He had done this before; too many times judging by his tired voice.

'It's OK, dear,' said my mother. 'Thank you.' She shook her head unconsciously as if she was comforting him.

His voice cracked. He found it impossible to look us in the eye. 'I'm sorry.'

We returned to the room where we'd been waiting all night for news. It was cold. There was another family in there too. Polite smiles were exchanged and best wishes and brief histories of the respective brushes with death. We compared probability of outcomes in our heads. Survival rates were tallied up behind the same smiles. We pretended that we wanted the best for them. It was a lie. We wanted the best for our father.

I sat and said something that resembled a prayer. If He was listening, I wanted Him to take *their* family member and not ours. Increase the odds in our favour. He couldn't take two men from the same unit on the same night at the same time. Could He? A few days later that family was gone. The man was gone too. As dead as yesterday. It was a tragedy, we all said. Of course it was. But I was glad. We all were. The odds were with us now.

A week passed, perhaps more.

I began to miss him. But he was still here. I could still hear him talking.

He would tell Michael and George about all this when he was back in Quins and they would have a Guinness and a whisky ready for him upon the night of his big return. The boys in Quins would sing a wee song for him. Strike up the band. 'Haul Away Joe' or 'Wild Rover' or 'Shoals of Herring'. They would laugh with their pug faces, lifting their pints with fingers the size of overripe bananas and they would put the highlights of the Celtic matches he'd missed on the television screen just for him and they'd say, Christ, he's some man, that big John Tierney.

They would tell him that Larsson had scored two against Hearts. They'd say the team looked tired but they still fought their way to a fine victory. They were League leaders after all, that's what they did. Fought to the end. With ten minutes to go Larsson steered a header passed Niemi and five minutes later struck his second with a right-foot volley.

My father would have smiled and said, he was a great player that Larsson, and did we not deserve a great player like that? And the men in Quins would look at him and say, no offence, John, but what are you doing in the pub? And would you look at the great, big hole in your head? Size of a dirty great hurling ball.

They'd say the surgeon was actually *in* his head. Inside his head. Would you credit it? And they'd found all sorts of stuff in there. A bigger brain than Bob Crampsey for a start. Big as County Mayo. And the boys would laugh. Too right it was. Bigger than all the counties of Ireland. Or St Patrick's mission.

And make sure that young fella pours that pint right, George. Up to the line. Did me out of about half a pint the last time. I could plant totties in the space he leaves in a bloke's pint.

Visitors had been arriving steadily: Donald, Iain, Katie, Gerard, Anne-Rose, Morag and Nancy too, my mother's brothers and sisters. Mary was in Barra and couldn't get down on the ferry yet. Roddy had been dead a while now. The drink had finally caught up with him. Neil was sick and had been for some time. Elizabeth Anne was in Australia but sent her love and prayers.

We took shifts at the hospital, checking for any movement and signs of life. We tried to talk him back into consciousness but that was for the dreamers in us. They said his brain was still working, but what we were seeing now was the result of the damage that had been done in roughly two minutes at the very beginning of the stroke. The area of the brain just around the burst blood vessel would have felt the full brunt, and this tended to be the area that didn't recover as well.

My mother returned home daily to candles and grief. Tea and candles were the solution to just about every predicament. Even during exams at school a candle was lit and that just about got us through. We wouldn't need to study a lick. A candle for every occasion. Both my grannies used to light them all the time for us. And that was fine too. I had never heard of anyone dying just because someone had lit them a candle.

The Sussex weather had been kind to Francis. He looked well when he arrived and the contrast between my father and his older brother was marked. I couldn't help but feel a pang of envy at his health. But Anne was never far from his mind. It was years since he'd moved away from Glasgow. Even back then the change had seemed too swift, like the switching off of a light or the abrupt changing of a song on the radio. We no longer saw our cousins. My father never really saw his brother that much apart from when he drove to Horsham with my grandmother. Part of the past remained, but most of it became memory. And trying to recall a memory was never as easy as it first seemed.

After Francis had visited my father, we went to Quins for a pint with Vincent. A few of my father's friends said hello and how was your father keeping and to tell him that the men in Quins were all thinking of him and sure as fate he would have his spot back in no time at all. We drank a few quiet pints. The conversation was muted. All I could really think about was my father. Francis was happy in England. It was his home now. It always would be. It was difficult to really know how they felt about each other. I know that my father loved his brother. But phone calls had been sporadic. Christmas and New Year. A birthday here and there. It was never something I understood. I spoke with my brothers almost every two weeks while they were away, or while I was.

I remembered Francis being at the house one time, years earlier. He played the guitar and sang 'Mull of Kintyre' with my father in the dining room, before the living room had been decorated. The children were all crammed in. Some of my cousins too. The two men were both as happy as pigs in a peach orchard. And then the years disappeared.

He returned to England the following week. My mother would call to give him updates.

Early one morning, a few weeks later, the telephone rang. My mother was in the kitchen, all business round the cooker. My father had already been moved back to Stobhill Hospital from the Southern, following the surgery.

'I'm sorry, Mrs Tierney,' said the voice, 'your husband has taken a turn for the worse. We think you should come up now.'

By the time we arrived at the hospital my father was lying in the ward with both his eyes shut tightly with surgical tape. They looked like white St Andrew's crosses. 'We taped them down so he wouldn't look so frightening for you,' the nurse said. He was just staring at the ceiling as things began to shut down. A piece of tape had curled up at the edge, as if he'd tried to move it with his eyelids. But the nurse said he couldn't move at all. Apart from involuntary spasms there was nothing.

A loud sucking sound came from what appeared to be his throat. 'He's trying his very best,' said the nurse. My mother asked God for more strength while some man with a bushy beard had his head in his hands.

Another man was shouting, 'Nurse, nurse, help that man. Bloody hell. Bloody hell, where's the doctors? Is there no' a doctor?' It was a kindly act. He was shouting on behalf of my father. But he could see himself lying there too, abandoned. 'That's no' right. It's no' right.' The whole ward, it seemed, was rooting for him. Everyone stared across at my father, as his search for breath got faster and faster.

Thank God, they all thought, at least it's not us.

Christ Almighty, would someone do something here.

My father kept sucking at the air. We sat in a small room stuffed with empty cardboard boxes and a few broken chairs. It might have been a store cupboard once. A junior doctor was on her way. Neat and precise and pretty as a picture, she spoke softly and with practised concern. But she was too young to be dealing with this. It wasn't her fault. The shifts were getting to her. She had pen ink on the back of her hand. The ink had run up her sleeve.

'It's very serious,' said the doctor. 'Do you mind if I speak to Mrs Tierney alone?' She turned away, showing me her back for what seemed like an age.

'I'd rather be here,' I said. My mother nodded in agreement.

'Fine.'

I flashed her a look. She noticed immediately. She looked down at the ground. His condition had deteriorated very dramatically overnight, and they suspected it might be another haemorrhage. Her voice was gentler now. If that was the case – she paused – then we might have to prepare for bad news. She would let us know the result of the new scan he was going to have. Another staff member appeared and asked if we wanted my father resuscitated if things got any worse. My mother rocked back and forth. Someone dropped a metal tray on the ward. I stood shaking my head.

'I don't want him in any pain,' said my mother. 'What if he's in pain? I don't want him to feel anything. He looks like he's in pain. Oh, please God, what are we going to do?'

'If the situation was reversed,' I said, 'he would never, ever let you go. Ever. No way.' He would have spat the answer out. 'He wouldn't, Mum. You know that.'

'I know, Michael . . . I don't want to. I won't. But the pain? I don't want him in pain. He looks like he can't even breathe.'

My father would tell the doctors to keep working on my mother, if she was the one lying there, till their fingers bled to the bone. He'd stand over them and make them fix her. He'd make sure they fixed her, and woe betide any one of them who got in his way. If they couldn't fix her he'd put on one of their green tunics and do it all himself.

The doctor appeared again. They were still waiting for the full results of the scan to come back but she did think it was a second haemorrhage, although she couldn't be 100 per cent sure yet, but the scan she had seen looked very cloudy.

'Do whatever you can until it's impossible,' I said. 'Really impossible.'

The doctor asked my mother if that was her decision.

'Yes, please,' she said. 'Yes, please.'

He was critical but stable.

He was dead but alive.

Am I dealing with chumps here? Switch that thing off? If there's any switching off to be done it'll be done by me. I'm the electrician. I'm the one that switches stuff on and off. Switch it off? Are you all half mad? I'll switch off the lot of you! Eedjits!

I wanted to tell the doctor about my father.

I wanted to tell her that he'd raised nine children with my mother with nothing and that he fixed our house until it almost killed him. I wanted to tell her that he took us to the Campsies on Sundays, and we sat drinking diluted orange juice and ate crisps and played in the waterfalls and lost our football in the craggy hills. I wanted to tell her that even though he never went to university he was one of the smartest men I had ever met and that, a few years ago, he'd delivered medical supplies to Bosnia, and smiled all the way on the long van journey across Europe.

I wanted to tell her that his father died in France fighting Germany when my father was just a baby and I wanted to tell her that he used to drive my mother from Crinan to Glasgow on the back of his black Norton when they were young and in love. I wanted to tell her that although he believed he was Irish he'd really never been happier than when he visited my mother's family home in Barra and collected shells in Vatersay and later ran cables for electricity into the house and it was like performing an island miracle.

I wanted to tell her that he took me to see Sporting Lisbon when I was fifteen because he couldn't afford to go before that and, one day, *one* day, we would go to see Celtic again. And I wanted to tell her he'd been through enough already what with the drilling-in-the-head routine, and about the bone that had been left out of his head like a lost piece from a jigsaw puzzle. And about the mighty draught that it had left in his head during the winter and how would she like to wander about the town with a great big hole in her blonde head?

Could she not just *fix him*?

My father interrupted.

Listen to me, young lady, I'll be fine as long as you don't turn that electricity off . . . I know about these things. There'll be trouble if you do, I'm telling you. Who exactly is running this show? John Bull's men, no doubt? There's no one going to turn me off at the mains, that's for sure. I'm fine. Lucozade or boiled lemonade. Hurry up, please. There's a man dying of thirst here . . .

We were allowed back in to see him before he was taken to the

Intensive Care Unit. The curtains were pulled around his bed. The whole ward smelled of disinfectant, sour milk and diarrhoea. There was a crusty dribble on his chin from saliva dripping out of his mouth. A clicking sound was coming from a machine that he was attached to.

His hair needed cutting.

His eyes were still taped shut. I kissed his cheeks. We all did. A priest appeared. Last Rites again. I wondered if that got you extra points when you were trying to get into heaven. The girls told my father he was the best dad in the world, and that it was OK to let go this time. They said it over and over. More kisses, more tears. My mother was trembling. Someone said the words 'Bye, Dad'. I don't know if the words meant 'Bye, Dad, we'll see you soon,' or simply, 'Goodbye, Dad, we'll *never* see you again.'

His head was stroked a hundred times. It just made him more annoyed.

And where are you all off to now?

The girls recited all the names of the people he loved and who loved him back. The priest began throwing holy water over my father and the machines surrounding him and praying loudly. How much of this was necessary I wasn't sure. For my mother's sake he was doing the right thing but I couldn't help but feel uncomfortable about it all. The public display. My father would have hated it. My mother needed it. It didn't really matter what I thought. The clicking sound from the machine grew louder.

Last Rites? What about my First Rites? My Rites to live a long and lasting life without some nutter turning off the electricity . . .

A porter arrived to take him to the ICU. We should go and have ourselves a coffee, he said. Just round the corner. The Americano was good and the tea was proper stuff, he said. 'And by the way . . . they're good upstairs. Down here they just tell you what they think is wrong. Upstairs they fix it. They'll sort your da out there.'

He had moved thousands of bodies around the hospital before. He knew who lived and who died. He could tell by looking at them. He was someone who knew the ins and outs of stuff, he said.

He knew where all the bodies were buried too, if you know what I mean. He winked and tapped his nose. 'Don't worry about it, big man. Your da will be fine.' He tapped his nose again. 'I know who gets a handwritten tag on his toe. See that guy over there?' He pointed. 'Aye, him. Nae chance, mate. Deed as a herring in four days straight. Listen to someone who knows.'

Celtic man?

'Probably, Dad.'

Good. Tell him to wheel me away.

I kissed my father one last time on the forehead. 'Come on, Dad.'

And the band played 'Waltzing Matilda'. You're all daft. Stop listening to these people . . . I'm fine.

We sat amid laminated menus that were sticky, evidence of a thousand fellow mourners. Some men and women were in pyjamas and gowns. A few wheelchairs were in the corner. There were crutches too. A man with one leg sat beside us, his pyjama trousers pinned up to his thigh. We didn't say much to each other. My mother's hand shook when she lifted her tea.

I picked up the *Daily Record*. He used to call it the *Daily Rangers*, suspecting that most of the sports writers supported the Ibrox outfit or had some close affiliation with the local lodge, and it wasn't for hunting. He wouldn't have the paper in the house. But you couldn't accuse him of bias because he wouldn't have the *Sun* either.

He called Rangers *that lot*. That mob. That outfit. Them.

They called us a lot worse, I'm telling you. Taig. Fenians. Bead-rattlers. Paupers. Papists, Gypsies, Bog-jumpers, Harpies, Mackerel-snappers, Micks, Paddies and Pot-lickers . . .

'Some things have changed, Dad.'

He said they weren't changing quickly enough. You couldn't believe some of that stuff in this day and age, he said, and he took great enjoyment from the fact that Protestants had always played an active role in the success of Celtic.

Jock Stein, the greatest manager of all time. Protestant. Kenny Dalglish, one of the best ever Celtic players. Protestant. Danny

McGrain. Greatest left-back in the world. Protestant. I couldn't care less if we had a team full of Yemeni Arabs, Wee Frees or Church of the Latter Day Loonies. We're all the same. It's a pity that other mob never thought the same about us.

He would shake his head, not quite understanding how anyone could belittle his religion and the religion of the people who'd come before him.

They just don't like the Irish. That's it in a nutshell.

He never disliked other men's faiths. But he disliked the fact that other men disliked his.

And what about Murray? We'll spend a tenner for every fiver Celtic spend, he says. Trying to buy their way to everything. It'll come back and haunt them, mark my words. I warned you about the moneymen.

Up until a few years before his stroke, Rangers had been going through almost a decade of domination and every Celtic fan felt dread to their marrow. You could tell just by looking at them. You could tell by the shame-filled eyes. You could tell by the way no one looked directly at each other back then. It was just too painful. It would have been easier walking around with a dead penguin around your neck.

Rangers fans, on the other hand, strutted. They marched.

My father always told us to watch the way we walked. We were never to march. It was too much like them. We weren't invading Poland.

It was impossible to escape the scrutiny. Every year from the 1988–89 season until the 1996–97 one, Rangers won the League title, equalling Celtic's nine-in-a-row achievement. Rangers were spending money hand over fist. The club's owner, David Murray, had vowed to spend double what Celtic did. In November 2000, Rangers bought Norwegian Tore André Flo for £12 million. Celtic had not lost in the Scottish Premier League that season but had not won at Ibrox in thirteen matches. Flo scored on his debut when Rangers beat Celtic 5–1.

If there was any kind of comfort for Celtic's fans at that time, and it surely was a crumb, it was the knowledge that the achievements of their great rivals came many years after Celtic's own nine-in-a-row.

There really had been no getting away from it. It had been a tough number of years for Celtic fans. For too long Celtic had all the style and elegance of a one-legged man in a bum-kicking contest. Celtic had won just one League title in eleven years and there was no one alive who could argue that was enough. McClair, Provan, McGrain and MacLeod were disappearing into history, to be replaced by players like Brian McLaughlin, Chris Hay and Rudi Vata.

The club had almost gone bankrupt in 1994. Fergus McCann, who was originally from Croy, not far from where we lived, saved it at the last minute. He would stay for five years. He would make money too. He would change how Celtic operated. But he would *save* Celtic. And he did. Some of the men from Quins said they knew his family. The Quins men drank to them all.

In 1997–98, Dutchman Wim Jansen as manager prevented Rangers from winning ten-in-a-row. I was in a bar in Woodside in Queens, New York, visiting Mark, when Norwegian Harald Brattbakk scored the goal that stopped Rangers reaching the magical number. It would be a lie to say I remembered it. I don't. Not a single drunken minute.

The following season Dr Jozef Vengloš, Celtic's gentleman manager, and Jansen's successor, was ill-equipped to take on Rangers' big-spending manager Dick Advocaat and build on the success of the previous campaign. Vengloš lasted a season. Celtic were being rocked back on their heels.

And it was getting bleaker.

Beginning in 1999, Celtic played under the inappropriately named 'Dream Team' of John Barnes and former Parkhead hero Kenny Dalglish. My father shook his head. Barnes? Murder. The man was killing us, he said. Couldn't put a stick in a toffee apple. In the 1999–2000 season Celtic had finished a mind-numbing twenty-one points behind their oldest rivals, and Barnes and Dalglish were on their way out.

Barnes had brought Celtic nothing but misery, limbo and a sports headline that would reverberate for many years to come. In February 2000 Celtic were thrashed 3–1 by the journeymen of Inverness Caley Thistle in the third round of the Scottish Cup, a result that led to the downfall of the former Liverpool star. It was a headline writer from the *Sun* newspaper, to the tune of Mary Poppins, who helped seal his fate.

SUPER CALEY GO BALLISTIC CELTIC ARE ATROCIOUS . . .

Barnes had been having a torrid time since his arrival at Celtic and his team of big-money signings, including Eyal Berkovic and Stilian Petrov, had still allowed Rangers to run away with the SPL title. During the half-time break in the Caley match Celtic striker Mark Viduka had been collared by Barnes, a falling-out ensued and Viduka childishly refused to go back on to the pitch. Caley duly completed their rout. Barnes was summoned to the Chairman's office. Dalglish took over the managerial duties until the end of the season.

It had been a devastatingly awful period. Each week the fans stared hard and angrily at the players. And the players couldn't hit water if they had fallen out of a boat.

Then came Martin O'Neill.

If he had been a child he would have arrived at Celtic on a bike without his hands on the handlebars. Not a one-handy. A *no-handy*. He wasn't scared. And he certainly wasn't scared of Rangers. O'Neill came to Celtic from Leicester City in June 2000 and decided, quite emphatically, to stop the godawful rot. No longer would Celtic be bullied on the park and no longer would they haemorrhage goals. Celtic fans stopped sitting in the damp and the gloom of Parkhead with their hands over their eyes. The worry left their faces.

O'Neill's first Old Firm game was in August 2000 and I was there while my father watched it at home with my mother, who could barely look at all. So she spent her time in and out of the kitchen making sandwiches and tea and shouting, 'Oh, come on, Celtic, come on!' My father, running his finger along the arm of the couch, just smiled.

In truth, both of us expected a sound, baptismal thrashing but

O'Neill – an Irishman to boot – led Celtic to a 6–2 demolition, their biggest over their rivals since the 1957 Scottish League Cup Final, dubbed 'Hampden in the Sun', when Celtic ran off 7–1 winners. It was surely a portent for the good. The chapels filled up on Sundays.

'See. An Irishman. I told you that's what we needed,' said my father after the match, when I went home to see him.

I looked at him. 'An Irishman? What we needed? And how do you explain Liam Brady . . .?'

'Who?'

'I rest my case . . . and anyway, you didn't. You didn't say anything. Not a word. You said we'd get gubbed.'

'Rubbish. I said we should have got O'Neill from the beginning . . .'

'Did you? Who did he manage before Celtic?'

'Ach, behave yourself . . .'

During the next Old Firm game we were solemn as the local bishop. Celtic lost 5–1 with the help of Flo, but it was a point worth arguing that even to the most entrenched Rangers fan, a 6–2 drubbing of your ancient rivals would be much more welcome than a reasonably close 5–1 encounter. In fact, any right-thinking observer would have noted that, given the lack of a fair wind or of a decent referee, that 5–1 game was almost a draw . . .

It would be easy to say now that Flo's signing and the 5–1 win over Celtic had all the hallmarks of a Pyrrhic victory. But they did. No one knew it then, but all that spending would come back to haunt Rangers in spades. There was a monster lurking behind the door.

I told you . . .

I hadn't been to a match in more than a year when my father was first taken into hospital. Work was taking me away more and more from home and it was difficult to return after a trip and argue for a Saturday or midweek game when the children were only small. But it wasn't simply work. It was also me. Somewhere along the way I'd slowly begun to change. Counsel and refuge were sought elsewhere. I wasn't sure exactly when the change happened, but I'd got married, had two children – growing to three – bought my first flat and my first car and started knowingly to shop for furniture that didn't come straight off the St Vincent de Paul lorry.

And I rarely listened to Irish music any more. I was gradually becoming a confirmed Irish agnostic. It had all happened, I think, without my noticing. Or maybe I had but didn't care to admit it.

My father noticed. Slowly. He definitely noticed.

I had spent my last couple of decades listening to my father talk about his people's history, and our team's history, and about an emerald island filled with surnames like mine and red-headed children who skipped and played in wheelbarrows by the Shannon. Occasionally, Ireland was something whispered. So-and-so was involved in this or that. A cousin, an uncle. Someone who knew someone else and they were on the lam from the peelers, but keep it to yourself.

The truth of the matter was that my father's Ireland had slowly become about as real to me as Paddy McGinty's goat.

In February of the previous year, I had been in Libya awaiting the return of Al Amin Khalifa Fhimah, one of the Lockerbie-bombing suspects freed into the embrace of Colonel Gaddafi. Later that same day, I met Gaddafi in his compound with a group of other journalists, all of us shouting and screaming questions while a camel was having its throat cut to celebrate Fhimah's release. The whole episode was surreal. The wretched camel. A big knife. A lot of blood. The fat guards. And Gaddafi looked like he had recently been embalmed. He appeared tired and only vaguely threatening.

I shouted at him. And he kept ranting. I shouted again, asking him if he would pay compensation to the victims of Lockerbie and he said, 'Who will pay for this?' before turning to the remains of the compound where, in 1986, the Americans had bombed a building, killing thirty-seven Libyans.

'Shall Libya pay?' said Gaddafi. 'No, no, America will pay.' It was a decent sound bite. A cameraman from ITN patted me on the back and said, well done. It felt weird. I watched the camel being dragged away. A Gaddafi aide said it would go to the family of Fhimah. And then we were all ushered on to a waiting bus to watch loads of Libyans waving tatty flags and bedsheets in the street. That night, while I was filing my story, my father called.

'Did you speak with him?'

'Yes. Well, sort of. I shouted at him. He answered my question.'

'Good, good. Well done. I saw a bit of it on Sky. I recorded *Sky News* on the video. We saw you in his compound. You can watch it when you're home.'

'I will, Dad. Listen, I need to get this copy over. The deadline's a nightmare and I've to call this story in to a copytaker somewhere in England who doesn't understand my accent and the phone keeps cutting off.'

'OK. Oh, and by the way, seeing as you're there, see if you can get me one of his *Green Books*.'

'His what?'

'*The Green Book*. Gaddafi's *Green Book*. All about his political philosophies and—'

'Yeah, right, I know it.'

'Seeing as you're there . . .'

'I know it. Chairman Mao-type gibberish meets Karl Marx. I'll try . . .'

'See if he'll sign it. Might be worth a few bob one day . . .'

'Sign it? Away and don't be so daft, Dad. Here, Muammar, any chance you could *sign* this? It's for my dad. And can you sign it for the men in Quins too before you blow something else up?'

'Ach, you're there, so see what he says.'

'I'll see what I can do.'

And then, almost in the same breath, he spoke about the up-coming Celtic–Rangers League Cup semi-final match. I shook my head and laughed: Gaddafi and the bloodied camel, and Celtic and Rangers. For a brief, shining moment I could see him standing in the hall at home, with the onyx telephone at his ear, grinning amid the absurdity of it all.

'Who's the ref?' I said.

'That Willie Young, I think.'

'You're joking . . .'

'Aye, nightmare. He would score David versus Goliath as a draw.'

The call to prayer sounded outside the hotel, across the onion-shaped mosque domes. My notes were spread across the bed. The part about the camel sounded promising. *They slaughtered a camel for the hero's return . . .*

'I need to go now, Dad. I'm back in a few days.'

'OK. Come round to watch the match when you're back if it's on the telly. Nighthawk to Danny Boy. Over.'

'Cheers, Dad. See you later.' I ran my hands through my hair and shook my head. 'Gaddafi's *Green Book* . . .'

The next morning I got him a copy from the hotel-lobby shop. They were everywhere, as popular as the Gideon Bible that was slipped into hotel drawers by the worldwide conspiracy of Bible elves. I told him Gaddafi was too busy to bother with a signature but sent his best.

Eedjit . . .

I closed my eyes again. He took Gaddafi's *Green Book* to Quins. He was looking at it and telling everyone in Quins that it was actually Gaddafi's *personal* copy. That I'd sat with him in his tent eating dates and drinking camel milk and smoking from a sheesha pipe, and we chewed the fat about the Middle East and about wee Yasser Arafat too, and that we'd spoken about the upcoming Celtic and Rangers match . . .

And then a nurse came striding towards us.

I put down the *Daily Record*. The nearby flower shop burst with carnations and chrysanthemums. The tea and coffee had grown cold. My mother could barely manage a sip. The nurse was smiling. My mother made room at the table, quickly clearing up the mess. The nurse sat down heavily alongside my mother and held her hands tightly.

'He picked up very nicely with us . . .' she said, with a pleasing grin and the emphasis on *us*. 'His blood-sugar levels,' she added, 'were not particularly well . . .' And then she paused. 'Not particularly well controlled earlier.' She looked around as if she was hiding from someone. She smiled again and got up, letting go of my mother's hands, but my mother held on. She needed to hear more. The nurse obliged. 'Took their eye off the ball downstairs,' she said. 'Wasn't another stroke at all. Just his sugar levels.'

'Thank you, pet,' said my mother. It was hard for her to smile. The past few hours had taken all her smiles right out of her. 'Thank you. Was it a mistake? Did someone make a mistake?'

The nurse raised her eyebrows. 'I need to get back. Take care.'

Sugar levels? I told you. All I needed was Lucozade . . .

I had always known Neil as Beretta. After the gun.

It was a few days later, while my father was still in the ICU, when the call came through. Uncle Neil was my mother's younger brother. Neil was fond, as they say, of a drink. He drank in that fast, concussive way that many solid, working-class Glaswegian men do. The drink posed short-term answers to long-term questions and these usually involved grief and a bloody fist. It was hard to beat the coruscating power of drink. He was a fairly young man who had suddenly grown very old. Photographs of him when he was younger always showed a beautiful-looking child with blond hair and an impish smile. Now he was pushing fifty and the years of alcohol had started to hurt.

The phone call said that Neil was back in the Southern General Hospital. It was difficult for my mother. Her husband was in the ICU and now her brother was very ill too. She needed to be there for my father, she said, every day and every night, to watch for any sign that he might be getting better. The next call told us Neil was being moved, to Stobhill Hospital, where my father was. The following day my uncle was lying in the bed opposite my father's. My mother melted like a packet of soft butter.

The medical staff had been unaware that the two men were related and though they apologized there wasn't much they could do. 'We're sorry,' said the nurse, 'but there's just no room anywhere else in the city. He has to stay here for a while.'

There was a chair beside my father's bed and they put another beside Neil's, and we swung between the two. Neil's body looked pale and bony. At the time he couldn't speak either. Meanwhile, my father's skull was on fire. He needed a cool bed and as many prayers as my mother could muster.

The bed allocation was a lottery. It wasn't Neil's fault that he was there.

My father liked all my mother's brothers. It wouldn't have bothered him that Neil was lying there. Not for a minute. He'd have laughed loudly if he could have seen him and called Neil an eedjit. Neil would have giggled and opened a book on who was going to die first. His odds, to be fair, would have been pretty decent.

They'd have chatted about Celtic too and Neil would have said that he loved watching Larsson and that he didn't fancy that Steve Guppy much and my father would have agreed, because he wouldn't have known who Guppy was.

'Have you got any ciggies, John?'

Away and don't be daft, Neil, you can't smoke in here, this is Intensive Care. The nurses will go mental. We're dying, remember? No point in making things worse.

'What about a wee drink? Can you get carry-outs?'

No.

'No? You serious?'

Aye, no.

'What's the Celtic score?'

I don't know. I've been trying to find out for ages. I think the doctors are all Rangers men. There's a wee porter somewhere. I think he's a Tim.

'Aye. That's probably about right.'

Neil must have stayed in there opposite my father for about a week before he regained consciousness. No longer was he the colour of old teeth. They moved him out of the ICU and I sat with him alongside my uncles Gerard and Donald and we told him that he'd been lying next to my father and he almost collapsed again, only it wasn't the drink that was killing him now, it was the laughter. His laughter filled the ward like a bucket filling up with water. And he told us all to shut up, *for fuck's sake*, because his sides were splitting open with the laughing and his liver was about to go pop.

Then we told him my father might be dying, but he was fighting it. And he started to cry. He cradled his head in his trembling hands and said, 'Ach, Jesus, no' again. Not big JT.' And then he said to his brothers, 'Remember *that* New Year with Big John?'

And they nodded and said they did.

Chapter Five

The Wrong Boat

We sat on the pavement and played in the tar on the road. We sat with an old, beaten-up football. We did it every summer, for years. When the tar bubbles had gone, erased by a million car tyres, we knew that we were growing older.

The house felt as if it'd been there for ever and that I'd lived in it for ever too. Occasionally, a deer would sneak into the garden from the fields way, way over the other side. The deer just wandered around, grubbing for food and listening to every sound and peering at us with its sad, saucer eyes. We looked at it from the kitchen window and my father smiled, rolled up the sleeves on his V-neck, and felt good about the life he was giving us.

The trees were climbed every weekend. We climbed up the tallest tree till we were holding on to nothing but skinny branches and fat clouds.

Then the developers came. He couldn't stand the sight of them with their finger-pointing and their clipboards and their telling us what's what. We watched them in their yellow helmets. Now and again they threatened to keep our ball if we kicked it again over the bushes and the trees into the black, dusty ground. And then we told my father. And he went down to see them. And the ball was returned quicker than a tadpole swims in a jar and the men in the yellow helmets looked paler than they had just five minutes earlier. And we didn't hear much of their threats again.

Mr and Mrs McIntyre were an elderly couple who lived next door.

Although both were so compellingly different from my parents, they were decent and polite and always had a look of wonderment at the number of children they saw running around the other side of their garden railings. Mr McIntyre was something on the Council and always looked very smart, seemingly dressed in his Sunday best even when he tended to his garden. With his slicked-back grey hair, green jumpers and corduroy trousers he might have been born that way out of his mother.

A little further up was John Brownlee, a bachelor and fishmonger and endearing eccentric, who fired golf balls from his back garden into the quarry at the same boys my father was aiming at with the rifle. His garden was vast and the trees at the bottom rose like fat varicose veins from the earth. 'Old John is a cracker,' my father said. 'A cracker.' And that was that. He admired old John because he was a private man, like himself, and why on earth would you want to make a noise about anything? Folk would find out soon enough.

The boys from the quarry were after the contents of old John's enormous shed, but they would get nothing from him even if his life and his good limbs depended on it. He swung his golf club like an executioner did an axe. None of us had ever seen a bigger shed. Or a bigger bolt to keep it locked. He lived in his shed the way most men lived in front of the television watching football.

The quarry separated us from Milton, where most of the quarry boys lived. We only passed through it when my father took us to St Augustine's now and again to show us, he said, what real church people looked like. A church for the poor, he said. We passed through it on our way to Maryhill to visit Auntie Lena, my grandfather's sister, who was avid in the Glasgow Irish Minstrels, a branch of Comhaltas Ceoltóirí Éireann, though we didn't even know what it was.

The children just said she was in the black and white minstrels if anyone asked.

The Tierneys were musicians and singers but the DNA hit a fork in the road when it came to me. I couldn't carry a tune in a bucket.

Although the quarry boys were still stealing from the garden, my father always said that you didn't blame the people, you just blamed their circumstances. There would be a few rotten apples but a few good ones too. They were just like the boys he had grown up with and hunger was a good kitchen and when you were hungry you would always go to the tables with the most food. Besides, Kenny Dalglish had grown up there too, so don't be making judgements now . . .

'You're the one with the rifle . . .'

'Wheesht.'

The quarry boys hid in the tall grass and the dark blackberry bushes and stinging nettles and the giant conifers, like Japanese soldiers from an ancient war. They hid from us so that they could take our sweets and school bags and maybe even the trainers off our feet if they were brand new. They would be so lucky.

They broke into the house and stole a watch and a jug that looked like silver and something else belonging to my father which made him furious. A few weeks later he had forgotten about it or he had made a phone call to someone who knew someone else. The something got returned but he still leaned out of the loft skylight, looking for movement beyond the pines. He said he was aiming for the trees but I have never heard trees shouting 'ya bastard' before or since.

The railway ran past the street on Kirkintilloch Road and over the back of the houses up the Drive and we would hide near the underpass after climbing down the embankment with my best friend, Paul, who lived in the next street, and his sister Katrina. There were lots of kids. We played like a swarm of locusts.

We played Best Man's Fall.

There were an infinite number of ways to die when I was a child. You asked the person who was *het* to describe to you three versions of the most gruesome way to die and, in return, you had to act out the death of your choosing. You could die by lethal injection administered by a mad German scientist or be killed by a Japanese kamikaze bomber. You might have a lethal injection by KGB agents or be ritually disembowelled by a medieval swordsman, no doubt

English (and a Rangers fan), who was torturing you to find out the secrets of Scotland's haggis.

You could be stabbed, shot, hacked to pieces, poisoned, skinned alive, boiled alive, have hot tar poured over you or have your bits eaten by ferrets. No one, as far as I could recall, had ever asked to die of a stroke. Years later I understood why.

We were on the tracks too often for our own good and often someone in a donkey jacket shouted, 'Gaun, get tae . . . aff they tracks, ya wee maddies,' at us because they didn't want the death of one, or all of us, on their hands. But we kept going back and gave the man the Vicky-sign.

Although we were best friends, Paul was at Balmuildy Primary and I was at St Matthew's, but it didn't matter about schools to us because they didn't teach you how to catch frogs in a net or how to camouflage yourself in the woods with mud, swimming goggles and two black jumpers. The only thing that really mattered to us, to all of us, was playing in the street and jumping from the roof of his dad's hut and hiding down the railway and collecting eggs from birds' nests and sticking a pin in the bottom and blowing all the gooey stuff out.

We'd heard that a man had killed himself by lying down on the track and he'd been cut in two by the train galloping from Falkirk to Glasgow. A small search party, in shorts and T-shirts, had gone to the tracks to look for bones and blood, but there was none as it had probably all been swept away already or was in black bags in a skip, and the rumours of the jumping-on-to-the-track carry-on disappeared into the recesses of our active imaginations, as quickly as the sun settled over the trees.

Still, a friend of the local minister up the street caught us on the railway embankment and, judging by the stern look on his face, he wasn't about to ask us to join all the wee snot-nosed Brethren children for a party. We doubted that he had ever been a child, such was the delight with which he gave away our hiding holes to my father. My father, eyeing him with suspicion, thanked him when he arrived at the house and knocked sharply on the front door. The only men who knocked on a door like that, my father said, were a polis or somebody on the hunt of a debt. Or the minister collecting his tithe.

Ignore the man, said my father, because he was half an eedjit anyways, and a friend of the Wee Free minister to boot, or whatever they were, and shouldn't they all be busy preparing for their Sunday sermon of fire and brimstone and hell damnation instead of pestering children? My father admired acts of treachery but he didn't like traitors.

'He's one of the Vinegar Hill mob, that one,' he said, and we didn't know what he meant but I'd've bet ten bob he was on about Ireland.

My father and religion were two separate and unfathomable universes. On the one hand he shook his stick at the Church of Scotland for the way they looked at Catholics. They stared down at us with all their stiffness and piousness and faces like boiled ham. On the other hand he secretly admired the fact that they were never as fancy-dan as some of the opulent stuff and the big shiny gold statues that went on in our own churches. He couldn't abide showing off. Especially if it was a church that lived on credit from the poor but had a stash of gemstones that would shame a foreign king.

Anyways, we were just to get on with the playing malarkey but to make sure we were safe and not to do anything daft when we heard the sound of the train approaching, like jumping on the track and waving at the driver or baring our bums. 'I think that poor bloke might be a bit touched in the head,' said my father, 'maybees a wee bit soft, you know. There's dogs lived in kennels that've had more fun than that fella. Just be careful. Look after the girls and the wee ones.'

The railway line was as far as we were really allowed to go.

It marked the bottom of the street and the start of another world. The world outside of family.

The quarry was haunted too by a gang of dead bank robbers. The robbers had stolen money, my father said, from a wee town post office or a small bank, and they had hidden their swag until it was safe to collect it. And he winked. And then other fellas who wanted their share of the loot murdered the robbers. The money was still out there. Guns and bullets too. The quarry thrilled us every time we ventured near it. The only way the quarry could have been improved was if my mother had sat there with us, making ham rolls and dishing out digestive biscuits or custard creams.

We were never allowed to stray too far out of sight of the kitchen window and, at weekends especially, I could see my father peering out checking where we were, looking over the crest of the small hill at the back of the garden and shouting if we'd gone too far out of view for too long. He looked all the time. Nine children meant you needed eyes in the back of your head.

When the older quarry boy approached Iain and me, we were just mucking around in the dirt with our ball. I was about eleven, and Iain about nine. It's hard to remember exactly. But I remember the boy: he was seventeen or eighteen and had teeth like a witchdoctor's necklace. He walked with an odd gait and had a bad haircut and eyes that were as dark as the bottom of a muddy canal. He beckoned both of us over. I hesitated but we moved towards him. I told Iain to stay behind me. And he did.

I looked up to the kitchen window but my father wasn't there.

'Where do you live?' he said.

'Over there,' I said.

'That big stupit house?'

'It's not stupid.'

'Shut it, you wee prick. If I say it's stupit, it's fucking stupit.'

I held Iain's hand tightly.

'What would you do if I hit you?'

My lip started to tremble. My legs felt like they were standing on quicksand. I had never been hit before. I'd had dummy fights at school and with my brothers but not with someone like him. But my father always said we were less than no one. My lips twitched. I bit them too.

Then he laughed. 'It's all right, I'm not gonnae hit you. Relax, wee man.'

I took a deep breath and tried to gulp in air. I looked up but I still couldn't see my father. The boy drew a line in the quarry dirt with his foot and then looked at me.

'Step over that line.'

I was as scared as I'd ever been. 'Why?'

'Just step over it.' His voice sounded like a bolt of lightning. 'Step over it. I won't do anything.'

So I stepped over the line that he'd drawn in the dirt and as soon as I did he pulled his arm back and punched me in the face and I jumped back, in shock more than anything, and Iain shouted something and started to cry. The older boy laughed.

'Sorry, wee man. I didnae mean it.'

I tried my hardest not to cry, stifling the tears until they burst over my cheeks. The quarry boy said something again and I waited for another blow to land. My father always said thunder followed lightning, sure as eggs is eggs. I waited for the blow. Iain was shaking his head. As long as he didn't hit Iain. That's what big brothers were for, said my father, keeping the younger ones safe. Making sure they're sheltered and looked after. That's their job. Fathers and sons and brothers, that's their *job*.

I looked up at the skylight first, with its rusting hinges, and hoped that my father was peering out with his rifle and I hoped he would shoot the quarry boy. I wanted him to shoot him through the eyes, like they did in films. As dead as tree bark. As dead as a doorknob. As dead as John Dillinger. I'd be happy to shoot him dead too. I'd be the trigger man any day. Iain would too. You just don't go hitting children in the teeth.

The boy was grinning. He asked me if I wanted a smoke.

The black gate at the bottom of the garden, the one with the broken lock that my father always promised to fix, flew open so hard and ricocheted back so quickly that my father had to shoulder-charge it twice to stop it closing. I could see his black eyes. His mouth was shouting stuff, I couldn't hear what, but I knew he wasn't inviting the boy in for dinner or a christening. His eyes were coal-black mad. Like they belonged to a horse that was trying to escape from a burning barn.

The boy turned to run but fell. He got up again and started to scramble away but fell again. My father was on top of him and he was squeezing his face into the dirt, with hands that could wring the sweat out of a rhino's hide. The teenager's face turned purple and changed shape in my father's hands.

The boy could *taste* the dirt from the quarry now. It was in his mouth and on his tongue. My father pulled him to his feet and looked four-square at him and the quarry boy choked back tears. My father let him go, kicking his backside as he went. The boy ran, spitting the quarry back into the earth and screaming that he would get us all.

'Are you OK, boys?' my father asked. He pulled us close to his chest and looked at the fleeing teenager. 'Don't worry, he's not coming back.' The boy was gone, up and over the quarry, past the black ash that we sometimes played football on and past the trees and through the fields, still shouting and cursing at my father.

'I told you not to go out of sight,' he said, but his voice wasn't angry with us. 'Come on, let's go back to the house. Mum will make you a sandwich and a glass of milk.' We wandered off together, holding hands. He just needed us all to be safe. He knew that the quarry was a world where empathy didn't exist. It meant he would have to build a higher wall.

My mother raised a houseful of children and none of it was easy, but her own mother had raised twelve so she had the better deal when you thought about it. She did it because it was the best thing she'd ever done and no mistake, even counting the times she had the sickness when she was pregnant. She said she hoped she lived long enough to see us all grown and come back with her grandchildren, and my father said, why would she want *any* of us to leave in the first place? And she said, John, you need to give them all a little space.

I knew she sometimes cried on the stairs, but only when the work seemed too much or the holes in the ceilings were still not fixed or the rooms were damp and cold. And she never ran out of work with nine so she was happy altogether.

The good thing, said my mother, was that my father was always around too and he never shirked his share, even the nappies when they were loaded with the stink. He worked as often as he could for as much money as possible but it was never that much even if you doubled it on a Saturday because you still had to divide it by eleven. And my mother said he was a terrible man for not charging people for what he did for them. Especially the older ones. They reminded him of his mother.

'She's an old woman, Cathie,' he would say. 'She can't afford it.' And my mother would look at the few pounds in her hand and wonder how she could afford to feed the lot of us and my father winked and said, all we need is a few loaves and fishes, and my mother said, you don't need to bring the Bible into it, John Tierney, neither you do. God forgive you.

'Don't worry, Cathie, it'll be fine.'

He emptied his pockets of all his money for the weekly shopping and she gave him a few pounds in return for Quins. The leftover shrapnel he saved for books and tools. I didn't know anything really about what the fathers of the other children who lived in the Road or the Drive did, but I knew that mine was always around. He could do most things but the only thing he couldn't do for sure was cook. If my mother took the bus to visit one of her sisters, or her mother, then we chalked it up as a day of fasting for Jesus.

He made tomato soup once.

He squashed tomatoes the size of shinpads – which he had grown out the back in a trough of mud – into a pot and poured in boiling water and covered the lot with a lid that looked like it was off a dustbin. It boiled away angrily for hours and turned to pips and mush. At first we thought he was joking and we laughed and then he laughed and then the laughing stopped suddenly like a broken clock and we were told to eat it because the black babies in Africa were starving and who were we to treat good food so badly?

We said the black babies in Africa could have it.

'Don't be cheeky. Those children have nothing and you've a good pot of soup . . .'

116

We looked around and swore we couldn't see it.

So he banged around the kitchen, mumbling about the poor and sweating like it was monsoon time. We all just looked at each other, made a face and tried our best not to choke. The younger ones sniffled. And the older ones shushed them and we all ate our measure till we were as full as a fat lady's sock. Boiled water and tomatoes had never tasted so unremittingly awful.

And then he tried it.

'Oh my God,' he said, making a face. 'It's not ham off the bone, is it? Sorry, children. I must have, uhm, forgot to add something. You don't need to eat *that*.' He pulled out his hanky and honked the lumpy red mouthful right into it.

It took two-dozen rounds of toast and creamy Heinz beans to quell the rebellion. He fed us cheese and onion crisps as well and told us not to tell our mother because she would likely be unhappy about the rotten-food carry-on and he might not see the pub too soon either. He handed out some Fruit Pastilles. He opened the bag of sweets and it was like opening a tin of breadcrumbs to pigeons. When my mother returned she asked about our dinner and he blinked over at us, nudging us with his eyes. We lied and said it was great but the wee ones said it stank to the heavens and could they not have more crisps and sweets to take away the taste?

The simple truth was that my father loved to be around us. He held on to us with a closed fist, determined never to let go. It was when my father was happiest.

Some people thought that a family of nine children really wasn't that respectable and my father would say, respectable? I don't even know what that word is supposed to mean. Is that supposed to be a good word? Jesus wasn't respectable, he said. He fought the good fight and he chased all the moneychangers and kicked out the tax collectors and he ate with sinners and the gas cookers too.

And my mother said, stop that, John. She shook her head. 'Gas cookers . . .'

It rhymed with something else.

Don't worry about being respectable, Michael.

Some people thought big families were a condemnation, a court case waiting to happen, but it all depended who was captain of the team. We knew that if we stuck together then everything would be fine. Sometimes people would make comments and pretend they were making a joke but my mother always said their opinions said more about them than they did about us and she'd scrub us harder behind the lugs in case anybody checked for muck.

She made sure that we were always immaculately turned out, even if our clothes were not always new or the most expensive. I went to school once in a green coat given to me by an aunt and I will swear till my dying breath that it looked like something Ginger Rogers might have worn. By the end of the day when the bell rang loudly for home I knew that if it wasn't Miss Rogers' then it must have been her sister's, the amount of slagging off I got. My mother said it wasn't that bad but she never troubled me to wear it again. Fiona looked better in it than me anyways.

She polished our school shoes daily and our Sunday shoes on a Saturday night because, she said, we always had to be well turned out for God. 'Just give Him an hour of your time,' she said, with a smile. 'And make sure you're dressed for the priest and Him too.' My father polished his own shoes till they shone. Not so much for the priest, but out of love of my mother and his respect for the inside of a holy place.

Come rain or shine, every Sunday we arrived at St Matthew's for Mass at 9.15. My father parked the van beside the chapel. Our hair was combed and brushed and our teeth were as fresh as a mouthful of cut hay. My mother said my hair had a cowlick, and a double crown too, whatever that meant, and she pressed my hair down and down into the scalp with wet fingers. We took up a whole pew when Mass began and sang like gypsies around a fire.

When the priest saw us – a procession of miraculously scrubbed and combed angels – stepping out of the van every week, he always delighted in exclaiming, 'My goodness, there's more . . . God Bless you *all*. Now that's a *good* Catholic family if ever I've seen one. Keep up the good work. Well done. Very well done. Well done now, Mrs

Tierney. A credit now, a credit to you.' My mother was delighted. My father said nothing, but looked on with a suspicious eye and hoped he had enough loose change for the collection plate for all of us when it was passed around.

He had a deal with God, he said. Sometimes he winked at me and put in a foreign coin if he came across one or an old Victorian penny. 'But I'm not always that lucky,' he said, laughing.

My mother said, 'John. Behave. The children will just copy you.'

And anyway, big families with big faith always got into heaven, said the priest. We would be at the front of the queue, he said. And, sure, wasn't God a Celtic fan too? Some of the men would smile. Some of the women frowned. The congregation was divided. Sunday Mass was not a place to be talking about football, neither it was.

Some of the priests made the easy connection between Celtic and their flock that attended on Sunday. A little joke here and there about getting back to the house in time to go to the match or watch the Cup Final on the television was enough to keep some of the men happy and guarantee their attendance the next Sunday, and away from Quins and the other shops too. Other priests made a clear distinction between the sacred and the profane and they had their eyes on anyone entering the chapel with a Celtic top on his back. The chapel was no place for football and wearing the jersey was a bigger sin than being seen naked. Or seeing someone else naked.

Sometimes the boys at Mass snuck their Celtic jerseys on under their shirts and you could see mothers smiling beatifically before the altar while hastily tucking the collar back into the neck of the young heretic who had placed it there that morning without his mother's say-so. There was always something warmly familiar about a mother delivering quiet admonition. 'Ssshhh . . . I'm warning you. Stop your nonsense. You'll get that thing off the minute you're home. Now be quiet. God's *listening*.'

We knew He was. But we also knew that He was cheering on the Cannonball Kid too.

My first Celtic jersey was rumoured to have belonged to Billy

McNeill, the former captain who'd lifted the European Cup in 1967. It was supposed to have been passed through many hands before being handed to me – probably mistakenly – by one of my uncles, Roddy or Iain. It certainly *looked* like the real thing. It was made from heavy cotton, and its slim green and white hoops were things of beauty. Although I was never able to authenticate its provenance, I wore it in the back garden almost every day after school with the pride of a first-team player making his debut at Celtic Park. The jersey had turned me into a liar of sorts. I told everyone that McNeill had given me his jersey *personally*, when he had come over to see my father for a drink and some ham sandwiches and to show off his medals, and they were all very impressed and lined up like cattle for signatures.

I worried that my tongue would fall out at the roots.

There was a strict rule about wearing the Celtic jersey. I was never allowed to go to the shops with it or wear it out, which is to say anywhere there might be any other human beings. The same went for the rest of the boys, although as they got older the same strict Celtic-jersey prohibition never seemed to apply to them. I convinced my parents that on our street was acceptable but even then my mother was wary in case any quarry boy of a Rangers persuasion would happen up the road with his big stick.

We struck a deal of sorts. I could wear it to our granny's house or when we visited an uncle in the van. But never on buses or trains.

After Mass we all trooped off to the shop for the *Sunday Mail* and the *Sunday Post*. My father got the holy papers too. The *Scottish Catholic Observer*, and maybe a *Universe*, at the back of the chapel. The *Universe*, he said, had a wee bit more in it than the *Observer*, which told tales of priests attending the birthday celebrations of old Catholic ladies in their dotage, and about younger priests moving parish and getting presents of new jumpers and boxes of biscuits from the same old ladies. I said I'd like to start a new Catholic paper called the *Rattlers Galaxy* and I got a scud round the ear for my cheek.

We went home and had Sunday breakfast and my father's plate

was the size of a town clock and filled to the edges with just about every kind of fried meat, including pelicans. When I could eat a plate like that then one day I'd be as tough as my father.

I liked Bishopbriggs. It was the only place I really knew.

As I grew older I was allowed down to the park with the burn running through it and to the Cross, and past the memorial to the fallen soldiers and the relics of the war. Maybe they were commemorating my grandfather too, I said to my father, but he would just look away or keep reading the papers.

I liked the way people said hello to you if you were out on your bike and they'd say things like, he's one of the Tierney boys and aren't they well turned out and I don't know how his mother does it. And the women, some of them as strutty as ducks and all affected voices, looked at each other with big eyes from under their brittle blow-dries. I was never supposed to hear but I did.

A big man called Alec stopped me once outside my house and he taught me to wiggle my ears. I can still do it now.

I liked how drunk men gave us ten pence in the late Saturday-afternoon sunshine when we cycled past Quins. I loved the library and the large, vaulted windows where a stray pigeon always got in and its flapping and cooing would mix with the perennial sound of a child coughing. And then it shat white goo on a book and we all laughed as the librarian's eyes went mental and she pretended she hadn't seen anything. The librarian, a pearlescent-haired lady, looked at me over a pair of half-moon spectacles and then stamped my new loan, adding the admonition that it *must* be returned by the due date or all the librarians in hell would come back to haunt me and I damn well near believed her.

I wanted to shout out that the pigeon had just shat all over the place.

But I didn't.

One day Paul asked if I was a Roman Catholic.

I wasn't sure of the answer.

'I don't think so,' I said, pondering the magnitude of the question.

'I think I'm just a Catholic. We've never been to Rome. But I might be a Barra Catholic, because we've been there. I'm not sure. Or a Glasgow Catholic? Or a Bishopbriggs Catholic. I think my dad is an Irish Catholic but we've never been there either. My granny lives in Ruchill so we might be Ruchill Catholics, I don't really know. Why?'

'One of my pals said you were Roman Catholic bead-rattlers and that you don't like Proddies.'

'What's a bead-rattler?'

'I don't know,' he said.

'Are you a Proddie dog?'

'I think so, but I'm not sure.'

Paul supported Rangers and I supported Celtic. But we just shrugged and went back to kick-the-can. Paul didn't go to Mass on Sundays and sometimes I wished I was a Proddie because I could stay at home too and lie in on Sunday or play football out the back. But he went to Bible classes sometimes and I went there with him one time. It was on the other side of Bishopbriggs, and my father made a face about it, and the Proddies there seemed really happy to see me when someone told them I went to the other school. At least I thought they were Proddies. They kept clapping all the way through the meeting and every time I stood up they clapped me too and I thought I must be doing something right so I clapped right back like an eedjit.

Another day I asked my father who was the Pope's Eleven and he laughed and said, 'Where on earth did you hear that?'

'I heard someone from school shouting, "Come on the Pope's Eleven." And they asked me if I knew who it was.'

'It's supposed to mean Celtic.'

'How come?'

'Well . . . the Pope is the head of the Catholic Church and Celtic have a lot of Catholic supporters, but not all. And so Celtic fans kind of say that the Pope is the head of Celtic.'

'Like the manager?'

'Ach, not really. Like a figurehead . . . never mind. It's daft really.'

122

My mother, who was doing the ironing, said, 'Don't be bringing the Pope into Celtic now, or I'll shoot the boots off the both of you, it's bad enough the language and shouting that goes on at those matches without bringing the Pope into that nonsense.' And she said something in Gaelic and quickly blessed herself. 'Don't be talking nonsense the both of you, I'm telling you.'

I looked at my mother. My father made a face like he was scared and we laughed together. And he winked.

We lived on the quieter edges of the city. There were incidents and mindless happenings, of course, but only my father really knew about them. There was the story of the murder of a boy in the park and someone's big brother being assaulted with a broken bottle after a football match between Celtic and Rangers. Bishopbriggs was a place of relative quiet and just the occasional burst of life. It climaxed on gala day and when someone put Christmas-tree lights on down at the Cross. The Boys' Brigade marched down our street and we watched from our windows and listened to their drums. It was never really my father's kind of thing, he said, harrumphing in his chair.

Spinsters who sang too loudly in church carried out the crimes we heard about the most.

Now and again, during Lent, when I attended early-morning Mass, another holy Joe and I would snaffle a few ten pences from the donation plate that sat at the back of the church. By the time Lent was over we had amassed a small fortune for a new Celtic top. Guilt got the better of both of us, and fearing the wrath of the Lord, or of my father, or both, we quietly returned the money under the pretext of donating it to the Black Baby Fund for all the wee black babies who were starving under an African sky.

'Bless you, boys,' said the priest.

'You're welcome, Father . . .'

'Now have you thought of becoming altar boys? Or perhaps joining the priesthood?'

I shoved the holy-Joe sidekick to the front and legged it home as fast as I could, pretending a pack of hungry wolves were after me just to help me along. 'I have now, Father. Of course I have. But the thought quickly passed. It was the Lord's decision, I think, and a correct one under very difficult circumstances, I'm sure you'll agree . . .'

I graduated from St Matthew's Primary with honours in mischief-making and overhead kicks. I fell in love with girls, but they had yet to fall in love with me. At Turnbull High School I fell further in love with football and it was, to my delight, reciprocated. We went out together, usually on Tuesday and Thursday evenings, and met up again at the weekends. After school I spent most evenings, in the garden, away from the prying eyes of my mother and father, practising till I got it right. I think they both felt I was still too young and that I should concentrate on my homework.

I would play for Celtic one of these days. That was my plan. Ever since I'd first set foot in the garden. Some of my team coaches said I could. They had been telling me for years. Some of the other fathers said it too. But my father nodded and I didn't know if it was up and down or side to side.

Turnbull High School was Catholic and Bishopbriggs High School was non-denominational, which meant that was where most of the Protestants went. Who, he said, was kidding whom? We mixed easily with the boys and girls from the other school and played in the same football team and went to the same discos and youth clubs. Separate religious schools were as much of an issue to us as private ones. There really was no issue at all.

We knew we were Fenians, Tims, Taigs and Left-footers, and we knew they were Huns, Proddies and Billy-boys. But everyone had labels. The private-school kids from both sides were snobby, short-trouser-wearing bastards, posh wee poofs and rugby-playing knobs. If you were any of those things and were fat and ginger too then school was a tough, tough crowd. Children didn't hang about with each other because of the schools they attended. They hung about with each other *despite* the schools they attended.

We never attended a different school from anyone else. There was nothing different about it. We just attended the one that we knew.

If we did ask about it my father simply told us it was because we believed in the Catholic teachings and that Catholic schools were better for learning about who we were and where we came from.

As far as we knew, the Protestants didn't really want us in their schools anyway and had never wanted us since that fella John Knox came on the scene shouting the odds about Mary of Guise and shouting the odds about the Virgin Mary and banging on about reforming stuff all over the shop, and could he not just have stayed in Geneva? So how was it our problem, said my father. And anyway, they had pictures of the Queen in the hallway of their schools and they had to sing the national anthem every day and dress up in top hats and blow trumpets and play big drums and some such malarkey, said my father.

'And there's no chance we would be doing that, now would we, Cathie?' My father would laugh. 'Snowball's chance in hell.'

Here's a memory.

Aviator sunglasses, old blue jeans and a mop of curly black hair. His white vest had a hole at the back where the wee ones poked at his skin. Then he ran his hands through his hair, exasperated, laughing, trying to herd us into the VW. His hair looked like it had been combed with a toffee apple. That was my handsome father, at his bareknuckle best.

The van was as animated as a carnival.

The Tierneys were going on holiday to Barra, with the croft and the castle and the black beasts that Granny Mac told us lived in the sea. Where the collies chased the cars by the petrol pump in Castlebay and the men chased the boys who fought in the freshly gathered hay by the pier, making a mess of their valuable stacks. It was July, I'm sure, the summer of '79. My father blew a plume of cigarette smoke out of the driver's window. He tapped the side of the van.

My mother said it was the most beautiful place in the world, and it was. God made it and it was a holy island with a good priest – even my father liked him – who preached at Our Lady, Star of the Sea, and the best place in the world for young children to run about without a worry or even a jumper.

We were packed and ready to go.

His sunglasses meant you couldn't see his eyes. But we knew he was smiling behind them. The sun shone on him and he was over six feet tall and he stood up straight because he didn't like to be talked down to. He said his glasses had once belonged to Glenn Miller, and he'd got them off a man he knew down the road, and we didn't even know who the Miller fella was so it might well be true.

'One, two, three, four,' he said, tapping each of us on the head as he leaned over the driver's seat, 'five, six, seven, eight.' A puzzled expression settled across his face. 'Number nine, number nine.' He sang it first.

'Where's number nine?'

Nothing. Silent as a dead begonia, as my granny would say.

'Where's Claire? Ach, for goodness sake.'

Lorraine, the eldest, got the first quizzical look, followed by Maureen who was born only twenty minutes later. 'I don't know, Dad,' she said. 'It's not my fault.'

He shook his head. 'Michael?'

I looked up and shrugged.

'Iain? Fiona? Mark? Where's Claire?'

Silence.

'I'd get more out a Republican in Tammany Hall . . .'

'Stop talking in riddles, Dad . . .'

He got out of the driver's side and walked round to the sliding door. Then he fiddled with his keys and pulled at another rusting flake of white paint before peering inside for a closer look. We were elbow to elbow together. 'Come on, we'll be late. Is she in there or not?'

Vincent piped up from the back, 'Here she is.'

He pulled a rustling infant from beneath a collection of brown wool blankets. Claire's instinct for self-preservation had yet to kick in. Catherine had been sitting on her. 'Get off her, you two,' said my father, grinning, while still picking at the paint, 'or I'll be sitting on you the whole way to Oban. Fine. Everybody ready? Good.'

The door of the van closed. We were packed together like loaves on a shelf. My father ran his fingers through his curly black hair again and sighed. He didn't know whether to laugh or cry. He laughed regardless. 'I'm going to leave you all behind,' he shouted, and sometimes he'd have meant it.

'Right, are we ready, now?'

He started the engine and it curdled into life.

'I'm telling you, children, there's nothing better . . .' he said, pausing expectantly, and waiting a little for a response.

Without looking up, everyone in the van finished his sentence: '. . . *than the sound of a Volkswagen engine*.'

He grinned again.

'Where's Mum?' asked Iain, proudly wearing a pair of Celtic sweat bands.

My father looked at the empty front passenger seat. 'For God's sake. Cathie. Cathie?'

'Stop saying "God",' said a voice from the back. 'You're not allowed to use His name in vain.'

He harrumphed.

'It's a sin.'

'It's not a mortal sin,' my father shot back.

'It's a *venial* sin.'

'Yes, I suppose it is. But I won't be going to hell for that. Now be quiet. Do you know how much petrol money I'm wasting with this bloomin' engine on, waiting for . . .' No one was listening.

He switched off the engine and the smell of the petrol mixed with aniseed balls, fruit salads, drumsticks and Stockley's barley sugars. It was a dangerous game opening up all those sweets in a confined space. 'Someone give me a sweetie,' he said, and Lorraine passed him a dark boiled lump that looked like hardened asphalt from her white paper bag with the twisted corners. 'What on earth? Could you not have given me a worse one?'

I sat with Iain going through our Panini football sticker album. There were seventy-two pages with the potential for 594 stickers and that included *shinys* as well. These were the club badges and more silky-textured fabric than shiny. But shinys was a good name and they were great for swapping.

Got. Need. Swap.

That was pretty much how all Panini sticker albums worked.

There was a Liverpool player on the cover jumping alongside the goalie from Club Brugge in the 1978 European Cup Final. I think the player was David Fairclough because he had a big rake of red hair. There were other pictures of stickers on the album cover: of the Nottingham Forest team (got), Bob Latchford (need), the Liverpool badge (a shiny/got/good for swapping), Cyrille Regis (got/quite good for swapping), the Dundee United badge (a shiny/swap).

And there was a picture of the Rangers team on the cover too. (Don't have/don't want.) Hold with the edges of your fingers and *swap, swap, swap* as soon as possible but, preferably, *dump* in the bin.

In all the packed sticker books we ever had we *never* collected Rangers players or teams or the badge. If we could've swapped them with Paul, up the road, we would have. But, to be honest, it was magic to see the players staring up at us from out of the bin in the kitchen.

Don't need. Don't want. Swap. Bin . . .

Half past ten in the morning. It had taken over two hours to get to this stage and we had yet to leave the driveway. Just then my mother appeared. 'All set. Just fixing my hair, John,' she said, before climbing into the passenger seat, snagging her tights as she went. 'Och, see.' She rubbed her leg. No matter the time of day my mother looked as fresh as morning bread. Normally, she was swollen with children but Claire was the last of our brood to appear. My mother looked as pretty as a petticoat.

'Suitcases in, Cathie?'

'Yes, dear. Two cases between the four boys and three for the girls, plus the twins' vanity cases, a couple of carrier bags with extra clothes in case it's wet, and some toys. Did you put in the sleeping bags, John?' My father nodded. Claire and Vincent would share. Catherine and Fiona would share. Mark and Iain would share.

Lorraine and Maureen would share. I got an itchy woolly blanket that might have doubled as an asbestos sheet, all to myself . . .

'Does anyone mind if we actually *go* now?' he said, a little impatiently. 'Did you put in the food? The packet soup, bread and square sliced sausage?' He looked at my mother and shook his head, smiling beneath his scowl. 'I was only asking.'

The engine sprang to life again.

'Brilliant, brilliant,' he said. He thought the VW would drive him right into heaven.

My mother smiled and touched his arm. 'You love your van, don't you, John?'

He ignored her momentarily.

The older ones said, 'Aaahh.'

He stifled a grin. 'You lot won't be laughing when there's no Volkswagen and you'll all be walking to school. A line of wee Tierneys in the skittering rain soaked to the bone.'

Thank God.

'Who said that?' asked my mother. 'Don't say *that*. Don't use the Lord's name in vain. You only say "God" in your prayers.'

'*See*. Told you.'

'It was Maureen.'

'No, it wasn't, it was Lorraine.'

'It was not, it was Michael.'

'Shut up, you, it was Iain or Fiona.'

'It wasn't.'

'*Don't say shut up either . . .*'

'It wasn't me.'

'It was . . .'

Vincent blessed himself and recited a prayer for a safe journey: 'On the name of the Father, on the name of the Son, on the name of the Holy Bear and Men . . .'

'Would you all shut up in there and behave and stop talking rubbish, you're driving me round the bend. Cathie, tell that lot to be quiet, for God's sake.'

'John!'

'DAD!'

Silence.

The morning looked on to a horizon of unbroken sunshine. For the next six weeks it would be nothing but cow dung, UHT milk and the beach at Eoligarry near where the plane landed on the seashells. It was the only place in the world, said my mother proudly, where planes used the beach as a runway. We would sit and watch them landing in the shallow bay of Traigh Mhòr.

My father rested his arm out of the window trying to catch as much of the beating sun as possible, the way all workingmen did. Catch the heat when it was there, he'd say. Make the most of it, because it was never around too long. Somehow, it never felt like that. Back then the summer was so bright you had to use your hand as a visor. We all went dark in the sun except for Fiona and the twins, who freckled like tinkers.

But not on Barra.

Our little island usually sat behind a fat piddling rain cloud on the television weather map. This time my mother had promised sun: the same sun that used to shine when she was young on the island with her brothers and sisters and my grandparents and Uncle John and all the dogs. It was the type of sun that made the landscape fade into the hills and the greenery too.

Uncle John was my mother's uncle and he whispered Gaelic in the pre-dawn dark at the house, when he visited, and late at night too and we barely understood a word when he spoke in English either. He would ask us how things were but all we ever heard was a beautiful sound, like the bow of a fiddle moving, or something being spread on a scone. Now and again we would make out a word or two. Schuul. Glas-cho. Sickarettes. Cel-tech. Blach Beasht. El or Catherine.

Cel-tech. We knew then he must have been a Celtic fan too.

When my mother talked about Barra her face lightened.

And we always mimicked her pronunciation of her golden island.

She said it with a soft Hebridean lilt and it sounded like a language from another world. 'We're off to *Barraigh*,' we said, laughing. She said something in Gaelic. But she was smiling too.

We would make it on time to the big ferry, my father assured us, the one that sat in the cold water of Oban. Be patient, have a little faith. The van trundled on. We spluttered through Ruchill and then Anniesland and then we hit the road to Crianlarich and he knew the route as well as he knew his van and all the while he shouted at any driver that got in his way.

'Look at that eedjit!'

'Flippin' man's a bampot.'

'Looks like all the dafties are out today . . .'

And we all said, 'Dad, you're the daftie!'

All the drivers on the road stood between him and my mother's island. Who was causing the hold-up now? Why was the lane suddenly slow? What's that fella doing in my lane? What's going on here, lads?

'Would you stop that, John,' said my mother. 'The children are listening. You're supposed to set an example.' She looked over her shoulder at all of us. At least your father didn't swear, my mother added. She was right. He never did. Why use a real profanity when a gentle 'wee eedjit' would do? He never, ever said the words we'd heard other men using. He said 'flip' or even '*frip*' sometimes. Frip was really a softer word for flip, to help it cushion the blow even more. Even flip sounded too close to swearing. But the boys knew it didn't matter what came out, it's what he meant that counted. And sometimes he meant a lot more than he let on in front of my mother.

It was no skin off his nose, he said, if we wanted to get there. Hey ho, he said. Hey ho. We went over bumps that made our bellies heave and lurch. You never remember the roads, said my father, but you always remember the bumps.

He was singing now. 'Hi-ho, Hi-ho.' From *Snow White and the Seven Dwarfs*. 'Come on, everybody, join in.'

No one sang a peep. We all nodded heads and acted like we were busy, but you could hardly hide in a van.

'Rubbish. Absolute rubbish. Come on, we're on holiday. What's the matter with you? Come on, all of you. Hold hands and we can all contact the living . . .'

'John . . .'

It was about a three-hour drive to Oban and then a six-hour crossing to Barra. We all had to remember to get off the ferry at different times once it arrived in Barra and say that our mum and dad were behind us with the tickets so that we didn't need to pay the man on the pier. It was my father's idea to do the skipping of the fares. He would pay for maybe four of us, the younger ones.

'I'm not paying for *nine*, Cathie,' he said. 'No way. You can't pay to get into your own home, now can you?'

'It's *my* home, dear. None of your Irish nonsense . . .'

He took one hand from the steering wheel and lowered his sunglasses with his free hand before giving my mother a mock-sad look and shaking his head. Although my father loved Barra he would never admit to it. Barra was real. Barra was a place you could stand on. It didn't belong to the land of imaginings across the water.

He started to sing again. Eloquent and true. All about Danny Boy and how the pipes were calling from the glens and the mountainsides and all manner of maudlin. He sang for my mother. He loved her and she loved him. And then he sang us all into silence.

'If the ferry keeps going,' said my father, once the singing had all but died down, 'if the captain forgets to land in Barra, where will we be? Where will we end up? Anybody? Nobody? Come on, it's easy. I'm trying to give you all an education, children. We'll get to America. *Amurikay.*'

He said *Amurikay* with an Irish accent. 'America. The Irish own America. And where are my people from?' Nothing. We were quiet as a box of eggs. 'That's correct . . . Ireland. So if the Irish own America, what do we own?'

'Nothing,' shouted Iain. He peered up from the Panini album, while peeling back the sticker of Stewart Barrowclough, who played for Birmingham. We shared an album but we collected our own stickers.

I had managed to offload Barrowclough to him for Peter Marinello, of Motherwell, because I knew I could swap Marinello for two or three Celtic players from a pal who needed Marinello to complete his Motherwell team.

'Nothing!' the rest of us shouted.

'Don't talk rubbish. The Tierneys own loads of America, there's loads of us there. What about Gene Tierney, the American actress, eh? Was in *Leave Her to Heaven*. We're flippin' Hollywood stars, to boot! We're related.'

But he couldn't tell us she was also in *The Mating Season*. He couldn't even say the words.

What if the captain did keep going, we started to whisper to each other. What if the captain did get to America? What then? Vincent got out a tattered map of Scotland, from under one of the benches my father had made from an old couch, and looked to see if America was anywhere near Barra. Or Ireland.

'Look, there. It's there.'

'Where?'

'*There*.'

'If your wee Granny Quinn had got on the right boat from Ireland,' said my father, his voice newly chirpy at the thought of America, 'instead of landing on the flippin' Clydeside, we'd all be living in New York now, proud as natives.' He paused for effect and a drum roll. 'And I'd be driving a big black Cadillac instead of this old thing.'

He squinted against the sun and looked into the distance ahead of him, pretending he was driving his Cadillac over the Queensboro Bridge and on to the streets of Manhattan lined with a thousand electrical workers from Local Union Number Three. Later, after making a few dollars, he'd have disappeared out west in his Cadillac and then ridden cattle, he said, and then he'd have bought an old house made of wood and a ranch and fixed it up and drunk cold beer from the bottle while we drank Coca-Cola too. Pretty as a picture.

'How would we?' said Fiona, interrupting his dream.

'How would we what?'

'If wee Granny Quinn got to America then your mum wouldn't have met your dad, and they wouldn't have married and you wouldn't have met Mum and then none of us would have been born, except, maybe to someone else who married Mum because she was born in Glasgow and you were born in New York.'

My mother stifled a smile.

My father looked like a dog had just emptied a load in his hat.

He turned silent, his face a thousand-piece puzzle. He never used two words when one would do. Now there were none. My mother hid the grin on her face with the back of her hand. He muttered something inaudible and we knew that Fiona was right. If wee Granny Quinn had got on the right boat we wouldn't be going to Barra. We wouldn't even be *here*.

'Thank-God-for-wrong-boats,' Iain shouted out. And everyone was thinking the same. Thank God For Wrong Boats.

'Iain . . .' my mother said. 'I've told you, don't say "God".'

But she didn't mind. Not that time. And we knew he was thinking it too. Thank God For Wrong Boats. He was looking at my mother, wondering who on earth she might have married if wee Granny Quinn had got on the boat to America from Ireland, away from her father, or grandfather, who was hanged from a tree or whatever it was that my father had told me once before.

He always liked the idea of the New World, but not that much. He dreamed of America but never got further than the end of his street. His head was going ten to the dozen. Who would my mother have married? He would get the eedjit . . .

'How did you sleep last night, dear?' asked my mother.

'Rotten. My leg's killing me. I flippin' just want to lie down and drain the blood out my feet. The whole flippin' lot of it. Empty my feet into a big bowl . . . killing me. I'm all twisted inside.'

'I've told you to go to the doctor but you won't listen.'

'What's the doctor going to do, Cathie? Waste of time. I've told you a million times, the medical profession only exists to keep the working classes healthy enough to work but sick enough not to do anything about their sickness.'

'Well, I don't know about all these things,' she said, half smiling, half in anger and fully annoyed at his pride. 'But I know this much. I'm fed up listening to you complaining all the time, every night, tossing and turning, the same thing. Your right leg one night, then your shoulder, then your arm, then your feet, then your bloomin' toes. I listen to it and I feel like screaming. It's the same thing all the time.'

'You don't care, you don't bother what happens to me, Cathie.'

He looked straight ahead, unblinking.

He was trying not to laugh because he knew that my mother cared for him more than the man upstairs did, whether it was a Tuesday, Friday or twice on a Sunday.

We could always tell my father's mood by how he had slept the night before. We could tell even before he'd got down the stairs and had a cup of tea and two bits of burnt toast. The mood arrived, like a coffin on wheels. We could tell his mood if his leg was sore, or if someone mentioned a terrible injustice about Ireland, or if Rangers had beaten Celtic, or if someone threw out an old piece of his wood, or if someone mentioned France and the place where his father was buried.

He disliked it when my mother mentioned the doctor's and how he should go because he just thought it was pointless and a waste of everyone's time. He never took tablets, never swallowed pills. What was the point? You might as well smell the scent from a dead cat, all the good it would do you. And for the love of all that's good and wonderful, said my mother, don't get him started on the banks or the lawyers or the accountants.

I watched my mother and father.

The two of them, sitting together in the front seat of a big white van. It had tyres as bald as a crow's egg and engine oil unchanged since he'd bought it, second-hand, three or four years earlier. The hubcaps had long lost their sheen, the window wipers were creaky, and the exhaust pipe was two bumps away from collapse and held to the bumper with a twisted, coughing coat hanger.

None of that mattered. She loved John Tierney.

Her big strong man, she always said. I never heard my father *say* he loved her. But he loved her more than anything that breathed.

Not long now, said my father, for the eighth or ninth time. But we didn't care. I was lying up the back with Iain, on the slope that rode up to cover the engine. The engine was in the back of the VW, not the front, and it was warm up there and the smell of petrol and fumes was sweeter than ginger ale. We had our comics and books and Panini sticker albums and Celtic programmes from George.

And then he told us.

He couldn't make this trip on to my mother's island. Once we got to Oban he had to turn the van round and head back to the city because he was working in Glasgow, putting light in people's houses to earn us all some money because there was precious little left in whatever pot or cupboard they kept it in. The wee ones were crying. They offered their piggy banks.

He said it might have to be bigger than that. He wouldn't be there on my birthday in Barra to light up the cake with a pocketful of candles. Not to worry, he said, if I climbed to the top of Ben Heaval I would see him waving out of the loft.

I climbed the hill because I thought it might be true.

Chapter Six

A Horn Sounded Over Kisimul

He always said that spectators never won matches. Fans did.

By the middle of March 2002, nearly two months after my father's stroke, the speech therapist said he was following simple commands slowly and that he could indicate what he wanted by a wavering nod or by moving his eyes. We had to look closely. Sometimes he moved in the shadows. But my father could no longer eat or swallow or talk. The stroke had left him in a voiceless void, silent as a ruin. Depression had quietly set in too and he was put on antidepressants for several weeks, perhaps the first real medicine he had ever taken, while being PEG-fed until August when his swallowing slowly began to return.

More than anything he looked frightened. Deep, black fear.

At night, said the nurses, when he woke alone he was scared almost half to death. Who knew the terrors that visited him with the noises of the dying and the nearly dead all around? The ward was full of others who were suffering much the same. Although the one he was now on was much more private, it was still filled with the incapacitated and incapable, the disorientated and the mute, and those calling out in private agony and abject despair. They were all in a similar condition to my father. Their brains and their bodies had let them down. Sometimes, as they wandered about in torn pyjamas and hospital gowns, they looked less than human.

The extent of his brain damage had also rendered the control of his bowels meaningless and the nurses changed him constantly and the bag beside his bed filled regularly with orange, brown and yellow fluid and residue. There was no room to worry about dignity. Dignity didn't matter.

The tube that had been stuck through his abdominal wall would have been uncomfortable but he had to bear it. Liquid nutrition went straight into his stomach. It meant that from January until August he had no solid food pass through him. Regardless of how it was being achieved my mother was overjoyed at his progress. We all were. Slowly, despite his dreams and the ghostly night figures in the shadows of the ward, he was returning back to his life.

More than anything we wanted to hear my father's voice. That would connect him back with us. A word. An old phrase. A song or laughter too.

We could feel the tension hidden in his jaw.

'Come on, Dad.'

I'm trying my best here, Michael.

'I know, Dad. We know.'

Everyone keeps asking me questions. Can I feel this? Can I hear that? Does this hurt? Does that feel uncomfortable? I don't know . . . I don't know anything any more.

'You can survive it, Dad. Of course you can.'

The swelling had gone from his brain, along with part of his skull bone, and now the top of his head resembled the dent in a car bumper. I wished now I'd asked the surgeon for that piece of bone. I'd have kept it at home in a jar, alongside his other jars filled with nails and screws. Part of the hole in the roof.

The sutures were gone and in their place were small white scarred holes. Harsh dots on a gnarled landscape. He was fragile. The huge bags under his eyes looked like they had been darkened for comical effect or some kind of theatrical performance. Sometimes we thought we heard moaning sounds. Other times nothing at all.

It was a time of worry and fear.

There were simple facts we had to accept. His brain was no longer functioning properly and might never again. It would be unlikely that he could ever tell my mother anything private again, but she grasped his hands hard enough that she might just be able to squeeze the words from him if she held on long enough. He looked at his children vaguely, as if they were strangers by his bedside, opening and closing their mouths for no reason. Circumstances had changed him and would keep on changing him. How much we didn't fully know, but it was happening.

On deeply quiet mornings and busy afternoons he would slowly begin to forget everything. His new brain was helping him forget all of us. It was taking our entire father away. And yet, he was alive.

The days and weeks passed and turned to months. Whoever was around took turns trekking back and forth to the hospital and my mother's house. My mother visited twice a day, blunt with emotion. It was hard, she said, watching other visitors bringing food or fresh fruit for their husbands and watching them sit up and eat and talk and ask how things were going at home, and they talked back. Instead, she brought fresh pyjamas and clean T-shirts daily.

She whispered to him that she was keeping candles lit in the hallway of the house, beside the large stained-glass window. The candles, as thick as piano legs, sat alongside cards with pictures of Padre Pio and Jesus, and both of them looked imploring. The cards kept curling up. 'You need to say your prayers,' she said to all of us and, in the beginning, some of us did. 'The Holy Ghost moves in invisible ways.'

Listen to your mother . . . A bit more faith, lads, please.

'You're one to talk . . .'

The months lying on his back led to terrible bedsores that pained him with every movement, and the nurses, despite his bewildered and confused looks, had to shift him and stand him and shuffle him while he winced. Sometimes, he just lay awake for hours. It had been a while since I had seen him smile. The months had erased his identity, or parts of what we understood it to be. Occasionally he did smile, but it didn't light up the room the way we wanted. It just sat across his face, like a half-moon, and tried to break the monotony of his suffering. I had forgotten what he looked like when he smiled.

When we hugged his body it was foreign, strange and old and as stiff as an ironing board where it used to be soft. His bones protruded like kitchen matchsticks along his joints.

One day I sat with Catherine and we wrote his name on a piece of paper and asked him to try to copy it. Today was a good day and he obliged with a slow, defunct and wavering arm that tried and then failed. Catherine's eyes welled up. For weeks we pushed a yellow piece of paper in front of him, trying to elicit the same reaction, and he shook his head but tried anyway. Slowly, a spidery scrawl appeared on the paper starting with what looked to us like the letter *J*, before transforming into a long, squiggly line. Each time he left a small imprint, like little black bird feet on the page, we gave a cheer. He tried to bring that old smile out. He gave us a little smile, crooked and bent, but the partial palsy down his left side kept it anchored and rooted.

Then he tried other letters. *O* first.

'Yes, that's it, Dad.'

He drew a circle. Then he drew another one, and another. Then another. I wrote *Cathie* on the sheet. Could he try that?

A line, followed by circles and more circles.

He tried again. It was circles again. Then a few more squiggly lines. He moved slowly, as if his whole body was stuck in mud. Or a peat bog, he would say. An Irish bog. For weeks he kept trying but all we got was lines and circles. We knew he was frustrated. He looked up at the ceiling. It was an incredible effort to make his body move at all. He was writing in his head but his body was not responding in the same way.

On closer inspection of the paper, I could distinctly make out the image of a hangman's noose and part of a stick figure.

'What's your word, Dad? I'll write it down.'

_ _ _ _

'Is there an *E*?'

_ E _ _

'What about *L*? No?'

140

_ E _ _
'What about *D*? OK.'
D E _ D
'Dead?'
Yes.

'Dead? Don't be daft, Dad. You're not dead. You'll live for ever. You'll be fine. Listen, you're getting *better*.'

I shivered while I held his hands. I promised it would be fine, but what on earth did I know? How could I possibly know what the silent terrors of the night inflicted on him? He brought us up not to be afraid of people and certainly not of death because you could just be buried out the back garden, under a tree, and not really have left your home anyway and everyone would just look out of the window and say, 'See, there he is, the old da, out there.' And point while doing the dishes. But I was afraid now. The fear was compelling. How could it not be? Christ Almighty. I was utterly afraid for my father, the condemned man on a sheet of yellow paper.

My mother worried about everything. I hated to see her like that. Worried about running out of candles, or the candles blowing out. The hallway was a furnace.

She worried about the big things, like his speech, and the little things, like his hair. It had grown so long that he had begun to resemble Gandalf. But it suited him. Long and white and fine, and grey hair that curled below his pyjama collar and around his ears. It had never grown so long and derelict.

'We'll sort it out, Mum, don't worry.'

'I know, it's just that he would hate for people to see him like this. As if he didn't care about himself at all.'

There was a piece of card tacked to one of the hospital walls with the name *Tearney* in blue felt-tip. His name, one of the few things that gave his life any real meaning and identity, both in hospital and out, had been misspelt. It shouldn't have meant much but it did and we asked if they could change it and they promised they would but they had other things to do and it was still there in the morning. We took it down and put his misspelt name in the bin.

His right arm troubled him. It still lay lifeless, like a withered root. There were pinpricks along his arms and there always seemed to be dried bloodstains under his fingernails.

Televisions flashed their white noise. Everything smelled of uncapped medicine and old urine and sometimes the nurses and visitors talked loudly as if the patients had all turned deaf as Rodin's statues.

Over the previous few weeks I'd been having a recurring bad dream. It happened so often I couldn't *not* have the dream. It wouldn't go away no matter how much I tried to change it. I just couldn't undo the thoughts about how it must have felt for him, after so many weeks, to wake up in a hospital bed and survey his room. So I started to daydream the dream so often that I forgot what was the actual dream and what was the daydream of the dream. It was keeping him alive a little longer, I supposed. In the dream he stood beside his bed and began talking to us. But no one was listening. So he raised his voice a little, wondering why he was so suddenly and randomly being ignored.

'Cathie,' he shouted. 'Cathie!'

Nothing.

'Michael, what am I doing here? Why am I here?'

Then he shouted again. At all of us, one by one. Iain and Fiona and Catherine and Mark and Maureen and Vincent and Lorraine and Claire.

'For Pete's sake, why can't you listen? Why can't you *hear* me?'

And then, inevitably, he screamed, his voice like an angry creature from the depths. The screaming continued until the dreadful realization that, while his mind still worked, his voice had disappeared. It had simply gone.

I dreamed too that my father had shrunk and that he was trapped for ever in his own head, actually living *inside* himself. It was as if there were two of him, like with Russian Matryoshka dolls. One figure lay on the hospital bed while the other, smaller version walked about inside his body, chatting to the blood and the bones and the meat too and asking how it was all feeling today. He was actually living behind his own brain matter. And he knew that he would never be able to communicate with us again. He could look out, of course, through his own eyes, but the Matryoshka Tierney would be tiny, and he would know that he would never be able to talk about Celtic or Ireland or his mother and father or Coalisland and the boys who had got into trouble over there and had also wound up in bits and pieces.

I even wanted to hear him talk about *Rangers*.

I had no idea if the dream *meant* anything. It didn't matter. But it drove me crazy. But not as crazy as lying in bed without a voice drove him. I was scared he would just die of fright. Not of his stroke, but of fear. The fear of living like a Matryoshka doll.

I asked him to talk.

I asked if he remembered the Sporting Lisbon game because it was suddenly *important*.

I wanted to know if he remembered the next round of the UEFA Cup, the third round, when we played Nottingham Forest, who had already won two European Cups. Iain and I had wanted to go to Nottingham but that was never going to happen. Not in a million years. Not in a trillion years. We were just two boys dreaming up in the loft. I knew a boy from school whose dad had taken him down to England. He'd skipped school and gone on a Celtic supporters' bus and stood beside his dad in pubs and then gone to the match. Actually been to an *away* match. *In England.* Hundreds of miles away, it might have been the moon. It was ridiculous. *He was a year younger than me too!* You just didn't do that. It was just rubbing things in.

Especially as I had only just been to my first match. Ever.

The boy said something about the Brian Clough Stand and Celtic fans shouting at the Forest fans that *the Jungle is here*. He said there were big crushes and fans had broken arms and some got squashed in pens and found it hard to breathe and it was almost a disaster. When he was back in school he was like a hero. Not only had he dogged it – with his dad as a willing accomplice – but his dad had

143

let him sip from a can of Tennent's into the bargain. *At the match.* The boy talked about it for weeks. Iain and I just shrugged. I kept wondering how anyone could afford to go to a match in England if we were struggling for a match in Glasgow . . .

The match was a 0–0 draw. We would surely beat them in the return leg at Celtic Park.

We listened to the home match on the radio. Probably all of us did, sitting in the dining room eating crisps and toast. We'd have been shouting at the radio. Shouting at Clough, and Steve Hodge and Colin Walsh who both scored in the second half for Forest. Celtic lost 2–1 on aggregate. But part of me was happy. It wasn't all bad. It would stop the boy from school heading off on another bus, on *another* Celtic jaunt.

I also wanted to know why my father shot at the quarry boys when we were young. I wanted to know how to build a boat from a van like he had promised, and where the waterfall was in the Campsies that we used to go to in summer. And I wanted to know about my grandfather too.

He didn't talk about personal stuff.

That's why it's called personal . . .

The worst part was that everything was always the same. Every minute and hour and day and week and month. We sat with him and he just stared through us. It rained outside and even the rain hurt him. Everything seeped into his body. The hospital, the stroke, the people around him, the nurses, the visitors, the stainless-steel food trolleys, the medicine, the peeing into bags, the lifting, the television repeats and quiz shows; all of it and all of them became part of his body. Parts of his skin fell off, as easily as peel off an orange.

Listen, you need to get me out of here. Get me the hell out of this madhouse. For God's sake, Michael. The place is full of nutters! Look at the state of that bloke over there . . .

'Which one, Dad?'

Him. The one with the long, grey hair . . . bloke looks half-mad.

'That's you, Dad . . . I'm sorry.'

What the flip are you talking about?

'We can't take you home yet.'

Thanks very much. Say hello to the devil when you leave . . .

It was one thing for him to survive, quite another thing to survive intact.

My mother wanted his hair cut. Would I mind, she asked, cutting my father's hair? Of course I didn't. My father looked at me. He was sitting up in his wheelchair. The veins in his eyes were too red. They looked moist. I would cut it after work, I said. We'll get a new pair of electric clippers, like the ones the barber who worked at the Cross used on us years ago. He smiled. He blinked and he coughed. It took him a while to swallow.

The following afternoon the nurses moved him back into his chair. 'You'll look dead handsome,' said one, smiling. 'Sure you will, John?' She talked loudly at him, as if my father was deaf or a child or as dumb as a month-old cat. It was no one's fault, but it didn't make it any easier.

He sat in his chair and lowered his head when I asked him and slowly raised it when I asked him again. I hated his compliance. I wanted him to look at me with contempt and tell me not to be so stupid, and could I not see he was a man who would not have his hair cut by his own son? But he couldn't do anything now. My mother shook her head sadly.

The difference between a good haircut and a bad one, he used to say, was four weeks. And then he was off, laughing away to himself.

The barber down at the Cross was in a room round the back of one of the old tenements and up the stairs, with a few chairs, comics and a row of boys frightened enough to make their mothers wonder why on earth they had sent them there in the first place. The barber had a limp. We called him that too. The Limp. That was nothing, said my father. The man who cut his hair in Partick only had one arm and it was no joke. He was Greek. My father called him Jimmy the Greek and he could cut hair with hedge shears if he wanted, he was that good.

Once in The Chair each boy would get wrapped in a plastic sheet before being given the opportunity to whisper a lie to The Limp. 'My Mum said just a *wee* bit off the sides . . . Thanks.' And The Limp would nod, considerately and empathetically, and then ignore everything that was said to him before giving every boy a good shearing until his head resembled a tennis ball or the rough end of a coconut.

My father looked exhausted already and ready for sleep.

My mother helped me put the black cape around his neck, fastening the Velcro corners, and then she pulled it across his shoulders and over the front of his chest. She spread the cape across his knees so that the hair wouldn't get stuck in his pyjama bottoms. I had only ever cut snippets of the children's hair before, but my mother said he just couldn't deal with a hairdresser at the hospital.

I touched his skull and the recessed bone. A soft pulse came through the hole that was left behind.

The black box was like a small town hiding huge secrets. It was filled with clippers and several different attachments, numbered from one to eight, and a black plastic comb and something else for sweeping the fine hair from the clippers. There was a small bottle of lubricating oil. The scissors were silver with a crescent-shaped kind of spur attached to one loop that you rested your ring finger on for better control.

The electric clippers sprang to life. I ran them up his skinny neck and his white and grey hair tumbled to the ground. I worried his neck might snap like the pea pods he used to grow in the garden. His head sank like a pallbearer's. 'Lift your head up, Dad.' My voice sounded like I was admonishing a child.

'Sorry, Dad . . . a little higher, please.'

The brain was roughly three pounds of pinkish-grey matter and the most energy-hungry organ in the body, constantly demanding a disproportionately large percentage of the blood supply from the heart. Although the brain made up only about 5 per cent of the body's total weight, it used more than 20 per cent of the body's blood supply to survive. I could feel the blood pumping between my hands. I thought of the surgeon who'd had his hands inside my father's head. Holding it, like a crucible.

It must have felt odd.

Yes, very odd. Especially if he was a Partick Thistle fan . . . The fella probably hadn't been that close to genius in his life . . .

His scalp was thick and dry with old skin which crumbled in great flakes to the floor. He was losing even more of himself now. Remember that joke, Dad? 'A man goes for a haircut and the barber says, "Do you want your hair cut round the back?" And the man says: "What's wrong with in here?"'

His thin cheekbones rose, a micro-facial expression of approval. A brief smile appeared. With each movement he came back to life. My mother smiled too as the hair continued to fall, in long swirls of white. His hair smelled of oil from the van. 'You look so handsome, John,' she said very softly, before caressing the side of his face. She held it like he might break apart. Then she shook away his dead hair and skin.

The comb ran over his scalp again. I combed, lifted and cut, trying to remember the way The Limp would cut my hair. The loose hair kept falling and he sat there unmoving, not speaking. That was the hardest part. His silence. You could hear it screaming. I ran my fingers across his skull again and the tip of my finger curled under the bone. It was warm in there. Warm as a blackbird's blood. 'Just cutting more of the front now, Dad. Close your eyes. I'm going to blow the hair away. No, Dad, *close* them. Close your eyes. Please. Shut them over, please. Thanks.'

His eyes were closing over.

Hold on, Dad. Just a minute. Nearly finished. Don't fall asleep yet. Five more minutes. Nearly done. You'll look like Tony Curtis in no time. Another lopsided grin. Remember when we watched the old film of Celtic against Inter Milan? He lifted his head a little. Flicked his eyebrows.

Yes, he remembered.

Celtic fans of my generation had always suffered through *not* having witnessed the club's greatest triumph of all time. And, we liked to think, one of football's greatest triumphs. They won the European

Cup in 1967, becoming the first British side to do so. But that wasn't the *really* big deal. They won it with eleven players who were born within thirty miles of Glasgow.

It didn't matter how often the story was repeated. It was still a great story. Leonardo da Vinci only painted the *Mona Lisa* once and no one said, stop banging on about it, what else have you got in the bag, Leo? And if you didn't like the story you didn't believe in magic.

The nearest I got to the match itself was in the windowless confines of St Matthew's Church hall, many years after Celtic's victory. The film night was advertised by the regulars in Quins and by word of mouth amongst the stalwart attendees at St Matthew's and a few others who never made it quite so regularly but their hearts were in the right place if not their feet. No booze was allowed. I must have been around fourteen years old at the time, and we sat on rows of plastic chairs lined up neatly on what was variously the badminton court, the Cake and Candy area, and the meeting place for stiff-backed ladies of the Union of Catholic Mothers.

The first time the priest said it I misheard him.

I thought he was holding meetings for the Union of *Alcoholic* Mothers.

And so, for years, I believed that the priest was one of those radicals my father often spoke about, who believed in Liberation Theology, as practised by many of the Christianized Marxist priests in South America, and that his meetings for the Union of Alcoholic Mothers were just an extension of his radicalization. It did seem pretty radical for Bishopbriggs, but I admired the Church for looking after the welfare of a bunch of reeking and inebriated mums of a Sunday and was especially impressed when the priest mentioned that if any woman wished to join them they could easily find a form at the back of the church. I watched a few women pick up the forms and didn't think for a moment they were particularly big drinkers, but who ever knew about anyone really? Fair play that man.

My mother never joined because she didn't have the time but she would have because she probably had a lot in common with them.

'In the name of all that's wonderful,' said my mother, shaking her head, when I pointed out how thoroughly impressed I was by the fresh approach of the priest to the drinking habits of the flock. My father pointed at my mother and made a drinking movement towards her with his hand. And winked.

A few girls sat at the back of the hall for the screening, so pretty they made my stomach ache. Daughters of the sherry-drinkers, I presumed. They giggled and flicked their bouffant hair. Their painted eyes could stop traffic down the Cross. The hall was a familiar haunt filled with familiar, vibrant faces. Not an extension of our community, but the heart of it. It smelled of coffee, drying mops and sour men who had misspent their youths honing their skills at snooker. It still does.

Despite the prohibition on alcohol there were a few cans of Tennent's and Sweetheart Stout smuggled in by thick-necked fellas carrying Co-op bags and an overabundance of crisps. The hall was besieged by fathers and sons. My father pulled up some chairs for my brothers and me to witness what we believed to be the greatest football match of all time. For the Celtic fan, raised on romance and myth, and struggling to formulate their identity, this was our game. It was a truly heart-tugging romantic waltz.

Someone rang a hand bell.

It was 25 May 1967 when Celtic made history by defeating the much-heralded Inter Milan 2–1 in the Estádio Nacional in Lisbon. No matter how much time passed, Celtic fans, young and old, could still recite the names of the players in their sleep: Simpson, Craig, Gemmell, Murdoch, McNeill, Clark, Johnstone, Wallace, Chalmers, Auld and Lennox.

The Lisbon Lions.

In the 1960s, when Ronnie Simpson wore woolly jumpers and what looked like a pair of gardening gloves in goal, and football fans wore their smart suits on the terraces, Europe was dominated by just a handful of football clubs. Just four teams – none of them British – had won the major prize of the European Cup in its first eleven years to 1966.

The eleven young working-class men, all born within that thirty-mile radius of Glasgow, grew to conquer Europe. Celtic won everything that season: the League Cup, the League Championship, the Scottish Cup and the European Cup. The feat gave Celtic fans of every age a sense of elitism that remained unsurpassed in Scottish football lore. The absolute scale of the achievement was monumental.

And if that wasn't magic to you, you were probably already dead.

Every recollection was the turning over of a sod by an old man with a giant spade.

The story of 1967 was a staggering and compelling one. It was the high point in the career of each player who took part but also, more importantly, in the lives of successive generations of supporters. Celtic's identity was inextricably intertwined with its fan base that crossed creed and colour and country. Fathers, mothers, uncles, aunts, cousins, sons and daughters all ensured that we would all bask in reflected glory.

The match in Portugal was not simply about football, said my father. It was much more than that. It was about our identity, or lack of it; it was about the underdog, it was about overcoming adversity, both cultural and ethnic. It was about the fans. It made their work bearable, their lives acceptable, and their failures tolerable. Despite my father's suspicion of how some of the Protestant and the Presbyterian community viewed his religion, Celtic was Catholic men and Protestant men *together*. Players and fans. A team of mixed religion in a city of religious division. Rangers could choose to be separate if they wanted.

How did you think that made us all feel?

I know, Dad, I'm getting there.

It made him angry and bitter. They were not just saying no to him. They were saying no to his sons and his daughters.

They were saying that they were better than us. They were part of the whole problem. There were civil rights marches in America, for God's sake, so that black people could be treated as equals with whites. And flippin' right too. But Rangers point-blank refused to say we were equal to them. A football club? Telling Catholics they were inferior . . . It was the same with Ireland. Britain destroyed my family's home and then they billed us for the trouble.

When the footage of the film started, it was utterly sensual and full of life and it filled the hall. And filled our world of nostalgia. My father sat alongside me, enraptured by the game. My memory tells me the film was in soft, grainy Technicolor but I'm sure, in reality, it must have been in black and white. Some things simply were.

For a while I never understood any of it really. Just because one dog bit another didn't mean a man should dislike all dogs. I used to think that perhaps we looked different from the Protestants, that there was something obvious that must give us away. Like two heads or an extra arm growing out of our backs. I counted my toes and there were still only fourteen . . .

There was no difference. The men and women in the Portuguese sun were just like us. We were not second-class citizens at all. And Celtic didn't just beat Inter Milan; they destroyed the smooth, bronzed Italians with flair and panache and guile and excitement and grace and more than a hint of *gallusness*. If there was such a word. And if there wasn't, there should be. It was Jock Stein, the manager, who summed it up perfectly: 'We did it by playing football. Pure, beautiful, inventive football.' Stein wanted to win with style because he thought that was how football should be played, because football was a beautiful sport.

'You couldn't make it up,' said my father, after the show. 'Couldn't make it up. That was something else.' He whistled and shook his head. It was as if the result was something new, but it was already more than a decade old. It didn't matter. Watching it all again made it *feel* new. It made it real.

And seven of them ate fish and four had steak. They could put that in their pipe and smoke it!

He said Rangers never forgave Celtic for winning the European Cup before them. It wasn't supposed to happen that way. Something went wrong somewhere. 'That was *not* in the script,' he said. 'No way. No chance. People were fired in boardrooms for less, Michael,

I'm telling you, son. Masonic halls were cleared out and new, thirty-third-degree Masons were sworn in. I'm telling you. Rangers-supporting bank managers were queried about why they had allowed this to happen. Policemen were interrogated by some of their own. How could it happen on their watch? Judges were looked at closely, their surnames checked for any hint of Roman or papish ancestry. No one was safe.'

And he just laughed. And the men in the hall laughed with him. Celtic won, Celtic wonderful.

The hall emptied and we walked away, clutching our memories tightly, like an old man holding on to his hat in the wind. I walked with him. We all did, out of the door and into the future.

And then I crash-landed in the hospital alongside him, and wondered where in the name of the wee man it had all gone.

I snipped the sides of his hair, around the ears.

'Hhnn. Uhh,' he said, trying to speak. 'Ddnnaa. Mmuuhh.'

The sounds were a trickle, like blocked water in a pipe. No matter how often I heard them, his abbreviated sentences hit me like a blunt instrument. If you didn't know he was unwell you might think that he was only drunk.

I just needed to cut around his ears. Trim his eyebrows. Last wee bit now, Dad. A few more stories and we're done.

If I could rescue him with a story I would try.

'Remember, that time when Mum . . .' I said.

When I mentioned my mother he tried to speak again. His eyes moistened. His face lit up.

Here was my mother, plucked from air and memory, never far behind him: green-eyed and smelling bewitchingly of the kitchen. You never forget your mother's smell. She was thirty-five years old and a mother of nine and she took us all to Barra when my father drove us to Oban and he dropped us off to catch the ferry.

Remember, Dad?

Of course, I remember.

A few weeks after my father had returned to Glasgow, my mother, brothers and sisters were all sitting in the living room of the house in Garrygall that smelled of coal and toast and clothes drying near the fire. There was barely a stick of furniture. The house was empty apart from children. So it was never really empty at all. My mother sipped tea with her sister Morag and they talked in Gaelic and the children didn't understand a word of what was being said. Unless we heard *Micheal* or *Iain Ruairidh* spoken in her aboriginal tongue. Then we knew she was talking about us.

A little higher, Dad. Almost finished.

The muscles in his neck had atrophied and were sinewy and weak. His head tilted uncomfortably to his left. When I clipped his nasal hairs and eyebrows he sneezed loudly. His whole face recoiled, as if assaulted by a noxious smell. His head shuddered and the space where the bone had been removed from his skull reverberated. Each time this happened he tried to lift his good hand to his skull but it was a slow, arduous process. His hands, once large and vascular, were now the colour of greaseproof paper. I noticed how thin they had become.

'That's better,' said my mother. 'You look very handsome, John. You just look so handsome, John.' My mother's face was tear-striped.

On Barra we were sunburned and freckled and the days passed easily out on the croft behind us or at the great, white beach at Tangusdale where the sand filled our socks and Mother's Pride ham sandwiches and custard creams filled our bellies. Someone shouted that the ferry, which ran more often in summer than in winter, had arrived from Oban. Outside, the early-evening sun was reflected in the waters of Castlebay, in front of us.

Kisimul Castle had been the stronghold of the MacNeils since the eleventh century and it was filled with the ghosts of dead fishermen and some ancient, stern-faced marauders from North Uist and Lewis. A horn sounded as the ferry docked. One of us would be sent down to Castlebay shortly to pick up the fresh bread and milk that had been brought to the island. If we were not fast enough we would be left with the long-life milk that tasted like dog's pee for our cornflakes.

Ten minutes passed and someone pointed to the figure walking round the bend from Castlebay, past the sign that said *Garrygall* and in the long shadow of Ben Heaval, the highest point on Barra, with the statue of Our Lady Star of the Sea near the top, standing guard over sailors like Granda Mac and Uncle Roddy. Below sat the church which, my father never tired of telling people, had opened on Christmas Eve 1888 – the same year Celtic were formed, in Glasgow.

The figure carried a small suitcase and a smaller cardboard box and a cigarette between his fingers. He picked up pace a little and blew cigarette smoke into the air and put out the stub on the ground with his foot. My mother ran to the door. We all did. The figure walked to the small bridge, built by Uncle John, which separated the house from the main road. He crossed the bridge and put the latch back on the gate.

It was my father.

He caught us, as he always did, in a trance. I could see him in the lowering of the sun. The wind blew as always. He put down the suitcase and opened his arms.

'Hello, Cathie,' he said.

My mother disappeared into his chest. Shyly, he kissed my mother on the cheek. One at a time, he lifted up his nine children. Small kisses, big hugs. He smiled as he opened the box and distributed small packets of sweets – Love Hearts, cola cubes, Liquorice Allsorts. That was my father, kept alive in a story, always coming towards his family, never turning his back on us. He ruffled my hair. My head turtled into my slender neck once again. I could hardly feel him through my layers and his jacket and shirt. But I could hear my father's voice.

And I always would.

Some stories needed to be told.

It wasn't a dream. It was true. I was in a minibus a few years ago. It was going from Celtic Park to Archerfield Links, a golf club, in East Lothian. On the bus were Billy McNeill, Bertie Auld, John Fallon, Joe McBride, John Hughes, Bobby Lennox, Jim Craig,

Tommy Gemmell and Willie O'Neill. More of the surviving Lisbon Lions, and some of the other players in the team who didn't play in the final, were in their cars or making their own way there.

McNeill had got everyone on board and we headed off. After ten minutes I stopped taking notes and I decided just to listen. It was raucous. It was marvellous. It was sad. It was hilarious. It was like travelling with Westpark Under-15s or a bus filled with workingmen from the Maryhill Stanklifters.

I had expected it to be quite a genteel journey across the breadth of Scotland to the golf course, as the men quietly reminisced about the past. It was nothing of the sort. They called each other every-thing under the sun and then some. There would be less colourful language in a Filipino tattoo parlour. But that was their business and not mine. I would keep all of that quiet, I said, and they called me a few things too.

The men on the bus had history stamped on them, like letters through a stick of rock. But they'd been boys once too.

Some of them went off to play golf, while others sat over lunch and talked. Over the course of the afternoon and into the next day, I realized that not only did I like the men that my father, and my family, had spoken about for years, but that I *admired* them too. They were teammates. They were part of something graceful and special. Some things went beyond cups and medals. And it had been that way for decades.

Some of the stories I knew. *Most* of the stories I knew. But there were other things I hadn't heard.

John 'Yogi' Hughes, nicknamed after the popular American cartoon character Yogi Bear, was a fourteen-stone Apollonian giant of a striker who tested the resolve of even the hardest defender. He had a shot like clenched thunder. During a match against Aberdeen on an icy pitch, Hughes borrowed McNeill's old trainers that had wee suction holes at the bottom, because he didn't like his own rubber boots. He scored five.

During Celtic's second-round tie of the 1963–64 European campaign against Dinamo Zagreb, the team had been invited to visit

Mount Sljeme, a 3,000-foot-high peak on the edge of the city, before the match. It was the middle of December. Hughes didn't fancy the cable-car journey down so Sean Fallon, the assistant manager, said he could walk. He talked John Divers into going with him.

They walked and walked until a car pulled over and two Yugoslavian policemen with guns got out. Hughes and Divers were shouting, 'Celtic, Celtic,' and pointing at the badges on their clothes and the two policemen pointed up the hill and took them back up the way in their wee Fiat. 'I said to JD, "We're in big trouble." ' More than two hours later they got back to the bus. The team were livid. Because the forest was jumping with bears, a newspaper reported: 'Divers and Hughes lost in bear-infested forest. Yogi would have been all right but they weren't so sure about John Divers.'

'Nobody can take away our memories,' Hughes said. 'We never made a lot of money, but nobody can take those away.'

Jim Craig was smart and funny too.

In some ways he carried the burden of being the sole university graduate in the Celtic team. He gained a degree in dentistry, later wrote a couple of books and went to South Africa to play football, 'because I wanted to see what apartheid was like for myself'. He also liked to recite poetry, especially that of Robert W. Service, best known for 'The Shooting of Dan McGrew' and 'The Cremation of Sam McGee'.

'My teammates were all smart men,' he said, 'but they didn't all have the benefit of an academic education. I could pass an exam, but I wasn't necessarily smarter than the rest. People only had this nebulous idea of what university was like.

'One day during a training session I was paired with wee Jimmy [Johnstone]. Jimmy asked how I was getting on with my dental course. Fine, I said. "How you getting on with the Latin, big man?" Latin? He told me he thought we all spoke Latin at university. "No Latin?" He was perplexed. He was sure I spoke Latin. People presumed a lot back then.'

Craig went to Africa, he said, because he didn't want the thought police telling him what to do. 'I discovered that there were very many good white South Africans,' he said, 'who were trying to change the system from within, including the guy I worked for who treated both black and white people in the same dentist's chair. That was completely against the way they did things. I liked that . . . But I was seeing it for myself. I wasn't reading about it like others.'

The night in Lisbon, he said, was probably the most important in his professional life. He was twenty-four. 'But the night after Lisbon was the most important in my life.' He met his wife that night, when he arrived back to celebrate the victory.

Joe McBride always smiled.

But behind his smile he carried the memory of his omission from the European Cup-winning side around with him like a rusty shackle. McBride's goals had taken Celtic into Europe and provided the springboard for the Lisbon triumph. But he was struck by injury at the height of his powers and denied the chance to play in the biggest match of his life. It was a simple fact: Joe – everyone called him plain, simple Joe – should have been part of the starting eleven.

'I remember it all as if it was yesterday,' he said. 'And I still feel the pain of it exactly like that now. I really cannot describe it. Don't even ask me who would have been left out. The only thing I can say for sure is that I would have been there.'

Joe had scored thirty-six goals by Christmas during the 1966–67 season, but a career-threatening injury against Aberdeen ruled him out for the rest of the campaign. In the 1965–66 season he had finished with forty-six goals. If he hadn't scored them, Celtic wouldn't have been in Europe.

The night before his operation was the date of the second (home) leg of Celtic's quarter-final tie against Vojvodina. Joe was lying in hospital in Killearn. Celtic were 1–0 down from the first leg.

'Two young doctors came into the room I was in and said, "Joe, we're going to be attending your operation tomorrow. Is there any chance you can get us a couple of tickets for the game?" I said, "No chance." So the two of them walked out and I called them back. I said, "Any chance if I did you could take me to the game?" They just looked at me. "Jesus Christ," they said, "no chance, you're being operated on in the morning." No, no, no. "Our jobs" and all that.

'The two doctors weren't five minutes out the door when they came back in and said, "Look, Joe, if we could get this arranged, that nobody comes into this room, we could get you there."

'I called Big Jock and explained the situation. "You cannae come to the effen game before an operation," says Jock. Effen this and effen that. I told him I had my clothes and everything ready. So the two doctors drove me into Parkhead and I went to the directors' box and got their tickets.'

Charlie Gallagher hit a late corner and Billy McNeill met it and scored and Celtic beat Vojvodina 2–1 on aggregate to secure a place in the semi-finals of the European Cup. 'After the game I had to dive into the car of the doctors and get back to Killearn before anyone knew I was missing. Can you imagine that happening now? We were in stitches laughing.

'I was delighted for the team winning the cup and delighted for the way they played and everything. But all through the whole thing I was sitting there watching and knowing that if I was fit I'd have been on the park.'

No matter how hard he tried Joe could never get away from missing out on Lisbon. His voice quivered like an old man's hand. His dreams hung in the air like a child's balloon.

'I will live with it until the day I die.'

And he did.

Joe McBride succumbed to a suspected stroke and was buried in St Dominic's Church, in Bishopbriggs, in July 2012. The funeral was just up the road and round the corner from my house. I couldn't make the funeral though I wanted to. Later, I met one of his family and she gave me a copy of a photograph I had been trying to find for years.

It is of Muhammad Ali, in Glasgow, with some Celtic players. Ali, in his shirt and tie, stands in the centre of the picture, flanked by two black men. Also in the frame are Billy McNeill and Bobby Lennox, and some others too. Joe McBride is smiling as Joe always did.

The eight surviving Lisbon Lions and the rest of the squad who made the journey to East Lothian that day on the minibus regaled each other with tales and reminiscences about a time when they were young and indestructible. Seeing them was a privilege. Seeing each other, I understood, was a privilege too: an autumnal portrait of good men and the inevitable passing of time.

I listened and listened.

Sometimes that was all you needed to do.

Ali, I thought, was in some fine, fine company.

Chapter Seven

Sunday Shoes

The apple trees at the bottom of the garden doubled as goalposts and he strung them with the orange fishing nets that he had got from some of the fishermen on Barra, in Northbay or Castlebay, where he would sometimes go for a drink with my uncle Lachie or my uncle Roddy.

He would do a little work for the men who drank there too, putting a light in their sheds or running some old electrical cable into a cottage. Some of the men who lived there did so without wives and with maybe only a collie. Small jobs to help out. Or he'd put a new light in an outhouse where sheep might be slaughtered. Money would never change hands. A pint for yourself and whatever you might need, they would say in voices soft as bumblebees and they would look around at the bit of croft and he would oblige them and put the nets straight into the van, along with the crates of sand and maybe a crab or two.

'That sand on the beach is as good as any,' he said. 'No point in paying a quid for a few bags in Glasgow, eh? This is God's sand.' And he shovelled it twice as quickly, prouder than a cat delivering a bird to the back door. 'Paying for sand? I still can't get my head round that . . .'

He enjoyed putting the nets up, knowing where they had come from and knowing that they had caught thousands of fish. Fish on Friday, lads. Always fish on a Friday and never mind what they said. He tied the loose corners of the nets tightly and marvelled at the sight of them. The developers were starting to build the new houses over the quarry. That's where some of the wood came from when he built the second goal.

'They're ruining the view,' he said. 'And they'd better not put one foot on my property or there'll be trouble. I've looked at the deeds and I know exactly what land is mine. From here to there.' He pointed. 'I've measured it all out and it's my land and none of them will touch it, I'm telling you, or they'll get the old rifle or worse.' He rubbed his hands through his crow-black hair. I laughed and booted the ball. Then my father must still have been a young man but he seemed to me to have been old all his life. An older man hijacked by young flesh. That's what he was. The sun hit the grass. It made him squint. He raised a smile.

The bottom of the garden alone was bigger than a five-a-side pitch and when we had finished with the nets we painted white lines with emulsion across the grass including for the goalie's area so that all the children could play the game properly and learn the rules, and you never know where you might end up if you train and practise hard enough, he said, maybe Celtic. Or Rangers.

I laughed at that last bit.

The pitch was bone dry in summer and muddy and snow-covered in winter. We could stand on the grass and the snow would be up to our knees and we would be chilled to the core but he'd let us play out there regardless because what was a bit of cold snow to children? We played in flotsam. We only felt it if we ever stopped running and we never stopped running. In spring the world melted and he said we should let the ground breathe for a while until the grass had grown through the trampled mud and the earth feasted upon itself. The pitch would be brand new for the summer holidays and the whole street could come in to play, including the Minchellas, the Renfrews, the Galls and the MacPhersons, and they did.

We didn't really *go* places. Our house and our garden were as much as we needed. The garden was the open field my father had promised all those years ago, and it was where the neighbours' children congregated every day. Sometimes, there would be twelve or fifteen or twenty children in the garden at once, as if they had been instructed to gather there by a children's wizard or sometime magician.

The games never bothered my parents although, now and again, my mother would look askance when the strip of land at the bottom of the garden began to resemble a turnip field. When the boys played football Iain was Frank McGarvey, Mark was Packie Bonner (he was the only one with goalie gloves so had little choice in the matter) and Vincent was too young to care.

Me? I stood in the garden, wearing a second-hand Celtic strip and Celtic sweatbands on my wrists. I wore the same Celtic strip for years, and it stretched across my chest like a sausage skin. I had flash new Adidas football boots from Woolworths on my feet. My parents never skimped on my football boots and I was as happy as could be. I was playing for Celtic. I was Kenny Dalglish. King Kenny. *Kenny*. Always just Kenny.

It didn't matter that he had swapped his Celtic shirt for a Liverpool jersey. I was always Kenny.

If Celtic was in my childhood DNA then Kenny Dalglish was the most dominant strand of that particular genetic football structure. Growing up in Glasgow there were few boys who didn't want to be like Kenny, regardless of the colour of the shirt they wore. He was one of those few select players whose first name sufficed and he played the game the way *every* boy dreamed about it. He was faultless as my grandmother's old clock.

If you wanted to score a goal in your dreams it would always be the kind scored by Kenny: arms wide apart (the hands hanging loosely from the limbs), perfect balance, right foot swinging back and the left anchored to the ground. Open spot in the goal. Don't even look up. Devastating. Simple.

He was also a Rangers fan, having been born in the East End of Glasgow before growing up in Milton, across the quarry from us. He lived in Mingulay Street, which was named after my great-grandfather's island many, many miles away. All the streets across the quarry were named after Scottish islands. There was Berneray,

Mingulay, Westray, Scalpay and Castlebay. There were more. More than I could remember. They never planned the area right, said my father. They named the streets well but they forgot to add community things, like a cinema or a pub or decent shops or factories, so that the people there always looked out to what others had and, later, the drugs set in too.

But he used to drive us around and show us Mingulay Street and Castlebay Drive and say that it was a shame the people here couldn't see the real islands instead of having to suffer in the tough streets named after them. If they had seen them they might have smiled at the trick that had been played on them by the big city planners.

Kenny was too old to have been one of the boys we shot at. Separated by just a few years and a disused quarry. When you thought about it, and ignored his lifetime of adulation, it really wasn't that much. A goal from Kenny could set the sun in our back garden. The men in Quins would say that he was effortless. They said that you had to see him up close and my father winced at that. They said that he did things you couldn't even see with the naked eye. An old man said that Kenny *passed the baw aroon like some'dy firin' vinegar across a bag o' bilin'-hoat chips.*

Kenny was part of a hair revolution too. And we all thanked him for it, but maybe not The Limp because his custom started to dry up. Out was the short back and sides that had defined the era of footballers and children before him. Look at the Lisbon Lions and there was not a hair out of place on any of them. Kenny grew his hair long. We did too. The barber could chase himself. Kenny grew sideburns. Those would come to me later. He was also blessed with film-star good looks. We wanted them too.

Everyone, deep down, wanted to be Kenny.

He looked *majestic* in his green and white when football strips hung upon the less fortunate like a dead man's suit. 'To be fair,' said my father, 'he's some player.' And that would be the extent of his adulation. He never gave out compliments. He was as well handing out tenners all the good it would do him. Celtic fans loved Kenny because of where he was from, where he ended up and how he got there. They loved him in spite of the fact that he supported Rangers and then became a star for Celtic. They probably loved him more *because* of that. They closed their eyes and they tried to score goals like Kenny. And those who could barely even dream, well, they loved him anyway.

As long as you could wear the green and white hoops with distinction, that was enough. That was what Kenny did. And more. My father said he dealt with pressure better than any other player. Pressure revealed everything about a person, he said, and when Kenny played he looked like a boy out the back or in his ten square foot of garden.

My father remembered the boy who wanted to play for Rangers, and who stood over a penalty spot in Ibrox Park, about to take a penalty *for Celtic* against his boyhood heroes. It was August 1971, in a Scottish League Cup game at Ibrox. Kenny was twenty years old. My father smiled at the recollection. He had listened to the radio. And I was listening to him. In football, *that* penalty was pressure.

Kenny took the penalties in reserve games. But at Ibrox? He had waited a long time to be part of the Celtic first team and here he was, in this football cauldron. Celtic Park was being redeveloped and the club had three games in a little under a month at the home of Rangers.

Pressure.

Years later, when I spoke with Billy McNeill, he talked about Dalglish and that penalty. As a young man, McNeill said, Kenny was very, very assured that he could play in anyone's company. He had so much self-belief and faith in his own ability. It was astounding. Off-the-pitch shyness was a problem. Kenny would blush furiously if anyone spoke to him.

Seconds later the ball was duly placed on the spot as photographers gathered behind the goal in anticipation of the youngster's next move. The fans snarled and shouted. Endless vilification, like a subterranean growl. A snarling Rottweiler tied to a tree. The Rangers fans cursed him. Their curses floated in the wind. But for all those who sowed the wind, they would reap a whirlwind . . .

The crowd, the frisson of underworld glamour on the terraces, could inspire or make a man powerless and insignificant. It was all there, spiced with an edge of threat. Dark and empty faces staring back at him; black as colobus monkeys. Like standing in front of the Roman emperor before the royal thumb went up or down. Most waved scarves as if to ward off evil demons. Violent exhortations. Just something you grew up with. Another Saturday night on Sauchiehall Street. Or the streets of Milton.

How do I know this? I don't. But I want it to be true. It's my grown-up version of my father's memory. How do we know he was that good? Simple: *'Cause my dad said so*. And then you made a raspberry sound with your mouth. *'Cause he said so* . . . Sometimes you just needed to go route one. It's not a false memory. It's just a memory. A memory of how I needed things to be.

Kenny looked up.

Thousands of fans in the terraces and none of them could do what he could do. Although he was shaking inside he gave no impression of nerves. Even then Kenny handled fear better than most. He took a couple of steps back and then looked down at his boots. His laces were undone. Of all the times and of all the places in the world to have undone bootlaces . . .

Kenny bent down. Long, blond hair, high, articulated cheek-bones, flat-eyes, and always with goals on his mind. Thoughtful. Kenny always spent the day before a match sleeping, just to conserve his energy. He was never the quickest, but the first yard was in his head. The next twenty he owned while his opponent was left wondering when half-time would come. The youngster thought about the game. He *thought* about it.

Peter McCloy, the tall, lanky Rangers goalkeeper with legs like an uncooked turkey's watched Kenny as he prepared for his penalty. However long he was down there, one knee on the grass tying his bootlaces, it would have seemed like an eternity to McCloy. It was like a solemn ritual. A sea of Celtic fans were behind his goal, screaming, cursing, shouting and cheering. Arms raised in broken shapes: crucifixes and exclamations and a fat guy with a broken nose. The heart and soul of Glasgow spat venom from both sides of the football divide. Football was the core of life.

McCloy shifted on the line. Kenny stood up. But what the hell was he thinking? Payback because Rangers passed on him when he was just a boy? Final retribution?

Miss this and the Rangers fans would still think he was one of theirs. Miss it and the suspicions of Celtic fans would have borne fruit. Score it and the Rangers fans would turn their backs for ever. Score it and the Celtic fans would embrace him like the Prodigal Son. He drew the screaming curtain closed. The truth was he was no longer thinking about playing for Rangers. That was the past. Every part of him was focused on *beating* them.

Kenny knew that McCloy went the same way for every right-footed penalty-taker. A man of habit and routine. Kenny paused, made a mental edit of past shots. Memory traces interacted and accumulated in his brain. He felt cool. Cooling was good for the brain anyway. It protected it. If you're cooled down the cells switch off and you don't need as much energy to keep going because you're not doing very much.

He stepped back.

'I could never forget the moment I first set eyes on Kenny and instinctively knew that he was a unique talent,' McNeill told me. 'It was like watching a thoroughbred enter the parade ring. Jock only brought ones in that he knew could handle it and obviously Kenny was one. And it was patently obvious to me, and the rest of the senior professionals, that this fella had the ability to carry himself on.'

Kenny, before the eyes of the Celtic faithful, was already fulfilling the prophecy laid down by his father that his son would play football at the very top level. Dalglish Snr had made only *one* mistake: he thought it would be with Glasgow Rangers.

The Celtic crowd cooed him on, whispered in his ear as he rose from bended knee. He looked as if he was on a balcony drinking tea. The boy warrior stepped up (yes, Kenny could be a fighter too). Kenny turned away in the knowledge of a certain goal. McCloy, like a leper in search of a bell, went to pick out the ball now lying in the corner. A wrecked boat on the beach at Mingulay. McCloy struggled to regain his composure in such a public arena.

It was Jock Stein who pinned the number nine on Kenny and then played him in a slightly withdrawn role behind the front two. Link with the back four, sit off the front. Much later Stein would say of Kenny that you don't talk about positions. 'You just give him a jersey.'

In 1977 someone brought the shutters down.

Kenny was transferred to Liverpool for a then record transfer fee of £440,000 on 10 August, three days before the start of the new Scottish season, and six days before my ninth birthday. I found it unacceptable. I was still collecting tadpoles from ponds in the quarry, still popping tar bubbles in the street and still peeing out of trees into the neighbour's garden. I would never see him wearing a Celtic jersey in the flesh.

For fans of Celtic and, specifically, of Kenny, part of the country was plunged into mourning. King Kenny was leaving. How could things get worse? They did, of course they did. That's what happened in life. Someone threw a stink bomb and you ran in the opposite direction, but they were throwing stink bombs in that direction too because they knew how you would react. A few days later the news broke that Elvis Presley, the *other* King, had died, aged forty-two, although he must have looked about sixty. The radio itself almost broke down in tears as the doleful voices of DJs relayed the news.

For some strange reason they claimed Elvis was American, but we all knew he was from the Gallowgate. You could hear him singing there every weekend.

Scots men who grew up on Elvis and Kenny were stunned to silence. My father talked even more quietly for about a week. Days were spent glued to the radio and television. Two kings gone in a matter of days. As Elvis tributes poured from every radio station people in back gardens and tenements mourned the departure of King Kenny. The iconic status Elvis achieved in his lifetime coupled with his early death cemented his position as one of the most famous rock stars of all time. The departure of Kenny to Liverpool endowed Kenny with the same status. For the Celtic legions it was a bitter blow.

Who would have believed he would have gone?

The Celtic faithful believed that an imperious Glaswegian such as Kenny would rather have his eyes rubbed with leftover shards of metal from the Govan shipyards than leave for England. It was more than a venial sin, it bordered on a mortal one. Why would *anyone* want to leave Celtic? The fans were aghast. Yet he duly left his northern constituency like the King always promised he would. He simply had to go.

It barely mattered what age we were; back then, in the seventies and eighties, Kenny was still the only player anyone ever wanted to be – in the back garden or in the street. When schoolboys played five-and-in or head tennis each was Kenny. They were even Kenny in goal.

My father took us all out into the back garden to forget.

'Shots-in,' he said. 'There's no way you can score.'

He let in at least ten. He understood how we felt.

If my father ever had to barter his way into heaven he would be able to cite all the time he spent with his children – and our friends in the street were witnesses to the fact – out the back in our garden. From the minute we were born he was the most reliable of our play-mates. Other children used to wonder how he could spend so much time with us when their fathers never seemed to be around apart from at weekends. The truth was simple. He liked our company. And we liked his too. And work was sometimes hard to find and that was another truth.

Children knew things.

If his sandwiches weren't lying wrapped in empty bread paper on the kitchen counter in the morning then he probably didn't have work that day, so seeing him as soon as we were home from school became less of a surprise. The house kept him busy and he never hid from us, and him in the garden all the time was just his way of saying to us, look, I'm here. You might not need me and you might not always want me, but I'm here.

My father stayed with us in the garden in all weathers until the dark drifted in from the Campsies and we sat down around a fire he'd built from the wood he'd pinched, before heating (till they burned) potatoes from the Fruit Market that he'd covered in tin foil. He sang 'Black Velvet Band' and 'The Men Behind the Wire' and 'Folsom Prison Blues' and 'My Dixie Darling' while we sang 'Rivers of Babylon' and 'Grease' and 'Follow You Follow Me'. He played badminton with the girls till their arms were sore and the wind stole their shuttlecocks and they landed in the new gardens being fashioned out of the quarry.

I talked a lot about my father with Iain. We knew that it hurt him sometimes when he didn't have work, but he rarely wallowed. He gave us his time, we said, because his own father was dead and he knew how sore it was *not* to see your father. The passing of my grandfather was like a brutal argument that had gone wrong and neither of them would ever be able to resolve it. I think he wished there had been an argument. Something, at least. But there was nothing except a space and a void and a young man dead in a hedgerow or an orchard in a land his son could never get to. My grandfather was the Holy Ghost.

At the time I was playing for Westpark Boys' Club and my father took me to every Saturday match and training night, in the old van, without fail. He took Iain to his matches too. There were times that I knew even the smallest expense of petrol for an away match would catch up with him that week, or later in the month when the bills came in, but it didn't seem to matter.

Sometimes there was also a midweek game. He drove constantly and the van ran on fumes. He drove the girls to their running club in Springburn and to their cross-country races over the other side of

Scotland, where the wind lashed at them because it came from the east, and you couldn't do much about it except shelter in the freezing van till it passed. We would go regardless because his arms tingled when he saw us play and his eyes filled when he saw the girls running and winning medals, and the money would be found somewhere.

You couldn't call it poverty. My parents would have belted our backsides or chased us with the wooden spoon if we had. They were never poor. They just didn't have any money. The difference was so vast you couldn't walk across its canyons. A layered life, some said. They took a deep breath and looked at what they did have and my mother turned it into a collection of miracles.

That Sunday it rained cats and dogs.

There was a fundraiser for Westpark Club when coaches and managers and parents and some of the boys would play against each other, while hoping that no one had a heart attack or got terribly injured or both.

He had already taken us all to Mass in the morning with plenty of time to get back to the house and get changed and for me to get my boots ready. I'd cleaned and polished them the night before. I'd shined my boots to perfection. Sometimes I loved the ritual of a football match more than the game itself. Cleaning the mud or ash off them from a previous game and unscrewing the rubber studs out of the soles and checking to see if any of the metal threads were worn through. I would remove them using my father's black pliers, then wash them in the bath, and my mother would shout up not to make a mess because the children would be getting their bath later, and then I'd put old newspaper inside them so that the leather would dry slowly into the paper and not crack like a cheap mirror.

If you put them over a heater the leather would turn as hard as asphalt, so the best way was newspaper. Once the boots were dry, but still with a little moisture in them, they were covered in polish or dubbin. Black polish left them a lot shinier, and I used it when the weather was fair. Dubbin, like a sticky wax, was better for wet weather, and it softened and waterproofed them all over.

My boots ritual was always part of the match. It was my only ritual. It was my only football *thing*. I was never a football anorak. I couldn't retain anything really about football other than the rules and where the goals were. I had no arcane knowledge. I didn't really *get* statistics. They just sounded far too much like homework. Recalling numbers and stats made me shiver: they left me, physically, cold.

Some of my pals knew *everything* about Celtic. They could name reserve-team members who'd played in the semi-final of such and such a cup. They knew the middle names of all of Celtic's forward line since 1978. It felt like a lifetime of punishment exercises from the history teacher: 'Name a whole Celtic team with blond hair.'

'What?' *What?*

'When did Danny McGrain suffer a fractured skull at Brockville?'

'Where's Brockville?'

'When Jim Craig graduated from the University of Glasgow what was his degree?'

'Graduated? I didn't even know he had gone.'

'When Celtic beat Rangers in the final in 1977 who sponsored them?'

'You're just being silly now . . .'

Football was for *playing*. Those who could play did, those who couldn't, well, they just remembered stuff.

My father had no rituals. He had no uncanny ability to remember Celtic statistics or facts. And that was fine. The problem on this occasion was that he didn't have a pair of boots either. Or anything, really, that resembled sports footwear.

He wore his sandals in summer, and his good Sunday shoes for Mass. They were simple, sturdy and black. Nothing ornate. He even wore his *old* Sunday shoes for working in. Wore them till the soles grew holes and leaked and he would say, they're fine, but they were nothing of the sort and dirty great puddles of water filled his socks. Despite him being an electrician I had never seen my father in anything so effete as a pair of insulating shoes or rubber safety boots in his life.

'Water conducts electricity, Dad, remember . . .'

'Only if you don't know what you're doing.'

He liked to tell us he was an artist with an electric cable and I believed that he was. Why did a man have to use paint and a canvas to be considered an artist? He could put a light in anything or run a line and wraggle a wall and not leave a hint that it had been touched by a hand or fist save for when the room lit up and someone remarked that the man who did it knew what he was doing. Light, he said, shaped the environment. The light bulb was a work of genius. Put light in a man's house and he'd thank you for ever. 'But you just need to know what you're doing,' he said. 'You just have to remember that it could kill you too. Once you accept that you'll be fine.'

He looked at his Sunday shoes. He would play the game regardless. It was a game of football. It wasn't going to hurt. Not a bit.

The truth of the matter was that I'm not sure my father properly understood the rules of football. The litany of important ones anyway. And I didn't really know much about anything *apart* from football. I'm not sure he understood even the basic things like off-side or the very idea of a direct or indirect free kick. These were beyond him despite the fact that he always pretended otherwise. He understood the laws of kick-the-can more than of football.

Ask him about the *details* of a match or the *tactics* and he would mumble his way around the topic. He said they were just rules and who made them up anyway?

Matches on the television followed the same, predictable pattern. He harangued referees from his corner seat in the living room convinced that their decisions – *all* their decisions – had been pre-arranged in one of the local Masonic halls or Orange lodges with a whisky the size of a small dog and an untraceable twenty-pound note. There was no other possible explanation. Not now, not ever.

'Did you see that?' he'd say, his heart pounding while pointing at the screen, arms flapping at the temerity of it all. 'A joke. An absolute joke.'

'Dad, he was a mile offside . . .'

'Ach, behave yourself. Offside's got nothing to do with it. A joke. I'm telling you, that referee's been *bought*. The bloke can't even run the length of himself. Hope he chokes on his pint down the lodge later on. They're as well putting us all in chains and be done with it . . .'

He sat there seething in his short sleeves. 'Scoundrel . . .'

And what right did old Queenie have to lord it over the working classes and then there was the bowler-hat mob that ran London and what about their secret banks in Switzerland with their numbered accounts? They got it in the neck too. The list was endless and it was hard, I had to admit, keeping up sometimes, but I rarely found myself disagreeing.

The fundraiser match was to be played on the big grass pitch at Bishopbriggs High School, round the corner from St Matthew's Church and past the library. It was the best grass pitch for miles around and you could dance a sailor's hornpipe across it without a stumble and he used to raise his eyebrows and say that it was funny how there was no grass pitch like that in *our* school. And he would leave his comments just hanging there like a hand grenade in a trench, long enough for us to start to think the same.

We drove to the pitch in the van and the sky looked like it had been turned in a blender.

There were other fathers and sons already there and I prayed quietly to Mary, the Mother of God, that someone might have a spare pair of size tens or elevens or even twelves in their bag. I asked around. He certainly wouldn't be asking anyone for a pair of spare boots himself, you could guarantee that. There were none anyway. He sighed a little bit, his chest exhaling like a shot pheasant, and glanced a little forlornly at his feet before laughing and shaking his head at the absurdity of it all. Someone passed him a jersey and shorts and looked him up and down and said, 'Christ, John,' and that he didn't think they would fit but maybe he should try them anyway. There were no spare football socks either.

He straightened up, trying to loosen the jersey up a little and his hands gripped like steel wire around it, pulling and stretching. There he stood, a giant about to climb over another hill into a cornfield. His joints clicked and you could hear the sound in his knee from an old bike crash.

Back of the van to change. He sucked on a cigarette.

I was surprised my father had agreed to take part in the match. He certainly wasn't a bad player. But I didn't think he would agree to become public property for the day. My father was born quiet and stayed quiet his whole life. His shyness in public was the thing that held him back the most. He didn't like to be around people he didn't really know. It wasn't fear. He just didn't like it. My father would rather walk ten miles barefoot in the rain than take a two-minute car journey with someone he didn't know or who was known to be a talker and wanted to know his business. 'Can't listen to that fella,' he'd say. 'Asks too many questions.'

He went shopping with my mother in the van for the messages, dutifully attended Mass, drove us all to football or the running track for training, and went to the pub when he was thirsty and sometimes if he wasn't. But it was a rare day when he was involved in anything public other than as a bystander. If my mother asked him to drop off some old clothes for the St Matthew's jumble sale – which meant he had to go *into* the hall and *speak* with someone – he made sure one of us was with him to do all the needful chatting stuff with the priest or the women running the stalls. He wanted to donate the clothes, and if it was to the poorest family all the better, but he just didn't want to talk to anyone while doing it.

He didn't care for small talk. And he didn't care if you knew he didn't care for it either.

He would sing in the house till his heart was content, even if he was hunched and sore, while he fixed something else that was broken, and we loved to hear his voice across the landing. Charley Pride, or Jim Reeves, or Slim Whitman. He might even stand up in front of us and ask us to join in. 'Michael Row the Boat Ashore'. Elvis when he was in a good mood. Maybe a Celtic song in front of his brothers-in-law at New Year when they were all as drunk as boiled geese. But that was always the extent of his public performance.

Decent men could still shine from a distance.

Some of the men told me I was a good player. I could go all the way. A lot of boys heard the same. The compliments could hook and snare a child. They said I was better, but what did they know? Most children were good at some things, even if it was just destroying a piece of paper with a crayon. I had played so much on our pitch in the garden that the big teams were starting to look at me. In a few years there would be even more.

I would have trials with Dundee and Morton and St Johnstone. I went to England with Middlesbrough and across to Firhill with Partick Thistle. A few seasons earlier, Benny Rooney, the Morton manager, came to our house with Mike Jackson, his assistant. They were a formidable pair and both former Celtic players, and they wanted me to sign some forms that, in the cold light of day, would commit me to little more than legally binding indentured labour. I could expect to work through the football ranks for lukewarm pea and ham soup and some train fares.

They first asked my father and mother's permission, outlining to them their plans for my future. They drank tea from the good cups and ate chocolate biscuits my mother laid out on her best plates before they told my father I would be offered a few pounds' expenses and two pairs of football boots, and my father said that the decision was entirely up to me, before inviting the two men to go through their spiel all over again when I came into the room.

My father was adamant that they should run through it all again to me.

The two men just looked at each other.

I didn't know what to say, but I nodded this way and that and said I would think about it and get back to them.

My brothers and sisters were hiding in other rooms fantasizing about how we were just about to become . . . thousandaires. They would have a fat television in each room and probably a brand-new van and the girls would have perfume too and they would no longer have to share the same bath water. My father later told them that I had decided no and not another word was said on the matter.

He said, 'Are you sure?'

'I'm pretty sure.'

At Middlesbrough I stayed in digs for a few days with some other young players, including Derek, a club-mate, from Bishopbriggs, with whom I'd travelled down. It was 1982 or '83 and Malcolm Allison was the manager. For some reason, and I still don't know how, I ended up in the back seat of his car with another of the boys, either going to or coming back from training. I'm sure he must have talked to me and I'm sure I must have replied but I just remember thinking that I didn't really fancy being down in England much because the food in the digs was nothing like my mother's, in fact it was awful. Egg and jam sandwiches. And something with gravy that looked like something else and it didn't work hot or cold.

I don't remember the trial and I don't remember any of the professionals we trained with apart from one. At the time Gary Hamilton was a young Middlesbrough player, either in the first team or on the verge of it. He was from Glasgow too. Whoever was taking training – all I remember was shuttle runs, back and forth, over and over – said, speak with Gary. He's a sweaty-sock too. I laughed and didn't have a clue what he meant. Someone explained it meant a *Jock*. A Scot. It was a bad start. I didn't say anything, but I thought it. English pricks . . .

Hamilton might have been about seventeen or eighteen but he looked enormous, with massive thighs, and everyone seemed to bounce off him. A lot of the players admired him. He was confident and brash. His advice was simple and to the point: 'Don't take any shit off these English pricks, wee man.' I liked him straight away. I was a lot quieter than he was, and I'm pretty sure I took a lot of shit during those few days, especially in our digs.

At the end they said they would keep their eye on me. I

176

think Allison drove a Jaguar. It was a decent way to be let down.

My father once drove me over to have a trial with Celtic. It might have been at Barrowfield, the old training ground. A group of boys had been selected from the north of Glasgow area to play against one of Celtic's boys' teams and there was talk of S-form traineeships being up for grabs for standout performers.

Signing an S-form was the start of the first, long step on an even longer road to a potential professional career, they said. I played well, but not exceptionally, and I remember feeling completely over-whelmed by the experience. Celtic Boys wore the hoops and we wore yellow bibs. It felt like I was playing against the *real* Celtic. I just couldn't get into the match at all. My father watched from the side. The only time I would hear him was if he shouted something positive. I'd never heard him saying anything negative during a match, or even after one.

On the drive home he knew that there was no chance of an S-form being offered now. Not now, I thought, not ever.

'If you signed for Celtic I think you would disappear anyway, son,' he said, biting at his lip, not wanting to say the wrong thing. 'They'll sign up as many young boys as they can and then they'll put those forms in the drawer.' I nodded and shrugged. We stopped off for chips. We shared a bag and a can of Irn-Bru.

Later, I travelled to Dundee on the train and returned with an offer of a year's contract or traineeship, under Archie Knox and Jocky Scott. I landed there on a frighteningly grey and awful morn-ing and believed the city had been raised in the shade and that I had travelled back in time. I normally played centre-forward, or centre- or left-midfield. Dundee wanted me to sign as a left-back and I could never quite understand why. Someone said it was because Tosh McKinlay, who used to attend St Peter's Primary where I was once also a pupil, might be leaving sometime soon.

On the way home, I decided not to sign anyway. Someone had stolen the sun in Dundee. And they took my football boots too. They were nicked from my bag as I stood on the platform waiting for the train home. I never went back.

Manchester City were sending a scout after I'd been at a summer football camp down there. There was talk of Newcastle too. There was always talk. Young boys were desperate for talk. Adults thrived on it. Fathers especially. Sometimes they wanted it more. My father didn't. He said, whatever made me happy. Slowly, somewhere deep within those fleeting moments, youthful enthusiasm gave way to the dawning of adulthood. And I didn't like it one bit. Sometimes the truth hurt. The years passed. And they're still passing.

On the pitch I ran around like a twisting Galway salmon. I was aggressive too. I wanted to play football. I wanted to play for Celtic. I just didn't think I wanted it *enough*.

Before the match started, someone found my father another jersey and shorts that were just a little bigger. My father exhaled the smoke from his cigarette. Veins popped in his hands. There were folds now in his jersey. He could breathe. A man he knew asked him if he was any good. He spoke with his cigarette between his lips and a cloud of smoke masked his face. 'The older I get,' he said, smiling, 'the better I *was*.' He looked happy to be there and I was happy too.

He kept his nylon ankle socks on and slowly he tied the laces on his Sunday-best shoes. They were as shiny as the smartest Edinburgh lawyer's. His shins and ankles were hairless. The shorts left red rings on his thighs when they rode up. We both ran on to the grass and joined the others. The pitch had a fine sheen to it from the last heavy rain. It was as slippery as glass. 'You be all right with those shoes, Dad?' I said. 'Course I will,' he replied.

Someone had put up corner flags and they flapped in the breeze. The railway track ran behind the pitch and away towards the city. Andy Dodds, one of the coaches, ambled over. He was dressed for goal and he chatted with my father. They knew each other from school years ago in Ruchill or Maryhill and they caught up for ten minutes before the match began and spoke about the past and what they were doing now and was so-and-so dead yet? They laughed and nodded, maybe they would grab a pint later.

Andy always had good things to say about me. He told me then I was the best player he had ever seen at my age. Thirty years later he told me the same thing when I met him in Morrisons and he asked how my father was doing. He always asked after him and I always enjoyed hearing that. He said he'd have put his house on me making it in football, and his car too, and I enjoyed hearing that as well. Why did I stop playing? There must have been a good reason. I said, thanks, but it was a long, long time ago. Everything was, I said. But I couldn't explain it, really, in the frozen-food aisle.

I didn't really want to *be* a footballer.

All I'd ever really wanted was to *play* the game . . .

My father just stood on the pitch in his shoes.

He stood with his big, tough wrists showing below the cuffs of the jersey stuck halfway up his arms. Lorraine and Maureen and Iain and Fiona were waving and cheering from the sidelines by the old grey fence. *The Tierneys! The Tierneys! Come on, the Tierneys!*

My father waved back. He looked slightly embarrassed and then stretched out an arm and a leg but only because everyone else seemed to be doing the same. Someone shouted something about a warm-up and my father looked at him quizzically, wondering what he was supposed to warm up for. Sure, he had warmed up by taking us all to Mass and eating breakfast and fixing the front-door bell before he left. He wouldn't be warming up in front of anyone. Don't be daft. He finished the last draw of his cigarette and blew the drag into the sky and watched it rise and disappear before flicking the butt to the ground and stomping it into the dirt.

He hadn't yet given up his Benson & Hedges. He would do that the next year during Lent because they were too expensive. He bought one more packet, and we all watched as he picked out and then slowly smoked his last cigarette ever at the back door of the house and then put the packet on top of the kitchen cupboard. For the six weeks of Lent, whether he was in a good mood or bad, he walked past the cigarettes and never touched a single one. There were nineteen left when Lent finished and nineteen went straight into the bin and he said he wouldn't smoke another, not for love or money, and nor did he.

I'd only ever played football with my father in the garden. I called my father Hot Shot Hamish after the Hebridean giant from the *Tiger* comic, because he had a shot like a sledgehammer. That was his thing. His left-foot shot was like a concrete block. But we both knew he always found it impossible to get the ball from me in the garden once I had it at my feet. The grass was our own battlefield. Our contests were good-natured. Sing-songs and slide tackles. A glancing header. We shared the adoration of the invisible crowd in the garden. But we always competed. That was the thing though, with fathers and sons. At a certain age they *always* competed. I think that's what he always missed the most about his own father. Two sets of footprints on the grass, not one.

The pitch flickered in the fading light of a dank afternoon. I could see the flats in Springburn and the face of a clock staring down. A train muttered past before the game began and I could hear men swearing and Fiona counted all the words she'd never heard at home.

After a few minutes he was already out of breath and holding the stitch in his side. He missed easy passes and easier lay-offs while back-pedalling furiously. The ball went over and across and around him while he was left lumbering somewhere in between. He took a deep breath as he looked across at me. Other men pointed their fingers or shouted. A late tackle here and there. Someone went down in a heap. You couldn't bend wire that shape. A pulled muscle and a swollen knee.

Some of the men took it a little too seriously, whipping balls around in a fury, forgetting that their chance to make it in the big leagues had long since passed them by. Others were nursing a hangover and spat gobs of saliva that the wind carried to land on your jersey. 'Come on, Dad,' I said, shaking a fist. 'You need to get into the game more. Keep up.' He was slow as good honey in January. His shoes were nailed to the ground.

Off the pitch I was quiet like him. My father always said you need two people to have a conversation, one to talk and the other to listen. Neither was more or less important than the other. But he always stressed that if you really wanted to be heard, you needed to listen first.

The problem was that on the pitch I never stopped shouting and directing. It must have come from being the eldest boy in a big family. Even when I was young, he said, as a freshly pulled weed, I always directed the others. The habits were hard to break. Before either of us knew what was really happening I was directing my father and shouting at him to run or sit or press or pass and he would look over, mildly irritated by my incriminating voice. I was oblivious. The magic of fatherhood was leaking out of him with every raised shout.

I could hear the ground swelling.

At first he laughed when he slipped, but when the tackles went flying in he quickly realized that if it wasn't a completely serious game then it wasn't far from one. He held his ankles and rubbed his knees. His Sunday shoes were the death of him. The twins shouted and pointed. Should he not be wearing proper boots and might he not get hurt or something out there? They were right, and he was floundering. There were few things as graceless as a father of any age playing football on a muddy pitch wearing black, Sunday shoes.

Someone swore as loudly as bullets and my father drew him a look.

'Hey,' he said, jamming his gaze at the perpetrator. 'There's children playing this game, and there's children watching too.' He pointed at his children. 'This is just a *game*. OK?' He bared his teeth and stopped running. The player, a man with sloping shoulders and a bulldog face, considered the admonition for a moment and then lowered his head towards the wet tufts of grass to avoid my father's stare.

But it didn't stop him falling.

My father slipped and slid on to his backside, covered in dirt and mud. I could hear laughter from the sides each time he did this. A small man, as fast as a fox, took the ball from him and, even before half-time, I wanted the game to end. Hope died quickly on a football pitch. 'Shut up, you eedjit,' he said, snapping at someone on the sidelines.

The tone in his voice had changed. Now the shoes *were* funny and he might have said the same thing to someone else if he had seen him wearing them too. But the joke was wearing thin. There was no escape hatch here. He was being watched. And he didn't like being watched. He was the centre of attention when he was just supposed to be having some fun. He was just supposed to be helping out his son. Now, in the middle of the Bishopbriggs High School football pitch, he was exposed.

Half-time couldn't come quick enough and, when it did, my father hobbled back to the side of the pitch and he just sat on the grass and said nothing and then he lit up a cigarette and threw the burning match to the ground. My brothers and sisters ran across the pitch shouting that he had played great, that he was brilliant, but the more they said the more uncomfortable he felt.

'It's the shoes, Dad,' I said to him.

He shook his head. He looked sharply at me.

'The shoes? There's nothing wrong with the shoes,' he said. 'They're good shoes. Look at them. They're great shoes. Good leather. Your mother got me them. I clean them every Saturday or Sunday. There's nothing wrong with the shoes. You see anything wrong with those shoes? Tell me what you think is wrong about a pair of shoes that get polished every week for Sunday Mass and get me into the chapel without so much as a grumble about the shoes. What's wrong with the shoes?'

'It's the shoes and the pitch, Dad,' I said, quietly. I could see his teeth. I felt about a foot tall. 'That's what I mean. The shoes can't grip on the slippy pitch.'

He pursed his lips and then nodded sideways. He groomed his hair with the palm of his hand. 'The pitch is fine too. A bit wet but it's fine. It's good grass and the man who tends it keeps it well. The grass is brand flippin' new. It's like a bowling green compared to most.' He pulled some grass from the ground, dropped it and watched it fall. 'It's a bad workman that blames his tools, don't you think?' Then he dug a hole with the heel of his shoe. 'You're doing good out there, Michael. I know you're good but you're playing better than I thought amongst the older boys and the men. Well done . . .'

'Thanks . . .'

'You know why?'

'No.'

'Simple. Because you prepared. And you practised. I'm thirty-nine or forty years old, I don't even know, and I smoke all day and I haven't done anything that might pass for exercise for over twenty years and I wear a pair of good Sunday shoes to a game and I'm disappointed that I'm not playing well. It's not the shoes. It's not the pitch. It's me. I'm disappointed . . . in *me*.'

'It's just a game, Dad. You don't need to prepare for a silly game like this.'

'Son, there's people laughing out there. And I'm your father. I know you're embarrassed when you see me falling about.' He looked up at me and I diverted my gaze. 'I wasn't supposed to prepare for the game. The game is irrelevant. I was supposed to prepare for you. And for the twins. And Iain and Mark. And the children up in the house.'

'I wasn't embarrassed,' I said, lying.

'You were. I could see you. I've known every line on your face since you were a baby and I know every look. I know your brothers and sisters too.'

'Sorry, Dad . . . I just wanted you to play well.'

He nodded and rubbed his hands and fingers together. He made a clicking sound in his throat. 'You shout quite loudly when you want to, don't you?' Both of us laughed together. 'It's good to laugh, eh?' We kept laughing, like a couple of happy evangelists with their toe in your front door.

'I don't know why. It just happens like that on the pitch,' I said.

He looked over at the rest of the players, some eating a slice of orange and others drinking from a bottle of Irn-Bru. He reached to undo his laces and then took off both shoes. A plume of steam rose from inside. He cleaned the mud using the sleeve of his jersey and said that my mother would be upset to see them so dirty so he'd best give them a wipe. The rain was slowing down to an imperceptible drizzle. Then he put his shoes back on and tied the laces in a tight bow.

His shoes glittered. He was right. They were good shoes.

I heard the tune to *Rocky* in my head. He would overcome the odds like Rocky did against Apollo Creed and get one last shot at the title.

But football is cruel. It isn't like the movies.

It would have been a great story if he'd gone out in the second half and played his heart out and scored a hat-trick, but he didn't. When he stood up that's exactly how I thought it would be. I watched as he walked on to the pitch with purpose. The tune was in my head. But things never worked out that way. That was for his stories and the myths and the songs and the tales we were told in the loft.

Another forty-five minutes to go. My father still slid around the pitch and some of the spectators still laughed. But he kept playing and tried his best to keep on his feet. And then he landed on the grass like pork chops on a butcher's counter. I watched him.

There were also parts of the game I didn't see. I didn't see the heavier tackles coming until they landed right on top of me. I didn't see the grin on the face of the older boy with the sharp scowl who was pointing at me, or the father of another boy who elbowed my father in the head and my father elbowed him right back and the man grimaced. Someone told me about that later. It was men, literally, against boys, and the game developed an edge. The score is impossible to recall, but the tackles are not.

Some of the men felt they had a point to prove and today would be as good a day as any to prove it. When I was hit I felt hit. I stayed hit. The tackles arrived like buses: none at first and then four at a time. Sunday-afternoon competitors: all of them hating to lose.

Then I heard someone crying out loudly and realized it was me. I'd been battered once again. I thought my youth was protection enough, that they might lay off me a little. I got up off the ground, wobbled a little and then fell over again like turnips off the back of a lorry. I clutched at the gash on my shin and felt the tears welling up and I tried to hold them in. He had gone right through me. The player was lying beside me on the grass. He looked over and winked and then started to get up. 'Man's game, wee man,' he said.

So he tried to get up. But for some reason he couldn't. My father was standing on his ankles. He just stood on him like a parrot sits on a man's shoulders. I had seen the man before. He had a bit of a beard and a head like a refrigerator. I couldn't remember his name. He was a few years older than my father. My father bent down with meanness disguised as a smile and said sorry, and could he give the man a hand up? He put out his hand and the man put out his and my father squeezed as tight as he could and the man recoiled as his fingers started to crack. The man kicked his feet into the mud for enough leverage to move my father but couldn't. The man's eyes lit up. My sisters shouted, 'Dad! Get off him!'

I looked at my father.

My father looked at me.

'Good tackle,' said my father. 'Up you get now, pal.'

My face was chalk pale. 'No, it wasn't, Dad,' I shouted. 'He battered me.'

'You were too slow . . . it was a good tackle. It was fair.'

He still held on to the man's hand, squeezing and crushing, and the man yelped but my father ignored him and looked at me. I could smell his cigarettes.

'You want to play football when you're older, Michael?'

'Yes . . .' I said, stammering.

He nodded. Then he pumped a few more times on the man's fingers. A leg twitched like a cat's tail.

'You think you can dance about there all day long? Sometimes a tackle like that can help you *see* things a little more . . . clearly. You know what I mean? Don't be Mr Showy all the time.'

He didn't say anything else. Whatever happened next didn't matter. The game continued. I hobbled around and it ended soon after. We shook hands and we might even have hugged. He was covered from head to toe in mud and he walked off the pitch with his shoes in his hands, cleaning them with his sleeve and some spit. He left invisible footprints in the mud. The following Sunday he wore the same shoes, black as a liquorice stick, with his pressed Sunday clothes and he put a few pence in the collection plate as he always did.

That game of football passed quickly into memory and was rarely talked about. But it was a small death in our relationship. A small, deep cut. I was never sure then if he was trying to teach me a lesson and I'm still not sure even now. Whatever it was he intended, he showed me that, as well as heroes, sons needed ordinary fathers too. They needed men who wore jerseys that didn't fit and shoes that belonged in a pew.

I once heard it said that we glory in our fathers in victory and success. But we fall in love with them in defeat.

I would have liked that game to go on for ever.

And I still do, even now.

Chapter Eight

Returning Home

The weather had turned as warm as my mother's prayers.

We all wanted to get him home just to sit in the garden in his wheelchair with the Campsies in the background, the sun warming his skin to brown. He would enjoy the heat pressing down on his face and deep into his bones. It would be a relief to see some colour. He was already as pale as the moon.

Years ago he would sit or work in the sun and bake and his skin turned purple as a berry. He would tan in a coalmine, he said. The Black Irish. His people came from everywhere *before* Ireland. They were Iranians and Spanish and Africans and they came on armadas and they were dark-eyed tinkers too. His summer skin told the story of the past.

The nurses said he had passed the might-die stage but if there was still a chance they agreed it would be better that he did so facing the hills and the greenery and in the garden, with the long grass that needed cutting after his absence. He could sit under the big trees and think his private thoughts. He would trace our lives, and his, from childhood to now and remember it all. And my mother would be near him, in his daydreams, making dinners and hanging out so much washing on the line that the garden looked like it was a cotton field, and he would recall everything through sunshine and sometimes rain and be happy as the day was long.

He would be home soon, they said.

How long have I been in here?

'One day, Dad, that's all. Tomorrow is your first day and it always will be. Just one day in hospital. That's all you need to know for now.'

What month is it? June? August?

'It doesn't matter, Dad. At least you're here.'

His physiotherapy was helping now. To do what, we weren't really sure. To help him mumble more clearly? To help him stumble better? To recalibrate the cog inside him that had stopped? The nurses supported him on a frame. You couldn't call it walking but they were trying to show him what his body was once able to do by going through the memory of motion. Every step was met with a clap of the hands from my mother and half a grin from my father. He was like a man wading in a snowdrift, unable to fall, held up on both sides by the nurses and the great weight of something unseen.

There was a downside. The more conscious he became of his predicament the less inclined he was to receive any treatment from anyone. As he came back to life he remembered that he was a private person and he shrank back towards the past. It was a good sign too. It meant a lot of his old, grievous, recalcitrant habits were still there.

I'm trying. Just give me some time . . . You know the story of the scorpion and the frog? That's me. You can't just expect me to change overnight because I've had a stroke. It doesn't work that way . . .

Iain was still in America but was planning to return to live in Northern Ireland with Natalie and Quinn and their new baby, Aaron. Mark had returned for a brief visit before going back to New York. My father responded much better to those he hadn't seen for a while. When Iain, Mark or the girls called from abroad his eyes bulged with white. It was always a huge effort on his part to communicate but he tried as hard as we'd seen him over the past six months. He loved to hear their voices, talking about Abu Dhabi and Dubai and New York. Their voices helped him to escape his bed and to wander.

Before his stroke I'd sensed a few changes in him. The boys also had. They mentioned it in their calls when we spoke. The warts of the past were being shed. He was no longer as strident in his opinions about Ireland and about how he wanted to go there to live at some point. Perhaps the Irishmen we all got to know in New York were not the Irishmen of his imagination. Perhaps it had struck him one day that Ireland might never welcome the returning Prodigal Son that he'd imagined himself to be, somewhere in Cork or Tyrone or all the villages and towns with freckled children lolling in a stream.

Whatever the cause, he spoke less and less about the past and wanted to move forward. Dubai was the place. Portugal was the place. He retained some affection for New York. My mother and father had even been planning a trip to Australia. I think he realized too late that the world was vast. He also looked relieved that it was.

Mark had got married in Portugal and we'd all gone there for the wedding. 'This is the place,' he said, over a brandy and ham in a late-night café along the road from the in-laws' house. 'This is the place. I mean, look at it. Just *look* at it.'

We were all staying in a small village near the fortified town of Óbidos and it was as if he'd stumbled across a new spiritual home. It was quiet and respectful and no one swore in the streets and you could drink brandy into the evening in the sunshine and no one would ask any questions of you. He loved it as much as he'd loved any place. He submitted to it. And then it ended. Mark returned to New York and we all went home and my father shook his head and said, this is it, lads. This is it.

Not a whisper more.

But there were few protocols when it came to forgetting. He couldn't *escape* Ireland, nor did he truly want to, but something had definitely shifted. Bigger things affected him too.

The September 11 attack on the Twin Towers in New York, in 2001, also seemed to change him because his sons were there and that was as good a reason as any. Iain and Mark were working in Manhattan at the time. Iain was high up on scaffolding on 14th Street and Sixth Avenue and he could hear the Twin Towers exploding and he saw the immense swirl of black dust clouds as they fell against the cobalt-blue sky.

Mark had been laying blocks in the basement of the Metropolitan Museum of Art, on 87th Street and Fifth Avenue, from early morning. He took coffee with Gary, his friend and a contractor on the job, at 8.40 a.m. and then they heard people talking about a plane crash downtown and they saw the same black smoke rising. They heard that another plane had crashed and then they tried to get home but couldn't so they headed uptown to the Kinsale Tavern, and he managed to speak with my father from a phone box before all the communication lines went down.

My father talked with Iain too and the news unsettled him. Just like everyone else, he couldn't fathom what had actually taken place. It was only a few months earlier that he'd stayed in New York with the boys and had been to the Twin Towers and the Empire State Building and walked around Broadway and visited Barnes & Noble bookstore and a few more Irish bars than he'd initially planned. Years earlier, I'd worked downtown with Iain and Mark around Fulton Street and John Street, and all over the city and various boroughs, labouring for an Irish company that was building schools and apartment blocks. I knew the bars and the places where my brothers were working. My father loved it there as much as I had.

He called me after the boys had called him.

'Terrible,' he said, 'just terrible. There has to be a big rethink here. Terrible waste. Absolutely terrible waste of people.' His phrase struck me. The only time he ever really said people was when he was referring to his own. The Irish. But the people he meant now were everyone. I noted it and then I put it away. My editor had called me a little earlier. It was my day off and I was making breakfast in the flat and I hadn't seen the television reports yet. 'You'd better look,' he said. 'Call me back when you've watched it. I think you should go over.'

My bags were packed and the office tried to arrange flights but everything was cancelled within hours. I was disappointed that I couldn't travel. Angry too. Part of me believed that if I was there I'd make a better job of telling the story than anyone else. It was a terrible conceit to feel that way. To believe that because I wasn't part of it, it was somehow less valid. I shook myself and headed to the office.

Later that evening, I sat with my father watching all the events unfolding. He hoped the boys would call again but they didn't, not for days. He knew they were safe, but it never lessened the worry. What if something *else* happened? The newsreels ran. The planes crashed over and over and over. They couldn't be undone. Nothing could. They just kept crashing and then exploding. I don't think I'd ever heard him being so vocal about something. The events confused him. The world had suddenly shrunk. He had two boys working in Manhattan and they might easily have been working down there too. He still had fresh five-dollar bills from his recent trip, which he used as bookmarks.

There was always a time when some doors closed and other doors opened. They'd been opening a lot back then. He looked like a man with glasses who was constantly pushing them up to his forehead and scratching. Scratching and wondering.

Another month passed as quickly and easily as a word written on a page. He was sitting outside the rehabilitation unit in his wheelchair, gaunt as a skeleton and, despite our obvious presence, alone. He was lost. My mother stroked his arm and then his cheeks but he'd simply disappeared somewhere unreachable. A pause turned to a long silence. Another man from the stroke unit sat nearby. He'd been in the unit for a few months but now was sitting up, talking with his wife. She smoked a cigarette and the smoke spun in the air. The man took an occasional puff. They were laughing together. Suspended in conversation and recollection.

I watched my father as he looked straight ahead, out towards the unmoving hills where he used to take us for walks, past the sleeping cattle and the fat sheep. He could see the stiff chimneys of the houses in Bishopbriggs. They were reluctant signposts to where he lived but hadn't been in months. I pointed out the chimney of my parents' house and, with his cold fingers, traced the road from the hospital, down to the traffic lights at Colston.

'There, Dad. I live there now. Can you see it?'

He smiled while I held his finger.

'It needs work, Dad, just like yours. A lot of work. We're neighbours now, eh? Three streets away.'

He nodded too. I let go of his hand. He pointed slowly at his own house, nestling beneath the hills and just up from the Cross and near Brackenbrae Road and the Men's Own.

I see it. I see it. I need to go home. I want to go home.

Although I'd been away from Bishopbriggs for years, in truth, I'd never really left.

Football had come and gone. I stopped playing when I was sixteen. Some of the trials went well, others less so. But I knew, deep down, that I wanted other things in my life. Maybe I was just never good enough. Perhaps I'd always just wanted to write. When I stopped playing I didn't call the coaches or go round to their houses.

I wrote them all a letter.

For a while I studied at the University of Glasgow, in the west end of the city, streets away from where I'd lived as a child in Partick. I liked studying, or at least the idea of it, but I wanted to travel too and I took a year out to go off to America and Australia and Thailand and India and Europe. At some point after university, between mixing mortar in New York while dreaming of writing stories, I became a journalist and eventually arrived at the *Glasgow Herald*, which later became the *Herald*. I hatched a plan to travel and write as much as possible and, for a while, I did.

The newspaper work was exciting and so was the travel. I wrote about things at home but felt a greater need to go away. I went to China to write about the Yangtze River and the thousands of people who lost everything to the world's biggest hydroelectric project, the Three Gorges Dam. The people had to move and their belongings and their homes and their possessions became nothing but artefacts in a river to be discovered in the future. It was terrible the way poor people took a lifetime to accumulate the little they had only for bureaucrats to take it all away, said my father.

I travelled to Palestine and Israel to try to write about a conflict that had been around since biblical times and decided that I could barely understand any of it, so what I tried to do was write about some of the people I met there in the hope that they could tell stories of their own. He nodded then too. The Israelis, he said, had a lot to answer for and sometimes so did God, while we're at it. That part of the Middle East was a strange world of batons and bombs but, much like Ireland, I knew that every cut of the loaf left two pieces.

His interest in my career was absolute and he called me wherever I was in the world to check that things were going well and whether, if I had the time, I could bring back a souvenir. It didn't matter what. Just something that showed I'd been there.

'Only if you can, Michael,' he said. 'If you've got the time.'

I brought all kinds of stuff home: a postcard, a banknote, a magnet, a weather-polished stone from the ground and a bullet casing too. I brought him shells and old floor tiles and a small rug and a music cassette and an older smoking pipe and some ancient, dried wood and some twisted metal and local newspapers and inane hotel accoutrements. They were small treasures but it allowed him to be part of the journey. He put the totems upstairs beside his bed or packed them away in the loft, marking these scenes like a crime.

He liked me to tell the stories.

Like the time I was in Bethlehem and my driver, in a battered old Mercedes, took me near Rachel's Tomb, the traditional burial place of the biblical matriarch, the wife of Jacob, and revered at various times by Muslims, Christians and Jews alike. And wandering inter-lopers too.

It was night. The driver took us too close to an Israeli Defence Force checkpoint and a shot rang out above our heads, hitting a wall and breaking the plaster rendering. I can't say for sure who fired it but I could feel it and hear it and I knew which direction it came from. The driver shouted and quickly spun the vehicle round and tried to get back to the hotel where I was staying. They hadn't shot at us, just *near* us. I understood that. It was a warning, nothing more. I'd heard warnings like that before. I lay awake that night and knew that I wanted to keep writing. About why people did what they did, even if I didn't agree with them. And why things were done to other people, even if they didn't ask them to be.

My father listened, in his living room or at my flat, while I told him my stories. He cared. And he'd have packed his bags to travel with me that night if he could have, gathering up his stuff before standing on the runway and not looking back. At least not for a while.

I got on and off planes. Bishopbriggs never seemed so far away, and I wasn't counting it up in miles.

I wrote a lot for the *Herald* magazine and I didn't want any more than that. Space and inches and trust were everything in newspapers and sometimes I had all three. In March 2000 I made a trip to the Falkland Islands but I can tell you now that the real reason I went was because I really just wanted to stop off in Argentina to try to find the former president, General Galtieri. I didn't know for sure I could find him so I told my editor that I could definitely get a story on the Falkland islanders and then hatched the plan to stop off in Buenos Aires before anyone was any the wiser.

There was little time and not much money and that has never helped anyone find a former architect of a doomed invasion of an island in the South Atlantic. A few hours after my arrival, sweating and virtually penniless, I stood in a downmarket suburb outside the modest brown apartment block of the former president while the generalissimo stood upstairs at the intercom. Neighbours told me that he helped out doing small jobs around the apartment block. He didn't appear to have profited very much from his previous power. He went for walks every day and sometimes took the wife of his friend, a hardware-shop owner who lived nearby, to church on Sundays in his old, dark-blue and reliably British Ford Escort.

Neighbours and shop owners and a nearby hairdresser spoke with me too. Some liked him for who he'd been earlier, others were angry at what had happened. More wanted to forget the past. A woman said he drank too much whisky. I kicked myself for not bringing a bottle of anything that might help loosen his tongue.

At night when I visited again and pressed the buzzer, a woman answered and Luis, my taxi driver and translator for the day, explained to her why I was there. 'No, it's not possible,' she said, politely. He did not speak to Argentine newspapers and he would not speak to me. She said she was sorry. She had to go. Luis explained I had come a long way. She could do no more, she said, and was sorry if I'd had a wasted journey.

I had to fly back that night. The newspaper wouldn't let me stay any longer, especially since they never really knew I was going. Expenses and budgets were more important than some stories. I'd been in the Falkland Islands for the past week already and the clock was ticking. From the pavement I looked up at the apartment window and the white-haired figure hovering there. The figure quickly moved away. I left Galtieri with his thoughts of the Dirty War, the Falklands, his Ford Escort and another empty glass of whisky. Time caught up with everyone.

'Did you bring your camera?' asked my father on the phone.

'Yes, but it's not any good. In fact it's rotten.'

'You could have taken mine.'

I laughed. 'I know, I know. How's things?'

'Good, good. Everyone is well.' He paused. I could hear him smiling. 'Galtieri? His apartment? A flippin' Ford Escort? They used to drive him about in a motorcade. Well, if the old spooks didn't know where he was they do now! Over and out . . .'

Luis was just as disappointed as me. He said he would take me somewhere else before I flew home and we headed off for a quick visit to see Diego Maradona's house instead. He might have been showing me a bowling alley for all I knew.

In New York I sat for hours with the wildly effeminate writer, actor and raconteur Quentin Crisp and I doubt there was a more interesting man or woman in the whole of Manhattan. Crisp lived in an apartment that, by his own admission, he'd never cleaned in years and never would. I practically slid into the small, dank room, such was the filth. I stayed for hours and it was a privilege.

'New York,' he said, 'is just like the movies.' And, of course, it was.

Sometimes journalism was just like the movies too.

I applied for a Stern Fellowship at the *Washington Post* around March 2001, and was interviewed by the London Bureau Chief, and Ben Bradlee, the then Vice President At Large of the *Post* and perhaps the most glamorous and renowned newspaperman of the modern era.

Like many young and ambitious journalists of my generation, I held Bradlee in high esteem but, if I was being honest, I knew Bradlee's Hollywood character more. He was played by Jason Robards in the film *All the President's Men*. Bradlee's two reporters, Bob Woodward and Carl Bernstein, had investigated the Watergate scandal and eventually forced the resignation of President Nixon, transforming in the process both politics and journalism. It wouldn't be long, I imagined, before the boy from Bishopbriggs was bringing down the United States president too.

My father always admired the tenacity of Bradlee, Woodward and Bernstein, particularly as they were up against the right-wing resident of No. 1600 Pennsylvania Avenue, and my father never really had much time for anyone who took up residence on the right wing of anything. And now Bradlee was interviewing me in London for a three-month fellowship. Bradlee met me in the corridor and I followed him into a room. They already had some examples of my work. One piece was on politics in Ireland and another about Lockerbie and my recent meeting with Colonel Gaddafi in Libya. The Bureau Chief asked me to describe myself in a few words. He probably meant my career.

'Working class, Catholic and Scottish,' I replied.

I'm sure I caught him looking over at Bradlee, stifling a grin.

Then he asked if that was the order that expressed my identity best and I replied that I was less sure about the Scottish part, but the other two definitely. I'm sure I mentioned Celtic somewhere in there as well. I knew that Bradlee had married a Quinn and *we* were also Quinns. Surely he would make the connection? The words were out of my mouth and inside I was shaking my head and I'm sure I must have shouted at my father too: You eedjit, what did you make me say that for?

Slightly flummoxed, he asked me to explain. Bradlee listened intently while I tried to untie the big, fat Irish Celtic knot.

I wasn't sure, really, why I said it myself.

I was born in Scotland to Scottish parents but my father's influence was such that I felt a more natural and certainly emotional affinity to Ireland than Scotland. I admitted that I'd never quite truly understood why I felt so. Though Celtic *were* the first British team to win the European Cup and they had done nine-in-a-row before anyone else . . .

You said what? You're as daft as I am . . .

Yet my mother was Scottish. She was *island* Scottish. She spoke Gaelic and there was the house on Barra and the walks down to Castlebay past the fat, squishy cowpats, and the kittens that Uncle John used to drown in the river. But I never *felt* Scottish. At least not in the sense that other Scots people I knew seemed to feel it, with their tartan and their kilts and their Saltires and their lodges, and wistfulness whenever they saw a scrag of heather. And, besides, how could I ever truly understand a country that had only ever given Jimmy Johnstone twenty-three caps?

There were some things that were simply *impossible* to ignore.

The rest of the Lisbon Lions got hardly any Scottish caps at all: Ronnie Simpson (five), Jim Craig (one), Tommy Gemmell (eighteen), Bobby Murdoch (twelve), Billy McNeill (twenty-nine), John Clark (four), William Wallace (seven), Stevie Chalmers (five), Bertie Auld (three) and Bobby Lennox (ten). I couldn't remember what year Scotland had won the World Cup but they must have had some team . . .

It was all the things my father had told me over the years. It was the music he played and the songs he'd sung and all the conversations we'd had. It was the loft and the roof and the tired house and the garden too.

It was the Old Firm Scottish Cup Final, 1980, at Hampden, when Celtic beat Rangers 1–0.

The Tierney house was full for the match. We all sat in the dining room and the old brown television was on, and the radio was also on in the kitchen for my mother. Crisps and peanuts in small, silver bowls. Someone pressed the button for the BBC and we all had to shush.

All the players looked just like my uncles and my father's friends. Davie Provan, young and cool with his white socks at his ankles, and Danny McGrain with his beard, who looked like Jimmy Ward down the road with the ice-cream van, and Frank McGarvey with his wavy hair and Bobby Lennox, who looked about fifty-eight and tough as a honey-badger. They didn't look like the footballers of today. They just looked like fellas who were told to turn up at 2.30, after a shift at work, and play.

The game just went back and forth in a wave of green and blue and it went left and right too. It went up and down and side to side but it was still 0–0 and it went to extra time. And then Celtic scored. The ball came out to Danny McGrain who sclaffed a volley and it was going a mile off target until George McCluskey redirected it past Peter McCloy into the empty net, and the Rangers players looked as happy as a deer being swallowed by a boa constrictor.

When Celtic's goal went in all our crisps and peanuts were thrown in the air and the girls started screaming because the boys were jumping up and down all mad and my father was laughing and the peanuts were choking him, and my mother ran in and said, what's all the commotion, have they scored? It *was* possible to nearly die of happiness by eating too many packets of Fine Fare crisps and peanuts, and drinking too much diluted orange juice while watching Celtic. And my mother started hitting my father's back and he was laughing and shouting, the eedjits, the eedjits! We've won!

When the match ended the Celtic players went to the supporters to celebrate the victory. That's what everyone did. We clapped and cheered with them. The girls too. Then the Celtic players lifted the trophy. There were Celtic fans on the pitch. Five minutes later it was bedlam. The place went mad. Rangers supporters were on the pitch now too.

The fans were on the pitch running rampant, scarves tied around their wrists and their hair swirling about. I'm sure I saw Uncle Gerard or Uncle Neil. Bottles, iron bars, cans (thousands of cans) and bricks were thrown. Both sides started having a right old rammy and tear-up, and the police were on too with their truncheons and their horses and a commentator was calling it *Apocalypse Now*.

There was a big, white horse with a policewoman on it that was just like King Billy's old horse. The pitch had turned into a boxing ring but the rules had gone out of the window, all gone to pot. You could hear the horses' hooves on the pitch. It was a full-scale riot and it wasn't just the young ones, it was the old men also, and we watched wondering how it had all come to that just because we'd won.

The girls were shouting and my mother was saying, that's terrible, that's awful isn't it, look, they're battering each other. My father wasn't too happy either because it wasn't a good example to be setting the children. We could hear them shouting 'Fenians' on the telly and I heard 'Orange bastards' from Celtic supporters so my father turned down the sound.

It was just a fight now. A stupid, horrific fight between the two sets of fans. There were pictures of a wee boy crying beside his dad and that wasn't right. My father said there was an unwritten rule that the losing team in a final always left the ground early, or first, to let the winning team get on with the celebrating stuff. 'They couldn't accept their team lost on the day,' he said, and kept shaking his head. Rangers had been favourites for the Cup. We had a couple of players missing. Tom McAdam and Roddy MacDonald. But we had beaten them. My father knew there would be trouble in the town that night and in all the pubs too and there was.

It was mad watching the horses at the end. There were eight horses and they went galloping backwards and forwards, rounding up the fighting fans like something out of a cowboy film. Some people said it was caused by sectarianism and it probably was, said my father, but it couldn't have been us because Celtic had five

Protestants on the pitch that day, including the man who lifted the cup, Danny McGrain. He'd supported Rangers as a boy. So how could we be to blame, he said.

But it wasn't just Celtic and football that was in my head.

It was my grandfather dying in a ditch and my grandmother crying out when he fell. It was Granny Quinn and her father, Francis, and the tales from over by and the stuff that everyone whispered about while glancing over their shoulder. All of these things made me believe that day with the *Washington Post* that my Scottish identity was not as important as my class or my religion. And maybe it wasn't.

Perhaps there was a medical definition.

Celtic-Irish-itis . . .

The interview continued. Bradlee, in his perfectly pressed shirt and braces, looked impressively patrician. He was Georgetown, the Hamptons, Capitol Hill and shiny penny-loafers. He was the real deal. Mostly, he just listened.

A few days later I received a letter from the Bureau Chief. My application had not been successful. I was not unduly surprised. I felt savagely average and mediocre. Even without my rambling interview about identity, the rest of the candidates were from national papers, based in London, and had a little more gravitas and hinterland. I told myself that I was truly delighted to have been considered and never believed a single word I said.

And that was the end of me bringing down US presidents.

About three weeks later there was an airmail letter in my pigeonhole at the office of the *Herald*. On the envelope, in typed letters, it said: Ben Bradlee. The letter had the address, and stamp, of the *Washington Post*.

Dear Michael Tierney,
I just wanted to drop you this short note to thank you for your interest in the Stern Fellow program, to regret with you that you were not chosen this time, and to tell you that you impressed me as a journalist that I would be proud to work with.

I would also urge that you apply next year. I think you are at a time in your career where it would be good for both of us if you plied your trade in Washington.

Sincerely,

Ben Bradlee

I remember sitting in my chair and smiling serenely, like the face on an old pocket watch. I asked around to see if other applicants had received a letter from Bradlee and a previous Fellow checked around and doubted any of them had. My father loved the letter, and encouraged me to think about Washington. 'The man brought down Nixon,' he said. '*Nixon*. You don't get these chances too often, Michael.'

I couldn't say with any certainty that I would ever have got to Washington and I couldn't say for sure that Bradlee's letter was little more than polite flattery. I couldn't even say if I was anything more than a mediocre journalist. But sometimes choices get made for us. When my father had his stroke there was never any question of where I would be the following summer.

After his stroke I began to spend a lot more time in Bishopbriggs and started to feel some contempt for my work. It seemed utterly point-less. I hated the office and every day I wanted to punch a hole in a wall or a fat man's face or even for someone to *hit me*. Kathleen said that my father's illness was making me depressed, but if anyone was going to be depressed it would be my father trying to claw his way out of a dark hole.

I put up a front. Or at least I tried to. We all did. My mother remained seemingly impervious to despair, although I knew how upset she was, but she just kept getting up and getting on with things. I worked and I travelled but I wanted more than anything to be closer to home. My mother needed things done around the house in his absence. The boys were away. At that time I simply preferred going backwards and forwards to Bishopbriggs and being with my father. There was much less noise.

Bishopbriggs still had its busy row of shops next to Quins and the bank on the corner and the schools and the park. The familiarity of it all remained. I had always liked the park with the burn that we used to run through in our school uniforms at the end of term. The rows of neat houses spoke of normality, patience and order. The house Kathleen had seen advertised in May was old and honest as a confessional box and only a few streets from my parents'. I could see the spire of Kenmure Church from one of the upstairs bedroom windows. I loved that church at the top of the street and I think I always had.

The property we wanted to buy needed extensive upgrading. The list of tasks had begun to sound terribly familiar. But the house was filled with life and not a little love either. There had only been two other families living there since it was built in 1904 and the current owners had outgrown all the rooms. There was no bitterness at the sale, only hope that it might go to a family who would look after it. It turned out that I desperately wanted the house even though I didn't really know it at the time.

The lady who was selling knew I worked in newspapers and that my family lived down the road. She'd once delivered a bag of clothes to my parents' house for a charity fundraiser. One day when I was viewing the house, she asked me to hold on for a minute while she went to look for something.

'And do you have a sister called Catherine?'

'I do . . .'

The lady went upstairs to find what she was looking for. I sat down on a chair to remember.

Not long after I'd graduated I volunteered to deliver medical supplies to Bosnia during the break-up of the former Yugoslavia, for a Glasgow charity. It wasn't wholly altruistic. I wanted them to let me report about the trip for a community project I was working with. Weeks later, having borrowed some recording equipment from a local radio station, I was on my way to Bosnia, driving a large van filled with medical supplies and second-hand clothes.

I drove across Europe with two other volunteers, Anna and Mohammed, who I'd never met until a few days before our trip. We drove to Split, in Croatia, and from there we were to take some supplies into Mostar where there was a great deal of trouble and an even greater need. In Split the army said we would not be able to go to Mostar directly due to an escalation in the fighting, and so we were forced to leave the majority of the supplies in a refugee camp filled with women and children from Sarajevo, in the hope that they would later be taken further inland.

The roads back to Zagreb were rutted and dangerous and filled with roadblocks manned by teenagers wearing army fatigues and Guns N' Roses T-shirts, and drunken soldiers. For reasons I still can't fathom I crashed on a tight bend. The van dropped around forty feet into the Adriatic and landed us upside down in the water. Anna was thrown through the windscreen and ended up broken and battered and wedged between large rocks. I went through the windscreen too and finished up in the water, but though bruised I was mostly fine. Mohammed was unable to swim but a large jerry can helped him to stay afloat.

Hours later Anna was in intensive care and would be operated on when the electricity generators were turned back on. About ten days or so later and we were back in Glasgow. And Anna eventually recovered from her injuries. The trip had been tragic and exhilarating and sometimes crazy and even funny and I wanted to go back. The draw of finally getting into Mostar and Sarajevo would be too much. After a few months a return trip was planned.

Although my father had been worried about what had happened during the first trip I could tell that he was eager now to go as well. We could always tell by the way he *didn't* mention certain things that these were exactly what was on his mind. Eventually, we agreed that we'd go together, along with my friend, Alan. The charity was delighted.

Some time later the replacement van stood in the driveway of the charity's premises. It was like something off Noah's ark. It had a double clutch, usually found only in very old commercial vehicles, which made it virtually impossible to drive it if you weren't wearing a flat cap and selling Hovis from the back. I didn't actually know what a double clutch was so I listened while my father explained. He was in his element. 'Easy,' he said. 'Once you get used to it.' And then he grinned like a muddy schoolboy.

I understood then why he wanted to make the trip. It wasn't that it was a trip to Croatia or Bosnia; it was a trip *anywhere*. The first time he'd ever been abroad was when he was in his late thirties and he went for a week with my mother to Calella in Catalonia, after Iain had won a raffle at St Matthew's Primary School. Calella was talked about for years as if it was the greatest thing since sliced bread. For my parents it was.

It was also another chance just to get away from the street, St Matthew's, the Cross and even Quins. He didn't mind discomforts at all. He'd dealt with them for years. It was just that a trip like this one to Croatia, in a big old van, might never come around again. Two jumpers, a pair of jeans and some pants in a bag. That was about all he took. And his camera too. He just didn't need anything else. Just the journey.

It made for great watching.

He was going on his *holidays*.

'Cathie?' he shouted. 'I'll maybe take a clean shirt as well. We'll stop somewhere over there for Mass.' My mother kissed him and laughed and said, you're too old for this, dear. We hadn't left the house yet but the trip had already transformed him. I hadn't seen him smiling that much in years.

We took turns driving the van and eventually got the hang of things and survived on conversations about the Bosnian war, the Middle East, Ireland, football, the family and Celtic. Alan was a Celtic fan too. Celtic was always the fallback conversation when we ran out of things to talk about. So-and-so was good, but so-and-so was really bad.

Celtic ended up third behind both Rangers and Aberdeen in the season 1992–93 and we wrote it off as yet another criminal aberration. The whole period was an aberration too following the appointment in June 1991 of Liam Brady, a brilliant Irish footballer who'd played for Arsenal and Juventus. He fitted the Celtic mould and his Dublin-born Irishness was a bonus for many. But in terms of his football management skills, well, he didn't have any to speak of, even if he'd been interrogated at Confession. In terms of management he couldn't have hit the Confessional door if he was swinging on its handle.

In Brady's first season (1991–92) Celtic ended up third behind Rangers and Hearts. We'd have finished second too if we hadn't thrown away our last game of the season to Hibernian and we only actually needed a point to go second and it meant that we were out of Europe. But then we were back *in* Europe . . . because of all the troubles in the former Yugoslavia.

Given Brady's past European form we might as well not have bothered. In October 1991 Celtic were humiliated in Switzerland, beaten 5–1 by Neuchâtel Xamax, a team with such a ridiculous-sounding name it might have been a headache tablet. It was one of those awful games when anything that could possibly go wrong did and hardly endeared Brady to the Parkhead faithful.

'I went to the return leg,' I said. 'I still have no idea why.'

'One–nothing, wasn't it?' asked Alan.

'Yep.'

'George gave me the programme,' said my father. 'McStay was on the front. It's up in the loft.'

I looked at Alan. I'd sold it to some Celtic diehard pal for a fiver. Who could possibly complain about a four-pound profit after such a horsing? I changed the subject to something equally miserable: the League. Rangers had won the domestic treble in the 1992–93 season. We quickly changed it back again.

We drove on all day and all evening and into the next day too. Something happened as we drove. I think I heard my father *listening*. It was summer. It was warm and it was dry. He looked fresh and young. He might well have been driving to pick up a new screwdriver from B&Q. My eyes got sore thinking about it.

It happened with people, especially with fathers.

They were right in front of you your whole life, fixing a car, going shopping with the wife, going to work, tending a garden, and you didn't really see them. Sometimes it took a journey to change them, or to allow you to see them. I could see him now. Now he was there, away from the quiet and safety of our house. The van banged and rattled and he said, hold on to your hats, boys.

There was singing too.

We listened to the radio and I changed channels without asking his permission. He said nothing, barely noticed. Raidió Teilifís Éireann had been left behind in the hallway and the shed and the loft. He laughed a lot, especially when Alan struggled with the double clutch. So my father and I drove the majority of the way to Croatia and back again.

He would have been almost fifty years old. I noticed a few extra hairs around his ears and nostrils but his physique had barely diminished. He resembled a languid movie star from the fifties. His hands were blue-collar though: they were like shovels. Although my father had always been as hard as the Old Testament and took a lot longer to understand, the trip helped him relax. It was as if he was shedding some hidden part of himself. And he was. He didn't worry an inch or part of a mile.

It wasn't easy for him, but gradually he spoke a little about my grandfather and how he'd enlisted in the Territorial Army for the duration of the war. It was, he said, under some provision of the National Service Act of 1939. He was with the 3rd Batallion Scots Guards when they headed for France, on 20 July 1944. And he would die less than two weeks later.

The conversation had an almost magical power. The past started to fill up almost randomly. But there was still a long way to go. It had started at the bottom of a well.

It was in a Churchill tank, he said, somewhere in France, perhaps in a field, or an orchard, or on a road, or a town that had been under attack by German soldiers. It wasn't particularly hard recalling the facts. The hard bit was just thinking about his death. He talked. We listened. He talked again. There was a lull. He was happy.

There was no late-night drink to draw his bitterness and anger. He just talked. He sat up and stared at the road ahead. He talked about Operation Bluecoat and Caumont and Major Willie Whitelaw, who was my grandfather's commanding officer at the time in S Squadron. For years, my father would always mutter something whenever Whitelaw, who became a Tory Cabinet minister, was on the television. He didn't like Whitelaw. I think he wondered if he'd actually witnessed his father's death. And if he did, why did he not find his mother in Ruchill and come and pay his last respects? And if he didn't witness it, well, he should have paid his respects regardless.

With the Guards disembarking on the Normandy coast, near an artificial harbour at Arromanches, my grandfather would have spent a week or so there before moving forward towards Caumont. But if my father knew any more of the details or particulars of his father's death, he never let on. It was enough that he was dead. The details were for him alone.

He slept for a bit, his head resting against the window. He woke up and ruffled his hair.

Remember we went to Stevenston and the water crashed over the pier? I got soaked and the girls were laughing and Auntie Anne and Francis were there too. Remember you used to scare us with stories about Maggie Murphy and the Mad Carrot and if we didn't get up to bed you would shoot the boots off us?

Remember Granny Tierney made her soup and you said we could dance across it and it was the best soup ever, and remember the time we all jumped down the giant sandbanks in Barra and we went hunting for fish with the bamboo poles from the wee nets that you sharpened with a penknife and you said if we caught a fish we had to eat it so no one caught a single one?

The European sun crept out of the ground. It grew easy to like my father then.

We continued on, past fields and farms and even a Ferris wheel that stood empty somewhere in Germany. He directed us through villages and cities and across motorways and to small roads leading to bigger roads, abandoning any sense of nervousness that he might end up lost. By the time we arrived in Zagreb, his sense of achievement was palpable. You could touch it with a stick and hang it on a wall too, like a framed picture of a good marriage.

The years did not diminish the death of his father, not for one minute. His absence worked on him quietly: water dripping on a stone. And the stone was breaking in two. But he was with me now. And I was with him.

The signpost for Zagreb was up ahead.

Alan, my father and me: we all burst out laughing. We'd arrived. Double clutch and all. There was only one thing for it. A song.

> 'Hail Hail, the Celts are here,
> What the hell do we care,
> What the hell do we care,
> Hail Hail, the Celts are here,
> What the hell do we care now . . .
> For it's a grand old team to play for,
> For it's a grand old team to see,
> And if you know the history,
> It's enough to make your hearts go,
> OH-OH-OH-OH!'

We sang the song with such gusto that the van shook as we pulled into Zagreb. The locals just looked at us, singing away like grey linties in an old van that had *Humanitarna Pomoć* stencilled across the top of the windscreen. We hoped to God that it said something like 'Humanitarian Aid', as the charity had promised us. And not 'Three Eedjits from Glasgow' . . .

A few *Hail Hails* later and his suggestion that we head to a church quickly put a dampener on proceedings but, as he explained, the local priest would likely know the location of the refugee camp we were heading to. The priest might also help us understand the politics of getting there. A van with medical supplies might suddenly disappear. The rules were different. In any case he was right. The priest spoke decent English and we explained why we had driven all the way from Scotland and what we had with us and asked where was the best place to take it to.

He smiled and thought we might just be a little mad.

The further we drove down the coast towards Split, he said, the greater the likelihood that the roads would be busy with soldiers and they might take it upon themselves to confiscate our supplies, either for themselves or for selling on. My father nodded. He was the oldest and the priest looked at him first. There was no question he enjoyed the authority. The rhythm was established. My father talked and asked questions. He was part of something. He was part of something *important*. The people here were being affected by war and he wasn't just watching it unfold from his living room.

It would be the closest he could ever get to a war. And maybe that's exactly why he went.

There was food and some drink. There was conversation about the war and there were rumours of terrible things done to women. He baulked at that. The Church in Croatia was mentioned. My father listened again. Phone calls were made. Supplies were dropped off. Photographs were taken. Things had changed so much since the war began, said the priest, and people were so suspicious of each other. My father listened once more. There was suspicion the world over, not just in Glasgow. Tribalism too. He put on his sunglasses. The words spilled around him like scattered seeds. We drove home.

He sweated at the prospect of returning to the old life.

The lady who was selling us the house returned, clutching a few photographs. Two of them were of my sister Catherine. She must have been nine or ten years old and as pretty as a butterfly. She had been crowned the Gala Queen at the local fete and the lady had been on the organizing committee all those years ago and had had her picture taken with Catherine, who was wearing a neat dress and a plastic tiara.

It was strange to see a photograph of my sister in someone else's house, but I liked to think that Catherine had been making the rooms ready for us for when they might be needed. And now they were.

'She's very pretty,' she said. 'Lovely dark hair.'

'The old photos are the best,' I said. 'The colour always seems to last longer.'

A few days later I returned to the house with my daughter Mahoney in her child seat in the back of the car. I sat outside and thought about my father and the day he took me to see his new house all those years ago. Although Mahoney would be too young to remember anything it was good to have her with me. The sky was clear and the roads were quiet. I peered in the window and felt the memory of snow on my face.

'See, Dad. We're neighbours now. Everything that's passed by, well it doesn't matter. The past is the past. We're neighbours.'

He was sound asleep.

There were days when we just dreamed him alive, when he got up from his bed and put on his clothes and walked out of Stobhill Hospital for ever. He simply walked home, past the Colston lights, wearing his pyjamas and slippers, and he shouted at passing cars to get out of the way because couldn't they see there was a man trying to find his legs? And then he sat in his favourite chair and said, 'I'm back.'

But that was just a dream. He lay as stiff as a pencil.

He tried to shut himself off too.

Mostly he just stared at the walls around him. Sometimes he resembled the despairing face in Edvard Munch's *The Scream*. My father's broken face told of the same blood-red and blackness. He looked utterly alone and lost, despite the love around him. Did he really remember anything about us? Did he recognize that I was his son? Did he know my mother and my brothers and my sisters?

Celtic had recently won the League, having beaten Rangers to the title by eighteen points. He wouldn't know that either.

There was a broad contradiction as well. Was he just reacting to sound and touch without knowing why? The number of visitors had also slowed down and maybe he felt it. Felt abandoned. I hadn't seen George for some months and, despite his gregarious nature, I think he found it difficult to see my father like that. It *was* hard seeing my father like that. He'd been replaced by a barely breathing corpse.

Secretly, I wondered if the best thing might be for him to die. I couldn't say it out loud in case it actually happened but sometimes his face held too much terror. How he died was irrelevant. It was simply a matter of when.

We knew that sleeping at night was still difficult for him and my mother couldn't bear to leave him alone. The unit was never still. There was always movement, hustle, crying, laughing, televisions purring, patients talking to themselves, patients sobbing, visitors sobbing, nurses gabbing and machines drumming. Every noise under the sun was there, said my mother, and a few more we'd never heard before. She worried it was all too much for his head and that the skull would burst open again.

She worried all day and worried at night.

My granny always said that worry would be the death of you. There was enough in the world to worry about without adding to the woes. Worry was etched on people's faces. My mother was dazed by worry. She worried like a long-tailed cat in a house full of rocking chairs.

Towards the end of July there was great news. He was allowed a home visit and his bright eyes told us he knew exactly what was happening to him. The first visit was on a Saturday. It was a day of smiles and rejoicing. On the short journey back to the house he took in everything, nodding slowly towards a new set of flats that were under construction. He could see the old BP garage being closed down, where he used to send us to buy his Lucozade.

When we turned into our street his eyes welled up so much that we thought he might drown. He tried to speak but there was nothing, just tears and silence inside. With two of us at his side he was able to shuffle very slowly with his frame. A few of the neighbours watched as he arrived home. It was more than six months since they'd last seen him. I noticed them waving from their windows as the sun's rays shone on his back while he tried to get up the steps and into the house.

Vincent's old room downstairs would be his when he visited and we filled it with familiar things: photographs of his mother and father, of his children and grandchildren, and books that he would never read again. Occasionally, I caught him looking around, lost and frightened, as if the raw horror had hit him all over again. Every day he shouted silently against the world, but the world ignored him. And so, quietly, without fuss, he returned to the island of his own grief.

A day visit turned into an overnight stay and July passed into August, then September. When they're written down, the days and weeks move fast and smoothly. But for him they were painfully slow and hard and they always would be. At the hospital he shuffled more easily along the corridor with the help of the nurses. If we listened closely enough the empty noises from his throat slowly turned into words.

'Are you OK, Dad?'

'Yye.'

'Are you tired, Dad?'

'Nnn.'

'How do you feel today?'

'Ffffnn.'

'Who do you support, Dad?'

'Ccceell.'

'What's that over there?'

'Ggrrapp.'

'Who do you love?'

He just smiled at that one.

'Where have you hidden your money?'

He smiled again.

His body was trying to work by itself. To connect the wires to the muscles and the bones. The neurons in his brain were all reconnecting and the wheels were turning and the cogs broke from their stiffness.

I told you not to switch me off. See. It's all about connections. You connect A to B and sometimes C will work . . .

He wanted to be alive again. He wanted to sit and talk and say stuff that didn't really mean anything. He wanted to look out of the window at home and say hello to strangers. He wanted to be part of a welcome-home parade. There would be cheering and pats on the back. He'd survived. They would smile. All of them. Even the ones he said were for the watching. But sometimes it was too much. He looked away too, as if all that *being alive* was just too much effort. Too horrendous to even contemplate. He turned off the light in his head. Not a sound or a glance or a movement. He lay as still as a run-down dog.

While the occasional home visit was good for him he still needed round-the-clock attention. One day a nurse found him lying on the floor of the hospital rehabilitation unit and there was a glass of mixed-berry juice spilled on the floor beside him. It looked like blood. The wheelchair was on its side. The only witnesses to the incident were the faces in the photographs of his grandchildren and a photograph of my grandmother Jane holding a raisin and fruit dumpling like the ones she'd made many years earlier.

His right hip was now broken.

He spent the next eight days in the Victoria Infirmary, in a new ward with car-crash victims and men who'd been assaulted and were broken and maimed. The noise and the light of the busy Glasgow hospital caused him problems. Each evening we visited he had the covers pulled up tightly, right up at his face, like a frightened child. His eyes darted about. If it was possible, my father's brain would be having a heart attack.

The fog lifted when they returned him to Stobhill and the familiar faces of the nurses there. James, another patient, waved his hand and said, 'Hello, John, good to have you back.' James's stroke had not been nearly as serious as my father's. 'Good to see you back, John. I'll away and get some biscuits for you.' It didn't matter that my father couldn't really eat them. But it might have been the kindest act I had seen for years.

I felt terrible for my father lying there, in the land of digestive biscuits and small talk. James lay down and began singing, as he waited for his nieces to visit him, which they had been doing for over five months. My father smiled through his thin lips. James didn't know it, but we knew his kindness had helped to save my father's life. The months passed more quickly than ever and my father gradually began to pick up again. The tubes to his hand, chest, mouth and stomach were gone. So were the foam and elastic slippers.

James died sometime later.

Finally, he would be going home, in the half-light and cold. It was November 2002, more than ten months after his stroke. As he was leaving the hospital ward, walking awkwardly with the nurses and his frame, and bent as a cigarette ash before it falls, he stopped when the physiotherapist came by. His eyes, spider-webbed with tracks of purple and red, were soft with emotion. I still don't know how he managed it, but very slowly and very deliberately he spoke up.

'Thnnk. Yyu.

'Frrr. Lokkng. Afftrr.

'Mmee.'

My mother just said, 'Oh, listen. Oh, dear goodness. *Listen!*'

Chapter Nine

A Dead Man's Bag

We lived amongst dead things.

His collection of wrinkled books and grey tools and Kodachrome photographs and yellow magazines and stiff clothes, and some bicycles and instruments and more tools, and broken machines and things so old that they must have belonged to the saints. My father loved all of these things. They had meaning. It didn't matter that most of them didn't make sense to us. They were his way of making a dent. They were totems. They were a life lived.

We lived in a time machine and its hidden components all resurfaced when he fell ill. My father had built the time machine years ago and later it slowed down. That summer, we stepped inside and stared at the dials and dashboard and the mechanical entrails for the very first time. It was ornate. We picked it apart.

It felt good. It felt sad too.

He filled the time machine with his stories. He filled it with our lives. His *things* were an anchor against a storm of forgetting and the erosion of memory. They clung to the loft like dead skin. They were like love letters.

The narrow wooden stairs were built from reclaimed floor joists and we climbed the steps past the small set of shelves that were crammed with everything that could hold dust. With each step my mind drifted to the past. If my father's unconscious could be turned to flesh and bone it would look like the contents of his impregnable loft. I hadn't been in the loft for months following his stroke but I knew it was no longer the same. We all did. You could *feel* it. Nothing was the same now. Part of him was gone. Most of him was gone. And he would never, ever be able to step into that loft again.

The loft was an extension of my father's head.

The loft *was* my father's head. We already knew this, Iain and I, years ago when he visited us up there at night.

He shaped the things in his life and then the things in his life shaped him. As we grew older my father knew that his children would one day all leave home, so he filled the loft with even more of our things, or the things that connected us to him. He filled it with so much stuff that it blocked the escape route for all the memories that were contained up there. The boys might leave, my sisters too, but we'd be taking nothing with us. Not a box and not a memory. Not if he could help it.

We protested. They were just things.

My old bed was still there, as was Iain's, although it had been joined by derelict wardrobes filled with clothes that Maureen collected constantly to send to children in Africa. She'd been a teacher for a couple of years in Malawi, living in little more than a stone hut, and her new habits forced her never to throw anything out. She hid clothes and shoes and blankets and toys and wrapped them up and posted them to Chintheche where she'd been staying, and the children jumped and sang when the parcels arrived.

Although they were much smaller than my father, the men in Chintheche wore his old clothes with distinction and a sense of pride at the big, white man who'd given them away, half the time without even knowing about it.

He dreamed of seeing Africa.

Five years before the stroke he travelled to Chintheche with my mother to visit Maureen and when he saw that his daughter had donated a pair of his old shoes and a suit to one of the men in the village, he decided to leave behind a jacket and pair of jeans he'd brought in his suitcase. The man was called George and he cooked my father bony fish with their eyes still in and my father never stopped talking about it in Quins, about the offering of a piece of crunchy fish with the cooked eyes.

'These people are as poor as hell,' he said, and he wanted to swear but couldn't break his habit of not doing so. 'It's flippin' disgraceful. There's children eating *roasted mice* out there too . . . I mean, what is the world coming to?' The old Africans, he said, got the world on top of them pretty *tight*. He said their fate was worse than that of the Irish.

If it wasn't nailed down to a floorboard Maureen sent it away. Over the years she took his clothes and he never said a word about it. We should all go over, he said, and help them build something, like a hall or a school. He would do the electrics. We could all chip in. Mark was a builder. We could lift and carry. Why not? Of course we could. It was easy. Things were easier than you anticipated, not harder.

He said the place was greener than you could imagine and that the people in the villages were happier than frogs in a pond and we had a damn cheek to complain here and the priests down the road should do a lot more for them than they were doing, starting with selling that bloomin' parish house and moving somewhere that was less shameful.

Sometimes he'd sit with us with a drink and talk about the African skies as if he was David Livingstone himself and the first man to have ever set foot on African soil. Ireland became Africa and the battle with the past was slowly receding over the Mulanje Massif or the Dwangwa River. It was a big leap in a tiring body. He was utterly moved by his induction to a new, previously hidden world.

'A disgrace,' he said. 'There's men and women and children living worse than animals there and look at all the flippin' waste here. The old colonialists have a lot to answer for.' He held his drink in his legendary hand, where the veins popped like a ploughed field. Maureen played some African music on the CD player. He closed his eyes and tapped his feet.

Up in the loft I switched the light on.

Over there was a pile of rusting saws with broken teeth. They lay beside cream telephones, cables, hi-fis, a guitar and case, and my old radiogram that would never offer another tune better than it had done twenty years earlier. The snooker table was still there, as worthless as one shoe. There were gold-painted picture frames and brown ones too. The clocks had all stopped; each suffocated by time. Back and forth I went, like a greedy child on a swing. I could see the boxes of photographs, thousands of pictures of the younger Tierneys, and pounds of old nails, and empty jars and full jars, and holy medals and well-thumbed Celtic match programmes and books and his motorcycle side guard. The air rifles were there too, in their long cardboard boxes and polystyrene packaging. Years ago my father had got another one for Mark.

Maureen was under the eaves, looking for jumpers.

I picked up an air rifle. At roughly nine pounds it felt heavier than I remembered it. I wanted to shoot it again, at the trees and the telephone poles and the boys from the quarry who scared us all throughout our younger lives till we grew up and realized that some of them were just as scared of us. We told my father we didn't shoot at the crows. We told lies when it came to hurting animals or birds. But that's what boys did. They hit each other, they hurt each other, they fought, they shot and sometimes they stabbed and stole. Some even grew up and still did it. Some went to war too. And no one ever really complained about that. But people always said we should never hurt the birds or any animals.

'What are you doing?' said Maureen.

I leaned out of the window. 'Just one shot, Mojo. Just like when we were boys.'

'That's dangerous.'

'There's no one there. Just once . . .'

It was hard to know where to start.

My father never earned enough money in his life to walk right past a drum of electric cable while the foreman was away, or if there was some spare wood, well, it might just end up in the back of his van. He'd pick up empty wooden pallets from the back of superstores and toss them into the van, having convinced himself that throwing away something as beautiful and natural as wood was a mortal crime anyway so he had, in fact, committed no crime, merely tried to prevent one from ever taking place.

Much to my mother's despair he could not throw out the smallest item, even if it was the stump of a dead man's chair. There was nowhere in the loft where I didn't see my father. There was nowhere in his life that he didn't see *his* father.

I wanted to find the bullets too.

I *had* seen them. I *had* held them in my hands. I held them tightly. There was one unopened box and around two hundred other bullets in a tin box that looked like it might have come from the army. The box said *.45 Auto Colt Smokeless CF Cartridge*. There were fifty in the unopened box. The bullets as real as a dog bite.

I don't know where my father got them or what they were really for, but I understood what they could do. Two hundred bullets were two hundred dead men. Way back when I found them as a teenager I never told a soul. Over the following few months I'd regularly take a bullet from the tin box and go over the back of the garden and into the quarry. The new houses were still a dream. I followed the small hill and wandered the tracks that had been made over the years by the men going to Milton and I found a peaceful spot.

I'd take one bullet at a time and try to explode it with a rock or stone. I'd throw the missile at the bullet as it lay on the ground, hoping for an explosion. When it didn't explode I threw the bullet as far away as possible and hoped that the ground would swallow it up and turn it into grass before anyone found me out, especially my father. I think I wanted to get caught. Because I knew my father would ask me where I'd got them. And then I could say to him, where did *you* get them?

Then, one evening, in the loft, I looked for them and they were gone. All of them. He left nothing and he said nothing. But he knew and I knew about the bullets.

There was nothing in the loft now that had been planned or ordered and the space had grown like butterfly bushes and wild-flower meadows from the chaos that inhabited his head. I loved it all but I hated it too. There were plastic boxes of hundreds of old school jotters and toasters and light fittings. There was an anvil. And a birdcage. The list was a trapdoor to a life of hoarding the souvenirs of memory.

They were his things. And they spoke loudest about his life.

A dollar bill was still pinned to a wooden beam alongside a photograph of my grandmother with Iain. It hadn't been touched in years. I'd never noticed it before. There were traces of wood preserver he'd started to brush on to the wooden support beams, before being abandoned. All that was left was an empty glove that he'd used. Now it was bone dry and cracked, as if he'd simply left his hand there for another time and maybe he had. There were a handful of torches in a row, like mini lighthouses protecting him from an oncoming storm. I pushed their buttons to see if they still worked. One of them did to start with and then it failed.

On a far wall, behind the partition, was my grandfather's green and grey canvas kit bag. It had his army number printed on it, stencilled in white: *2699783. Tierney M F.*

He kept his memories in a dead man's bag.

The discovery of the black and white photographs of my grandfather meant that he suddenly became more visible. Until that moment Michael Francis Xavier Tierney had been little more than a ghost and a swollen conversation. I shook the dust from the bag and swept it from his face.

Here was my grandfather, in Sergeant Mackie's Squad of the Scots Guards. The photograph was dated October 1940, and was taken by S. H. Brock & Co., of Clapham. My grandfather was seated in the bottom row, second from the right. He must have been about twenty-six years old. He looked like Iain, slim and handsome, with a rifle balanced against his left knee. Alongside him there were other young men. Men named Duncan, McCran, Wallace, Fowler, Long, Logan, Gedders, Keddie, Ferguson, Milbourne, McKenzie, Bolton, Clark, Burden, Bostock, Cameron, Keay, Mitchell, Walker, Harvey, Silcock, Sgt Mackie, Amos and Davidson.

They were ordinary, nondescript and defiantly awkward men. And most of them, I imagined, were dead, whether through war or life or just old age. But their names survived: in sons and daughters and factories and shipyards and schools and villages and stories.

The next one, taken in January 1943 by P. J. Hart, of Streathbourne Road in London, was of the Guards Armoured Training Wing, just over a year before he died. He was smiling but there was a matter-of-factness about him missing from the previous picture. He was flint-eyed and square-shouldered and set to go to war. He didn't look the type of man who would tolerate fools and I hoped that he never did.

Another photograph was of Jane, my grandmother, holding a baby (most likely my father's older brother, Francis), while my grandfather gazed steadily at the camera. Jane was dressed in a wide-shouldered, patterned coat with a black hat, and was beaming like a dancer or a singer. She had Maureen's face, or maybe Maureen had hers.

My grandfather Michael was in a rough suit, a shirt but no tie, and his arms poked out of his jacket sleeves but there were no starched cuffs. He had no wedding ring on his finger and my father never wore his. I didn't wear mine either. I'd always seen my father's in a box in his room. You could inherit a nose, or a chin, I thought, and perhaps a dislike of jewellery too.

Here again was Michael with Jane. Smitten by the lure of the photographic studio.

Michael, in a suit, with a six-buttoned waistcoat and white hand-kerchief in his top pocket, dreaming of civilized things. He was smiling now while combing his hair back in grand gestures: something my father always did. Jane, wearing a polka-dot blouse and scarf, held her right arm and hand up towards Michael, as the sun rippled off both their faces. There was no scribbled date on the back of the photograph so it was difficult to tell exactly when it was taken. It could have been years before he died, or it could have been just months before while he was on leave, but there was no mistaking the way the young couple felt towards each other. You could hide a lot of things but you could rarely hide love.

Their heads were inclined towards each other, not away. I liked to think it was one of the last intimate photographs they shared when both of them were happy and smiling, with two boys in their lives and thinking of what lay ahead for them together in Maryhill. They fitted their photograph well.

The photograph that saddened me the most was the one with Michael, in his army uniform, kneeling on the ground, with his left arm clasped protectively around what must be Francis and his right hand holding something – a toy – alongside my father, who is barely more than a baby.

Michael looked healthy and tanned. Even though it was a black and white image on worn Velox photographic paper, he was the same colour my father used to turn every summer in the garden when the sky had cleared to firecracker blue. More than anything, I hoped that it was Jane who was taking the picture, smiling back at the boys and at her husband while Michael, Francis and my father were locked together in an embrace that, although it was only very brief, would span the horizons and last for a lifetime. It was a picture that connected all of our lives.

And then Michael was gone.

I knew that he would have fought to live, with bared teeth and a stone fist and angry voice, not for himself but for them.

My father surprised me on one occasion. He showed me his father's Soldier's Service and Pay Book and he held on to it like it was a paper shroud, and if you touched it, well, it might just break in two and never be the same. Then he put it away and I never saw it again.

It was in a box in the bag.

It smelled of cotton or the broken branch of a tree.

There were other papers in there too.

Michael was born on 23 April 1914, in Maryhill, Glasgow, and died in France thirty years later, on 1 August 1944. Although my father had always said that his people were Irish and our people were Irish and that, in some ways, we were Irish too, Michael was born here, along the road from where I lived, past the canal where I sometimes walked and near the back of the Botanic Gardens where I would take my children in fine weather. I'd mistakenly believed that he was Ireland-born.

Perhaps it didn't matter about the past. Perhaps it mattered all along.

He was the son of John and Eleanor, and husband of Jane. He lived in Duncruin Street and, before joining the army he was a builder's labourer and, my grandmother Jane once told me, perhaps in jest, also had a neat sideline as a bookie, taking bets along the winding Maryhill canal, part of the vast canal system of Central Scotland.

At five foot ten and a quarter inches he was reasonably tall, and had grey eyes, brown hair and when he went off to the army he weighed 158 lbs. He had a scar under his chin and there was some damage to a finger on his right hand. Someone had scribbled *DOW* in pencil on the book. I think it stood for Died of Wounds.

According to his Soldier's Service and Pay Book, his Approved Society was the Ancient Order of the Hibernians (AoH), which he'd joined in London on 19 September 1940, with Membership No: 118279. Under *Religious Denomination* it stated: RC (Roman Catholic). Under *Nationality of Father* at birth and under *Nationality of Mother* at birth there was simply a line of blue ink.

My father always spoke about the AoH. Sometimes fondly and at other times with a rusted, simmering anger. It was, essentially, an Irish Catholic fraternal organization whose members were either Irish-born or of Irish descent. The Order, which was founded in New York in 1836, was a bulwark against anti-Catholic forces in the mid-nineteenth century, and it assisted Irish Catholic immigrants who faced discrimination. My father said that it was just the Catholic equivalent of the Masonic Lodge and he wouldn't care much to join any society, Catholic or otherwise.

So Michael went off to war protected by his AoH membership card, but I preferred to think that he carried a photograph of his boys too, to protect and then cradle as he died.

The Tierneys later lived in the Butney, in Maryhill, a place where the first Temperance Society in the world was formed, in 1824. The locals never paid as much heed to it as did John Dunlop, the founder of the movement who encouraged abstinence amongst the men from spirits, but beer and wine were drunk by the wagonload.

My father always liked to talk of these places: Maryhill, Ruchill, the Calton and the Gorbals. Places filled with tall-tales, and villainy, and good Irish people and some not so good. Most of their flaws he erased, and why would you not? In the Butney it was said that a tough Irish priest would sort out the local Irish navvies building the canal, who were partaking of too much drink, by striking out with his shillelagh. The Irish fought, said my father, and drank, and cursed, and hurt . . . but there was always a good priest back then to sort it all out and drag them off to Mass.

Fine fella, he was. Now would you have another drink?

Back then my father talked about Ireland as if it was his One True Home. When I listened to his stories in the loft Ireland was never a myth. It was as real as the tools he had in his hands and the songs that came out of his mouth. I wanted to believe all of these things, even if they were not true and sometimes *because* of this I wanted to believe them even more.

All the Irish people in my father's stories, many coming to Glasgow from as early as the 1800s, faced antipathy and antagonism and were forced to live in slums, he said. Following the Irish Potato Famine yet more settled in Scotland and Glasgow. He never called it the famine. He called it the Irish Potato *Starvation*. And he took pains to correct anyone who didn't say it his way too. *An Gorta Mór.* The Great Hunger.

And another sip too.

He said we grew up on Irish land. I could never quite work out if my granny Quinn had been part of the actual famine hundreds of years ago – she looked every one of her years and a hundred more too – or if she'd just had the misfortune to be born poor and wanted to move away. What I knew for sure was that she died spitting tacks and Rosary beads to the bitter end.

'Our people came here on account of the total poverty they faced at home,' he said. 'They were forced to eat grass in order to survive. You imagine that? They don't teach you that in school, eh? They were up against plantationists. They didn't plant crops, they planted people. Imagine it. They planted people! Scots and English. They transplanted people and their descendants took land at will from the Irish people. From *my* people.'

'How do you know this, Dad?'

'You'll need to do better than that, son,' he said. 'I know because I know. And if it doesn't make sense then you're not even *listening*. That's your answer.'

My grandfather's record of employment as an army tradesman listed him as a Gunner/Mechanic, Group C, Class III (what I could distinguish from the handwriting), and, under *On enlistment, Re-classified and Re-mustered*, it stated: Mustered. The initials of the officer were hard to decipher. Under *Particulars of Training* it stated: Completed Rifle + LMG (probably Light Machine Gun): Partially Qualified Gunner and Passed two other courses that I could not distinguish.

Under *Next of Kin* it stated, in blue ink, Jane Tierney.

Latest Known Address: 69 Cowal Street, Maryhill, Glasgow, NW. It was written in pencil. Michael would have written this himself. His handwriting was just like my father's. There was no mention of children, father, mother, brothers or sisters. His sole signature remained, like a macabre fingerprint, on the first page of the Soldier's Service and Pay Book, in pencil, on 18 June 1944. He died around six weeks later.

There were also the red-ink remains of a stamp across the first two pages of the Soldier's Service and Pay Book. In capital letters, it simply said: DECEASED.

Jane Tierney was born Jane Quinn, and grew up in Maryhill too, with her sister, Nellie, and brothers, Michael and Peter. Her parents were Francis Quinn, a coalminer, who died on 3 December 1961, due to cerebral thrombosis, and his wife, Mary, née Mahoney. Francis's father was Patrick Quinn, an ironstone miner, and his mother was Mary Ann Keenan, a papermill worker. They were solid people, I imagined, tight-jawed, steely-eyed, tough as trees in a howling storm, and able to survive without much help or even the desire to ask for it.

And just as my father promised me, their names were as Irish as the stone and thatched cottages near Renvyle in County Galway.

In the Registrar's Certificate – Publication of Notice of Marriage – Jane was listed as a Domestic Servant. Today we might call her a cleaner, but she was more than that. Much more than history and a pencil could ever record. She grew up on Skye Street, Maryhill, and she and Michael might have known each other as young children and become childhood sweethearts. I never asked and was never told anything much about them as a couple. It was always enough for me to imagine that they *did* know each other and they grew to love each other slowly over the summers as they turned from children into teenagers.

Michael might also have known Peter Quinn, who became his brother-in-law, and who was a barman before joining the Queen's Own Cameron Highlanders in 1940. He was four years younger than Michael and survived the war, but was discharged for 'Ceasing to fulfill Army physical Requirements'. He was wounded in the leg, in Egypt, and I could always remember that he hobbled around the house in Ruchill in some discomfort, but always smiled and promised me a shilling next week, but forgot when next week came. His Military Conduct was: Very Good. His foot, he said, was: Very Sore.

Jane raised Francis and my father with the help of Granny Quinn while Michael was away and later, following his death, they raised the boys together.

I never really knew anything about that war. I knew some dates and some numbers and which sides fought for this and that. But my grandmother told me something that made me shake for thirty years. I might have been sixteen, and I'd walked over the quarry and over the railway line to visit Jane in the house in Ruchill, and we sat for a few hours watching snooker while I ate boiled eggs and luncheon meat and drank soup and we twisted the lids off pickle and beetroot jars before she put out pink biscuits and American Cream Soda.

The solitary photograph of Michael that we'd all been allowed to see, which sat behind a glass frame on the wall, always watched over us and it hung alongside Our Lady of Perpetual Succour.

I gently inquired about my grandfather.

The *only* answer I remembered was this.

She said that she knew that my grandfather was dead even before she'd received any official notification. She'd been sitting in her living room and she opened the curtains and saw a funeral procession passing by her window. There was a flag, a Union Jack, draped over the coffin and the men who marched with the coffin walked solemnly and quietly. They were soldiers too. 'I got such a fright,' she said, and she ran to the door of the house. Before she got there, she said, the muzzle of a rifle was placed through her letterbox and it began to fire, and she dropped to the floor and started sobbing uncontrollably into the carpet.

She told me this with the conviction of an angel, as if it was the most natural thing in the world, and I believed her. Her voice wavered but she didn't cry when she said it, she just talked as if she was telling a story to her children about their father taking the bus to work. I believed that she saw something, whether in a dream or in a nightmare, but something happened nonetheless. Perhaps it was because she was growing older and her memory had tricked her, or perhaps it was simply what she wanted to believe. Perhaps it really did happen the way she said it did.

In any event she spent the rest of her life suffering.

Michael's real death was revealed a few days later, in a formal letter from the Scots Guards, 25 Buckingham Gate, SW1. It was dated 10 August 1944.

Dear Madam,
It is my painful duty to inform you that a report has been received from the War Office notifying the death of:-

(No) – 2699783
(Rank) – Gdsn

(Name) – M. F. Tierney
(Regiment) – Scots Guards
which occurred – in North West Europe
on the – 1st August, 1944
The report is to the effect that he – died of wounds.

I am to express the sympathy and regret of the Army Council. I am
to add that any information that may be received as to the soldier's
burial will be communicated to you in due course.
  I am, Madam,
  Your obedient Servant
  Officer in Charge of Records

By October 1944, she'd received an Army Form B.104–126, from
the Record Office, Scots Guards. There was nothing about his
burial.

Madam,
I am directed to forward the undermentioned articles of private
property of the late No: 2699783. Rank, Gdsn. MF Tierney, Scots
Guards, and would ask that you kindly acknowledge receipt of the
same on the form overleaf:-

Cigarette case, Photographs, Cigarette lighter, Gold ring, Styptic
pencil in case, Rules of Communion, Prayer Case, Cloth badge,
Coin.

These are the only articles at present forthcoming, but should any
further articles be received at any time they will be duly forwarded.

Yours faithfully
For Colonel

At the back of the Soldier's Service and Pay Book there were two
small, empty pockets. I put the folded documents inside.

It was getting a little darker outside. I placed the photographs of Michael and Jane and Francis and my father in another pocket in the secret hope that, somewhere, beyond my understanding, the very act of proximity might somehow unite them all once again.

The photographs I found of my father as a boy, and as a young man, were crushing and tender in their innocence and beauty. There was a lightness, freedom and graciousness to the images of him that I'd not seen before. His smile, for once, seemed unburdened.

There was the photograph of him with Francis and the boys had their arms wrapped around each other. I had seen that one before. There was my father, dressed as an altar boy, standing beside two other boys and the priest. In the next one my father was in white plimsolls, while Francis sat on the grass holding a baby, perhaps a neighbour's. He was smiling widely and as happy as I'd ever seen him. In another he stood patiently in a line in his school blazer waiting for his school photograph. And look, there he was in swimming trunks.

He was a boy.

My father was born on 26 July 1943 at home in Cowal Street. He would no doubt have been delivered by Granny Quinn and so the first thing in his life he'd have seen, and heard, was Mary Quinn speaking in her quietly fading Irish accent that had been hardened by the passage of time and her harsh Glasgow surroundings. Mary would have proclaimed my father for the Lord and have offered ten Hail Marys and an Our Father if He kept my father out of harm's way and showed him the path of righteousness and the truth of the Catholic Church.

From one image to the next, I watched him migrate to his teens. A decade passed in seconds. We could cheat a life in photographs.

There was the bicycle again and then his record collection and then the boy with the pompadour hair. He constructed a darkroom in a cupboard where he developed his own photographs, and some of them I now held in my hand. I opened up a small, brown envelope filled with unprocessed negatives returned to him from the

229

Picturegoer Salon, Long Acre, in London. They'd never been printed but the negatives still preserved everything about him at that time. I held them up and as the light shone through the loft window the secret images came alive. It was preposterous. And my father came alive with them.

There he was again, with his Norton motorbike that he'd open up on the long, bending road to Crinan to meet my mother. My parents met in 1962 in a hotel where my mother was working as a chambermaid and I know that she was as beautiful then as a saint.

My mother was born in Glasgow, in 1942, and grew up around Ibrox and Kinning Park, areas of the city where Harland and Wolff, the great shipping behemoth, sheltered a large thriving community. She grew up in the long shadow of Ibrox where Rangers played their home matches but the MacMillans were Catholics and each of her eleven brothers and sisters was a Celtic fan because their father was too.

Uilleam, my grandfather, was born on Barra, a handsome local boy with deep-set eyes from nearby Eoligarry on the north side of the island. My grandmother, Elizabeth MacPhee, was born in Castlebay, and she gutted fish when Barra was one of the busiest ports in the Highlands, while Uilleam was a merchant seaman. Uilleam was never much of a talker and El always spoke for him and of the old ways. You could put your hand in a hole in the Barra earth, she said, and touch the memories of the past. They were all buried there.

Sunday was their most important day of the week.

And my mother never forgot that either.

She spent much of her youth looking after her growing band of siblings and every time my grandmother had another child she'd whisper in their ears in Gaelic that he or she would be the last but they just kept appearing. Children were a gift, she said, and offered prayers of thanks. Sometimes she added that they doomed you to a life of worry too.

When my parents met my father was only nineteen and as shy as a boy of faith could be. The hotel was being renovated and he was one of the electricians working there. When he finally asked her out, their first date was at the local cinema at Lochgilphead, and my father picked her up on his motorbike, wearing his leather jacket, and my mother rode pillion, a scarf in her hair like a movie star from the other sunnier side of the world.

They'd only been going out together for a year before they were engaged. In an Italian café on Byres Road he asked her to marry him, after sharing an ice-cold Coca-Cola from the vending machine and listening to some music from the mini jukebox. Her favourite was Pat Boone. Even by my father's standards he was unusually quiet and my mother suspected it was because she'd told him she was going out with some of her friends from the office where she now worked, and there was bound to be a group of boys there. He panicked, she said, and immediately asked her to marry him. She had no doubts, she said, and never would have.

Three years later, on 4 June 1966, they were married in Our Lady and St Margaret's, Kinning Park. My mother got a white dress, a beautiful day and a feeling that her tall and strong husband might live for ever. They held their reception in the Ca' D'oro, in Union Street, up the town, she said, and went on honeymoon to Margate, in Kent, and they talked about the future, and the future all happened very quickly. They never planned for a large family. My mother thought maybe six or so, and I laughed twice at that when she told me, but over time, they accepted nine as if God was giving out lucky charms and they were at the front of the queue. The twins arrived on April Fool's Day 1967, and they always laughed together at that too.

Then there was me.

I was born in August 1968 in the Queen Mother's Hospital in Glasgow, and was named after my dead grandfather. My arrival meant that my father could say the name Michael more easily now and no longer always think of the man in the ditch.

By the third day we'd sorted various things into separate piles for what would be kept, what would go to charity or what would be just plain thrown out. We tried to convince Maureen that broken Hoovers would hardly be a priority in an African village but she argued the odds and someone somewhere in Chintheche has the cleanest dirt floor in the world.

The Irish tricolour flag that I'd brought him from a trip to Sligo many years ago still hung on the wall, sagging with the weight of the passing years. It was sun-bleached and covered in dust. He'd joked that we could wrap him in it when he died and bury him in the garden along with a jug of drink. It didn't feel half as bad as I thought it might to let it go.

The loft gradually lightened.

It had been feeling the strain for years.

Every year my father had wrestled with the roof, like a hunter would a wild animal, trying to bring it under control. It was impossible. The rain always got through the trestles and the crumbling membrane of black felt that had all but evaporated. The roof had shuddered to a halt. No matter how often it leaked, or shouted out in a storm, like my father's voice, no one could hear it. No one was listening.

Bags, boxes. More bags. More boxes.

What was that for? And that? And this? And those? And that strange-looking thing over there? Should we keep this? And that? And what about that? That? No way? No chance. Maureen, behave yourself. This can go, that too. And those. But not them. For goodness sake, what was he doing with *those*? How did he even manage to get that *in* here? That's illegal too.

He'd lay traps for us, the unsuspecting poachers amongst his offspring and over time we learned to work them out, allowing us to replace seamlessly anything that we moved. A drawer was left just so, a bag of tools had the saw on top but the hammer below, and the jigsaw had been in the box not out of it, and his old guitar never left the case and the dust gave it all away.

His cameras, cheap and old, preserved everything in his life and in ours, while the handful of inexpensive watches reminded him that nothing would ever stay the same.

Downstairs, he was oblivious to the peering-through magazines and books, the shin-deep discarding of wood and machinery that had been there for longer than many of my brothers and sisters had even been alive. We had cleaned out so much stuff that the house seemed to realign itself.

I came across the old Celtic programmes from George and there were Celtic books that we'd got from uncles and at Christmas. I sat down and flipped through them. There they were. The men from his childhood and mine. And my brothers' too. Bertie Peacock, Charlie Tully, Jimmy McGrory, Sean Fallon, Billy McNeill, Kenny Dalglish and a raven-haired Lou Macari. There were more faces staring back at me. Hundreds of men I recognized but had not seen for years.

They caught me unawares. I sat with them, but I didn't feel anything really. They were part of us, but they were also *apart* from us. They reminded me, I suspect, of the times that I *didn't* watch Celtic, not the times that we did. Books and magazines and programmes. Celtic annuals, with fading green covers. They had been thumbed to death. Some of them had pages torn out that we must have used as posters or for covers of our school jotters, before the headteacher said you couldn't put anything to do with Celtic on the cover of your homework books.

We put them in a bin bag and out they went.

Maureen found another photograph of him.

He was wearing a blue V-neck sweater, drinking cola from a glass. There was a bowl of baked beans on the dining-room table and behind him the wooden fire surround that he'd made and the spider-web wallpaper that he'd put up and the cupboard doors he'd hung and painted. There was a small football trophy on the mantel, an air-mail letter and some correspondence that might have been an electricity or gas bill. He was deeply tanned, as always. We all had summers then.

We passed it back and forth, smiling, gently rubbing the curling corners as if the image might spring to life if we tapped it three times. 'Goodness, he was so handsome,' said Maureen. 'You forget these things about Dad.'

'He was.'

His hair, wavy and black, was touched with just enough grey.

Those were my father's great years. When he was still young and handsome and had a life that was filled with goodness and problems too. Then the world expanded and contracted. The loft was just his way of showing us that he would always try to fix things even if they were broken. Even when they were beyond repair. But not right now. He would keep them up there and he'd get round to fixing them later. Just wait a little longer, I'll fix them, you'll see.

But he couldn't, because he was vanishing under the eaves.

Some weeks later Gerry arrived at the house.

He was a decent man, quiet and hardworking, and he would do the job, he said, as quickly as possible. He wouldn't get in the way, not at all. He understood. Gerry's people were from Ireland so that made it easier when my mother explained to my father that there was a man putting up scaffolding around the house and the whole house would be the better for it. My father just sat in his chair unmoving. Food dried easily at the corner of his mouth.

The poles and boards were erected around the front and back of the house, as meticulously as the surgeon prepared my father's head for his operation. The chimney stacks were taken down and new ones put up in their place. Old lead valleys and flashing were replaced with new, and eroded battens were removed, and Gerry, with his forearms as hard as rivets, was true to his word in that he barely made a noise and never got in the way.

I climbed the scaffolding and went up on to the roof. Gerry showed me his work proudly and also his tools for cutting slate and we both drank black tea and ate my mother's sandwiches and I wished for all the world that my father could have stood up there with us because he'd have loved the clear view over the quarry, by now filled with new houses, and over the Campsies and beyond. He'd have loved to see the new slates being cut and placed and nailed. A nail and a slate. Simple. Things like that made him happy.

Gerry didn't getting rich repairing roofs. But when the job was the right one, he said, he loved what he did. He removed the layers and then replaced what he could and repaired what needed repairing. Gerry sheltered people and my father gave them light. It was, I always believed, a noble combination.

The roof was renewed, better than the day it was built more than a hundred years earlier, he said, and I believed every word of it. It took a month and the weather stayed fine. Gerry asked about my father and we chatted for a while. 'He sounds a bit like my father too,' said Gerry. 'He was from the old school. They had it tougher than us, to be fair. Things were different then.' I nodded. And he paused. 'But to get you a house like this with nine children . . .' He whistled long and hard.

For weeks my father said nothing, he just sat remembering. When the scaffolding finally came down he said nothing too, but he smiled. And that was close enough.

I stood at the bottom of the garden and looked up. I remembered his voice. If you couldn't smile at a child playing, said my father, there must be something wrong with you. If you couldn't smile at a new slate roof on an old house there must be something wrong with you too. He didn't say that but I knew he would have.

I prayed that night for rain.

It rained hard most of the winter and my mother didn't stop smiling herself until the following January. On the eve of the first anniversary of his stroke my father had uncontrollable seizures, and was admitted to hospital for another five weeks. It felt like bereavement without end. He arrived back home for the second time in February 2003.

His voice and his legs stayed at the hospital.

Chapter Ten

Notes from My Father

My father recorded Celtic games off the radio.

It was so that I would listen to them on my journey. They would remind me of my family and of home. It was just his way of saying, stay safe, Michael. He just couldn't really say the words out loud. Whose father could, really?

It was 1988. The previous year I'd worked in a summer camp in Poughkeepsie, a small town in upstate New York, with my mate, Brian. He was from Bishopbriggs too. Now we were planning to drive across America. My father had always wanted to make that same trip but he knew that it would never happen. It would be me that was taking his place.

He also gave me one hundred pounds of money he never had. I had no idea where he got it from because it would've almost killed him to find that kind of spare money anywhere. Brian and I bought a clapped-out car that would take us from New York to San Diego and a few miles up and down the West Coast.

The tapes were just his way of reaching out.

We were, for a while, free. That was the plan. Away from Bishopbriggs and university and family. And Celtic. I'd no longer have to listen to stories about Ireland or the Church or my father's people or the poor or even the rich or the things that mattered, I supposed, to others, but not to me now. I was just leaving all that behind. I had no time for the Croppies or the Legion of Mary or a Plenary Indulgence.

I didn't want to know if we needed a new left-back.

All we had in front of us was the open road to the West Coast.

At least that's what I thought.

My father would have none of that. The forgetting Celtic, and the forgetting Ireland stuff.

The tapes arrived in a large brown-paper envelope before we set off.

It was already a few games into the season. There were four, or five, different matches on the tapes. He'd taken the time to sit and record them and had written down the details of each match, and then parcelled them up. In its own small way, it was heartbreaking.

I pictured him in the kitchen, standing in front of the old radio with its cassette deck filled with dust and breadcrumbs, waiting patiently for the pre-match commentary to end and the play to start. He'd have cleared his throat and quietly, and self-consciously, said, *one, two, one, two*, into the machine. Then he'd have rewound the tape to see if it had worked. Then he'd have listened to his own voice playing back to him. 'I sound like a flippin' eedjit,' he'd have muttered, before clicking the red Record button again and hoping he had enough tape for ninety minutes, plus the half-time interval. He'd have kept going in and out of the kitchen, looking at the magnetic spools as they turned round and round.

'Aitken to McStay. McStay turns beautifully and passes it on to Burns. Celtic are driving forward at pace here . . .'

He also sent postcards from the Kelvingrove Art Gallery and Museum. And postcards with pictures of Glasgow buses and another of a drunk man. There was some Wrigley's chewing gum, the one with the yellow wrapper, because he knew I liked it. And a short note about the tapes:

Just for listening on the journey. It doesn't matter what the score is.
If you listen closely you'll hear Mum in the kitchen. The boys and
girls will be out the back garden. I'll be working on the front room.
Good luck. Make sure you send a postcard.
  God Bless, Dad.

I did.

But not often enough.

The car swung out from the gravel road on to a highway as big and wide as an ocean.

We'd never seen roads or country like it. It wasn't Scotland. I doubted it was Ireland either. To the west was Indian country and farmland and whatever lay in between. There were wheat fields and grazing pastures the size of mill towns and we plunged past like a lift down an elevator shaft as we gathered speed. Bruce Springsteen sang 'Glory Days' over the radio as a blast of coolness from the air-conditioner hit us. Brian rested his Dr. Martens up on the dash-board. There was a relish in his smile. Both of us sang along with Bruce. And then the magnificent 'Mary's Prayer', by Danny Wilson, the one-hit wonder from Dundee.

My father's Celtic tape recordings were still in the boot of the car and I felt guilty that I hadn't played them yet. There was just too much to see and to listen to. I wasn't quite ready for the dulcet tones of a Scottish football commentator on Radio Clyde telling us how awfully Mick McCarthy was playing.

For hours we followed broken yellow lines painted all the way to an unbroken horizon. There was barely another soul for miles except unseen farmers, busy with their own lives, and men attending to horses. I looked at them as we drove and believed in my heart that if my father had been born in America he'd have been one of those men, tending animals, and crops and farms and family. It was only a daydream, of course, but he'd have had land, and a farm and a shotgun and a Ford pick-up for work and the same Ford pick-up for Sundays, only he might have cleaned it for church. Or maybe not.

He'd dreamed of America. Dreamed of it for years. Secret dreams his whole life. And I was driving across it. But the tapes were with me. That was why he'd sent them. Right there and then, as the aluminium domes of silos decorated the beautiful blue skies, I knew that. I felt him *there*. Nodding away in his overalls.

Just to be safe . . .

The car rolled on, taking us away from the things that mattered to us most. But somehow it was essential. He knew that too. It was a break from the past. A book sliding off the end of a table. He was letting me go as well. I knew how hard it must have been for him. He never wanted any of us to leave. And now it was happening.

He just didn't want us to go. Anywhere. But I don't think he wanted us to stay either. It was an impossible conundrum. When I was about sixteen or seventeen he took me out with him to work. I helped him rewire a house. Up early, home late. We liked each other's company, but it was hard work and callouses quickly ran across my hands. He didn't say it, but I knew why I was there. Don't do *this* for a living.

A few hundred dollars and more than a thousand miles later, past sun-bleached road signs and gas stations with names like Weaver's Garage and Johnson's Conoco station, we shuffled slowly onward, as collapsed as an old man's vertebrae.

When Springsteen sang we didn't realize it but it was us – the future us – that he was singing about. The car kept moving. What little money we had was rationed. I became the banker, doling out single dollars to Brian when required. My mother knew the value of every pound note she'd ever spent and even the ones she hadn't. Had she ever seen a new fifty-pound note, a woman asked. She'd never even seen an old one. I'd inherited her housekeeping skills. Every dollar was a prisoner.

Brian just laughed.

'Thought I'd left my mum at home,' he said, shaking his head.

We both knew that if we hadn't left we might have lived in Bishopbriggs for a hundred years.

Desolate drive-ins and roadhouses were dotted across thousands of miles, desperate as a long line of mourners. America felt like outer space but it also felt like the most amazing place the world had ever created.

Sometimes we sat in silence, our conversation spent as a kite that couldn't fly. Fifty miles passed with barely a word. With the silence came the realization that we were just two boys from the same village outside Glasgow, who'd attended the same school and

239

university and had played for the same football team. We knew the same pretty girls, visited the same bars and chapel, and supported the same players from the same football club, while dreaming that some day our glory days would not always be in the same place we'd grown up in.

We drove until nightfall.

The heat shimmered on the baking asphalt in the morning.

In neon-lit diners weather-beaten locals nodded and glanced at the curious-looking young men with the strange, yet familiar, accents. One man tipped his green Plainview baseball cap in our direction. I could see my father there too, talking with his children before leaving and climbing into his battered red Dodge.

Everyone, no matter where they were from, did the same thing. They sipped on coffee and dreams.

I called my parents from a phone box, reversing the charges. My mother sounded worried. She hadn't heard from us in a week and the children wanted me to call. Was I going to Mass? 'Make sure you do, Michael,' she said. 'You need to take care over there. You're not as old as you think you are!' And then she laughed. 'Just say your prayers and you'll be fine.'

My father picked up the phone.

'Everything OK, Michael?' he said. 'Your mum's worried.'

I could tell that he was worried too. 'Fine, Dad. Nearly made it across America! We're going to stay there for a bit and then fly to Australia. We got the tickets booked. We'll stay with Auntie Elizabeth Anne and the cousins first. Then we'll get some work. Don't worry.'

'You OK for money? I could, uhm . . . I could maybe send a few dollars.'

'Thanks, Dad. I'm fine. We've got it all planned.'

'Did you listen to the tapes I sent over?'

I paused momentarily, but I hoped he hadn't noticed.

'Yes . . . they're brilliant. Thanks. Sounded really clear. We've got a tape recorder in the car. Still got a couple to get through.'

It was a terrible lie.

240

'How is Celtic getting on?'

I think he paused as well.

'Good. OK. Not bad,' he said. 'I think they're doing all right. I think your mum's listened to them on the radio more than me these days. They were battered by Rangers though. That goalie, what's-his-name? Andrews. He was rotten. I've got more chance of catching sandcastles than he has of holding on to the ball.'

'I heard . . .'

Celtic had been thrashed 5–1 at the start of the season at Ibrox and I really didn't need a tape recording reminding me of it. Before the match the Celtic manager, Billy McNeill, was asked about reports that striker Frank McAvennie might be moving back to London. He replied that there was more chance of Rangers beating his team 5–1 the following day . . .

It was Celtic's worst result in an Old Firm game since 1960. Rangers had players like Terry Butcher and Ray Wilkins and Mark Walters and Chris Woods. Celtic had Ian Andrews and Chris Morris and Anton Rogan. McAvennie left a short time later . . .

'How's everyone down at Quins? George and Frank and Michael?'

'All fine. Some of the boys you were at school with were asking after you. Stevie, Jimmy, Stef and Michael. Paul Flynn too.'

'Good stuff, Dad. Listen, I'd better go, this is costing you a fortune. I'll send postcards soon, don't worry. Love to the gang.'

'OK, Michael. Take care. God Bless.'

America had only ever existed in my imagination, much in the same way as Ireland did for my father. But I didn't really need to see Ireland. I didn't *want* to see Ireland. I knew it was there and what it was like. I had known that for ever. It wasn't that I wanted to go to America. I *needed* to. The difference was inescapable.

Onwards we drove, taking roads for the sheer curiosity of where they might take us. We passed like an apparition through countless tracks that seemed to have borne little trace of human passage. Sometimes we were loud, as loud as we could be. The music crashed from the car. Other times we moved on quietly, as quietly as a secret.

The tapes, what about the tapes?

'Do you miss back home?'

'Are you kidding?' Brian replied.

'I can't *believe* we're here.'

'I know. How did this *happen?*'

Mostly we wondered about back home. Friends. Family. An old girlfriend. The boys would be in Quins. They would be going to see Celtic no matter what the result against Rangers. Jimmy and Shevvy would be there, come hail or shine. They breathed Celtic. They would be in the town for another few drinks. Jack the Lads the lot of them. One hundred miles an hour. The girls from university – Steph and Sam and Gill and Vicky – would be in the Queen Margaret Union or in the library smelling of patchouli oil and wearing herringbone overcoats and reading something by Simone de Beauvoir.

Home was slowly slipping away. Brian and I barely discussed football. Celtic was there and they always would be. The players would change. McStay and Grant and Miller and Walker. Of course they would. But we knew Celtic wouldn't change. We just didn't need them right now.

The tapes stayed firmly in the boot.

If I listened to them it would be as good as turning the car round and heading straight back home. Nothing would have changed. I'd have sunk back into the quarry.

The air was warm and it stole past us like shadows. The cowboys drove their cattle just like they did in our childhood westerns. The cowboys were real though. We watched mile-long freight trains and people sleeping in hammocks in dusty trailer parks as crop dusters swooped and turned. The country was alive in cornfields and prairies, narrow roads and clapped-out motels.

Secretly, we wondered if our first trip together would be our last. We drove with the windows down and the music up. Brian fixed his impossibly black hair while we talked, as we always talked, about the future. Both of us laughed at the absurdity and beauty and vastness of our journey. We were both afraid and elated at what would happen next.

We arrived on the West Coast.

The truth is that I didn't *ever* listen to those Celtic tapes my father made. All his efforts disappeared into the air.

And I'm not even sure what I did with them.

I'd like to think that when we gave the car to the son of a family friend of Brian's, in exchange for his hospitality, he found them in the boot. And he kept them. And *he* listened to them. And I hope that, years later, every now and again, that American teenager plucked my father's tapes from an old drawer and played them. Over and over. That he listened to the radio pundits commentating on Celtic beating Hamilton Academical or beating Motherwell.

What I hope for most was that my father *didn't* record Celtic getting thrashed 5–1 by Rangers. It's likely he did. And he'd have sent it too.

Australia was the furthest part of the world that we knew about and it seemed even further away when we got there. The Irish, said my father, were sent there for stealing sheep and fish and a piece of their own land. They were sent to Botany Bay on convict ships. 'The Fields of Athenry', he said, told the story better than anyone could.

'I know, Dad, you've been singing it to me since I was about two . . .'

'Ach, don't be daft . . . you were at least five.'

'All I could hear was *doh dee doh dee dohdee dohdee*, all night long. It drove me nuts after a few years.'

'Very funny . . .'

Brian and I were living in Newcastle, an hour north of Sydney, with my cousins, aunt and uncle. It was November 1988 now. We were all watching another Old Firm match between Celtic and Rangers and Mark Walters put away a penalty early for Rangers before Terry Butcher scored a brilliantly headed own goal that turned the Rangers fans to stone and sent the Celtic fans into raptures. Butcher looked like he'd just swallowed a pickled rat.

We jumped up and down on the couch, and ran around the room, and rubbed each other's heads and then the heads of our cousins too and flicked a V-sign at the television and my aunt was laughing and wondering what on earth was going on in the quiet of her charming suburb. Mark McGhee scored a second and did a windmill thing with his arm and the Rangers defence stood stranded like children sipping from a jar of their father's home-brew. We were winning and I thought it was the prayers because I'd spoken with my mother a few days earlier and she reminded me about the game and promised she'd say a prayer for Celtic and we should too. I promised as well.

Cross My Heart and Hope to Die.

Brian shouted and pointed at the screen. 'Look, look ... it's Mark. My wee brother Mark.' Mark was a ballboy at the match. It took an age for Brian's grin to disappear. He was already halfway home.

And then it was three. Billy Stark shot and it cannoned in off Brown. Celtic went off at the end to rapturous applause and my cousins laughed because although they'd been born in Scotland they'd moved away when they were young and had never seen anything like it either. You couldn't see that on a surfboard.

Months later, Brian and I were living in a wood and brick shack, in a fruit pickers' lodge in Mooroopna, with a handful of other travellers. We picked apples and pears from morning till late afternoon. The whole area looked like a beautiful, outdoor sunny prison with two bars nearby and pretty much nothing else. One was for drinking in and the other for brawling, and sometimes they altered the venues at short notice. Home had never seemed so far away. The months passed. We saved some money. I missed home more than I admitted. I missed Bishopbriggs and my brothers and my sisters and my mother and my father too.

He wrote to me as often as he could. More than I wrote to him. Sometimes he stuck a five-pound note inside. He sent this letter a lifetime ago. It's dated Friday, 10 March 1989. I lost a lot of his cards and letters, but not this one. It was the camouflage over a good man's heart.

Hello Michael,

This is just a little note to let you know how we all are. Everyone is fine. Lorraine and Maureen are just about finished their teaching practice, and are quite glad about it!

Hope you and Brian are keeping well; I suppose you get to sleep at night counting pears! Well, we got the video. It was very good. Have you ever thought of trying acting for a career? (Ha! Ha!)

Are you sure it wasn't a gum tree you were up when you had the inspiration to drive in Europe? Kidding apart, it might be more sensible if you left that until next year and you could take the van which would be more reliable and more of a mobile home, as the car hasn't been really tested yet. Anyway you can think about it.

(Sunday 12th)

Well, Celtic won 1-0 against Hearts yesterday. They signed Tommy Coyne and MacAvennie might be leaving.

When you leave Australia remember to send a postcard from wherever you stay when travelling. I don't know if Turkey will be a good idea, but watch yourself if you do.

Well, look after yourself, Michael

God Bless

Hope to see you soon

Dad

My father's letter sustained me throughout the rest of my journey. No matter where I went, I believed that it held all the love in the world a man could muster for his son. He never said much, he just said enough.

Brian injured his arm and had to fly home to Scotland for an operation and I waved him off at a train station in Australia and then he was gone. I stood there by myself wondering what lay ahead and worrying about it. Later on, I travelled to India and Thailand alone, and a lot of the time I felt exactly that. But the world was expanding. I wanted to see more.

*

My paternal grandmother was dying when I returned from India and Thailand. It seemed like we'd hit that patch in our lives. We were due the death of someone close. She was dying of cancer. But I had one more summer before going back to university and wanted to return to America.

Jane had been living at home with my parents and the rest of the family for the past three months, having moved into my parents' room while they slept downstairs. Claire, who was young and didn't understand what was happening, asked what was wrong with Granny. 'She's not too well,' said my mother, keeping the details to a minimum while looking grave and worried. My mother, who still deferred to my grandmother as Mrs Tierney, treated her as if she was her own.

Jane was dying quietly and without making much of a fuss.

Although my father could barely acknowledge the situation he was desperate to make her death as gentle and easy as possible, and endow it with as much decency as an old woman could expect as she lay hopeless in her son and daughter-in-law's bed. My grandfather had died badly and he wasn't about to let the same thing happen to her. It wasn't really dignity he wanted to give her, because that was just a word to help the living. He needed to make sure she was warm and fed and enjoyed the smiles and stories that came out of the mouths of her grandchildren.

We all knew that old people only moved into their children's rooms near the end. My grandmother didn't complain because she knew that the wait was nearly over and that she'd finally be going to see Mick – that's what she called him – and she called him that as she lay dying. It wasn't stressful hearing her call out for him. It was comforting. You knew that when she closed her eyes at night she remembered when she was young and pretty and so in love with Mick and his workingman's hands, and the scar under his chin and his pressed suits that he wore on Sundays to early Mass.

She loved him then as she loved him now, when the door was ready to close.

The pain was hard to begin with and she tried not to take

246

painkillers but in the end she had to. When I returned home the hardest part was watching my father.

My grandmother had been the centre of his world since he was a child. He visited her weekly, sometimes twice a week, and she came over to our house every Thursday and she brought her chicken broth and boxes of Mr Kipling French Fancies or Battenberg. My father picked her up in the van or she'd get the bus, until her legs began to fail and the bags she carried got heavier.

She didn't have a telephone for a long, long time and so he'd drive across to her house in winter regardless of the weather or walk across the quarry in summer, wending his way past the Glen Douglas bar and over the fence and across the railway tracks and up past the municipal golf course that led to her street. He collected stray golf balls along the way, and my grandmother would keep them for the younger ones and put six of them in an empty egg box for their birthdays and they'd have to act surprised at her little acts of kindness.

He loved to walk there and we did too. We dragged broken branches from the trees and sticks from the quarry all the way to her door. We went up past the broken gate at the top of the street where old Mr Davidson lived and my father would wave at him out of courtesy and he'd wave back but I don't think they said a word to each other in all those years. I juggled a football there till my feet hurt. We played kirbie across main roads.

I remember the time she got her first telephone.

'Isn't it lovely,' she said, sitting beside it and pointing at the new-fangled contraption in her living room. It was a yellow or cream General Post Office phone, with receivers as fat as a lemon.

Right after it was installed my father told me to cycle over to explain to her how it worked and to let her know when he'd call that same evening. My grandmother and I sat there together on the couch, two excited bookends killing time waiting for a ring that would change her life for ever. Before my father called she went into her bedroom and came out with a small, tartan-covered autograph book. It belonged to my father.

'That's for you,' she said. 'But don't tell your dad. He'll shoot the boots off me if he thinks I've given it away.'

My father had written his name on the inside cover and his address too: *John Tierney, 35 Huxley Street, Ruchill, Glasgow*.

Some of the autographs were difficult to decipher but there were the names of some great Celtic players, including Sean Fallon, Bertie Peacock and Bobby Evans, and players from Partick Thistle whose ground was little more than a few streets away from where we sat. My father had a scribble from Tommy Ledgerwood, the Thistle goalie who was a Scotsman by virtue of being born twenty-five yards from the River Tweed. He had Frank Pattison, Colin Liddell and Bobby McNichol of Stirling Albion, and Tommy Baxter, Jimmy Patterson and Roy Henderson of Queen of the South.

That my father had taken the trouble to get all these autographs was unexpected. His only heroes were the saints in heaven. I imagined him going to Celtic Park or Firhill as a youngster, on his bicycle or by bus, asking Fallon and Peacock and Ledgerwood for their autographs and the players smiling and tipping their flat caps back and saying, of course, son.

Years later I mislaid the autograph book.

Then I found it in the loft in my grandfather's kit bag. I'd scribbled my own name on the inside cover, just below my father's, and tried to copy some of the autographs of the old players in a pencil scrawl of my own. I'd ruined the whole book. He must have found it and put it away. But he said nothing.

I asked her about my grandfather and if he liked football and she said yes and she said something about Celtic when they won the Empire Exhibition Cup Final in 1938 and she mentioned Johnny Crum and Jimmy McGrory and John Divers and I laughed and said, you know more about football than my father.

I said I wanted to know if my grandfather was a big Celtic fan and I wanted to write down everything she could tell me about him, but the phone rang loudly and I never did.

'That'll be John,' she said, laughing excitedly. Her eyes lit up the room like fireworks. 'That'll be your dad. What do I do? Do I just pick it up? Och, here, you do it, Michael, I'm no' good with these fangly things . . .'

'No, Granny, you pick it up. Hold it close.' I motioned for her to lift it. She picked up the receiver. It was about three feet away from her head.

'Closer . . .'

'Hello. Heellooo . . .'

'How are you, Ma?'

'Fine, John. Fine. Oh, goodness me, it works. That's amazing, isn't it? Oh, for goodness sake. I can hear you fine. Yes. Can you hear me? How do you turn the sound up?'

'Yes, Ma. All fine.' I could hear him laughing.

'I still don't know how they do it, all they brainy scientists. How do they make our voices come out the phone, John?'

'It's not that hard, Ma. Copper wires and vibrations . . . Is Michael there?'

'Oh, it's really amazing, isn't it? Talking wires. Very posh. Yes, Michael's here. He's fine too. How's the wee ones?'

'They're fine, Ma. I'm just going . . . down the road.'

'Quins.'

'Aye, Ma.'

'Good, John. How's Cathie?'

'Fine. Did you watch the snooker?'

'Aye, it was good. We've just had some tea and toast and a biscuit.'

'Did you get the shopping in?'

'Yes, I went to the Co-op, and I took the bus up the road after a cup of tea.'

'OK, Ma, tell Michael I'll pick him up tomorrow. We'll put the bike in the van. Goodnight, Ma.'

'Goodnight, John. God Bless.'

'Night, Ma. God Bless.'

My father never felt any sense of forced duty towards my grandmother. He was around her because he loved her. He called her *Ma* when he spoke with her, and called her *my mother* when he spoke with anyone else about her. He gave her a place in the world when he could. And he was right about the soup. It was the best a man could ever taste. It wasn't reminiscing that made the soup taste good, it was just the right amount of barley and chicken.

On Sundays, after morning Mass, we went to Leighton Street.

Sunday at my grandmother's was a ritual that was rarely broken, and Jane made dumpling and she put ten-pence pieces under each slice for us and it would have cost her nearly a pound every week and that was a lot for a widow of long standing. The table was laid especially for us, with a neat linen cloth, and there'd be some ham slices and bottles of Barr's American Cream Soda.

There were slices of tomato and slices of chicken that you sprinkled with salt then placed between some white bread and that was enough to fill you for the day. Some days there was turnip and potato but that was in winter when it was cold. The summer food was simple and easy and it tasted like you'd just been on holiday somewhere sweet.

My grandmother and my parents blessed themselves and we did too and we all thanked God for the food we were about to eat.

Watching snooker or darts or *Scotsport* or *Bonanza*, with the adventures of the Cartwright family, followed our eating and drinking tea, and there was ginger and lemonade for the children. Watching snooker was my grandmother's favourite pastime. But she liked to watch football with the boys and my father, once she'd finished in the kitchen. Sometimes, the younger ones would go outside while the older ones might listen to stories about the olden days and of her brother Peter who got shot in the war and wee Granny Quinn who admonished Jane if ever she got to talking too much about the past, or even the future.

'You should be thankful for what you've got. Not what you had or might even want.'

Peter had lived with my grandmother and Granny Quinn for years until they died. Their passing was as inevitable as Christmas but their memories lingered, like perfume in a discarded shawl. Jane showed us postcards from Ireland. From Francis and Anne who'd been to Inishowen, in County Donegal, and from her friend Mrs

Chisholm who'd been to Connemara. There were postcards from Lourdes, and Girvan, and New Zealand, and Mayo and Armagh and Dungannon and the Mourne Mountains. There were postcards from my mother and father from Barra addressed *Dear Mother*, and one that I'd written in a scribble to my grandmother and great-grandmother, in 1978.

Dear Grans,
Having a wonderful holiday on this beautiful island, the weather has not been good but the food is great. Missing you all but hope to see you soon.
    Love
    Michael

My grandmother smiled when I asked her to show me the post-card that always made me laugh. She knew the one. It said: 'We shoot every third salesman. The second one just left.'

They were private people, and that was their way and you couldn't change them supposing they had a dial attached. My father was exactly like my grandmother. If the doorbell rang they would ask each other who could it be and then peek from behind the curtains or simply wait until the interloper had gone away. They didn't like outsiders and they didn't like people asking questions. Who knew who they were or what they wanted?

They were suspicious.

My father inherited the suspicion like someone inherits a chair.

If he saw a stranger in our midst his face would twist and his eyes narrow, and then his shoulders tensed and he clenched his hands to the size of cooked turkeys. My father didn't do subtle. If he didn't like you, or was suspicious of your motives, you soon knew. And you stayed that way regardless.

He protected the Holy Trinity. Their memories too.

When my great-uncle Peter, who'd been wounded in the leg in Egypt during the war, was in hospital they made him make stuffed elephants out of old, discarded cotton as part of his rehabilitation.

He'd cut out the template and then the material, sew the pieces together, inside out, and then fill them up with rags.

'Elephants,' he'd say to me, when I was old enough to understand the difference between a conversation and a curse. 'Bloody elephants. I went to war, got shot to bits and ended up making elephants.'

My father kept them. I've kept them too.

After my great-grandmother Mary Quinn died the only thing I could ever really recall about her death was the ten-pence pieces the children received from the men in black suits and work shoes at my grandmother's house. They gave them to us for trying to sing 'Hear My Song', the one sung by Josef Locke. My father sang her song long, long after she was dead.

He told us to get the paraffin heater. That would fix it.

There was that one winter, when my father took us over to my grandmother's and it must have been one of the coldest known to man. Every day of December grew colder than the last. He had to push a couple of penguins out of the way, he said, just to get a Christmas card off the postman that very morning.

Driving was impossible. At least it should have been. But my father insisted on seeing his mother and there would be no excuses, especially not from a bit of snow. If the winter was that bad then just think how cold it must be for your grandmother, he said, in a house with a three-bar fire and a kitchenette without a proper door and windows like tissue paper. The snow fell and the temperature dropped. 'We're still going.' He said it in a voice that simmered.

My father's van was little more than a lump of metal. It didn't have a name, and it didn't have fancy paintwork and was worth double, he said, when he filled it with petrol or a box of tools. But the van never saw a full tank of fuel in its life.

It seemed indestructible and he drove it that way too and often without seat belts, tax discs, insurance documents, fit-for-purpose exhaust pipes, or working windscreen wipers. It could look wretched to the neighbours. But through the eyes of a child, it could look like a thing of beauty. And it was.

The van was white and large, with rust on the sides and back. Others might have been ashamed to ride in it, and sometimes we were when we got too close to our school, but mostly we loved it. It didn't have any side windows. It didn't have any rear seats until he built his own from the old couch and later pallets of wood he screwed together into a long, box shape before adding upholstery made from curtains and some comfortable foam. It would have to do, he said. And anyways, if someone wanted to look down on us they had better be perched up somewhere pretty high themselves. He'd bought and paid for his house and van and doubted they could say the same for their own.

The benches helped us to pretend we were travelling in some style, like a sultan in fine silk clothing. His set of wooden Rosary beads swung from the mirror.

We laughed along with him.

'Everybody in the van,' he said, and the battle cry reverberated around the house. 'Come on, let's go, children.' The sound of hurried footsteps was drowned out by the noise of the stampede for a warm coat or a blanket to wrap around yourself.

The cold gripped like barbed wire.

It would be a year or two before my parents could afford to install central heating in the house – which my father would do himself – and the house was always freezing and you could almost catch your breath in any of the rooms or kitchen then freeze it and then carry it downstairs like a lolly and as evidence of the onset of winter. We blew our cold breath out between our fingers and pretended we were smoking. Each room had a storage heater filled with clay bricks and my parents had recently bought a paraffin heater too for wherever happened to need some extra heat. It was about three foot tall and as stout as a piano and it gave off welcome warmth from the blue flame inside.

Once he had started the van he cleared the ice and snow from the windows with a piece of stiff cardboard and some warm water from the kettle. The engine spluttered and tried to warm us all up but the weather had turned the van into an icebox on wheels. 'The van's *really* freezing, John,' said my mother. 'It's too cold to go over. Maybe we should leave it till next week?' My father sighed. The house was freezing, the van was freezing and we were all freezing. My mother wrapped us all up as best she could. We drew pictures in the condensation on the back window. But we couldn't get away from the cold.

'Maybe we should leave it, dear?' my mother said again, but my father would not be missing a visit to his mother's on account of a little bit of cold. The temperature plummeted. The snow fell. We would be going to my grandmother's come hell or high water or whatever lay in the middle.

'Michael, Iain . . . give me a hand a minute,' he said, his eyes twinkling. 'Clear that stuff up to the back of the van. Move that bench. Big ones look after the wee ones. OK? Come on, you daft galoots!'

'Yes, Dad.'

We moved the bench.

I followed my father into the house and we came right back out carrying the paraffin heater, its flame already flickering, as if it was the most natural thing in the world. I could already feel the heat surging through my fingers. Iain, a kindred spirit, looked across at me and stifled a laugh. 'Right, let's see if we can warm this thing up,' said my father.

At first I thought that he wanted us all to go back into the house while the van got all warmed up. But the best thing for it, he said, was for the boys to *hold* the paraffin heater, blue flame and all, in the van. We would save a lot of time if we simply *brought* the paraffin heater with us.

'John, you can't take the paraffin heater *in* the van,' said my mother. 'That's . . . *dangerous*. And you'll need to leave it in the house anyway to keep the house warm.'

'I'm not leaving the heating on while we're out. What's the point of heating the place up and no one to enjoy it?' He looked at us as if everyone else was daft and maybe, in the middle of winter, we were. 'And anyway, what if the house went on fire?'

'What if the *house* goes on fire?' snorted my mother. 'What if the *van* goes on fire?'

'Ach, don't be silly. The boys will be holding it.' He lit a cigarette and blew the smoke out and waved the plumes away. There were eleven of us in the van. My father always reckoned the odds were always stacked in our favour. I'm not sure if he ever meant against fire.

We were travelling in a Zeppelin.

I took a pair of his oversized, black driving gloves from him and Iain was presented with a pair of my mother's woollen mittens. 'Aw, you're kidding, Dad,' he said. 'This is em-barr-a-ssing.' My mother called for calm, and shouted at us all in Gaelic. My father smiled at her warm voice. His wife. Talking Gaelic. It always softened him.

Our job was simple. We were to hold the paraffin heater steady while we drove the van past Colston and Milton and Possil and to Ruchill, up Mayfield Street where the incline could worry a mountain goat. 'And for God's sake, make sure that thing doesn't spill,' he said.

'Stop it, John. You know what I'm talking about. The children are listening . . .'

In no time the van had heated up nicely, as did our hands, and we drove along the streets, all of us singing along to Johnny Cash's 'Ring of Fire'. There would have been an almighty glow from inside the van, like the flickering lights of a movie, or the Ready Brek advert, and passers-by or the drivers of other cars must have wondered what on God's green earth was going on in the back of that old van.

Even now I wonder about it too.

'Hold on tight,' he shouted, half laughing but trying to be serious. 'We're nearly there. That's some heat in there, children . . . that takes the flippin' biscuit, doesn't it? Ya beauty. That is a cracker. Listen, I'm going to patent that. Heaters for vans. Big paraffin heaters. Make a fortune. I reckon that could take off. Miners driving to work in heated lorries. There's something in that . . .'

I can still see him, smiling to himself, amid the warm glow of his family and the warmer glow of a blue flame from a paraffin heater that got us over to see his mother on one of the coldest nights of my life. My grandmother greeted us with a smile at the door when we arrived and ushered us all in and said, 'Och, see, John, you shouldn't have bothered today. It's too cold for the children to be out and I've got the three bars on anyway in the front room. I've got the hot-water bottle under the blanket for my bed so you didn't have to worry.'

My mother said, 'It's not too bad out there, Mrs Tierney. We're fine.'

And my father just smiled and said, 'It's fine, Ma. It's fine.'

Not long after that, the white van developed bronchitis or something equally deadly that old vans get. My father shook his head sadly and replaced it with a yellow one, although it was hardly new but second-hand. Much to my mother's consternation, and the neighbours' curiosity, my father kept the white van in the front garden at the far wall, still convinced that one day he would turn it into a boat.

He looked at it every day and said the same thing to all of us: 'I'm going to turn that into a boat. It's got a good engine. I'll weld some plates on it to stop the water soaking in. You'll see. Just wait and see.'

I believed him too.

One day, my other granny, Elizabeth MacMillan, called. She needed a van. It was for the nuns who needed help with some stuff. At the time she was cleaning and cooking for some of them at Nazareth House in Cardonald, a convent and occasional retirement home for older priests. He said, yes, he'd help.

It happened that there was a well-known high-street shop in town that sometimes had too much food and didn't think it right to throw it all away, and the nuns and the priests and some of the poor and the homeless might benefit if they were quick, because someone here knew someone there and it had all been rubber-stamped and nobody bothered too much. If my father was happy to help with his van, and he kept it all hush-hush, then we might get some of the food too, and I don't think I'd seen him move so fast in a long time.

'If you get over here, John,' said Granny MacMillan, in her Highland lilt, 'there'll be extra for the family.' Her voice, like the opening of a child's music box, sang through the telephone. They chuckled together, my father and El. My father was delighted and told us that the priests wouldn't mind if some of the food made its way to our table, though we all knew enough about some priests to know that some of them would.

The head nun called our house while he was at the vigil Mass on a Saturday night or the Sunday morning and she asked my mother if he could head over. When she explained where he was, the nun asked if my mother, or one of the children, could just go down there and get him out of Mass because the food needed delivering and it wouldn't be that much of a sin if he left early, now would it? God, said the nun, was a benevolent soul. And he didn't keep a Mass-attendance card. At least not when it concerned feeding the poor.

Everyone swore that nun was a saint.

My father set off in his van.

Every time he went on one of these runs, he'd sing the same song before setting off. It was 'Birmingham Jail', by Slim Whitman, and if I live to be one hundred and ten I'll never forget him singing that song and smiling as he took the benches out of the van and asked the boys to stack them round the side of the house like we were stacking sacks of flour. Then we'd brush the van out and put the brown blanket in there for covering up the pallets of food that he'd pick up later.

He said he'd be back after dark and we should make a little space in the fridge. He said it with a smile.

He went to the big shop in his van and said the nuns had sent him and they helped him reverse in the back way and he took boxes and pallets of food to various charities and groups down by the river that looked after the homeless and the poor of the city. While the food was perhaps a day past its sell-by date it was never enough to worry the men and women who lived by the kindness of the Missions and who had hunger in their bellies and couldn't read or count regardless.

While it was true that the priests still received a great deal of the food earmarked for them, my father felt that, now and again, it was his Christian duty to hand out cooked chickens and beef sandwiches to those less fortunate, and he included hungry Tierneys in his schedule. So the poor dined on chicken and fresh fruit and, now and again, the priests wondered as to the sheer volume of cabbages and lettuces and tomatoes and potatoes that had been left at the doors of Nazareth House instead of their usual delicious fare.

He smiled when he told us that.

When my father arrived back at the house we'd swear it was a miracle and he'd say, help me, boys, and we'd all rush down, laughing like drains, and take out bread and meat as big as dustbin lids and it stood us in great fettle for the rest of the week and more. Now and again a persistent priest would ask what had happened to the load that was supposed to arrive at the convent, and the nun would tell him that the poor were hungrier than ever this week and why should he mind if the Lord's work was being done?

And she'd wink at the priest and say that as long as the poor were being fed, now then, surely he'd sleep well in his comfortable old retirement bed?

My father drove his van across the city like a prince, listening to the football scores on the radio if it was working, and smiling at the thought of the food in the back. If the radio wasn't working he still drove the van the exact same way. He dropped food off at my granny Tierney's too.

Her cancer spread and she deteriorated quickly. By the end Jane was disorientated and getting up by herself in her nightdress and talking a little to herself. She shouted out for Mick. And she told him she would see him soon. And it didn't matter to some of us if we weren't always convinced by God. That was our problem, not hers. We knew that she would see him quicker than the time it took to recite a decade of the Rosary.

She said *Mick* like it was a talisman.

On the day of her death I went back to America. Reluctantly I said my goodbyes, and told her that I loved her while holding back tears as I left the house. She smiled, but I doubt she knew who I was.

I said not to worry. It's Michael.

All she could see was Mick.

'Should I stay?' I asked my father.

'No, no, it's fine. Granny would have wanted you to go to America.' He bit his bottom lip. We hugged. 'Call when you arrive. You can reverse the charges.'

'OK, Dad. I will.'

I left while my brothers and sisters were upstairs. They were talking to my grandmother, coaxing her gently into the quiet.

I remembered that she used to draw cartoon Easter chickens on our cards and let us sleep in her bed when we were small and the spare room that was colder than the park.

I remembered that she let us make budgies from plasticine and let us hang the soft clay birds around the house and on curtains. I remembered that she looked at the photograph of Mick on the wall as if it were Scriptures itself. I remembered that as she died she was leaving my father alone and that he truly didn't want her to go.

There were days I remembered everything.

Chapter Eleven

Then and Now

My father put a lot of my grandmother's stuff in the loft, and he'd sit up there and look through photographs and read some of her old postcards and sift through much of her correspondence. Insurance letters and bills mostly. Still, they were hers. Change happened right in front of us. But no one could ever really see things changing until they had.

One night after Quins, I sat up with Iain and my father. I was back at university and living in a flat directly opposite the primary school where I'd gone, but I was over at the house for the night. There was still enough space in the loft to sleep up there.

We discussed America, and the way my father talked I knew he wished that he could have gone there when he was young like us. We'd been working in construction with some Irish lads and, give or take one or two, we wouldn't have swapped them for an old shirt. Most of them were nothing like the boys he'd known in the past and told us about. Some of them called us 'Brits' and that annoyed us far more than anything else. There were always brawls and a bit of this and that too. You couldn't come from a family of nine and not have a fair old go.

He poured a glass of Jameson's as big as his arm. He could drink, no fear about that. He had a head like an oak bucket. The glass got bigger and so did the tough Irishmen from way back, or so he said, but I was growing a little tired of the Irish stories. He said Granny Quinn was tougher and more pugnacious than them all. I told him she'd scared the living daylights out of me once. I'd walked in on her while she was sitting on the toilet and she screamed, Mother of Mercy, and shouted for all the saints in heaven to help and preserve her, and she shouted once more at her daughter Jane and ordered her to make sure we never, ever went near the toilet again, even if we were on fire.

Hell would mend us if we did.

My grandmother scolded us loudly out of eyesight of the Terror in the Toilet but laughed as she did so, and put her finger to our mouths to shush us so that we didn't laugh back. She loved her mother. But sometimes the old soul could be awkward as a horse on a bike and I was never convinced Granny Quinn let Granny Tierney have a life at all after she became a widow. But that was the way of things back then and you couldn't really judge too much because someone would likely point the big accusing finger at you.

He laughed and then sighed. With nine children there was no going further than the length of yourself without getting into bother or running out of money and that was a plain fact.

And then he was a little quiet for a minute or two.

'He was a bastard,' said my father.

I'd never heard him swearing properly before. The way he said it sounded bitter and cruel and he wasn't walking through the servants' entrance on that one. 'That doctor . . . my mother's doctor. A bastard. If I ever get my hands on him.'

Iain sat at the table drinking tea. My father said the doctor should have done more and how he was harsh when he spoke to my grandmother about managing her pain before she died and how this happened and that happened. His face turned black and he went quiet in that dark, noiseless volcanic way. He was crying too. Iain went upstairs. I didn't want my father to feel embarrassed in front of both of us. Better one than two. The television hummed as my father cried and I could feel his tears salting my neck.

His mother was gone. He'd known it for months, but it was as if she had been spirited away that very night. The tears stunned me but I was glad that he'd let them out. His mother, he said, was the one person who linked him directly to his father and now they were both gone. He was back to ghosts. Francis had his life in England and they rarely saw each other now. They spoke when they needed to come up for air.

He talked a little about my grandfather but it didn't make much sense. He said they'd killed him and that he'd kill them too in return. He'd make sure of it. The whole lot of them, and anyone else who'd been involved. He talked about the Ancient Order of Hibernians and of Ireland and he already knew who he could count on and who was just playing games with him. He said the Hibernians had done nothing for them and they were just like the Masons. They were just like the Knights of St Columba or the Catenians too. They all thought they were something but they couldn't hold a candle to her. None of them had said a word when she'd died.

The past was crumbling.

Maryhill. Ireland. Ruchill. France.

Everything about the old days, with the moss-covered cottages that were built from stone in his imagination, was disappearing into the ground. There were gaps in his life now, like a mouth with half the teeth missing. The old blood that had bound everything together had seeped from his pockets quietly. And my grandmother's death bled him almost to the bone.

'Granny's with my grandfather now, Dad. She's happy.'

'I know . . . but that bastard hurt her. She never harmed a breathing soul.'

'I know, Dad. I know.'

The next morning he was quiet. Nothing more and nothing less. He drank good black tea and ate blackened toast and pulled his bag of tools from the downstairs cupboard. He put on his shoes and went hunting for the front door and it closed and he never swore in front of me again.

Everything collided slowly. But still it collided.

Mark had moved to America and was pretty much settled there. Iain stayed on too and his first child, Quinn, was born

262

there. Vincent, like me, took jobs for extra money during the busy summer months, before we finally worked out what we might do with our lives. As brothers we also just wanted to spend some time together. We put our feet under the table of a few bars and liked the feel of it. We were the same. And we were also as distinct as fingerprints.

So in New York we worked in places like Fulton Street and John Street and the Rockefeller Center and Grand Central Station and Fifth Avenue and Madison Avenue and Park Avenue too. Anywhere someone wanted something broken fixed, or something fixed broken. There were always simple reasons. And they turned into dollar cheques that we cashed behind the bars. No banks. Just bars. Anonymous. No questions. Just the way it was supposed to be. Quietly about your business.

We fell in with groups of Irish workers who, like us, were there without visas and paperwork. Nobody asked and nobody was told and if they had asked, well, they still wouldn't have been told. Manhattan, and the strong Irish community there, provided a refuge for anyone who liked a late night that ended with whisky and beer, and a rebel tune and a slice from John's. The work was backbreaking and you could be hauling blocks up scaffolding ten storeys high for the bricklayers, in constant fear of the union man, or be mixing grout for concourses on subway lines all night long. The raggedy arse would be hanging out of you by the morning.

My father said we could take over the place. Brains and muscle, he said, were all anyone ever needed. We laughed and told him to behave himself. If anyone was going to give it a go it would be our Mark. He had a head for the work, a throat for the drink and a fist that was as mean as a dog shitting brass carpet tacks.

There was Belfast Tommy, Johnny Cornflake, the Horse, Pat the Head, Big Noel and the Irish Gypsy. There was Crocket and Fifty-Fifty and the Bold Boy and Frank the Gun and a fella from Cork whose name I can't even remember but he was a carrot-cruncher if ever there was one and said so himself. The names told their own stories; every last one of them was a damn liar and as mad as the moon. And we lied too. If you didn't lie there was something very suspicious about you altogether. A fella could be hauled out of a bar for telling the truth. No one wanted any of that truthful nonsense in there.

We drank in the Fenian, the Copper Kettle, the Irish Rover, the Breffini Inn Bar and, when we had guests and were being respectable, the Parlour Bar and sometimes Curley's Inn.

Everyone called everyone else 'horse'.

'How's it goin', horse?'

'Fine, horse, how's yourself?'

'Grand, horse.'

All the brothers did too.

I never hid the fact that I'd been studying but I never advertised it either because a lot of the time mixing mortar beat the devil out of learning from books. Other days, when the city boiled and the buckets weighed as much as a grey mule, it was the last place I ever wanted to be. The lime burned you and you couldn't get the Portland out of your skin for weeks.

Some of the men were downright decent and others you wouldn't spit at sideways or round a corner. A few were running from something and a few learned to run when they got there. But running was good. It kept them on their toes. The occasional sober day was thrown in as a truce until the next few dollars arrived.

The smart ones, and there were plenty of them, had set up their own construction companies and they bought the bars as well and filled them with Celtic scarves and jerseys and Republic of Ireland shirts and shirts of GAA teams like Meath, Kilkenny, Roscommon and Antrim. There were signed souvenirs everywhere you went. The fellas spent their evenings looking at all the fine jerseys that reminded them of home and they spent all their wages drinking. The smart ones had already bought cheap apartments to give the men somewhere to drop their rent money. They paid their men on Thursdays and the place was dry by Saturday. There were fights and women and gambling. But it wasn't always as much fun as it sounded . . .

Sometimes, I began to think that I had people too.

The music began to get under my skin again, as it had all those years ago. It was a little rougher around the edges than the music I'd heard before. It was foot-stomping and head-birling and we all banged our knees to it for sure. Up all night. Up all night again. And once more for good measure.

Yet repetition is always the death of magic.

Even though part of me wanted to stay there and leave behind university and all the studies and the books, I needed to get back home. New York was a dream and always would be. I ended up hating it. It didn't matter where our people came from, or who I supported, or what my politics were, or who had died at the hands of this one or that one. We were a million miles different and we always would be.

Mark stayed and grew forearms like my father's.

My younger brother was born with genuine warmth and an open smile. He was in New York at sixteen or seventeen and he learned to be tough there and he was afraid of no one. They were easy words to say but it was a fact. As clear as directions for putting on a sock. You couldn't be scared when you worked with men from Mayo and Clare and Belfast and Armagh and Donegal and Cork and Limerick for over twenty years and, especially, in boroughs that preferred prize-fighting over preaching.

He promised himself that he'd never be less than anyone else, least of all the Irish, he said. If a contractor talked down to him Mark left him wondering why he suddenly had a swelling the size of an egg growing out of his head and maybe just a little more. The Coalition, who were like a black mafia, never troubled him. Neither did the Italians nor the Puerto Ricans. My father said Mark was a throwback. But it was never to Ireland. It was to the bone-hard Atlantic fishermen of Barra.

When I told my father I wanted to become a journalist he said it was a closed shop in Glasgow. It was impossible, he said, for sons and daughters of a working-class Catholic to get ahead in that kind of world. But the Glasgow workplace was changing. Had changed.

It was his generation that had taken all the hard blows, and the low blows, and had usually gone back for more. Besides, I never really cared much what anyone thought about me or where I might be from. That would be their problem, not mine, and if we had to discuss it at the back door that was fine too. You took a hit to land a hit.

Even football in the west of Scotland was changing.

Rangers' unwritten rule of avoiding signing Catholic players had finally, and very publicly, been altered. Maurice Johnston, a former Celtic player to boot, signed for them in 1989 under the dapper but deadly Graeme Souness, who'd just arrived from Sampdoria, and who'd been married to a Catholic.

Rangers had been under increasingly intense media scrutiny and pressure since the 1970s to change their signing policy. With this new acquisition Souness tried to put to rest some of the religious apartheid that had haunted the Ibrox club for decades. Yet it wasn't simply altruism on his part. There was more than a hint of mischief in his motives, as he understood perfectly how the signing of Johnston would infuriate the Celtic fans. Johnston was something of a Celtic poster boy in those days and, in 1986, during the League Cup Final against Rangers, he'd made the Sign of the Cross when he was sent off.

There were angry noises from both camps at the signing, of course, and they were loud as the drums of Lambeg and a Wexford bodhrán. Many Rangers fans wanted the club to remain resolutely Protestant and many Celtic fans believed that Johnston, once known as Super Mo, was akin to a red-haired Judas. There was still cheap hatred between Celtic and Rangers and perhaps there always would be. But at least now it could be on a level religious playing field. The divisions that had existed for many years slowly began to crumble at the edges.

Wherever I was when I heard that Johnston had signed for Rangers, I knew that something verging on the profound had taken place. I was stunned, everyone was. Because there was such an out-cry it meant there *had* to have been a corresponding issue in the past. My father had been right. Johnston's signing was a validation. Their unwritten rule was being rewritten. It seemed ironic that praise from many quarters was heaped on Rangers for moving to end their signing policy: a policy that many denied had ever existed in the first place. I *was* bothered that Johnston had signed, but not because he was a Catholic signing for Rangers. I was only bothered because he'd already agreed to re-sign for Celtic from French club Nantes, and Celtic had earlier announced their new capture. He'd even posed in a club jersey along with Billy McNeill.

Johnston's agent was a Rangers fan and a deal was quickly put in place behind Celtic's back. But that was business. And Celtic were often caught napping on that front. Johnston joining Rangers was an act, purely and simply, of finance. The motives to destroy the old ways of the past should have been about more than simply cash. It wasn't reason and decency and integrity that was changing Rangers' policy, it was money.

The period in question was an era for Rangers of huge success on the pitch but also of greater financial promiscuity and fiscal imprudence off it. Rangers spent money by the wagonload, most of which they didn't really have. Celtic fans all secretly hoped it would come back to haunt them. Candles were lit furiously at St Matthew's just in case. Maybe it would.

Regardless, you had to admire Souness for his sheer agitation and brass neck.

I fell into my first journalism job after Sunday Mass. And that doesn't mean I suddenly got more spiritual. My father had picked up the *Scottish Catholic Observer* and there was an advert for a trainee journalist or something close to that. Before long I was writing about priests and the Pope and nuns of all contemplative orders and the general tittle-tattle of Catholic life in Scotland. I took the job because it paid something and also because the editor was a fine former tabloid journalist in Glasgow and a bit of a rascal to boot. He told me a few stories and showed me a few tricks and I became a better journalist for it.

Later, I worked for the *Evening Times* and then the *Herald*, and had the best working time of my life, acquitting myself as well as I could. Despite some of the things I'd heard about the Glasgow papers I felt no more, or no less, prejudice than I had when I worked with the Irish boys in New York. And I gave out no more or no less too. Sometimes it was like working in a shark tank. At other times I had no problem even if I wasn't liked. I had no issue if they ever thought I was arrogant. I had a real problem if they thought I was an arrogant Catholic.

I was told that when I was barred for life from the Press Bar that the fault was all mine. There was no way that it was. But everyone knew that big families rarely produced wallflowers. The incident spilled out into the street and it included some printers from the plant next door. Des, the owner of the bar, was quite fair about the whole thing and explained that the other fellas spent a lot more money than me. It was a cash call. I could see his point of view. He wasn't being prejudiced either. After all, I'd gone to school with his daughter.

Although I worked locally, the stories I really needed to do were much further afield. They were always my father's type of stories. They were about all the conflicts and politics he'd ever watched and listened to over the years from the living room in Bishopbriggs. Soon I was going off to places like Gaza and Ramallah and Libya. I went to Lebanon and Iraq and Jerusalem. I flew to Liberia and America and Australia. And to China and Cuba.

The years slid past. He was ill and I kept travelling. I loved it and I hated it.

In early 2005 I arrived in Banda Aceh, Indonesia, a week after thousands of people were killed by the Indian Ocean earthquake and tsunami that devastated the region. Covering these stories was never hard for me. It was hard for the survivors who had to stay there. It was hard for the NGOs and the medical teams and the journalists who worked there for weeks and months at a time.

It was hard for those who covered wars long term and saw every nasty and ordinary piece of a conflict. I was in these places for a week, ten days or sometimes two weeks. I was just a visitor. They flew me in on a nice plane and flew me back out again. I wrote a few stories. It was a good life. It was a *great* life. If there was ever anything difficult it might have been the cumulative effect of what I saw.

Being on a plane with smiling air hostesses and the soft, comfortable seats and pre-cooked dinners and free drinks was easy, but the coming back home and thinking about what had just happened there posed some problems. There were thousands and thousands of dead in Banda Aceh. The ones I saw, bloated and black, looked like burst link sausages. Nothing more and nothing less. The dogs rooted around at their flesh. Whoever they'd been before – children, mothers and fathers – was already gone.

Sometimes, I sat bolt upright. When I'd stood on that dead child's crushed head, it was still a dead child's crushed head.

I was lucky though.

While the *Herald* didn't exactly give me free rein, they allowed me to put up an argument and I spun the globe and tried to tell simple stories, about the people who lived in the places I was sent to, and what exactly did their life mean? They might even help me find out a little more about mine. I wrote about the things people might not know too much about because I wanted to know about them too.

Like, why did a child have to walk twenty miles every day just to get drinking water, and why did a child called *Kill the Woman* even exist, and why had he had to carry a gun just to get through a day and the rest of the week? And why did that old English priest, who rose at five to drink water and to pray, get kidnapped in one of the darkest parts of Africa and then go back to the same place to defend the poor people he'd been kidnapped from?

There was a young boy, of about eleven, in a Palestinian refugee camp in Gaza. I never knew his name or even spoke with him but when he saw me he kicked his tatty football towards me and we started kicking it around together and we played keepy-uppy, trying to prevent the ball from touching the ground. The sun was scorching and we grew thirsty. He motioned for us to get a drink of water. He scooped some stagnant water from a big oil drum and offered me a dirty cupful. I shook my head and showed him that I had a small bottle of my own. Avnan or Talfen, I can't remember. But it was clean. Or, at least, cleaner than his.

He shrugged and started drinking from the oil drum.

I unscrewed the cap of my bottle and drank my water.

We played a little longer and then the driver arrived to pick me up. I watched the boy disappear in the rear-view mirror and he was smiling and waving at me and trying to play keepy-uppy with the ball. My bottle of water was still half full but I hadn't given him one sip of it. I had let him drink from the oil drum. There's barely a day of my life that goes by now that I don't think of that boy.

Sometimes, it was hard going from children who killed to children who wouldn't tidy their room. How did you go from young people who were willing to strap explosives to their bodies and then detonate them to why hadn't the dinner dishes been put away? Or you need to clean your plate, son, because there are children starving in the world. And, listen closely to me, young lady, I've seen some of them up close and it looks a lot worse than it sounds.

My wife, Kathleen, always said I was quiet and moody when I came back. I might be in a bad mood for days, and it wasn't the fault of the children that they didn't like broccoli or carrots, but sometimes it seemed like it was. And then the old routine kicked in. That's what travel did. It expanded and contracted you like an elastic band. I think my father realized that, but he knew it was already too late for him. He'd always wanted to see more. He just hadn't known it at the time.

But that wasn't the only thing. The truth was more prosaic. I wanted to go to these places and be part of something ugly and beautiful and sad and brutal and sometimes a little crazy too. I wanted something so different from Bishopbriggs and table manners and Sunday Mass and 2–1 up at Ibrox. It became something of a game.

And I lied to myself. We all did, if we were being honest.

I pretended it was because the story was important, and others did too. I still pretended to myself that the story couldn't exist without me. It was yet more conceit.

Once, I tried to get press credentials in America to do a story on a man who was going to be executed. I followed the protocols for weeks, speaking to the right people, and it looked like I would be going over. The story would be about Death Row and how inhumane it was and I'd write about the tragedy of the whole event and how immoral the whole circus was and how the machine of justice was prejudiced against the prisoner whatever he might have done. They understood, they said. They would help. Did I have a prisoner in mind?

I flicked through my list. Yes, I did.

I told them it was X. They took notes. I called them. They called me. I emailed. They said it might be possible. They said that X would be getting executed soon, and yet it went on and on and on, and the whole process itself felt like an appeal to the courts. Weeks passed. I called again and then one day they said no. It wasn't possible. They had to stick to the rules. Rules were rules. They didn't want a foreign journalist there.

I was livid. It was my story! *Mine*. It was a great story.

'What do you mean?'

'Sorry. That's the rules. Protocols . . . you know how these things are? It happens. Last-minute change of plans.'

'Unacceptable. I almost booked my flight . . .'

'Sorry. You need to understand.'

I had planned it. It would be great. It would be the cover of the magazine. We'd arrange for photographs and for the victim's family to give us some quotes. The prison governor also. It would be a great piece. Understanding and descriptive. There'd be emotion. There'd be death, of course, but there'd be resolution too. People would feel vindicated. So would I. The readers would have gone on a journey. They'd have wanted to follow it to the very end, even though it was distasteful and improper. If it was told well it would be fine. It would be palatable. The man would have deserved to die. They'd all have agreed. But I'd have written it in a way that certain liberal sensitivities felt moved.

The woman said no. Rules were rules.

I told her it was ridiculous. 'You mean I can't go over and watch that man die? Who made these rules? It's utterly ridiculous. I've been planning for that man's death for some time now.' I grew incredulous. I'd spent months trying to arrange to watch this man's death and all they could say was rules were rules . . .

That's when I woke up.

What was I doing? They told me I couldn't witness the death of another man and I was *disappointed*. That's when I knew it was almost time.

Then there was the crucifixion.

A few years after my father's stroke I was in the house of a young man called Harry, from Poleglass in Northern Ireland. Harry was taken by a gang of six men and crucified on a stile in Seymour Hill, Dunmurry. He wasn't crucified in the metaphorical sense. It wasn't *like* being crucified. He *was* crucified. In the absolute physical sense. The physical land of nails and hammers. He was beaten up badly and nailed to a fence through the palms and knuckles of his hands, as retribution for joyriding and stealing cars and entering areas in his surrounding community that, really, he should have known better than to enter.

He was no innocent. But *crucifixion*?

When Harry, who was legendary amongst Belfast's joyriders, arrived at hospital two blocks of wood were still attached to his hands by large nails – the firemen had cut him from the stile – and his family could identify him only by a tattoo of his daughter. The nails were bent over into his palms to make it harder for his rescuers to set him free. I sat with him in his father's house. Harry showed me three nail-sized holes in his palms and in one knuckle, and the holes in his knees where he was beaten with a baseball bat spiked with yet more nails. They were brutal stigmata. He was paper thin, with the kind of grey look that freshly dead people acquire. Harry was a Catholic, and a Loyalist group believed to be the Ulster Defence Association crucified him.

The only people I'd heard of who'd really been crucified were Jesus and Harry.

But for every brutality such as the one to Harry there was an equally horrible punishment beating, murder or attack carried out by Catholic members of paramilitary groups like the INLA or the IRA. Eighteen months earlier, at the behest of his *own* community, the IRA had smashed Harry's ankles with hammers for stealing cars on his own estate. The attackers wore balaclavas. One held him by his belt, told him to kneel down. Five or six of them broke his ankles with hammers.

The area where he was crucified was a decent place. Neighbours tended their gardens and said hello to each other every morning. But they feared people like Harry, in much the same way he feared them. They were individually ordinary and collectively very ordinary and their tribalism and prejudice was reared quietly – perhaps not always quietly – in their decent homes and their not-so-decent homes. The one thing they had in common was fear, or suspicion, of the other.

The story of Harry, and the other young boys I met, confused me utterly. They didn't make me feel sick. They made me feel *stupid*.

Another time. Another youngster.

Barney hanged himself from the scaffolding of the Holy Cross Church in Belfast. He, and a friend, had received punishment beatings a while back, meted out by certain members of their own community. His friend had had enough and hanged himself in the attic space of his Ardoyne home. Barney followed suit after the funeral. His skinny body jolted and wriggled. A fish trying to breathe in human hands. I sat with his mother and she was crying when she remembered how he'd asked her for a kiss just hours before he died. It was one of those kisses, she said, that had a message in it. She could feel the trace of his teenage moustache on her lip.

The priest climbed the scaffolding to the top of the tower and, unable to reach him, administered the Last Rites from a platform. In the distance, they could see the outlines of Cave Hill and Belfast Loch. When the fire brigade arrived and brought him to the ground the priest watched as the boy's father cradled him and whispered quietly in his ear. He would never forget it, he said. The cradling. And the tears.

I also met Sean who'd had his right knee shot off by the IRA. He was a burglar and known to the IRA and had been warned before about his activities. Once more and he would be done, and you'd better tell him now boys to behave, or else.

When he was sixteen, in an act of defiance, or bravado, against the paramilitaries, Sean had got a tattoo on his left kneecap with an arrow pointing downwards that said *Shoot Here*. The IRA blew his right leg off below the knee and told him not to be such a smart-arse and that if he did it again they'd come for the other one.

It was a much shorter flight home from Belfast. So much closer to home. But I still asked the children to clear their dinner plates.

Of course there were lighter stories too.

There had to be. There couldn't *not* be.

In 2003 I sat in Sean Connery's delightful house in the Bahamas and we talked about politics and nationalism and football and a bit of this and that. Connery was much more down to earth than I could have imagined and he seemed genuinely eager to chat. When we arrived at his house, Gordon, the photographer, was explaining that his luggage had been delayed at the airport and he had no other clothes apart from what he was wearing.

Before we left, Connery went to his room and brought back a polo shirt and a pair of Bermuda shorts for Gordon, telling him he could change in his bathroom. 'Put these on,' he said, in his distinctive Scottish burr. 'It's roasting out there.' Gordon dutifully obliged and when he returned Connery was laughing. 'Christ,' he said, at the apparition before him with legs whiter than a snowball. 'A Fife boy right enough.'

Gordon was laughing too. He'd tell me why later, in the taxi. 'You'll not believe this.' He pulled the band of his shorts back to reveal black underwear. 'I'm wearing his pants as well.' The following day Gordon was still wearing the actor's pants.

A few days after I'd returned home Connery was trying to get hold of me to clarify something he'd said. He'd missed me at work and tried my home number. The phone rang while Kathleen was upstairs. She heard his deep, sonorous voice on the answering machine and jumped up to grab the phone, but she wanted him to speak as long as possible into the answering machine before she picked up. She waited for him to say bye, or cheerio, or whatever. But his voice simply cut off before she had the chance to chat. She was livid. No one would believe that she'd been talking to James Bond . . .

Five minutes later she found our video recorder and took aim at the phone and pressed Record before pressing Play on the answering machine. So now she had a video recording of our telephone recording of Sean Connery's voice. Then she called her sisters and they came round the following day and all sat and watched the answering machine speaking.

'And this is the bit where I came down the stairs and he hung up . . .'

'That's brilliant . . .'

'That's amazing . . .'

On and off over the next few years Connery and I spoke with each other. I called him more than he called me but, occasionally, he'd call and talk quietly and with a great deal of care about Scotland and nationalism and identity and football, of course, and a little about Celtic and Rangers. He'd been following Rangers for a number of years, ever since owner David Murray had invited him to be his guest at Ibrox. Although he'd grown up in Edinburgh, in a two-room tenement flat, and supported Celtic when he was younger after being introduced to the club by his father, he later switched his allegiance as his friendship with Murray grew.

I called him *Sean* and he called me *Tierney*. A few years ago, I tried to call him but there was no response. About six weeks later my phone rang while I was in Dubai.

'Tierney,' said the voice.

'Is that you, Sean?'

'Yes. I'm just back from Switzerland. Been feeling bloody awful.'

'Just a minute,' I said putting my hand over the receiver. 'Kids, be quiet for a minute. I'm on the phone . . . it's Bond. James Bond!' I laughed loudly and my shoulders heaved. The kids laughed too. They knew exactly who it was.

'How are you?'

'Fine. Just back in the Bahamas.'

And he talked for a while. I was working on a new project. He might, he said, be able to help. And then he laughed. 'I know a few guys in Hollywood . . .'

I asked him about our bet. We usually bet a pound on Old Firm games or who would win the League between Celtic and Rangers. I was sure he still owed me. Celtic had been playing well against our old rivals recently.

'Double or quits, Tierney. Double or quits . . .'

There would always be one image of him that remained. It was when we met at his house. He'd been, and still was, one of the genuine movie stars of my generation and the generation before that. He was older now but he still carried great presence. An immensity of self. He always had something.

There was a tiny hummingbird hovering beside the feeder outside his office window. 'They're amazing,' he said. 'Sometimes I'll sit and watch them through binoculars from my room.' A few leaves shivered and rattled, while the small bird skipped in and out of the feeder. The scene lasted no more than a few seconds but it was a touching moment. It was a brief inkling of vulnerability.

Adjoining his office was his personal bathroom. Gordon had changed in there. He kept a battered street sign – Fountainbridge – above the door. It was a present from the former Rangers owner. Many of the familiar aspects of his life had vanished. His Edinburgh home, his parents – both dead – and much of the place he'd grown up in as a boy, and the sign, I suspected, was more than a battered remnant of a street or district. It was, quite literally, a sign to a life that was gone and that he could no longer reclaim.

There was a quietly autumnal feeling about our conversation.

I took his bet. He still owes me . . .

I never set out to but I'm sure that I wrote a lot of these stories for my father. I wanted to explain a world that he might never see but was curious about. I wanted him to hear about the world that existed beyond Bishopbriggs or anywhere else. They were my words. But they were written with his eyes too.

After a while I no longer really understood why I wanted to write them. Maybe, like the football of my youth, I no longer really wanted them enough. And I'd grown tired, I think, of listening. And asking the children to clear their plates of food.

I left newspapers in 2008. I think they wanted rid of me anyway.

We were raised to believe that God would fix everything and that God would heal the wounds of the sick and clean their very sores. He would clothe and feed us. But if it was true then someone had made a mistake. It was my mother who did most of His work. And we helped her out when we could.

It was my mother who saved my father. She was the one who brought him back to life. She never stopped. She did everything for him, and more. She would do it alone. She didn't want to trouble us, she said.

Once, when she needed a new ladder, she took the bus to B&Q without telling us. She couldn't take the ladder back on the bus and said it wouldn't fit in a taxi so she carried the ladder over her shoulder all the way home. She wandered across roads and pavements for three miles, like a pheasant wandering in a field. If she hadn't turned sixty-five yet it was because she was keeping it all a secret.

We all gave her a telling-off over the ladder.

'It wasn't that heavy,' she said. 'It just got a wee bit heavy towards the end.'

The months turned to years. My father was lifted from his bedroom into his chair in a hoist. It was done to him every day with barely a complaint. Occasionally, he'd make a face or try to shout but mostly he smiled. There was nothing else for him to do.

We took turns helping my mother clean and change him when the carers were unavailable. My sisters called home all the time. They spoke softly and reassuringly to my father even though he couldn't say anything back. He grinned when he came off the phone and sometimes he'd cry a little. He'd grown older quickly. You could tell time was passing as his bones began to stick through his clothes.

It was impossible for him to look at me while he was being changed. I could *feel* him glancing over at me before turning away or looking downwards. When we moved him from his chair I wrapped my hand tightly around the flesh above his knee to hold him upright and his sense of shame was harder to bear than the loss of his speech. Sometimes, when I was near, there was so much emptiness in his eyes, like a distant field or a broken For Sale sign.

No matter how difficult or sick he could be, or how often he needed help during the night, my mother was there. Every day, fixing him. When his illness happened it was all she ever wanted to do, she said.

He'd been home for some time now.

It was possible he would have more seizures, and something – anything – could trigger them. The doctors didn't know for sure. But my mother raised her right hand to God and said she would make sure that he would get better. He had to. A fire was lit under her and it never went out.

More than anything she missed him talking, but at least she could speak to him and she did. Every day. And he nodded. And she talked. And it went on like this for years. Every day he sat on the large automated armchair, eyes fixed to the television screen while a cup of cooling tea rested on a tray on his lap. You could have set a clock by it. The cup slid to one side, and my mother would reach over and stop it from spilling. My father's eyes remained fixed to the screen, oblivious to the sliding of the tea. This episode took place every day. His eyes were always just fixed to the one spot.

It took a long time for us to adjust to our father being like this. It took him a lot longer. The chair wasn't a place he went to for comfort. It was the place he now lived. When my mother told him that I was there, he might slowly look up and stare for a few seconds, and then he'd try to say something. But the words wouldn't come out. In their place was that now-familiar rumble, of disconnected and tantalizing sounds.

'Nnnh-nnhh. Uhh.'

His voice had evaporated over the rooftops, like one of his old songs.

One day, I lied to him and said that soon he would simply get up, like Lazarus, and his voice would have returned too and his legs would be strong enough to carry his body around the house and outside into the garden and to Quins and down to Mass.

I thought he might smile.

But he just looked away.

'OK, Dad?' I said, knowing the answer would never come. A smear of dried toothpaste nestled on the edges of his mouth, caught in a little of his stubble. Although his mobility had been sabotaged he always touched the left side of his head, trying to scratch at something that was bothering him. An itch was like a jail sentence. His long fingers wavered while he probed the deep indent that scarred his skull.

As a result of his injury, and because the left side of the brain was responsible for language and communication, my father had been transformed into something unrecognizable. He was voiceless, semi-paralysed and prematurely aged. His brain, the control tower that had made my father function his whole life, was broken. There was no machine more advanced than the brain, but his was deceiving him now. Whatever had exploded inside his head had spirited away his capacity to think his own thoughts, and his ability to plough his own furrow. It was the thing that drove him.

Now it had all gone.

There was some improvement at times. He'd put on weight and no longer looked desperate and gaunt. But most of the time he was simply lost. Much like an infant who could not yet speak, in signs a smile was a *yes*, while he turned his head away emphatically for *no*. But each movement was a slow recalibration of personality. There were also moments when he could not contain his emotions. A noiseless tear was usually triggered by music, something Irish, of course, or Jim Reeves. Occasionally, Elvis singing about Christmas.

If we talked about my granny Tierney and the steaming-hot

dumpling she used to make before leaving ten pence under each slice, he would crumble. It was an impossible sight to witness. Not just the tears, but also his inability to wipe them away.

The tears were for mourning.

I'm sure he was mourning his own death.

Back then he had almost twenty grandchildren and there were more to come. Each of them reminded him of the long days in his garden when we were younger and played football and tugged his sunburned ears and threw water over him with the green basin for washing clothes.

The children brought out the light in him.

But they were sometimes scared. Of the old man, known as Granda, who'd sat in his chair for ever and said nothing apart from a grunt.

'He's dying,' we used to say to each other. We all felt it. The boys and the girls. That's what we always called each other. Really, it was all we ever were. And he was. 'He's really dying.'

Yet my father, so close to death for so long, remained with us. The sadness was that he was now terribly troubled by life. One evening George came to visit my father. It had been years since I'd seen him. He was sprightly and eager to hear how my father was.

'You're looking well, John,' he said. 'Doesn't he look well, Cathie?'

'Oh, he does, George.'

'You look well, John. Can you hear me OK?'

The passing years without seeing George had become just another marker of my father's new life. George was older too, but he still spoke about my father with great reverence and respect. He said that the boys in Quins were asking for him and wishing him well and that he'd get his spot back in the bar when he returned one of these days. Of course he would.

We talked fondly about Celtic, and mentioned the match against Sporting Lisbon, but I'm not sure if he really remembered it as well as I did. It was just another game for George and he'd have been to many before that one and even more since.

My father loved to see George.

He loved to hear him talking about Celtic and Quins and the Brothers Bar in Possil and their good friend Michael, who'd died some while back. Michael was a kind and gentle man. And my father enjoyed his company more than most. He had a staunch decency about him and my father developed a protective instinct for the older man. But he admired Michael for more than Ireland. He just admired his goodness. A man who walked with his head up.

It was hard listening to my father trying to speak but George said, not to worry, John, that we should let him do the talking and he always had stuff to tell. He talked about Ireland. It might have been Arranmore, or Gweedore, I can't remember. Someone had a place there. It might have been Michael, before he died. Or George himself. Or Charlie, or wee Frank Cairey. It happened that way. The stories got muddled. But they were part of everyone, they *belonged* to everyone, so it didn't matter. That's what happened with Irish stories.

My father had been to Arranmore and Gweedore, a long time ago, and spoke about it often before his voice was stolen away.

George was getting older too and things were changing in everyone's lives. It never seemed to any of them at the time, when they were younger and drinking Guinness in Quins, that they would end up here. As old men. It simply never struck any of them that it would happen. The surgeon had cut out the malignant part of my father's skull, and part of everyone else seemed to go with it.

My father tried to speak again. But the words remained hammered tight inside him, like a nail in a tree. George just rubbed his hands together and told more stories. My father smiled. A lopsided beauty to it.

A short while later George finished his tea and got up to leave. I laughed a little to myself. It was the first time in my life I'd ever seen my father and George sitting together, in a living room with the curtains pulled tight, sharing tea and biscuits. They'd have hunted you down with a bow and arrow if you'd suggested that in the past.

'Thanks, George,' said my mother. 'See you later.'

'Bye, Cathie. Bye, John. Bye now. See you later, John.'

My father tried to wave but couldn't.

EastEnders was on the television and my father stared at the screen, watching intently. I thought my head might explode. It was never supposed to end up like this. I went up the stairs to the loft and found the air rifle. I loaded it up with pellets and came down the stairs and my father looked at me as I raised the rifle and I started shooting at the screen. It exploded before our eyes.

I didn't really.

But I wanted to.

It was good to see George. But it opened up too many old memories. It had already been some time since any of us had really mentioned Ireland. There were so many occasions when I sat with my father listening to stories about the time they went out in a boat to Burtonport. They spoke about Leabgarrow and the old middens along the beach and the spot that men used to look out for U-boats in the Second World War. I missed them talking about the villages of Fallagowan and Pollawaddy and Plohogue. Maybe he just dreamed it? Maybe I did too.

It was different now.

Talking about Ireland without my father made no sense. And a lot of things had simply vanished from our everyday conversation. I was glad that they had. My father was almost dead. And all the heroes in Ireland couldn't save him. Not now, and not then.

He was falling asleep in the chair. Slowly, I believed, my father also had resigned from all his battles. The news barely moved him.

It was funny. The thing that kept him wicked now was football. It stoked the fires of the past. But there was a glint of excitement in his eye, not anger. He always found the strength to wave a finger at the television screen. It was always football. It was always Celtic.

It was even Rangers.

He laughed loudly if Celtic beat them. I mean he *laughed*.

I could hear him too.

Eedjits . . .

Chapter Twelve

One More Time For the Road

However implausible it seemed, I liked to believe that my father's stroke changed the rocky path of history and guided Celtic towards retaining the League title in the 2001–2002 season, for the first time since 1982. Not only did they retain the title but Martin O'Neill, Celtic's manager, led the team to their first domestic treble that season, the first since 1968.

'Celtic cruised it, Dad,' I told him. 'Must have been down to your stroke. You know what they say. One single occurrence can change the course of history for ever. A butterfly's wings can cause a tornado and all that malarkey.'

Of course it was . . . If I hadn't had that stroke, well, who knows what would have happened to their season.

'Anything for Celtic, eh?'

Happy to take some of the credit for sure!

I also liked to believe we laughed together. But he just sat there unmoving. The room was dim as an aquarium. I talked to myself again for a little longer and the warm afternoon disappeared as easily as cheap ice cream in my hand. The foreboding remained. I guessed it always would.

Back then O'Neill allowed us a brief respite from my father's illness. The green half of the city surged. You could feel it, pulsing against the sky. My uncles, friends and brothers were ecstatic too. Even my mother, who could only ever listen to matches on the radio, never watching them on television, kept saying, 'Brilliant!

Brilliant! He's really good that Martin O'Neill, isn't he? Your dad would love it!' It was good to hear her laugh at ordinary things. She was still as adrift as my father.

O'Neill, whose love of Celtic had been ingrained in him by his father, a barber from Kilrea, County Derry, had watched Celtic unfolding from a distance and then revived the club's fortunes close at hand. Barnes and Dalglish were long gone. By 2003 O'Neill had become the greatest thing at Celtic since Jock Stein. Beating Rangers became almost monotonous. The difference was that O'Neill was of *my* generation and not part of folklore and fairy tales and black and white images. He was the man Celtic had been waiting for for nearly forty years.

O'Neill brought inventiveness and improvisation. His arrival transformed the fortunes of the club. Celtic took the entire 1990s to win the three trophies and O'Neill, with his quiet, professorial demeanour, delivered them in his first twelve months as manager. Celtic fans grew fat on success. They wanted more. So he gave them Seville.

Now was our time. No more would we subsist on hand-me-down memories. Celtic were playing in the UEFA Cup Final against Porto after an astonishing run of results had got them to within touching distance of their first European trophy in four decades. It was Celtic's first European final since 1970.

It was the Liverpool game that really did it for us. We instinctively knew something amazing was happening. We all did. Even the Rangers fans knew. It was the quarter-final at Anfield. It was March 2003. My father was home. But we couldn't watch it together. My mother wouldn't let us. She shooed me away and said that the shouting and screaming at the television would kill him, never mind his stroke.

'But he'd want to watch it,' I pleaded.

'You'll kill the poor man with all that noise,' she said. 'You know what you're like. He's not well enough for that yet.'

My father stared straight ahead. Maybe she was right.

I went round the corner to my brother-in-law Mark's house.

Mark was on the phone to his mother, Sandra. She'd been going to Celtic matches since 1977 after Mary, her next-door neighbour, bought her a ticket for her birthday. The doctor had advised Sandra to take up a hobby after she'd been diagnosed with arthritis. She was hooked. She was also very superstitious when going to matches. Always had to be the last one out of the gate at her house. The bus always had to park in the same place at Parkhead Cross. And she always needed to find a coin. So she'd go around looking for coins to ensure a Celtic victory.

Mary had been going to the games since she was twelve, on the Holytown supporters' bus. She took a holy statue to the games. Sandra and Mary said Rosaries together. She said she'd take her zimmer-frame to Parkhead too if she had to.

'Did you find the coin?' said Mark.

'Yes, son. I've got it here.'

'Magic, Mum. See you later.'

Liverpool were favourites to go through after a 1–1 draw at Celtic Park. The match was memorable only for El Hadji Diouf spitting at the Celtic fans.

Now it was the away leg. Celtic needed to go on the attack.

Mark and I just stared at the screen. Praying.

Alistair, the next-door neighbour, was a good-natured Rangers fan. He had a Rangers flag and Union Jack in his shed. Fraser, his son, hid Rangers flags in Mark's garden when he was out at work. We could hear Alistair howling in his own lounge every time Liverpool went close. When Alan Thompson scored Celtic's first from his perfect daisy-cutter free kick on the stroke of half-time, Mark and I banged on the wall and Alistair went as silent as an old man having his neck shaved.

The wall shook. 'Are you watching, Alistair? Ha, ha! Come on, Ally, give us a wee Rangers song!'

Celtic pressed and pressed. Liverpool had sat back, content that a 0–0 draw would have been enough to see them through. But they hadn't planned on Big John. Big Bad John.

John Hartson took his football seriously. But sometimes he

looked like a wagon-train cook in a spaghetti western. He couldn't help it. He was big-boned. He had a backside like a fridge. But when the ball came to him, from a Larsson one-two, he looked like he had angel wings as he dropped the shoulder away from Jamie Carragher and let fly from twenty-five yards. The ball settled in the top right-hand corner. Curtains for Liverpool.

The wall got thumped again.

'Alistair! Alistair!' shouted Mark. 'Come in and see the champions play football! Come on, big man. In you come for a wee party.'

Silence.

Fraser planted another wee Union Jack in Mark's garden the next day.

As well as Liverpool, along the way Celtic had beaten Blackburn Rovers, Celta Vigo, Stuttgart and, in the semi-finals, Boavista. The names of the vanquished floated in memory now. We had discovered thirty-three new ways of winning. A whole new world was unfolding.

It was Brian's idea to make the trip.

We hadn't been away together since America and Australia over twenty years earlier, but we'd seen each other virtually every week since.

He still lived in Bishopbriggs too, initially in a house only four doors from mine, with his wife and children. Then they moved next door to our old school. Brian had never really moved away from Bishopbriggs although we'd spent a year sharing my grandmother's house in Ruchill after she died, living off toast and beans and Monster Munch from the ice-cream van. I cooked badly and cleaned reasonably and he made sure there was enough beer in the house while we watched repeats of *Dallas* in the afternoon. Somehow, someone at the university saw fit to hand us our degrees.

I called up my mother. 'Have you seen my scarf?'

'What one?'

'My old Celtic one. The one Dad got me years and years ago. The one with the cloth badges sewn on. Remember? Tell me you remember, Mum.'

I knew my scarf so well.

It had a Celtic FC Supporters' Club badge, a Celtic FC badge, with a green shamrock, Celtic FC in the shape of an arrow, and two conjoined circles with Celtic and The Bhoys on them. I had sewn all of them on myself when I was about nine or ten. I'd sat down with a needle and thread and the patches looked like someone wearing boxing gloves had stitched them.

The scarf had *power*. It was like a rare insect tacked through the thorax to a board.

'I haven't seen it. Sorry, pet.'

'I'll pop round and have a look.'

Three hours later I found it in the loft, hidden in a box we had set aside after freeing the space of my father's stuff. It was a little dusty and smelly and the wool had seen better days. But it was mine. My Celtic scarf from childhood.

I hadn't worn it in years. It was too short to wear to everyday matches without looking self-consciously like an overgrown nine-year-old boy, but I just wanted it with me and then I could pass it on to the children. Totems everywhere. The scarf was part of something. A speck from my father's past.

'I'll call you when I'm there, Dad.'

He sat erratically in his chair in the living room. Some people called it the lounge. But the living room seemed more apt. His feet were crossed at the ankles. He smiled but it was barely there.

'Take it easy, Dad. Relax.' I kissed his forehead.

'Can you cut his hair when you're back?' said my mother.

'Of course.'

By the time Brian and I arrived in Seville there were thousands of fans milling around the streets and in and out of pubs. There were slick-haired men with bellies that promised short lives and youths with dapper haircuts and others with faces that looked damaged by more than just genetics. Scars ran deep in pink, Glaswegian flesh. A group of three girls had smiles that could light a bonfire.

Drink was in abundance.

The *supermercados* had been emptied of anything liquid that looked or smelled like alcohol.

'Jesus,' said Brian. 'This is mental.'

There were Celtic fans of every hue. There were bankers and milkmen and lawyers and bricklayers and postmen and surgeons and a motley collection of boys from the schemes, all congregated together. There was an Irish mother from Kilkenny alongside old barflies with slack, ropy skin. There were women in green bras, and vendors selling scarves and Celtic buttons, reminders to everyone that they were there. Not that you could forget. Sing-song faces with sing-song voices. Old women carried sandwiches in plastic Co-op bags. The hubbub rose. Everything swirled. It was Sauchiehall Street in the sunshine.

'Buckfast is fine, we prefer Spanish wine . . .' they sang to the tune of 'That's *Amore*' by Dean Martin. The melodic line travelled like a plague. Everyone joined in. By God they were murdering his song. The number of pubs was equalled only by the number of stories spilling out of mouths about how they'd got here. How they left their wives behind. How they spent all their life savings. How they sold their wife's jewellery and the daughter's second-hand car. How they brought fathers too old and too frail to ever see another match like it.

'My dad would have *loved* this,' said Brian.

'Ach, mine too. Unbelievable.'

Brian's father had died of cancer a few years earlier. I'd been away in France when I found out and I couldn't get back to Bishopbriggs for the funeral. It had always bothered me. We spoke on the phone, when everyone had gone to celebrate his life in Cawder golf club. It couldn't have been easy. His father was a good man and the cancer hurt his body till the end.

'It was a great turnout,' said Brian. 'Amazing.'

'I heard it was incredible.'

We'd chatted briefly and then he went back to the wake. I couldn't remember the last time I'd seen Brian's father but whenever it was he'd have been smiling. You couldn't get the smile off the man's face.

Brian and I stood in a bar and listened to the stories. Celtic stories.

These were the people my father had spoken about for so many years. They were his people, but they were not just from Ireland. They were from Scotland and America and England and Australia and Africa and Azerbaijan and China and Japan too. There was even a van filled with fans who had driven from Barra and we talked to them about my grandmother and my grandfather and Eoligarry and Our Lady Star of the Sea and the race up and down Ben Heaval and the Castlebay Hotel from where my father and my uncle Roddy would fall out drunk and roll all the way home past Garrygall.

Roddy swore he'd seen a ghost and my father blessed himself and said he'd seen it too. And the two men said they'd better have another drink, just to calm their nerves, you understand.

There were Catholics and Protestants in the Seville crowd. There was dark skin and light. There was young and old. I knew one Celtic fan, a regular attender in the Church of Scotland, who knew where and when he'd been for the past thirty years by his proximity to Celtic Park or whatever away match he happened to be attending. He was there, grinning like an old cat. Happy. Smiling.

The stories were a lot like my father's stories. Half-truths and easy myths. The stories were made for easy listening, and were turned on and off like cheap electric light in the Chapel of St Mungo. Were they true? I had no idea. But I listened anyway. The first bar sagged with the stale smell of sweating bodies, almond milk and old laundry. A yellow canary was perched above the dark-oak panelling beside an even darker gilt mirror. On a wall the horn of a champion bull. A collection of old photographs of fishermen, touched so often their edges had curled. I kept similar ones in my pocket. But none of them had fishermen on them. Just a tall man with an open-necked shirt.

Every corner of the bar was crammed full. Thick-shouldered men, with hands more used to sausage rolls at Henry Healy's in Trongate, dipped into tapas with a little fear.

'Jesus, man, what's that?' said one.

'Octopus or something . . .'

'Och, you're joking. How am I supposed to eat that?'

'One tentacle at a time . . .'

Outside, masses of wide-eyed Celtic foreigners, white as bed-sheets, had invaded Seville. Pasty faces the colour of week-old newspapers, alongside sparkling faces the colour of red lobster. The lure of the Andalusian sun after another spiteful Scottish winter had taken its toll. In ancient jerseys and new ones, as clean and fresh as new tennis balls, they were the Scots conquistadores.

Seville was draped in green, white and gold. A young woman wore a T-shirt that said, '¡No Hay Huns En Europa!'

I called home.

'Hello, Mum. All fine? Good. Crazy here. Brilliant though. If you put the phone up to Dad's ear I'll have a wee chat with him. Yes, I'm on the mobile. Don't worry about the cost. The phone belongs to the work. Don't rush.' The heat stung my eyes.

'I can hardly hear you, Michael,' she shouted. 'It's so noisy. I've seen some of it on the television. Be careful. I'll put Dad on.'

My mother shuffled him in his chair and told my father I was in Seville for the match and that if he sat up OK she would get him the phone. She put the phone to his ear. He dropped it and then she helped him again. I could picture his hands contorting, like a Chinese burn. 'Careful, John, that's it.' A few minutes later and he was trying to speak.

'Hello, Dad. Can you hear me OK?'

'Mmm nnn.'

'Good, Dad. Brilliant over here. There's thousands of fans. Thousands. I've met a few of the boys from Quins. A few boys from the town. You'd love it here, Dad. There's Paddies everywhere too!'

'Dddnnn aaahh.'

'It's OK. I know what you mean. Don't worry. It's fine, Dad. Watch the game with Mum. Have a wee beer. I left a couple in the fridge. I'll ask Mum if it's OK. Never mind the doctor, eh? Just the one for the match. A wee can of Guinness.'

'Sssaa nnn. Ggeerrrnnn.'

'I know, Dad. I know. It's murder, I know. Let me speak. Let me do the talking. I wish you could have been here. And the boys too. And the girls as well. And Mum. All of us! It would have been brilliant. You'd love it. Next time, Dad. We'll get in the Champions League next year, eh?'

'Sssaaann Gghhh . . .'

'Don't worry, Dad. Don't worry. I know what you're saying. We'll get to a match one of these days. Don't worry. OK? Now I'd better go. I'll call you later. Make sure Mum's got the right channel on, OK? Talk in a bit. I'll tell Mum to give you a beer.'

My mother took the phone and my father slid back into the arms of his chair. A dead man falling. Even though he could not talk, he still had the whole world in his head. All of it. His family and friends and his childhood too. His mother and father and all his winters and summers. Celtic and Ireland and his motorcycle and the trips to Crinan with my mother. It mattered, of course, that he couldn't speak. But it didn't. He still had his bank of memories. They were still there, locked in the trunk of his past.

My mother took the phone. 'Och, that was great. He's smiling. Poor Dad. Enjoy the match!'

'Give him a wee drink, Mum. I left a couple of Guinness in the fridge.'

'Of course. Come on the Celts!'

'Call you later, Mum. Bye now.'

She'd be drinking tea now, and he'd have a half-glass of Guinness. He would never finish it. He couldn't. But it still tasted good: that creamy top hat and then the dark fleshy and bubbly blackness below.

The assembled crowd had swollen to around 80,000 souls, a migration of kilted and tricolour-waving revolutionaries. A few rival fans shook hands with us and swapped shirts and scarves. Every bar stool and hotel room had been snatched up and slowly this ancient, beautiful city had been turned into a suburb of Glasgow. Bishopbriggs and Cranhill, and the Gorbals, and the Wine Alley and Jordanhill and Shawlands and the Port and Robroyston.

Even the stone statues wore green Afro wigs.

At the Plaza del Salvador fans were multiplying by the minute and thrashed around in the nearby fountain, as if they were children stumbling through tall, uncut grass. At the cathedral wide-eyed, green-shirted urchins blessed themselves. The cathedral was so perfect that you imagined, momentarily, that it might not be such a sin to live there amongst all that incense and beauty. There were a few fans on their knees, genuflecting beneath its stone magnificence. It was something they had always done beside a church. But none of them prayed for recovery from sickness or to heal or build a safer community. They all just prayed for a win.

I prayed too.

God would have forgiven us. Everyone knew that He supported Celtic.

We bumped into this one and that.

Friends. Friends of friends. Cousins. Neighbours. Two Glasgow grannies. Black suits and Roman collars too. Over there an African face. A man waded slowly. Just like my father. Another man whose sons had bought him his ticket to see his beloved team in the knowledge that he would shortly die. Small things. He knew it and they knew it. He would die with the memory of the sun on the pitch and his sons' hands across his thin shoulders.

There were fans who'd been there for two, three, maybe four days. In the daytime they'd been drinking in bars and feasting on miscellaneous poultry and garlic sausages while declaring, *The grub isnae really as bad as it looks.* Many had already slept in the rough-hewn stone streets and in railway stations and on the occasional bar-room floor. Others had opted for the air-conditioned cash-dispensing areas of banks. They slept like discarded rubbish bags on the concrete steps of the cathedral. Hardy souls in three-day-old underwear and short-sleeved Celtic away strips. Glasgow, that post-industrial behemoth, would always suffer much stiffer hardships than a football match in the sun. It always had and it always would.

I called Mark in America. The phone rang for an age.

'Hey, how's it going, horse?'

'Fine, horse. Not too bad. All well? You in Seville now? Amazing. I wish I was there.'

'I know. I wish everyone was here. The girls too. I just called Dad.'

'How is he? I need to call him too. Been busy upstate the past few weeks.'

'He's fine. He'd love it here.'

'So would I. Must be amazing.'

'Keeping out of mischief?'

'Not too bad, Mike. Bit of this and that with the fellas. Doing some work for the Italians. Is Dad going to watch it on the telly?'

'Yeah. He'll watch it with Mum. But she hates watching finals. Her nerves can't cope. She'll just keep popping in and out of the kitchen. He'll have a beer.'

'Good stuff. He'll know it's Celtic, won't he?'

'Of course he will. It's *all* there. It's all in there.'

'OK, good. Drop me a line later. Hail, hail.'

'Stay safe . . .'

I went wandering with Brian.

We bumped into his brother Mark. He was with a group, including an old schoolmate of mine called Francis. We'd all been at Turnbull High together. They were a couple of years younger. We took photographs to mark the occasion. We grabbed a slice of the here and now. Francis held his arm aloft. Handsome and blond and staring at the camera, in his Celtic jersey. Frozen for ever. Francis would die aged forty-four. Just a boy, really. We didn't know that then. The photograph held him up a little longer, a little higher. A million dots together that preserved him for his family.

There were hardy souls from the Gallowgate and dinner ladies from Possil with faces like delicately veined hams. We could see it already. Seville was never just a sports story. It was the living history of our team, unfolding before us like it had for our parents in 1967, in the match against Inter in Lisbon. It was the stuff our fathers spoke about while we were growing up and we didn't understand and, sometimes, we never even cared because how could you ever really *know*?

I loved the thrum.

Seville was filled with the people I'd known for years, yet I didn't know them at all. Everyone drank as if prohibition was going to be announced in the morning. And the pale, amber light outside matched the liquid in the glasses. Nearby, a young man pushed a woman in a wheelchair. She was wrapped in a scarf and the people around her parted like the Red Sea.

They'd come by plane, train, bus, boat, scooter and bicycle and on foot. They'd borrowed Council vans – a bottle of whisky and the gaffer turned a blind eye. Say no more. He was a Tim too. It was only for three days, after all. Have it back Friday. They arrived in Transit vans with sofas in the back, pinched from the front rooms of their houses, and the wife was none the wiser because he'd paid for her to go away for a few days with her friends or the mother. They'd driven in a 1967 Volkswagen Beetle called Jinky. They'd told the wife they were off to the pub to watch the match and might be late getting back.

They never told her the pub was in Spain.

Onwards. Onwards.

We headed past Triana, the working-class quarter housing flamenco dancers, bullfighters, gypsies and prostitutes. The stadium was a few miles away and already we could hear the drum of excitement peeling over the rooftops. Distant shouts of Celtic – *Sell-ick* – banged off concrete and roads and glass and mixed with even more singing, while other happy voices writhed around the nearby streets like freshly caught fish. Everything appeared so unreal and unbelievable.

'Remember that time at uni?' I said, as we strolled.

'Haunted by it, mate. Haunted . . .'

We'd known each other since Turnbull High School but it was when we went to university that our friendship was cemented. Together, we turned up a day early for enrollment in our classes and stood in a non-existent queue until the janitor, a man who was stirring a spoon in a plastic cup, informed us that the signing-up stuff wasn't until the following day. We came back together and that was that.

A few days later we were at the Queen Margaret Union, during Freshers' Week, and we were walking back to a flat we were staying in that belonged to a friend. A taxi pulled over and there were four girls inside, about our age, slightly drunk, and they all looked like they were from the American girl band The Bangles.

'Hiya,' said one of the girls.

'Hi,' we said, in unison.

'We saw you at the QM.'

'Yeah, we were there . . .'

'D'you want to come to a party with us? Jump in, there's loads of room.'

We looked at each other. I remember a kind of Amish silence descending on Brian. For nearly thirty years I've run that question over in my head.

'Nah . . .' said Brian. 'It's OK, we're just having an early night.'

Brian had been the goalkeeper in our school team. He'd started out playing right-back but was quickly moved to playing in goal. When Brian queried this with the manager, he nodded sagely for a minute or two before explaining how deceptive Brian appeared in the outfield. He was a lot *slower* than he looked.

The taxi sped off.

I looked at him and shook my head.

'What the hell did you say that for?' I said, stunned.

'It was you,' said Brian, lying through his teeth. 'You made me . . .'

'What? *Unbelievable* . . .'

If Brian had sat down, chewed some straw and plucked 'Foggy Mountain Breakdown' on a long-necked banjo I wouldn't have batted a single eyelid.

I heard my voice again as we walked through Triana and to the stadium.

'Unbelievable . . .'

After another hour we headed across a narrow road, past windows

295

with wedding pictures and photos of someone's grandchildren. How easily we passed through other people's lives. We continued walking. Past women snapping peas in the doorway of their homes, past men eating steaming plates of paella in quiet street cafés. Children with dried flowers in their hair nodded in our direction and we nodded back, and waved. The air was filled with sweet herbs. Someone was frying vegetables in oil.

'When was the last time we were away?' I said.

'Must have been Australia.'

'Where the hell has it all *gone*? I mean, what happens to it all? Does it all just float away somewhere? A billion billion memories since time began . . .'

In Santa Something-or-other, stuffed with white-washed walls and narrow streets, a few more recognizable faces emerged from the crowd. People I'd known in the past and people who'd known me through my family but I'd forgotten their names. Over there was Paul Duffy. A hug and a laugh. He'd been like a wee brother to me for years. Handsome and dark, like his father. Later, Paul would die young too, just like his father. It was heartbreaking. Utterly heartbreaking.

There were more faces from Quins. Hellos and how's it goings exchanged like birthday cards. A friend of my father's was there. He asked after him and said he would visit one day, but people always said these things out of politeness, or embarrassment. We all did.

I watched people hug each other, some of them obviously strangers, but they just clicked through the colour of their jerseys. See you there, big man. No problem. *No problemo.* 'For it's a grand old team to play for . . .' Someone said out loud that they just didn't know it was possible to feel this good.

'I'm telling you he would have loved this,' said Brian, of his father.

'I know. I know.'

'My father always said to me, "You'll always find your level, son." He was right. You find the thing that works for you.'

'I know what you mean.'

The cancer had been bad, he said. Horrible to watch. Brian

quickened his step to the stadium. We had a purpose now. We talked about our fathers and all the games we'd missed together. Nature never gave a reason. Neither did fathers, to be honest, when you thought about it. They didn't tell you things. They gave you some clues to a bigger puzzle. You just had to figure it all out most of the time.

We walked faster and faster.

My father had always liked Brian but he'd never have said it out loud. That wasn't his style. But now I remembered that time he'd told me in his own way. My mother's sister Elizabeth Anne had come over from Australia to visit. Brian's parents asked her to theirs for dinner, along with my parents. Brian was there. I was away somewhere with the newspaper.

My father and Brian's father never knew each other that well. Brian's father played golf and my father wouldn't be seen dead at a golf club. I think it was the clothes that worried him most. He didn't understand leisurewear. The two men talked occasionally in Quins if Brian's father was in for a pint, or they chatted after Mass or at school football matches. But it would have been small talk.

That night the two older men shared a few whiskies and beers while the women enjoyed their meal and talked about their children and their husbands and their worries. My father left, as quietly as he'd arrived, thanking everyone, and shook Brian Junior by the hand, telling him that he was welcome to our house any time. A few weeks later, when I was home, my father said that he'd enjoyed the night over at Brian's parents' and that Brian had seen him and my mother to their car. His old yellow van had also gone by now. The girls had bought him a car.

'You know what?' said my father. His voice was quiet.

'What?'

'Young Brian . . . he's got some head of hair.'

'What?'

'He's got some hair. Jet-black. I used to have black hair like that, but not quite as black. His is black as black.'

That was all he said. It sounded like a poem.

I think it was one of the greatest compliments he'd ever given another man in his life. It was more than that too. It was about acceptance.

A passing Spanish brewery lorry filled with barrels of beer was greeted by half a dozen fans throwing themselves on their knees, praying as though still at the cathedral. In a city of strict religious observance it gave new meaning to blasphemy. But nobody seemed to care. Nearby, a nun read a book in the shade of a tree. I'm sure that she was laughing. We heard again the crescendo chords of *Celtic, Celtic* spilling from an army of mouths. *Hail, Hail.* Every song bellowed excitement. Thousands of feet ambled this way and that, back and forth, as we turned up a side street past a small marching band of fans in campaign hats. *Trrritt, ttrriittt.* Someone struck up a snare drum, and then a penny whistle, as little flags flew from the bumpers of old taxis.

¡Verdiblanco! shouted the locals. Green and white.

A thousand voices sang 'The Fields of Athenry' . . .

I joined in too, more self-consciously than ever before. We sang about prison walls and a girl calling and how Michael was taken away for stealing corn from Trevelyan. We sang about the prison ship and how we all once watched a free bird fly . . .

I wanted all the good to come out of the song. And a bit of the sadness too. I could hear my father in his chair, singing it, tapping his fingers and feet and spinning his glass of whisky. He'd have been warm as a scone and happy too. It had been a while since I'd belted out that song. It was a folk ballad, by Dubliner Pete St John, set during the Irish Famine.

You mean the Irish Starvation?

Sorry, Dad. I forgot.

The fictional Michael of the song was sentenced to transportation to Botany Bay, in Australia, for stealing food for his family. It was also the unofficial anthem of Celtic. My father always played the version recorded by The Dubliners while delighting in the fact that St John was also once an electrician, like himself.

Some collapsed around us, with the drink and the sun, exhausted and overcome with, well, everything. The boys were on the lash now. They wore green sashes and an array of uniforms, old and new, and I thought of Halloween and the time we'd been together in New York for St Patrick's Day. Even in Glasgow my father always wore something green on St Patrick's Day and we'd send him cards. My grandmother Jane always had a row of them at home. Usually from my father, and Francis, and her sister-in-law, Lena.

It was St Patrick's Day in New York. The Puerto Ricans and the Brazilians and the Jews and the Mennonites and the blacks and the Chinese were all Irish too that day. A woman was selling words in the bar, a handful of Irish-themed badges of every conceivable size: 'Luck o' the Irish' and '100% Irish' and 'Proud to be Irish'.

My father eyed her suspiciously. 'She's a plant.'

'What *are* you talking about?'

'A plant. A spook. *A spy.* Planted in here by the CIA to see who's buying what . . .'

'To see who's buying? Away and don't be daft. Just buy a badge.'

He shook his head. 'I'm telling you, that woman's a spy as sure as the day is long.'

Iain bought one. My father, somewhat reluctantly, picked the smallest badge there. The others were large and extra-large. Then he pinned it on, mumbling to himself. Then he took it off quickly.

'That's it. No chance. No way. You see all those other badges? Big ones. How come she's only got one wee one? And she's sold *me* that one? Practically pinned it on me. Why that one? I'll leave here and the flippin' snipers on the roof will get me. "Get the guy with the wee badge. Roger that." Boom. I'm a dead man. No way. No chance . . .'

A momentary silence. He mumbled into his pint, 'I'm serious.'

The table collapsed with laughter.

In their green garb and dress-up clothes the fans in Seville were his people too. The anointed ones. He always said that Celtic were never about the players. Players came and went as sure as day followed night. Celtic were Granny Tierney, Granny Quinn, Uncle Peter, the men on their knees outside the cathedral, the women with the plastic Co-op bags, Auntie Lena and her harp, and his father with his AoH membership card going off to do battle against the Germans. They were all there. The streets of Glasgow were empty again, just like my father said they were in '67.

We stopped at a bar next to a shop selling religious souvenirs and plaster statues and holy medals. It was closing down. Drink and devotion in such close proximity and it felt like home now. A Sunday drink after Mass and then watch the football. There was the sameness everywhere of small things. Finish up now. Keep going. We were almost touching the stadium.

I called home again. The lament of the ringtone.

'Yes, he's having a wee drink,' said my mother. 'Are you at the ground? What time is it?'

'Nearly time for the match to kick-off, Mum.'

'What's the weather like?'

'Goodness sake, Mum,' I said, laughing. 'I'm not on my holidays!'

'Och, see you . . . Dad's getting tired already, but we'll see how he goes. The carers will be in soon.'

'OK, Mum. Enjoy it. See you soon.'

I daydreamed them together, my mother talking to him, asking if he needed anything. My father gently nodding. A single piece of flint held no spark, but hit two together and they could start a thunderous fire.

We marched on. Life could be brutal.

Then we arrived and were soon *inside* the stadium. You could see the green-coloured sawdust that had been sprinkled across the pitch to hide the dry, scorched areas of the grass. I look around. Brian looked around. And we both started to laugh.

'Holy shit, Briany-boy.'

'This is just . . .' He shook his head.

'You'll Never Walk Alone' rang out across the stadium, the noise like thunder. No one ever sang this song better than Celtic fans. Not the massed chorus of Liverpool supporters, not Gerry and the Pacemakers, not Doris Day, not Frank Sinatra and the cast from the 1945 Rodgers and Hammerstein musical *Carousel*, where the song, my wife once told me, was first heard. Not even Frank the Kitchen from down the road.

The crowd, the incessant noise, the rumble, the changing shape of people, the rhythmic clapping, the songs, the fear, the whirling and singing, and the shoulder-to-shoulder intimacy. It was all there. All of *it*. This was *Celtic*. In Europe, where they belonged. We were inside the cauldron of the Estadio Olímpico, on an island in the Guadalquivir River. An Andalusian Celtic Park.

Did the result matter? I suppose it did. But no, not really.

Derlei put Porto ahead in stoppage time at the end of the first half. Brian's voice was nearly hoarse from shouting. 'I knew we did the right thing. I *knew* it,' he said. I held on to his shoulder, while shouting at something on the pitch. 'I know, *I know*.' The second half was all about Larsson. I watched him as he rose to equalize, moving gracefully and as beautifully as Victorian handwriting. How did he score that? We rubbed each other's heads. 'You wee dancer!' We rubbed the heads of strangers. Delirium set in. Larsson had jumped with an unknown energy and the stadium, most of it, jumped with him. Men to the left and right, women to the left and right, they were all jumping. We were all jumping. The fans pushed Celtic forwards. We pushed Celtic forwards.

Alenichev! Porto again. Two–one.

Larsson! Celtic again. Two–two.

The utterly improbable nature of Larsson. 'You are my Larsson, my Henrik Larsson, you make me happy, when skies are grey . . .' The stadium sang his song. Larsson was a nudge footballer. When he did something amazing we all nudged the guy standing beside us and said, 'Did you see that?'

Full time.

Extra time.

Thirty-five thousand Celtic fans inside the ground singing with such assuredness it gave us delusions of immortality. There was an eerie green light hovering in and above the stadium. Surely God was on our side. Of course He was. He must be. Surely God was a Tim.

That's what our fathers had told us for years. Maybe *their* fathers told them that too . . .

We'd been called Fenians and Taigs and Paddies and Tinkers and bead-rattlers for years. And all the while we'd gone to Mass on Sunday and on Holy Days of Obligation too. Surely God was a Tim? All around us fans had been blessing themselves. If God wasn't a Celtic fan then there needed to be some kind of inquiry . . .

We'd come back twice. *Twice*. In a European final. It would be all right. Everything would be fine. We held our hands in the attitude of prayer. We prayed out loud.

Hail Mary full of Grace . . .

Our Father who art in Heaven . . .

Glory be to the Father and to the Son . . .

St Michael, the Archangel, defend us in Battle . . .

Grace Before Meals . . .

Grace After Meals . . .

An Act of Contrition . . .

Would you just Shoot . . .

We prayed to God that Celtic could score *one more goal*. I looked around and saw thousands praying with me. Praying with us. It wasn't that much to ask of a benevolent deity, surely?

Christ has Died, Christ has Risen . . .

What the . . . ?

Shit! Shit! *Shit!*

Come off it . . .

For the Love of God, who let the prince of bloody poachers in? Derlei again. It was 3–2. It was gruelling, draining and debilitating. The gnashing of teeth. The scalding of a cartoon cat. It wasn't supposed to end like this. Larsson had scored two and Porto got three, and if you thought that was fair you were just plain dumb as a toothbrush. Two men beside me were crying. My throat had a childish lump in it. The show, and it was a show, was over. The steam of a Sevillian night covered us. We shuffled away, like an old man off to bed.

*

Brian was silent in the taxi from the airport to Bishopbriggs. I was too. We could barely breathe. The driver was laughing. 'Better luck next time, lads . . .' Definitely a Hun, said Brian. We paid our fare in our leftover euros. Who was laughing now? 'Change them at the bank, big man,' said Brian, with a wink. 'They'll give you the Queen's rightful currency!'

'Fly bastards.' He tossed the money into his cab.

We bought two rolls and sausage and a newspaper each. I'd never known anyone in Glasgow to buy a roll and sausage without buying a paper, even if they had no intention of reading it. The paper merely confirmed the result from the night before. Bin that. We sat for a short while, at the end of my street on a neighbour's wall. Christ, that was good. Despite the loss it was good. We chatted for a while longer, reluctant to let it all go. And then we parted. Brian walked the rest of the way home to see Babs, his wife. Her family were Rangers supporters. Andy, her father, would have been laughing with the rest of the handshake mob down the road . . .

'The worst bit is that he'll pretend he cares.'

'I know . . .'

'He'll say we were unlucky.'

'Better than watching *Coronation Street* like his lot . . .'

A short time later, I was lying in my bed at home. Brian had just called. He was in the park with his children. We still couldn't believe we'd been at a European final. I closed my eyes to sleep. It was raining outside. Best place for it, my father used to say. I laughed to myself.

I was dreaming that I was in heaven and it was warm and smelled of olive oil and lemon and beer and octopus. And Derlei, the prince of Porto poachers, was placing a winner's medal around my neck. It was a stupid dream. But I was happy.

My Celtic jersey hung in the wardrobe. I'd bought it for that match only and I would never wear it again. My children might, you never knew. It smelled of clams and parsley and smoky bits of pig cheek from Seville. But the team came from the east end of Glasgow.

*

303

It was May, the following year.

I was at my parents' house, watching Celtic against Rangers, and the match was heading to a draw as the Ibrox side held on against an incredible Celtic onslaught. Celtic had had the ball in the net after only three minutes but the referee said it was a foul by Henrik Larsson and my father, despite his immobility, was nearly out of his seat. He filled his lungs. His chest rose and dropped.

Celtic had already beaten them five times in succession but a sixth win looked impossible. That was until Chris Sutton latched on to a long clearance by Celtic keeper David Marshall and then collected the return from Larsson before beating Stefan Klos, in goal at the other end, with a magnificent surgical chip, sending the home support wild. Celtic had completed a whitewash of their rivals for the first time in over thirty years.

The Rangers fans despaired. Some looked like they were chewing Styrofoam. My father waved one shaking hand at the television, his eyes as big as teacups. He finished his glass of Guinness and soon fell asleep. The phone rang not long after and he woke up. It was Mark calling from New York. My mother held the phone to my father's ear and we could hear Mark chattering down the line. He was in a bar in Yonkers. My father just nodded, bony-shouldered, and smiled as Mark talked.

Mark must have asked who scored and my father, in as clear a voice as he'd spoken in twenty years, replied, 'Su-tt-on. Sutton.'

And we all jumped up. *What? What!*

'Say it again, Dad! Who scored? Who scored? Come on! One more time for the road!'

He smiled. But that was all he had in him.

Although he tried we'd never really hear him saying anything as clearly as that again. Mark would call in the hope of getting my father to respond to his voice, but it was gone. The wind had carried it away to rove elsewhere. Lorraine and Maureen coaxed him too, confident that there was still the potential for words deep inside him. They called from Abu Dhabi, and Vincent called from Kuwait. Iain called from Bangor, in Northern Ireland, and we kept talking from the hallway and the kitchen and the living room, but it didn't make much of a dent.

'One more time for the road!'

By God, I'm trying.

In 2008, long after Henrik Larsson had left Celtic, I went to his house on the outskirts of the prosperous and pretty ferry port of Helsingborg in Sweden.

Larsson had arrived at the club in 1997, and no one then could have predicted the impact the player would go on to have, not least given his debut against Hibernian when he gave the ball away, almost mindlessly, to Chic Charnley who proceeded to score and give the Edinburgh side a 2–1 victory. It was, perhaps, the most misleading debut in Scottish football. For the following seven years, Larsson grew to be as ruthless for Celtic as a switchblade and a bat down a Glasgow alley. Defenders hated coming up against him, playing, sometimes, as if they were appearing in a town hall panto. During this time he consolidated his reputation as the greatest Celtic striker of the modern era.

Despite scoring those two faultless headed goals in a world-class performance, Seville hurt him. He never watched the game again, he said, in a voice that was immediate with regret. His memories of it were too tortured.

'I don't want to,' he said. 'There's no point, we lost the game. I know where we might have won it.'

'Where?'

'I can't tell you . . .'

'Tell me.'

'It doesn't matter. It doesn't matter. It's history.' He waved the questions away. Neither did he ever look at his medal.

'You don't score two goals in a European final and lose, you know. Do you?' He left the question hanging momentarily in the air. 'To be honest, after that game I was distraught. Totally. I didn't want to do anything. It was one of my best performances in a Celtic jersey. Unfortunately, you don't get anything for that. Yes, you score two goals, but you don't get anything. I still wake up sometimes and think about it, about trying to win the game. It's still in my head to win it.'

I spent a few hours with Larsson. We played a little keepy-uppy out the back, before he drove me around his town and then to the train station. Football was always really just a hobby to Larsson, ever since the long days he'd spent playing on the large field below the apartment he grew up in, until his mother, Eva, called him in at dinner time. It was the same with Celtic. The hobby was just more serious. He was still just a boy. As a youngster he stretched his arms out wide and found that his reach was longer than he'd ever imagined. Such a beautiful hobby, such a beautiful game.

But life was funny. My father was desperate to talk. Larsson was desperate not to. At least not about *that*.

Chapter Thirteen

The Fields

My grandfather had been dead and buried in a country of strangers for more than fifty years, having lived only thirty years in the place he'd known as home. I wondered sometimes if that could ever change a man's nationality, his absolute identity, even as he lay underground.

It was a long time to be buried alongside strangers, so maybe they were not strangers after all. Maybe they'd become friends. Maybe they talked when visiting hours were over and said, man, that was *some* war. Glad it's gone. Even though he was dead maybe my grandfather, somewhere between the dream world and the real world, had learned to speak French too. Actually learned to speak French while he was under the ground. Who knew? Who could ever know?

People believed in ghosts.

They believed in God and angels. They believed that there were a billion planets and that torchlight could travel through a vacuum and that the average left-handed person lived seven years less than the average right-handed person. They believed a donkey would sink in quicksand but a mule couldn't, and that Albert Einstein never wore socks. They also believed that sending men to war was a sure way of stopping other men from going to war. If they believed all that then I believed my grandfather had learned to speak French.

We decided to pay our respects to our French-speaking grandfather. It was impossible, really, to let the dead lie without paying a visit, no matter how many years had passed. You might be dead one day yourself and it was best to lay down the ground rules early.

'We'll hire a car, Dad,' said Vincent. 'No point in taking yours, in case we have trouble with it. It's almost five hundred miles away.'

'That's fine,' said my father, biting his lip.

His questions followed.

Who's going and where are we staying? Did we know how to get there? Did we have a good map because he had a good map? What would we bring? Would we need a change of clothes? Would we need a warm coat? He was smiling, beaming. Shop talk about distances and speed and time to get there and the best place to stop off and have a break. And he'd be fine, he said, sleeping in the car to save money on hotels. No, of course not, we didn't need to sleep in the car. But we would get a map and follow it.

'Aye, of course, no problem.' He sighed, but he was happy. So happy. He was going to his father's new home.

We'd been talking about it for a while, about the boys and girls all going there together one day, like we'd once gone to Barra together, but it was impossible to find a date that suited everyone. I'd talked to Vincent about it and we just agreed we should go, and we arranged the car and told my father and my mother too, and then we said that we'd drive because he just needed to sit back and relax and close his eyes and wake up in the place where his father had died and was buried under the orchard leaves.

But we never mentioned that he'd actually *died*. We didn't say the words out loud. That would have been too much. I believed it was possible to make someone more dead just by saying it out loud.

He cleared his throat.

It was November. It was 1999. It sounded like a year of spaceships and time travel. He went up to the loft to find the letter from the War Graves Commission. 'They keep a list of all the . . .' he said.

My mother smiled in the hallway.

'Your dad would have loved to have known his father,' she said, discreetly. 'He's hardly ever spoken about him throughout our marriage, only said that it wasn't fair on his mother. He spoke about him years ago when we were younger. He'd have liked to have known what kind of man he was. It was hard on your dad not having his father around.' She paused, before whispering, 'He's always wanted to go.'

He rubbed his head and his hair in front of the hall mirror. Then he filled up a small bag, his expression opaque as rolled steel. For all he was the same, he looked different. Nothing obvious. He just sagged less. His clothes bag was practically empty and he was bringing his camera and a large video recorder that looked like it belonged to a television film crew. I'd never seen it before and had no idea where it had come from. It was something else that had found its way into the loft.

The bag and the cameras were in the car.

A few deep breaths.

And then his quiet smile appeared, like it had emerged from the tip of an artist's pencil. He looked content. I hadn't seen that face for a long time. I remembered feeling like that when I was small and we went out together in the van to pick up some wood or went over to the grass football pitches near Paisley.

I often dreamed of my grandfather and how he'd died. I knew from books I'd read years ago and from history lessons at school that the men had died in ditches or in hedgerows or in farm buildings or yards. I couldn't decide if that was in the First World War or the Second. Maybe it was both. I'd just never paid enough attention. In my dreams I always wondered what they thought. The books never told you this. How they *felt* when they were dying. Or who they thought of. Or what the earth looked like. Or if they saw the person who killed them, their actual face and their eyes. Did the person smile and say, I'm sorry. Was the killer old or young? Did he look like their friends? Maybe it was the noise of the guns that got them first. Maybe they were just scared into death.

I know my father wondered about that too.

My daydreams were always simple. An extension of the games we played as children. Of Best Man's Fall, or Japs and Commandos, or Cowboys and Indians. My father said I didn't always need to kill the Indians or the Japs or even the Jerries. They were the underdogs.

They were the same as us. And there were two sides to every story. The bad guys were not always the ones you thought they were.

Sometimes I dreamed that he died by the whip of machine-gun fire or by the twist of a German soldier's knife in close combat. It was gruesome, but I could never un-think it. We used to stand on the low wall of Mr Davidson's garden, with the rest of the children in the street, and I'd imagine my grandfather dying heroically, fighting off a nest of Germans with their sub-machine guns or Lugers and killing every last one of them the way they did in the *Warlord* comic, before a stray bullet caught him, and then his dying comrades held him as he whispered to them to tell Jane and the boys that he was fine. It was a noble death.

That's what people believed we should think. That it was noble.

As I grew older I tried to soften his death. There'd be no more heroic deaths, just quick ones. There'd be no pain. The deceit of death was important. You had to make it less of a real thing. In the new dream, during another attack on the enemy, he simply fell quietly amid the buildings and hills and valleys and sweet orchards of northern France and closed his eyes and then just disappeared into the ground, like spilled water into the earth.

He died at the beginning of August and the sun would have been shining brightly across the fields and the heavy *bocage* and the thunder of tanks and guns would have been frightening, but he'd have been reassured by the presence of his fellow soldiers, perhaps boys and men from Maryhill and Govan and Paisley and Stirling and Cathcart and Aberdeen. And Milton too. They would have been my grandfather's friends and that would have been as good a way to die as any.

They would've all sat around after the killing sharing smokes.

I used to love watching my father smoke. Maybe that was where he'd got his habit. There was a rhythm to it. His strong hands, fixing something while the cigarette – Benson & Hedges – dangled from his dry lips. Then, as the ash was dropping, he flicked it away from his chin, looked up and smiled. And then blew a large plume of blue and grey smoke away. He turned the screwdriver, and then inhaled. He did it again. Exhaled.

Even though the Bible said no to killing, and the Bible meant a lot in our family, and he wouldn't have wanted to kill other men, my grandfather would have had to cast all those words aside for a while. It was other men who stood between him and Jane and his children. There was no choice. Put the Bible in the cupboard and bring it out when things are done. So he would have killed. And maimed. And destroyed. The labourer became the killer. In the tank or with his rifle, it didn't really matter. Death was death and the choices didn't make it any easier. And anyway, he could always go back to his Bible later when it was all over.

The hard part was always imagining my grandfather's face. He was only thirty but I kept seeing an older man, much like my father now. Trying to comprehend that even though he was my grandfather he'd died without ever *being* a grandfather was strange. When he died he was more than a year younger than I was as I made the trip to France.

You could keep people alive in dreams or kill them too.

The dreams were my birthright. I could make them go any which way. I got them instead of a grandfather.

Our street was still. We were leaving early. He kissed my mother tenderly at the door and she patted his back before he slid his long legs into the back seat of the car, a place I had rarely, if ever, seen him sit. But he went in there in good faith and hoped that faith might get him to France.

'Got everything, Dad?' I said.

'Yep, think so.' And then he paused.

And from his voice you could tell he had something else to ask and then he did. 'Should we get . . . uhm, flowers?'

'We can get them when we're there . . .' I looked at Vincent. 'Plenty of time.'

'OK.'

'All set?'

'All set.'

My father had grown more tired recently and the weight was

disappearing from his body. It had left him like a dropped anchor. At first it wasn't too noticeable and then it became enough for us to talk about it quietly amongst ourselves. He would have been in his mid-fifties, and still refusing to visit the doctor. Perhaps the only time he'd actually done so was when his foot had swollen up so much he said he wished he could cut the flippin' thing off just to let the blood drain out. But it was the tiredness we worried about more than anything. It had accelerated from somewhere, the way half-eaten fruit quickly darkens. He might have been slipping away right in front of us for years.

'Sit back, Dad. Relax.'

A few hours into the journey, he awoke.

'Where are we now, boys?'

'Somewhere past Morecambe,' I said.

'Is that where you and Mum went on honeymoon?' asked Vincent, who was driving.

My father smiled. 'No, it was Margate,' he said, 'in Kent.' And there was a touch of embarrassment in his voice. Not at where they went but because he was allowing a little of his personal life to leak out. I closed my eyes and pictured them both, young as flowers and fresh at heart, sharing ice cream and walking along the sandy beaches and past the Victorian pier holding hands.

My father would have had an open-necked shirt and his hair swept back and his wide shoulders and my mother a neat skirt with her slim arms and high cheekbones. She wasn't beautiful because she was my mother, she was beautiful because it was a simple physical fact. In Margate they would have made promises to each other that would last a lifetime and a little longer than that if they could. They sent postcards home to the people they loved. And they dreamed alive each and every one of us.

The car rumbled on.

We stopped briefly at a Little Chef near Birmingham for tea and toast and he took some photographs of us inside the café. Recording everything was essential, he said. It was all passing so quickly. People were knocking things down, building things they shouldn't be building, changing things, mixing things up, wasting good streets and towns and villages for no other reason than to make money for someone else who didn't need it. His photographs were proof. They were evidence. And when it all changed – changed for ever – well, he would show them. They would say, John Tierney's got all the information. He recorded it. He would show them all. Then they would understand why he never wanted to let go.

Before we got to the Channel Tunnel he was speaking of France and its vineyards, and how Francis lived close enough to almost touch its shores and he could drive across for cheap wine. He could have reached those vineyards with a straw. He talked about how he'd learned French in school and how Bayeux had a tapestry that celebrated the conquest of England by William, Duke of Normandy.

Idle chat. Nerves.

The passing years had done nothing to make the trip easier. As we edged closer to France everything he'd learned to forget and to put to one side like an inherited silver tray or torn photograph came rushing back.

It bore down on him as hard as a painful conscience.

'I used to wonder if he was cold,' he said, from the back seat, 'even though it was August. Hard to believe I'm almost twice his age.' He looked out of the car window. Still nervous. 'How much was it to hire the car?' I heard him sighing. And then we all went quiet.

The grey sky disappeared and soon a strong breeze cut across us as we rolled through back roads, near villages with names like Le Portel, Saint-Valery-sur-Somme, Yvetot and Cabourg.

'He was in the 3rd. The tanks. It was the Churchills. Old Winston's mob . . . Must have been murder in one of those things.'

'Nightmare, Dad,' said Vincent.

'Brutal,' I said, shaking my head. 'Boiling hot. Stinking.' But we had no idea what any of it was like. It was only the living bit we understood.

'Thanks,' he said, laughing again. 'I feel a lot flippin' better now about it . . .'

Sometimes my father's voice had an almost magical power once it came to life. You could hear the shuffle of angels upstairs laughing with us too. His voice had real laughter in it, but it was not always present. Gradually, I understood why. He sucked on a sweet to moisten his mouth.

We arrived in Bayeux.

Along Boulevard Fabian, near the cemetery, we found a small *pension-résidence* and were shown to a room on the top floor. The building was old and the floors creaked and the toilet was in the hall and the room had three single beds, almost touching each other, and there was a sink with a dripping tap. It was hardly a place for newlyweds.

'Just the job,' said my father. He took photographs in the room too. He took some pictures through the window and down into the back alley running past the pension. He took photographs of the sink and the beds. And then he went into the hall, even though it was dark, and tried to get a shot of something without his flash. He took more pictures of anything that was written in French.

After dinner in a small restaurant where the meat was cooked too rare he made a wretched face but ate it anyway, chewing each mouthful a thousand times and saying, there's some amount of blood in this old coo and a good vet would bring it back to life. We said it wasn't a cow it was a horse, and he just called us a couple of eedjits. We bought some wine and talked into the night.

'I wish Granny could have been here,' he said. There was a knot in his voice. He looked up at the ceiling. 'Granny always wanted to go. My mother . . .'

But he stopped.

'Why didn't she?'

'It's fine, it's fine . . .'

We talked about growing up in Bishopbriggs and the work he did on the house and how my mother made sure everything was done for him while he put the house back together again. 'Eleven breakfasts, eleven lunches, eleven dinners,' he said. 'Your mum did

314

everything without stopping to think of herself. She always ate last. No matter what, she always ate last.'

We talked into the dark.

Tomorrow he would see his father.

Before going to sleep he said, God Bless, but he said it quietly as if he hadn't really said it at all. His St John Ogilvie prayer, a kind of *memento mori* that he kept in his back pocket, was by his bed. My father believed in the power and intercession of the saints and all that they could do for his family, his people, the Irish, the Catholics and the poor. St John Ogilvie was the saint he believed in more than any other.

Iain had also heard the story. We often talked about it.

We thought, perhaps, that we'd misheard him long ago when he said he'd actually *met* St John Ogilvie. Perhaps he just wanted us to think he'd said it. Either way, I know what he believed. Over the years I talked with Iain about it and he remembered it the same way too.

'What do you mean, Dad, you met him?'

'I met the man,' he said, looking directly at me. 'I met him in Ruchill. Years ago, when I was younger. He came to the house. I met the bloke.'

'St John Ogilvie?'

'Yep.'

If an alien had branded my ear with a red-hot poker I could not have been more taken aback. Whatever he was telling me then I really didn't understand it, but I knew, deep down, that whatever was in his head, he believed it with all his heart. Truly believed it. I just didn't know what he meant. He might have meant it as a parable. An allegory, or an analogy, or a moral story. I wasn't sure then and I wasn't sure now.

'I *met* him,' he said. 'And I told your mother, and she didn't believe me. And that was hard. Imagine telling something to some-one who you thought would believe you and they didn't. Well, your mother didn't.' There was no malice in his voice, just a hint of sadness.

We'd learned about St John Ogilvie in primary school. I couldn't say I always paid attention but they'd definitely talked about him.

The story went something like this: Ogilvie was Scots-born into a Calvinist family, but was received into the Catholic Church in 1596, during a period of opulence and expansion, in Belgium. In 1610 he was ordained a priest in Paris after joining the Society of Jesus two years earlier. Following his ordination he served in Normandy and lobbied to be sent to Scotland to minister to the few remaining Catholics praying secretly in Glasgow. He returned to the city in 1613 disguised as a horse-trader and began preaching and celebrating Mass clandestinely without a thought to his own personal welfare.

After a year Ogilvie was betrayed, arrested and taken to jail in Paisley. He was tortured, and his blood spilled like a river, to reveal the names of those Catholics he celebrated Mass with. He refused. The following year he was hanged and disembowelled like a deer, at Glasgow Cross. 'If there be here any hidden Catholics, let them pray for me, but the prayers of heretics I will not have,' were reputed to be the dying man's last words.

Ogilvie, said my father, had told him about what it was to be a Catholic and how he should conduct himself, and the type of life he should lead and the type of man he should be. My father recited this as confidently as if he was offering me a childhood treat and I took it as eagerly as if it might be my last. 'It was like a light going on in my head,' he said. He never used the word 'epiphany', but I think that's what he might have meant. I asked him if it was a dream and he shook his head.

He gave me a flat look. 'No way. No flippin' way. I saw him. I spoke with him. As sure as you're in front of me, it was him.'

Even then I remembered standing there feeling marked by his stories and the curious and mysterious embellishments of the Church. Was I to believe this? Did my father meet St John Ogilvie in some kind of saintly vision? I swallowed hard and concurred, conceding that of course he'd met the very saint himself and why on earth would I doubt it to begin with? Satisfied, my father returned to talking in his own inimitable way, about his family, his songs and his people.

But, simultaneously, I dismissed his claim.

I put much of it down to the tiredness of a man caught in the crossfire both of middle age and of frustration at his own life. Yet, if I could have heard it again – any of it again – I would have celebrated each and every mutilated or hanged saint with him. 'You can never,' he used to say, 'keep God from the unfolding of his own plans.'

My father simply believed.

I lay in my French bed and stared at the ceiling and listened to the drip, drip of the tap in the sink. Things that my father used to say could haunt a person. They haunted me for years, well after the new houses had sprouted in the quarry and the quarry boys had disappeared and the memory of Mrs Horgan had become distant and we'd been to America and back and I'd got married and my hair had started to show the first sign of grey. They still haunted me. Before I fell asleep I asked him about our conversation all those years ago.

'Remember that time, years ago, Dad, you said you met St John Ogilvie?'

A deep, peaceful snore came from his bed.

I never mentioned it again. And neither did he.

He was dressed first. He threw a splash of cold water on his face before flicking some over to Vincent and me. 'Quick march, lads,' he said. 'You're in old Lizzie's army now . . .' His white vest covered his still powerful body. Despite the passing years he was as solid as a ball-peen hammer.

He put on a crisp, clean shirt that my mother had ironed specially and his heavy leather coat Mark had got him in America. We all headed downstairs for coffee and a pastry. The camera and video bag was at my father's side. The lady who ran the pension had a huge smile. She smiled like a can of open peaches. My father mumbled something quietly in French and she smiled at his attempt and nodded. She knew where we were going and blessed herself as she waved us away.

We went to the florist's nearby.

He pulled his coat in tighter. He was embarrassed to ask for flowers. I went into the shop instead, and the lady in there began putting a small bunch together even before I'd finished speaking. I didn't speak French, but I'd been practising the sentence for weeks on end. It was supposed to sound something like: *'Je vais rendre visite à mon grand-père.'*

I probably asked her for a large piano.

Vincent and my father laughed at my efforts and I laughed back harder for bothering to even try.

Mourners usually arrived in packs of black, wearing overcoats that had been dry-cleaned for the occasion, but here the funeral had been such a long time ago that the dead didn't care how you dressed. If they cared it was only about how you lived. The long-dead were happy just to receive visitors.

The Scots and the Irish were good at funerals and wakes. Mourning was in the blood. You weren't doing it to show off, you were doing it to show that you understood. A funeral in Bishopbriggs, while never quite the same as one on Barra or in Cork, was almost as popular as a wedding. Someone knew someone else who knew someone else who was close to the person who'd died. So you made a phone call or sent a card or some flowers or went to Mass or even the service if the deceased belonged to the Presbyterians. A Mass card was bought and presented as evidence of comfort for the loss suffered by another like-spirited soul.

But even for the staunchest believers, the honest ones too, funerals were occasions to remind yourself that it was you who'd avoided the joys of heaven – or the clutches of the devil, depending on how you'd lived out the last few years of your life – for yet another short while. Catholic funerals were great occasions, of burning incense and reverential sermons. But they always spat out a collective sigh of relief. My mother said they were as sad as sad could be.

'Always best avoided,' my father would say. 'Especially if you're the one who's centre stage before the altar . . .' And he'd look at you and raise his eyebrows.

The men had on the same worn, black suits, too long in the sleeve and too tight at the waist to hold in their bellies, while the women fussed with their yellow, lacquered hair and too-high shoes until they were nearly late for the event. Everyone worried at funerals. It was a good day, said an old uncle once, if he woke up and his elbows weren't hitting the sides of the coffin.

With the flowers in our arms, we arrived at the cemetery.

Upright white stone. Trees fluttered. The Bayeux Commonwealth War Graves Commission Cemetery. In the morning light it was actually pretty and that was something to say about a place where everyone was dead. It was a decent place for a man to be buried if he couldn't be buried at home with his family around him mourning.

My father shifted from foot to foot.

It was the largest Second World War cemetery of Commonwealth soldiers in France, and contained more than four and a half thousand burials. Burials? A fancy word for dead soldiers. The plots of land had been assigned to the United Kingdom in perpetuity on account of all the sacrifices made by men like my grandfather, and the graves looked like rows of white deckchairs in the fields. My grandmother would have liked it. Not loved it. She would have kept all her love for Michael and the boys.

She would have said that although Mick would have preferred Maryhill or maybe even Donegal or Galway or Cork he would have been quite happy to stay here for ever.

I was glad he was there.

My father held up a piece of paper with the details of his father's lair, and he read it out quietly, more to himself than anyone else, as he walked. But he knew the details off by heart regardless. He read it out again. People worried about the quiet in quiet places. Libraries and hospitals and graveyards. But the dead never worried. They were dead.

Plot 15, Row K. 19.

The grass, neat and striped, was the colour of an old, green rowboat. A gardener was gracefully cutting the grass with his British cylinder mower. He was not so much tending to the graves, as he was tending to the old and young. Each headstone had a two-foot flowerbed and these were replanted every year with roses and herbaceous and alpine plants. 'It looks very well kept,' said my father, slightly self-consciously, as he walked amongst the grid of skeletons.

The gardener did everything slowly and deliberately, rolling the mower around the stone, which seemed almost too hard and too cold. His soft, measured cuts complemented the graves, offering a belated comfort to the scything of the bodies that had gone before. But it was too late for being maudlin. They were a single entity now. The mangled dead.

I closed my eyes and listened.

The soil toiled uneasily beneath my feet. The guns sounded in the sky.

When he saw us nearby he turned off the engine. And then the man lowered his head, his shadow cast into trees. My father nodded in the gardener's direction. He was never good at this kind of thing. Politeness and gentleness with other men. I watched from the shadows. Vincent did too. He kept walking and walking. As he walked I could see him changing. In the shadows, my father disappeared. In the light I could see, for the very first time, my grandfather's son.

I liked the way it sounded.

'I think it's this way, Dad,' I shouted. But he knew where it was and we let him find the grave on his own. He'd earned the right. The flowers shook in the breeze. A few leaves covered the autumn grass. He stopped. There were no stories. There were no tales of old or myths from the past. The cold rooms of my grandmother's house were empty now. He had no more scorn. He bent his head.

He dropped slowly to one knee.

Sometimes I believed in God. At other times I wanted to but didn't believe a word that came out of the mouths of preachers. That day was one of the days when I truly did. I can't say for sure if my father shed a tear. He'd shed them for his mother but he knew her as well as his own flesh. He'd have said a prayer as surely as a boy would fire a rifle left unattended.

I knew that my grandfather would have liked him. They'd both given their life for Jane.

We joined him. It felt like standing in a neat, mirrored room. The dead and the living staring back at each other. My father said something simple again. 'It's very nice. I like the stone.' We stared along the row. Row upon row, like large chunks of fish flesh. The grave said *Michael Tierney* and I thought that my own grave might look something like that one day too. My father closed his eyes as if he was invisible. We all touched the gravestone, for no other reason than that this was the response that death seemed to require. A final touch, a need for proximity. A hand on the shoulder. Are you all right, down there?

I'm not sure who noticed it first, but it was there plain as biscuits.

'Have you noticed the graves on either side?' I said to my father.

He shook his head.

'Look closely,' said Vincent, smiling.

My father looked at the two graves. He squinted in the sunlight. Then he smiled a little. Then he smiled a lot.

On the left side of Michael's gravestone was a soldier named Mason. On the right side was a Star of David for the soldier who lay there. For most of my father's life he'd railed against the Masons and their secretive clubs and their perceived negative influence on Scottish life. He railed against the Israelis too and the Jewish lobby for their immense and provocative influence on Middle Eastern politics. And there it was carved in stone. A Mason and a Jew standing guard alongside my grandfather.

'You know what irony means, Dad?'

He looked away into the sky and shook his head. I remember that day and everything was bright.

'I'm taking a photograph of *that*. Like you said, Dad. We need to record it. As *evidence*!'

Later, we called my mother. 'He was fine, Mum.'

'Good,' she said. 'When will you be home?'

'Soon, Mum. He'll be home soon.'

The war had gone.

In its place was silence.

I knew that my grandfather could see his son. I knew that he could see and hear us too, across the endless, foggy terrain between the dead and the living. Beyond the long line of yesterdays. Michael sat with my grandmother and they had tea.

Every drop counted, my father used to say, towards the filling of a cup.

It was some years later when I received a call. The caller was from the Scots Guards Association. He was a polite and upright gentleman and, somewhat surprisingly, he happened to live in Bishopbriggs but we'd never crossed paths. We'd never needed to, I supposed. He'd seen an article I'd written in the *Herald* about war graves in France and, if I was interested, he had some information for my father. I explained about the stroke and that he was no longer able to communicate properly and that his mobility had gone too. We talked for a while and then he came over to my house.

The Scots Guards, said the man, had agreed to give a plaque to my father in honour of my grandfather, and I thanked him for it and said that I'd take it round later to my father's. The plaque had the cap star of the Guards with its motto *Nemo me impune lacessit*. 'No One Touches Me With Impunity'. We'd hang it on his bedroom wall alongside the photograph of Michael in his uniform that had once hung in my grandmother's living room. There were some of his service medals too. Iain had arranged to get them cleaned.

The man had looked into the circumstances of my grandfather's death and there was something he wanted to discuss.

The Churchill tanks were the heart and soul of the tank squadron and had been developed with the intention of supporting the infantry in an attack. The 3rd Battalion Scots Guards and others were part of the 6th Guards Tank Brigade and they landed on Gold and Juno beaches on 20 July. It seems their first action was an attempt to take Hill 309, on the Caumont-l'Éventé ridge, from the German 326th Infantry Division as part of Operation Bluecoat.

The first week would have been spent preparing and waiting in farmyards and orchards and listening to the stories of those veterans who'd been in the countryside for the past six weeks. By 28 July Michael, and his fellow soldiers, were given the order to move. The training was over. Now it was time to work.

They fought over farmland, over ridges and wide expanses, and over narrow tracks. It was summer and the stone farmhouses would have looked pleasant, but they would have hidden snipers and small arms. S Squadron was led by Major Willie Whitelaw, and a few days later they ran into shell and machine-gun fire coming from between Le Bourg and Lutain Wood. Fighting was from hedge to hedge. The *bocage* was thick and stopped the tanks making much progress. There were a lot of dead Germans found at the bottom of hedges.

The tanks crashed on, heading to Les Loges. S Squadron moved rapidly.

I listened intently. The man said he was still looking into the ins and outs of things, but there were a lot of casualties and it was a hectic time and there were shots coming from several different directions. But the tanks, he said, were tough and they fought on. There were maybe three German Jagdpanther tank-hunters in the area, and they ambushed S Squadron, 3rd Scots Guards, taking out eleven Churchill tanks. Two Jagdpanthers were later found abandoned too.

A lot of men died that day and many were wounded. The Churchills had been annihilated at point-blank range.

But my grandfather had survived. He was still alive.

Major Whitelaw pulled the men together and they remained on top of a ridge, anticipating more fighting, until the Argylls came. The tanks that were still working were refuelled, ammunition was handed out and the men ate what they could.

The first day had passed. The Battalion had suffered grievously.

Michael had survived that bloody battle. But he died not longer after.

'There was something else,' said the man, and he talked for a little longer.

I listened. I nodded.

'I see . . . Thank you.'

He finished his tea and left my house.

The following day I sat in my father's bedroom and showed him the plaque. He smiled and held it in his hands. There were tears. He held the plaque tightly and I changed the subject. I talked about the Norton, his old motorbike. I said as sure as God made green apples I was going to get it fixed up with the boys and we'd get it sprayed and chromed and then we'd park it outside his house and we'd wheel him out in his chair and he could sit and just look at it. For hours if he wanted.

Then I'd ride it to Crinan with the wind in my hair and with my daughter on the back seat, holding on to me. And he grinned and tried to speak. And Mahoney would shout and say, slow down, Dad. You're too old for this. And I'd say, I'm fine. He laughed and he didn't look sick at all. And then I held his hand. I started to tell him about the man from the Scots Guards Association and the things he'd told me and the things that I hadn't mentioned yet. 'There was this man . . . He said he had some information, Dad.'

But I couldn't. My throat dried up. It felt black.

'Never mind . . . You know what, Dad? I can't believe that you've managed to get through all of this, how you've kept so strong. Must be all that Irish blood in you, eh? You old flatfoot Mick!'

Maybe later.

Chapter Fourteen

Am I Dead Yet?

My father was now an old man on parade.

Time had passed by so quickly. It was eleven and a half years since his stroke and today was also his birthday. Apart from the soft fog of a little music we sat together in silence. He'd just turned seventy. Was that even possible? His stroke seemed like another lifetime away, as if the actual happening of it belonged to someone else. Someone else's body and someone else's father, not mine. He'd been so much younger when it happened. My mother too. We all were. I was a boy back then and now I was nearly forty-five. The numbers sounded absurd.

The photographs of me from that time seemed to belong to another Michael. I recognized him, for sure, with all his confidence and occasional arrogance and the indifferent smile too. But that was gone. At least, most of it was. *He* was gone. It saddened me. I wanted to be that young man again. I supposed that we all did. That was the terrible trick of growing older. Time was simply a con artist. You didn't believe that youth would end, you never believed it even when there was evidence, and then it did, and all that you were left with was confusion and photographs of your youthful and smiling self. And the smile mocked you. It said, you see. You weren't even *listening*.

In the right circumstances it might even be purifying.

It wasn't. It just seemed sad.

My mother had called that morning asking if I could cut his hair before we took him out for a birthday meal. We'd go early because he always got so tired. And she was getting tired too.

Gone was the girl in the photograph in my wallet, standing in front of the house on Barra, with Kisimul Castle in the bay in the distance. She was young, in her twenties, brown-haired, green-eyed and beautiful. I'm sure it was my father who was taking the picture. She doesn't remember but I can tell, the way she was smiling and laughing, with the intimacy and ease in which she acted in front of the camera. She was in full bloom.

Now she was much thinner than she'd ever been and her skin was pale, the colour of seashells. Translucent almost. Her hair, which had always remained dark, had rapidly begun to turn grey. My father's sickness was beginning to raise uncomfortable questions about my mother's health. She'd recently turned seventy-one and it was all too much for her to deal with, but she refused to have it any other way. She would nurse my father, she said. She always would. That's what they'd agreed when they were starting out and when they stood in front of the priest and when they had their children. 'In sickness and in health, Michael,' she'd said.

That's what they'd promised they would do.

I brought the clippers over. They'd lasted well, since the first time I'd cut his hair in hospital. I told him that I was keeping a tab and he owed me a small fortune by now. I figured about eight haircuts per year. Multiply that by around eleven years and it was roughly eighty-eight haircuts, give or take, at, say, a fiver a cut.

'You're family, Dad, it's fine . . .'

So he still owed me roughly £440. Factor in a little booze, Dad, on match days, and we could call it £500?

He laughed. His cheekbones rose.

Mind you, I suppose I did borrow your lawnmower and some of the tools. I had some decent use out of the good drills and the paint that you left behind. I took your pickaxe, lump hammers and work-bench and the skill-saws too. The boxes of nails came in handy. All the screws you had. I saw some roof guttering that I didn't think you'd need and that roof felt. Bitumen was good, because I needed it for when my roof leaked and the damn thing was like a sieve. I used your wheelbarrow until I broke it. I wanted some copper pipes for the boiler and you had a roll of lead that never came cheap, even at half the price. I took that also. Factor in the assortment of screwdrivers, pliers and saws that always came in handy.

He looked at me.

'So I probably owe you a few hundred too, eh?'

I handed him his birthday card. 'Happy birthday, Dad. Happy birthday.'

His eyes were moist. His scalp was still as dry as an old hurling ball. Seventy years old? I simply could not fathom it. It just couldn't be true. But it was. The mantelpiece proved it. It heaved with birthday congratulations. He couldn't escape from it.

He sat quietly in his chair, trying to open the card with his good hand. It was slow and awkward. I wanted to rip the envelope open and let him see what was inside. He was like a child opening his card. Every birthday he'd shake the card hoping to hear the money in it. Then he'd open it and you had to register surprise when the notes fell out. It was a mysterious kind of current inside him that still made him excited to open a birthday card. His good hand stuffed the notes down the side of his chair. My mother would take them and keep them for him. She'd buy him something nice.

By the morning he would have forgotten that they'd ever been there.

My mother was at midday Mass at St Augustine's, round the corner from my house. The old priest had been round yesterday to see my father. He was a saint of a man and had decency etched into his bones. Yesterday, my mother had walked into the room and both my father and the priest were asleep. She had a little laugh to herself. This was what it had all come to now.

The CD player was running. Johnny Cash was singing 'Don't Take Your Guns to Town'. There would be a football match on shortly. An English Premiership game but he didn't bother much with English football. I switched the television on but turned down the sound before pouring him a half-glass of Guinness. I left the other half in the fridge in its thick, brown bottle.

Seventy? I shook my head.

He looked at me briefly.

Am I dead yet?

'No, Dad, no. Not yet. God, no.' He was always asking that.

It's just that it's been so long. I think I feel dead, though I don't know what that feels like. But it must feel something like this.

'I know, Dad. It's brutal.'

He was clear-eyed and lifted a wavering finger out towards me, not in admonishment but to touch my hand. His hands were almost translucent. They looked like an X-ray picture.

Listen, Michael. I'm glad I'm here. Even if I look and feel like this and sound like this. I'm glad. For your mother. I'd go through it all again. I'd rather go after her. You know what I mean?

'I know, Dad.'

Just to make sure she's OK.

'She is, Dad. She's good. And she loves you. But we don't need to talk about that.'

I know that, Michael. I know, of course . . . but we do. Sometimes we should. It's just the way . . .

He shuffled a little in the chair, getting more comfortable.

'Later, Dad. Later.'

So you're writing a book about me?

'Yes. I told you, remember. It's called *The First Game With My Father*.'

I think you mentioned it. My memory's terrible these days. What's it about?

'It's about the first game we went to. Remember? No? I know it must be hard. Against Sporting Lisbon . . . and all the stuff in between. You know, the van and the house and Bishopbriggs and . . .'

I could see him thinking, touching his forehead. He shook it a little. And then he smiled.

'What's so funny?'

Nothing, nothing.

'Tell me. Come on, Dad. I've had to sit here for a decade and more pretending you can talk to me so at least tell me what you're thinking . . .'

It's just that . . . you know, that match. The Celtic match. That wasn't it. Definitely not. I would have remembered. That wasn't the first game . . .

'What? What do you mean? Of course it was . . . I can't have got it wrong. Not now. It's too late.' I sighed. He knew I was lying.

No. That was a match. You know there's a difference. The first game was when we played together at Bishopbriggs High School and I wore my Sunday shoes and you thought you were brilliant, and you were good, to be fair, and I was terrible and you were embarrassed about me.

'I wasn't . . .'

Oh yes you were, Michael. But I understood. I should have made an effort. I should have asked someone for a pair of boots. But that was never my style. That was our first game together. Father and son.

I paused. I was embarrassed now. He knew. Of course he did. He always knew. He was right. He knew from the minute it happened. He knew when I watched him in hospital.

The Celtic match, that was great though. With George and Iain and driving across the town. But the first game was when we played together. That was when it all started. Us. Me and you. Getting to know each other, eh? I could be awkward, I know. But you could be too. I had to show you that if you wanted something you might need a little more than skill. That tackle . . . you know the one?

'Yes. I remember. Of course I do. I've never forgotten it. How could I?'

You were right. It was a bad tackle. It was a terrible tackle. But that's what happens. You can't just tap dance through life. Sometimes you need to hurt back a little too . . . Hurt back the people who hurt you. That's reasonably fair, I think.

It was warm in the room. I could feel my father looking right through me. He knew. He always did. That was the thing with fathers. You told them one thing but they knew. You couldn't hide.

'When did you know it was that match I wanted to write about?'

I've known for a while . . . for years and years. I knew when I was sick.

'No one else would believe me. They wanted to believe it was something else. They needed to believe it was something bigger. But I couldn't tell people that the first game with my father was a football match in Bishopbriggs and he wore a pair of his Sunday-best shoes. I couldn't tell them that because no one would believe me. They'd have said you couldn't write a book about *that*. It needed to be something bigger. Something more important. It needed to have a crowd. It needed fanfare and fantastic goals and Celtic players of renown. The night sky had to sparkle. Famous faces. Old players too, digging up the past. There had to be singing and flags and waving. There had to be tension and rivalry.'

People believe what they want to believe. People will believe anything.

He paused for a while.

I was disappointed when you gave up playing football. I'll admit that now . . .

'I knew you were. I'm sorry. I wanted to try other things. But it doesn't matter.'

I'm sorry. I should have told you why.

'But I knew.'

No, you didn't. Not really. You always thought I wanted you to play for Celtic. But I didn't. Not really. The truth is I wanted you to play for . . . Rangers.

'What do you mean?'

I wanted you to become the first Catholic boy of the modern era to play for them. I wanted you to show them. I wanted you to show them that we were good enough. Not just at football . . . but as people. As Catholics. As a person. I really wanted that to happen. You would have showed them. They'd have watched you play and they'd have said, why did we even bother making all that fuss?

'A spy in the camp?'

No, no. I'm serious. Much more than that. Just so that they thought our people were fine and decent. I wanted them to admit that they were wrong and not pretend it wasn't happening. I wanted you to show them that they were wrong.

We sat for a minute saying nothing.

'It's all changing now, Dad. Time to let it go. They know it was wrong. There's some good people on that side too.'

I know. I've seen them these past few years from my chair.

We did this a lot, sat together and talked. We all took turns when we were around him. We'd been waiting for the miracle so long. Doctors had said that he might get his speech back. The priests had said it too. But that was a long, long time ago. He'd never get it back. So we just pretended. It made us all feel better.

'Look, I've got something to tell you too . . .'

What is it?

'It's . . . uhm, nothing, really. Look, never mind. I'll tell you later.'

Tell me now. I don't know how long I've got. That's not fair. I need to know now.

'To be fair, is it not time you were *leaving* anyway, old fella?'

No chance. Not yet, Sonny Jim! There's a lot in me yet and make no mistake.

'But it must be murder for you sitting there, Dad. What about we fix it so that it's nice and quiet. No fuss, no hassle?'

Away with you to hell, Michael. That'll be right. You're not touching me. Get lost, you eedjit!

'I'm just saying, if it gets too much . . . just give me a wee nod and I'll do the needful. Couple of blinks should do the trick.'

Beat it . . . I've my eye on you.

'Don't worry, Dad. Let's go on for a bit longer. I think you're fine. You're a strong big fella. So let's keep up the big old fight. We'll keep you going until we get old Lizzie's telegram, eh?'

Too right. Old Lizzie. She's not that bad. It wasn't old Lizzie I minded. It was Phil the Greek, the old hubby. Money for old rope, that fella. A telegram would be nice. And a Knighthood for Services to Raising Wee Tims! Ya beauty.

And he would laugh like a drain.

Now put that pillow down, you eedjit.

'Well, fine then. But stop being so cantankerous. You're as old as the ark now and twice as miserable.'

I talked. I tried to make him real. I tried to bring him alive through words that he would never utter again. Almost every day I talked with him and he talked back. Only he never did. Not ever. Not properly.

The early afternoon was golden and the flowers my mother had planted beneath the window were in full bloom. That was his life now. The whiff of flowers or of fresh-cut grass regularly greeted him in the lounge. The rain battered the windows, the sun shone through it, the snow sat on it, and the withering of autumn could be seen behind each pane. He could smell, and he could see. But he could not touch it. His senses were like a large silver key that opened the outside world to him. Still he said nothing. The seasons had come and gone more than eleven times each since his stroke and he just watched as it all unfolded effortlessly in front of him.

We sat for a while longer saying nothing. The quiet was only interrupted by his soft sigh and a smile every time he took a sip of his drink. I believed in my heart that he was content now, a man far removed from the anger and sadness that had travelled with him for so long when he was young and spirited and headstrong and brave and all the things I had ever wanted him to be.

We sat together in the sunlight and I tried to bring him to life with some memories. That was all I was ever able to do, really. And everyone else did their bit.

It was my mother who had saved him.

I just told a few stories.

Someone asked me once, what was the hardest part of remembering?

It was not being able to fix things.

This incident never seemed too bad when I told people about it, but it had stuck with me for almost thirty years and I'll never forget it. I might have been seventeen. My father received the call he'd been waiting for, confirming that the quote he'd given for a rewiring job had been accepted. It was for the son-in-law of someone he knew who'd bought a large tenement flat and it needed a complete over-haul, starting with the electrics.

It was summer and I wasn't doing anything much.

'Do you want to give us a hand?'

'Yeah, Dad, sounds good.'

'I'll, eh, pay, uhm . . . I'll give you something. A few bob.'

'Don't be daft, Dad.'

'Ach, no.' His voice was louder, now. There was laughter in it. 'Ten pounds for two weeks' work, not bad, eh?' We agreed and the embarrassment was gone. He showed me how a house should be rewired, taking care to leave little or no trace of disturbance on the walls. He wraggled the walls, ran cable under floorboards, and changed old switches for new. If he wanted to run a length of cable up a wall he'd carefully remove the facings around the doors, which were old but a particular feature of these tenement buildings. Every new cable he installed was buried from sight. Old sockets that had been cut into the wooden skirting boards were taken out as being a fire hazard and replaced higher up on the walls in the plaster. Carefully, he'd fill in the holes that had been left in the wood until it was impossible to see any gaps.

He took his time. He cared about how the house would look. Someone had taken care the first time round, he said, so we should do the same.

I unfurled lengths and lengths of electric cable, drums of extension cords; I mixed plaster and finishing plaster. When hammering a nail into wood he taught me how first to tap the sharp end of the nail lightly, to blunt it. That would stop the wood from splitting. 'Careful, just a light tap.' It worked. The wood never split once.

My mother had packed us ham rolls, crisps and soup. We unwrapped the tin foil. We ate while we worked. The food tasted like it had been made for a banquet. And it tasted better when you were hungry. We chatted some more. The flat looked fantastic. My father had lit up all the cornices and the ornate ceiling roses and the high wooden doors and the mitred skirting boards. My father brought light into people's homes and I always believed that it was such a magnificent thing to be able to do.

Three, four, five, six rooms later and he was finished. It had taken us about ten days. He paid me a few pounds, more than I'd ever earned, and I was delighted. I'd probably buy myself a new shirt. After a few days I could sense that he was being very quiet. I always knew instinctively if there was something wrong, we all did. The air had changed. He wouldn't look me in the eye. He was angry. He said it was nothing.

The stillness of some people. The silences. He did it best.

My mother told me that *after* my father had completed the work, someone else had told the son-in-law that they knew someone who'd have done the job for half the price. And that was exactly what the man paid my father. Half the price of the job. And my father had paid for most of the materials too.

I had the urge to be sick.

The guy was fairly young and had a very well-paid job. And he simply decided that my father had cost too much after the job had been done. I told my mother that my father should speak with his friend but she said, no, he'd just get really angry and that wouldn't do the family any good at all. The way I saw it, some people just needed to be hit at least once in their life. Twice to remind them.

Anyway, said my mother, my father never liked to confront people about something as ugly as money. Maybe there was a reason, she said. We both knew there never was.

Weeks later, I stood outside the man's flat and waited till he came out. He didn't know who I was or why I was there. I walked over to him and asked if he had the time. He looked at his watch. I asked if he knew John Tierney. I could tell by his face that he did. I told him not to worry, that I was pretty sure everything would be fine, but there were no guarantees. He should just try to forget what had happened. That was all I said. He became nervous. What are you talking about, he said. I walked away. I knew then, as I know now, that he'd be worrying about a knock on his door for a very long time.

It was hard to fix a thing just by remembering. But sometimes it was worth the effort to try. For a while I sat with my father and we reminisced.

My eldest son, John Gabriel, was born on 11 October 2000, just over a year before my father's stroke. I was writing about something in New York at the time and my father was also there with Iain, in Woodside. Iain and Natalie's first son, Quinn, had been born in New York a few years earlier and they lived together in a fine street surrounded by decent Irish bars. I think my father thought he'd landed in heaven.

My son was five and a half weeks premature so I couldn't get home in time for his birth. My wife called from the hospital and she held the phone up to him and I could hear the gurgle of his infant noises. Despite the distance, his presence rattled the walls like an earthquake. My father smiled and offered his hand and his congratulations and there was a knowing look in his face, as if to say, well, now you'll know. Raise a boy and you'll raise a shadow all your days.

The world hadn't yet fully committed to doing absolutely everything over the Internet, so I went into the city to find a travel agent and change my flight home to the earliest one possible. Trying to rearrange a flight in America over the telephone was about as simple as trying to nail blancmange to a tin ceiling wearing stilettos. My father stayed in Iain's apartment. Later, I found myself in a bar at 23rd Street and Tenth Avenue for a few beers, and I soon fell into conversation with a man who was heading to the Serbian Orthodox Cathedral of St Sava, in Manhattan. He whispered to me, 'Victory!' Or something like that. He'd spent the previous few days shouting outside the Yugoslav Mission to the United Nations on Fifth Avenue and we spoke about his beloved Belgrade and how he'd lost his son in the war.

'When you are free,' said the man, 'all you have to worry about is politicians. When you are a prisoner in your own country, you worry about things like food and your children. Politicians come and go.'

He talked more and more. The people in Serbia had broken the cycle of war. I asked him about the death of his son and he congratulated me on the birth of mine. Back and forth we talked about fathers and their boys, who later became men. And we touched on nations and the people who made them.

'Every time someone falls,' he said, 'someone else must rise.'

I enjoyed the chat. I bought him a beer. He left and I stayed for a few more. The only thing I truly understood then was that I had no answers myself, and I still don't. Only questions. My father was still at Iain's when I arrived back from the bar. I was probably a little worse for wear. We shook hands again, clasped each other's backs. He squeezed me and it felt like he didn't want to let go. He smiled and said he was delighted with another addition to his brood but there was also reticence in his voice. We both knew that I had my own son now and that my son had his own father.

I would always remember it as one of the happiest and one of the saddest days of my life. I think he felt that way too.

About six years after Gabriel was born – we had always planned to shorten his name – I was asked to write a story about Celtic winning the European Cup in Lisbon in 1967 and how fathers passed the tale on to sons and how my father had once told the story of that great triumph to me.

It had been years since I'd sat in the hall of St Matthew's Church watching a rerun of that match. Would Gabriel ever remember it if I told him that simple story, the way one generation passed on a trade to the next? I wanted to tell the story to Gabriel a little differently. So we packed our bags and headed to the airport.

'Can I bring Spiderman, Dad?'

'Of course you can, son. Bring Superman and Batman too. But they'll never beat the Lisbon Lions . . .'

We arrived in Portugal. The Atlantic coastline shimmered and glittered like a ballerina's dress. Beyond it were small houses with paint peeling off their walls and an impressive *avenida* lined with pine and eucalyptus. Children trailed their boards from the ocean, their hair still wet from swimming. The windows of our taxi were open to the blue sky and a few clouds hung like the folds on an ancient statue. I put my face out of the window to feel the breeze, the way I used to when I was a boy. The way my father did in his van.

The taxi drove on. And then I caught sight of the stadium. Little seemed to have changed over the years from how it looked in the photographs and the Super 8 clips I'd seen. Empty white seats were scattered around the ground, abandoned like shelled peas. There was a distinct air of yesterday. I went to pay the driver and the contents of my wallet spilled to the pavement. There was my perfectly folded five-dollar bill with *Gabriel* written on it. I'd forgotten it was there. G34116373F – the one I'd kept from the bar in New York the day he was born. Amazing how you forgot the little things.

The Estádio Nacional was all our football dreams made flesh.

'Wow, Dad,' said Gabriel. 'It's amazing . . .'

'It sure is, wee guy.'

A few hurried steps and we were standing in front of the gates, not far away from the pitch and the ghosts of the Lions. I closed my eyes for a minute and listened to my father as he talked to me in the loft. Over the years the myths of the Lisbon Lions had grown. But that was the *point* of myths. They had to leave an imprint.

Bertie Auld, lean and dark and hard as a billiard ball, raged like a fighting poet. Bobby Murdoch, metronome-steady, strode like a colossus, pinging straight passes in the midfield, ice in his boots. Tommy Gemmell, a cinderblock with legs, hurled his big frame around and fired a shotgun peg. Bobby Lennox shuttled with consummate skill and a smile. Catholic and Protestant together in a city of deep religious division. Come summer, come winter, Billy McNeill, with his unwavering gaze, arrived for set pieces like mist appearing across the water . . .

The Lisbon Lions. They stood over there. Can you see them, Gabriel?

And then there was Jimmy Johnstone. Wee Jinky. You always gave nicknames to the people you loved the most. Trying to catch him was like trying to catch pigeons. His skill was something God-given. Johnstone always made my father laugh. He made him sad too.

337

Some months earlier I'd been at the house of Johnstone's widow, Agnes, where she told me a great love story. And I told it to my father.

It had been more than forty years but Agnes still remembered the Viewpark Youth Club and the shy, red-haired boy who plied her with ginger and crisps. She was sixteen, as pretty as a picture, and a Docherty then.

Jimmy Johnstone was seventeen and content as a boy going fishing. They fell in love in that devastating way that can only ever belong to the young and the very old. They'd go to the youth club and then on to nearby Greyfriars, which used to be a monastery for Capuchin friars. Before it closed down Jimmy would seek sanctuary with the brothers in the tranquil surroundings, attending retreats and Confession when his excellence had been worn down like a brake pad on a fine car and years of extreme mood swings had taken their toll.

There was a hut at Greyfriars, where the Scouts assembled. The hut had a big coal fire in it, and it cost them a shilling to get in. Having got the bus down every Sunday night, the two of them would sit together and listen to whatever band was on.

They'd go to the pictures too and eat bananas given to them by Jimmy's mother, and Jimmy would insist on watching westerns and the films of American singer Al Jolson, over and over. He loved Jolson. They saw one of his films five times and he was always singing 'My Mammy', especially to his mother, Sarah, a kindly woman given to bouts of depression. Sometimes, when the couple went for a walk in the park, Jimmy would climb on Agnes's shoulders to get to the top of a fence and walk along it, for balance. (When he was older and they were married, he still used her shoulders to get up into the loft of their house.) He was obsessed with football.

But Agnes never bothered with football. Even when he became famous, Jimmy would always just be her wee man and, later, her husband, who went round to her mother's house on Sundays for dinner, played Scabby Queen, table tennis and dominoes. And who went to work on a Saturday with a pair of football boots and a grin.

Once, long after he'd retired and when he already had motor neurone disease, he went up to the park for a wee game of football with a bunch of kids. When he returned he was exhausted. She helped him shower and dress and then he said, 'Aggie, I've left my false teeth up in the park.' So Agnes went looking for them and asked two young boys if there were any false teeth lying about. Eventually, one wee boy came over with the offending object, flecked with mud and grass, and Agnes felt terrible because she didn't have a penny on her to reward the boys for finding the teeth of one of Scotland's greatest-ever football players.

The teeth nearly made them boak, she said.

Back at the house Johnstone just sniggered, all gumsy.

Johnstone made a name for himself as a brilliant, but often troubled, genius. He knew it, the fans knew it, and Agnes knew it. But Agnes had made a vow to deal with it. Love bears all things. That was the rule of love, Dad. Jimmy knew that. Agnes knew it too. A business failed. Jimmy became more depressed. The drinking increased with his sadness.

When Jimmy's mother, Sarah, was dying in hospital, he sat on her bed and, when the lights were low and the ward was listening, he sang her 'Come Back Paddy Reilly'. All the other patients, and the nurses too, heard Jimmy Johnstone singing late at night, and she died a few days later. He put a small statue for his mother in his garden.

The pressures of Jimmy Johnstone's nameless terrors were always there in the household and he even brought in a hypnotist to calm him down before he played. Friday nights. His anxiety was that severe. In 2001 he was diagnosed with motor neurone disease, which destroys the nerves sending signals from the brain to the muscles, and although Jimmy realized he couldn't beat the condition he knew, at least, that the triumph was in the hard fight. He fought because he'd been fighting his whole life. Since the very day he was born. Some men know how to do that.

Some don't, and that's just another plain old fact.

Agnes at times had to put her hand under his chin to help him breathe. But they laughed too. Jimmy would say, I'm dying, Big Yin, and she'd shout back that he'd said the same thing last month and he was still bloody here. The night before he died she was trying to get him up the stairs. A neighbour from next door, wee Alan, came in and gave her a hand. They carried the prone figure, like a wounded soldier, to the top of the stairs and got him into bed. On the Sunday Celtic were playing Hibs.

Earlier, Bertie Auld had called the house to tell Agnes he was snowed in. He was a regular visitor and he said to her that he was going to try and get over on the bus, but Agnes told him not to worry. Thomas, a childhood friend of Jimmy's, had phoned to say that if he could get down that night with Holy Communion he would. Agnes told him not to go out of his way. Jimmy never spoke about heaven. He was afraid God was likely to put him into hell for all his indiscretions so he erred on the side of caution, stayed quiet and hoped that God would forget. But he took Communion every week.

He couldn't really move by himself. For four years Agnes had been lifting his arms up for him as he lay in bed. That night she thought something might be happening. She just woke up and knew that he was going. He was just passing away. Right beside her. He wasn't suffering any more. She just gave him a wee kiss.

Agnes Docherty didn't marry a footballer, a star or a hero.

She married a wee boy who used to climb in through his neighbours' window to demand that Thomas, who would give him Communion the night before he died, come out to play the game that Jimmy would love all his life. She married the boy who ate crisps with her on plastic seats at Viewpark Youth Club, and the boy who sang the last song his mother would ever hear as she lay dying. She married a drinker, a depressive and a man ravaged in his final years by a withering disease that meant she had to dress and clean him like a child until the night he died.

But, mostly, Agnes Docherty, the pretty girl from Birkenshaw, married the man she loved.

My father listened intently.

I told him the story of Jimmy and Agnes and although he couldn't talk, I knew that he was silent by choice. There was a difference between being unable to talk and having the wisdom at the right time not to even try. He put his hand out and held mine.

Jimmy was a hero.

My father was a hero too.

Gabriel shook me.

'Why are your eyes closed, Dad?'

'Oh, just thinking, son. Thinking about some . . .'

'Superheroes?'

'Yep, just like superheroes.'

'Cool . . .'

I'd bought a football earlier at a nearby store. The logo on the ball was, suitably, Sporting Lisbon's, Celtic's victims in the first match with my father, back in 1983. Gabriel tucked the ball under his arm along with his Spiderman figure.

The gates to the stadium were open.

A security guard spotted the ball. '*Não!*' We could not go on to the pitch, he said, in stumbling English and gesticulating. I looked beyond him to where the pitch rose. Already I could hear the chanting from the fans who'd chartered their own plane. And from the man who'd sold his house to pay for the trip. For many of the 20,000 Celtic fans who travelled to Lisbon in 1967 it would've been the first time they'd ever been abroad. They came on trains – the Ham and Cabbage Special. They spluttered there in Hillman Imps and rusting Fords.

The hairs were up on the back of my neck already.

'Excuse me,' Gabriel said, 'can we play on the pitch? We support Celtic. Please?' The guard looked around him, then ushered us up the incline while making a sign with his fingers that I knew meant 'just a little'.

Obrigado, I replied. Thank you.

Gabriel took me by the hand and I walked across the track and on

341

to the pitch. I took a deep breath and the sky rumbled. The white Portuguese stone was magnificent against the verdant trees surrounding the art deco ground. The stadium looked as upright as a widow's back on a Sunday.

'Why are we here, son?'

'It's about Celtic,' he said, 'winning the *biggest* cup in the world!'

Gabriel took his ball and ran off into the distance. 'Who scored the winning goal?'

'Johnny from the *Fantastic Four*,' he shouted back. 'When he was playing for Celtic and when he kicked the ball it went on fire. That was Johnny. He's from another planet. Some of the superheroes are from planet earth or they live in other countries. They scored in the olden days.' Superheroes when you're six. Superheroes when you're thirty-six, or when you're staring at the other side.

I wasn't even born when Celtic captain Billy McNeill stood in front of the same classical columns I was now looking at. But that's what stories are for. Remembering.

In 1967 Inter Milan had muscled their way to the top of the football world like a powerful boxer. They bullied the opposition into submission, scoring one goal before reverting to a system – *catenaccio* (door-bolt) – that allowed for nothing in the way of counter-attack but everything in the way of defence. Quite simply they became an impregnable Italian wall.

Then along came Celtic, dancing and romancing in their green and white hoops. 'They don't shrink to fit inferior players,' said Jock Stein, in a voice made of stone. I'd always loved that. The new kid on the block was sharper and faster and more swashbuckling. Fans swivelled their heads, this way and that, just to keep up. Inter were the nightclub bouncer. Celtic were the underage Teddy Boys determined to get to the bar. It was a clash of styles and mentality. And Celtic had Stein, a manager steeped in the specialist knowledge of both.

'So what happened, Dad?'

I ruffled his hair, the way my father ruffled mine as I stood outside our new house. In the years before Lisbon, Inter Milan had won three Serie A titles in four years – losing the other in a play-off with Bologna – and the European Cup twice, in 1964 and 1965. Helenio Herrera, the Inter manager, had the choice of Italy's best footballers. Celtic, on the other hand, built a team not on money but on people. In the tunnel before the game Jinky was shouting to Inter's Facchetti, 'Hey, big man, you and me after the game, swap jerseys, OK?' Ronnie Simpson collected the false teeth of every Celtic player who had them, put them in his bunnet and stored them behind his goal.

After only seven minutes Sandro Mazzola stepped up to the penalty spot with the ball after Jim Craig was adjudged to have fouled Renato Cappellini. Craig still denies the charge to this day. Mazzola had already had one glorious chance saved by Simpson. It was hard for Mazzola as he stood in the glare of the spotlight.

When Mazzola placed the ball on the ground, as Simpson was moving on his line, he could have been forgiven for turning round and simply leaving the field. In May 1949, Mazzola's father, the great Valentino Mazzola, had died when his club's team plane crashed into the Superga hillside, near Turin. Sandro was six years of age – around the same age Gabriel was now – when his father died. The last game his father played was at the Estádio Nacional. His team, tagged *il Grande Torino*, were returning to Italy from a farewell match for José Ferreira against Benfica in Lisbon. All thirty-one aboard, including players, club officials, journalists accompanying the team and the plane's crew, perished.

Score, thought Mazzola, as Simpson tried to stare him down. Score. *For my father.*

Torino had lost the greatest team they'd ever had, a side that had won four *scudetti* in a row. Mazzola had lost his father. Mazzola placed the ball.

Thousands of Celtic fans in the stadium shouted and screamed for him to miss. It wasn't the first time he'd been back at the stadium since his father's death – he'd been there with the Italian junior side – but it was the first time he'd ever been on a plane. Mazzola was looking to see if Simpson was afraid, but couldn't find anything in his eyes that betrayed fear. The goalie moved on his line without nerves. Mazzola stepped up, his father resting on his shoulders, and eased the ball over the line. His burden had been lifted. One–nil to Inter Milan, the masters of *catenaccio*. Mazzola looked upwards to the heavens, to where he believed his father was. Both father and son wore the number ten.

Gabriel squeezed my hand. 'Is his daddy dead?' he asked.

'Yes.'

'That's a bit sad.'

'It is,' I said, 'but his dad's always been with him.'

He looked at me. 'It's good that his dad makes him really strong and he scores a goal. He can hear his dad, sure he can? His dad is a ghost and the man can't see him, but sometimes he can hear him and he helps him to score. His dad sometimes says to him, "Be brave and don't get an injury and have fun."'

I gave him a hug.

I could see Mazzola on the grass waving over at us, and he nodded. Then he waved to Gabriel. Then he pointed up at his father. And then he was gone and we never saw him again.

'I wouldn't want something to happen to you,' said Gabriel. 'I would think really angry stuff at someone. If I met that person that did something I would choke them. Is the man you waved at OK now?'

'Yes, son, he's good.'

'Does he miss his dad?'

'He does.'

'I hope you don't crash,' he said.

'I won't. I promise.'

At home thousands of Celtic fans were watching their televisions or listening to the radio. Kenneth Wolstenholme described the action on the BBC. Inter already believed that the game was over. They started to bolt the door . . .

Celtic were having none of it, swarming all over the Italians. It had the makings of a fistfight. The siege continued. But Celtic were relentless. Giuliano Sarti, the Inter goalkeeper, performed miracles.

Although Celtic had conceded the first and what most believed would be the decisive goal in the game, they refused to be disheartened. They outplayed, outthought, and outsmarted Inter, knowing that eventually something would come their way.

Then I heard a shout. It was the security guard telling us to leave.

'You're kidding, mate . . . come off it.'

Gabriel picked up his ball, but he wanted to hear the rest of the story. The guard insisted. We had to go. Back at the hotel, Gabriel ate toast and drank cola. I had a Super Bock, brown, firm and dense. I took out my translation book. *Por favor, traga a conta.* The bill, please. 'Come on, son, we're going back.' When we returned the gates were tightly locked. My heart sank and Gabriel looked at me, and his face crumpled. There was only one thing to do and we did it.

We'd climb up the embankment at the side of the stadium, past the trees and bushes and up and over the gate that was higher than both of us but that didn't matter. 'Just like climbing a wee tree,' I said, and Gabriel smiled. And then he carried his smile around like a toy for the next few hours. The stadium was desolate. A photograph album of empty pages. There wasn't another soul in the ground. I kicked the ball from the stands on to the pitch and then we ran together, across the grass – such fine, fine grass – where the Celtic team strode about forty years earlier. We had our ball and we dribbled and ran and shouted and screamed, like I did when I was a child with my father in our garden in the shadow of the Campsies, years and years and years ago.

Over there was the tunnel from where the players entered on to the pitch. A line of shivers ran down my back. 'Let's go, my boy.'

'What if the police come, Dad?'

'Don't worry, son, they've better things to do.'

'But I can hear the sirens. I think the bad guys told them we were in here.'

The tunnel was quiet as a back road in Glencoe. It smelled damp and, oddly enough, of stale cigars. A bird's nest rested in one of the rafters. The long passage had a shaft of light at the end where the players stepped out from their changing rooms, talking easily to each other. Unafraid. The ghosts were there.

I could hear them. It wasn't the ghosts I worried about. It was the living.

Bertie Auld was in the middle of the line-up, alongside the tall, swarthy movie-star Italians. 'Hail, Hail, the Celts are here,' he sang. 'The Celtic Song'. The rest of the team followed his lead. They were just about to go out for the biggest game of their lives and they were singing like a pub team. The Italians didn't know where to put themselves, so they shifted uneasily in their boots. They looked great, of course they did. They were Italians after all. Long and lean and handsome. But they couldn't sing for toffee.

By God the Celtic boys knew how to sing.

We all walked out of the tunnel together.

After half-time Celtic continued to feast on the retreating Inter through Gemmell, who moved quietly, making no more sound than someone dressing. He galloped like a racehorse and right at the beginning of the second half he struck a magical shot and the ball seemed destined for the corner. But the keeper somehow managed to dive backwards and stop it going over the line. Sarti was supposed to be Inter's weakest link but he produced yet another spectacular save.

The clock was ticking.

In the sixty-third minute, Murdoch received the ball and deftly touched it across the field to Craig who, in turn, zipped the ball to Gemmell, now Celtic's secret weapon. The big left-back, as big as a water tank, struck another glorious eighteen-yard shot that finally beat the despairing Sarti at his top right-hand corner. Justice arrived at last. The goal broke the ice. The hearts and the bodies of Inter melted too.

'Yeeeeaaahh,' shouted Gabriel, punching the air in delight. 'Are they the winners now?'

'Not yet, son, not yet . . .'

Years ago Uncle Roddy had said it best. In Glasgow, in Dublin, in Cork, in Australia and America news of the goal was greeted like news of a cure for hangovers. Thank the Blessed Mother. Sweet Mother of God. Praise Be to All the Saints, and have one for yourself and a wee nip too.

Celtic were flying.

Five forwards, three half-backs and two full-backs. They were throwing everything at Inter, something that manager Herrera had simply not anticipated. Celtic did not have a single failure. Discounting Clark, the brilliant sweeper, and Simpson, the goalie, Celtic had nine potential goalscorers. And hunger was always the best of kitchens.

Celtic pushed forward.

Johnstone attacked from the right. Angry, but having fun too, like a chastised wean skelping a ball against a grumpy neighbour's wall. Over and over he did it, in spite of his getting into trouble. Agnes would have laughed. Just to show them he could. His mother would have smiled at her wee ginger-headed boy. Red as a fire truck.

Lennox cut a swathe around the left. Wallace, quieter than usual, was still playing his extremely efficient, if not so spectacular, role of holding back. Stein wanted him to hang back a little to give the others room to breathe into his space. The only question now was how long could the Inter players hold out. The watertight defence was crumbling. Gemmell canned another eighteen-yarder.

'Every time someone falls, someone else must rise . . .' The Serbian man in New York was right. He was right.

The hardman of the Inter defence was Tarcisio Burgnich. He was like a mahogany sideboard. His team just shut down mentally, physically and emotionally, Burgnich would later confess. They just knew, even after fifteen minutes, that they were not going to keep Celtic out. They were first to every ball. Celtic just hammered them in every area of the pitch. Even in the dressing room at half-time the Inter team looked at each other and they knew they were doomed.

Celtic had turned into a beautiful football team.

After the match Burgnich would tell anyone who would listen that Celtic weren't like the English. They were technically gifted, with creative flair. They were just like the Latins. Burgnich was right.

And Herrera had no more to offer than a bucket of warm spit. If it went to extra time there would be another thirty punishing minutes and then a replay the following day in the same stadium. Stein told his men to take it easy. 'You'll get them in extra time.' Celtic had no intention of taking it to extra time, never mind a replay. They were proud men. They had families to go home to. They would earn their £40 a week and they would earn it now.

The pressure on Inter was intense and the legs of the now aged Italians were breaking beneath them. It was always the legs. Time caught up with everyone, no matter who or what. The athlete or the dockworker or the man driving the day-shift bus. 'My legs are going . . .'

It was nearly ninety degrees out there.

Forget the heat.

Five minutes from the end Murdoch swept a neat cross towards the Italian six-yard line and Stevie Chalmers – who would later settle in a house in Bishopbriggs – nudged the ball past the static Sarti and into the back of the net. Sarti looked around, confused and just a little sad, like a man wondering where he'd parked his car.

At last! At last! History had arrived.

'Blow the whistle, ref,' I shouted.

'Blow the whistle, ref,' shouted Gabriel. 'Blow the whistle!'

More than forty years on and the fans still bit their nails throughout the last five minutes, still hid behind their couches and radios. We could hear BBC commentator Kenneth Wolstenholme again.

'That's it. Celtic are Champions of Europe!'

Inter were gone. The clouds had gone. All their pain had gone.

It was over. It was finally over.

The green-and-white-clad tormentors had won. The boys from Glasgow, Catholic and Protestant united, had won. They sprayed champagne and some of them drank together. They drank enough of it just to be sociable. It helped them to sing.

We jumped up and down in the empty stadium. Our arms were outstretched, our faces and screams remained beautifully suspended in the Portuguese air. We were free. Inter had retreated. They were deflated and broken. The *catenaccio* system was no more. Celtic had saved the football world from that system, from the creeping paralysis that was Herrera's making. Herrera, the son of a well-known radical Spanish anarchist who was forced to flee to Argentina at the turn of the century, was later forced to flee himself. His football was finished. He'd been blinded by his own success. He no longer understood what he was doing to his players. He was hurting them. Time caught him up. It always would.

The following season, Inter finished fifth in Serie A. Herrera, and his clenched fist, was sacked. Stein's philosophy had come up trumps. Celtic had ambushed the history books and the ripples of their achievement would light a bright path for Germany, Holland, England and the rest to follow. The young men in the Estádio Nacional had gone from merely Celtic players to Lisbon Lions.

We both ran on to the pitch, arms aloft. The stadium was ours. Gabriel ran in circles.

All the Celtic fans went wild too, streaming on to the pitch with us. The players were cuddling the fans. The fans were hugging the players. I hugged strangers. We were with all of them. I was with my son. It couldn't get any better. Yet even the victory was not the whole story, it was just part of the thread of it all.

Celtic had brought back the European Cup to Britain for the first time in history. It was taken to Scotland. It sat in Glasgow, in the east end of the city. We all knew that British clubs could win it again – and they have done so repeatedly since – but no one else, no one else, could do it for the first time. Celtic did it the first time.

We ran together across the grass and Gabriel squeezed my hand. I'd told the story of Lisbon to my son. It was the story that my father had told me, of the superheroes of 1967. I'd told it in the Estádio Nacional where the light shone brightly on grass that could have been stitched to the earth by angels. I'd seen my son run out on to the pitch. And he'd seen his father too.

People shouldn't forget, I said.

My father said, don't forget your people.

On a scorching Lisbon evening, eleven young men from within a thirty-mile radius of Glasgow carried the weight and hopes of millions. It was a time when people dared to dream, when men went to work in bunnets and children played football in streets and the sun shone in the Gallowgate, but brighter still on the coast of Portugal. They took on the might of Inter Milan. And won. Oh, how they won.

Gabriel, my premature son, I'm sorry I missed your birth.

But we danced with the ghosts. We always would.

By the end of that summer my father began to look just that little older. His birthday cards that lined the mantelpiece were put away and the presents that my sisters had, as usual, showered him with had been put by too. The twins were home, but were going back to the Middle East in a few days. Fiona and her family had moved to Hong Kong two years earlier and had now returned. Claire and Catherine still lived nearby. The boys came and went.

It was a beautifully warm morning, the kind that made you wonder why you ever doubted things the way you always did. I went out the back to the garden. The grass was long, lush and sharp and I strolled down to the bottom where we used to play football, right to the bottom where the new houses hid all of our memories. It was a shame, I thought, for all the people who'd moved in there. They'd never seen it as it was before.

They'd probably never even seen a quarry boy. Or fired a rifle at one either.

I looked up at my father's house in all its beautiful stone majesty, with its roof that had been perfectly repaired over a decade ago, and I could see my father smiling. There he was, the ghost of his former self, playing badminton with Claire, fixing his Norton, sitting having a cup of tea and a biscuit with my mother, showing the twins how to get a real tan, and playing football with the boys.

I remember that day when he brought his bike back to life.

He dragged it out of the shed as if he was carrying it from the burnt ruins of a Mayan scrapyard. In no time he'd rigged up an old battery and attached it with some kind of clips or wire to a part of the bike's engine. After a few kick-starts, it slowly putt-puttered into life. He whooped with joy, laughing and shouting, and was quickly astride it and it started to move. He fitted the seat like keys in the teeth of a lock. He took the bike to the quarry and ran it and ran it, on the open expanse.

I watched as my father, sweaty and breathless, rode over the little mounds of earth, past trees and round bends, occasionally riding one-handed across the quarry's breadth. He laughed gleefully, like a child. We screamed and cheered as my father whistled past the trees.

He rode that bike like Steve McQueen.

Most of those trees were gone now.

Most of *his* trees were gone now too.

He planted every Christmas tree we'd had in the house when the celebrations were over and we watched them grow. One of them had grown to more than thirty foot and I had to cut it down when my mother said it was blocking the view. I climbed all the way to the top and sawed away, foot by foot, until most of it was gone. I could still feel its presence, like an amputated limb.

The ghosts of dead trees were still ghosts. They had seen everything around them too.

The garden and the house were everything he'd ever wanted and everything he ever gave us. Nearly forty years ago we stood there together rolling a snowman without a face. He promised me the best football pitch a boy could ever dream about and I got it. We all did.

A couple of hours later I finished cutting the grass.

I put the lawnmower away, raked what was left over and straightened out the small shed. My ham rolls were waiting for me in the kitchen, the slices of tomato on a separate plate, and some cheese if I wanted it, and chicken and a little salad. My mother called me in. Time for lunch. I always had time for my mother's lunch, the size and weight of a cobbled stone.

We sat together, my father and I, watching an antiques programme, and the two young, posh presenters encouraged a smile from his otherwise tired face. He was weak but he was strong. According to my father, the Bible always said that God would give no one a burden that he or she couldn't bear. More than eleven and a half years he'd been sitting in that chair. Immobile. Voiceless. I didn't know enough about what the Bible had said but I guessed the authors had got my father just about right.

He tried again to speak.

'I'm sorry, Dad, I'm not sure what you're saying,' I said.

'Ddnnaa ssshhhnn.'

'Sorry, Dad.'

He lowered his head.

'It's fine now, Dad. Remember when we came here from Partick when I was just a wee boy? Remember we looked through the window and all the stuff was on the floor? And Mrs Horgan? You remember old Mrs Horgan?'

He stopped fidgeting and looked at me. And then closed his eyes tight.

'I remember the snow was so heavy. It was stunning, really beautiful. And you lifted me up on your shoulders and then we went round the back and made that huge snowball. And I told you to buy the house . . .'

I remember it as if it was yesterday.

'I'm sorry, Dad, I didn't mean to upset you . . .'

He shook his head. He understood.

'Look, Dad, I don't know why this happened to you and I don't really know how we got here. I'm not even sure who I *am* any more, half the time. And Ireland? Well, you've given me a mystery, that's for sure. I hear it all the time but I just don't know. I never even talk to the kids about it. Maybe I should. I don't know. But I need you to know that you did everything right for us.'

I reached over and held his long-fingered hand. His nails needed trimming. My voice began to crack a little.

'Do you want to go and see Celtic again?'

Chapter Fifteen

A Boat to Carry You

My mother heard the sound coming from the kitchen downstairs, a slow humming noise, almost a song but not quite. She'd heard it before but it was much clearer now. It was 'Crystal Chandeliers' by Charley Pride, the song Iain and my father used to sing when we were all children. Who on earth could it be at this time of the morning, she thought.

Strange. Maybe she was dreaming.

It was barely six o'clock, and the light from outside had just begun to filter into her bedroom. She always woke early but it was the singing that had got her, sinking inside her, so she shook herself awake and put on her dressing gown and tiptoed gingerly on to the hall landing. 'John? Is that you?' My father was sleeping downstairs, as always. 'Who is it?'

She felt fear in her stomach. An open wound.

Now there was a sweet smell of cooked breakfast, coiling around her like rolled smoke. Bacon, sausage, potato scone and fresh toast. Sunday breakfast, but it was only Friday. She could hear the tea being made. The kettle began to boil. She pulled her dressing gown a little tighter. Her arms shivered.

'John?' she said, quietly, wary of disturbing my father's sleep and whoever was in the kitchen. '*John?*'

The voice in the kitchen was now singing louder. The melody now.

My mother knew the song well. My father used to sing it all the time. He sang it while hammering wood and when he was installing the central heating. He sang it when he was in the van and Iain would sing it too when we all went visiting our aunts and uncles and grandparents. My father would ask Iain to sing it and eventually he would, and my father would sing along in the background too, his knees nodding to the rhythm of the tune. The person downstairs was singing my father's song. Her heart lurched. She felt like she was falling.

My mother began to shake. A tear welled in her eye. 'John? John. *Stop it, John.* You're scaring me.'

She went downstairs past the large stained-glass window where the candles were still burning from the night before, and every other night before that, alongside the prayer cards and the small, holy statues that looked like Army Men, the green plastic soldiers from my childhood. The candles burned as if they were alive. Love was something that you must be prepared to fight for, she would say. It doesn't just come to you. My mother fought to keep my father alive every day and night of the past decade and more. Some were ten-penny candles, others more elaborate. White and gold and purple. And red and blue too.

The colours didn't matter. She would take her hope from any corner of any field. And they'd never gone out.

Her hands touched the soft embossed wallpaper. The hall had been freshly decorated. It used to be his job. The men came in and made no fuss and left no mess. The bacon sizzled and she could hear my father singing now, as clear as Waterford crystal. She started to cry. Fear was paralysis. She stopped on the stairs, like she did years and years ago when they moved here and my father promised her that he'd fix up the house for her and that she didn't have to worry about anything. 'John! John!' Her heart was beating loudly, as loudly as it had ever done, and her insides were breaking. She ran to the kitchen, losing a slipper as she went, and my father was standing there, quite steadily, buttering fresh rolls and making a mess of the kitchen surfaces and the wooden chopping board.

There he was. Standing.

He looked weak but he was still standing. Holding himself up.

When he saw her he smiled and gave her a look as if to say, it's OK. He switched off the kettle. Then his whole face lit up. My mother ran into the room and screamed and they held each other close and the happiness was knocked into her with his touch. Then he cradled my mother because her legs had given way. Now he stopped her from falling the way he'd fallen all those years and years ago. It was part of a lifetime ago.

She sobbed into his chest.

Tears ran in sweet tramlines down her cheeks. The bright light in the kitchen hurt her eyes so early in the morning and she blinked to focus and then they held each other and it felt like he'd never been hurt. The kitchen smelled of breakfast and fear. 'It's all right, Cathie,' said my father. 'I'm here . . .' She nodded and her eyes shone through the water that had gathered. It was her right to cry. She'd been saving it up for years.

My father said it was holy water. You had to believe, he said.

She looked at his hands and they were soft and clear. The years in the chair had washed away the dirt and the oil and the paint. Even the scars were gone, the lines that had been cut by chisels and saws and Stanley knives and drills. His knuckles were still the size of walnuts. And his strength was slowly coming back. She could feel it when he held her. It wouldn't be long. He would get all his strength back.

And then she stopped and shook herself and then picked herself up, remembering that she had yet to go into my father's room to check if he was still asleep. She tried to shake herself from the dream but she was standing there. My father laughed. 'I'm not asleep, Cathie. I'm *here*. Look, it's me. John Thomas Tierney. Look. I'm here.' But she looked away from him. 'It can't be you . . . it *can't* be you.' Are you sure she wasn't dreaming, she asked him. And he said that no, he was there, in the kitchen, and that something had happened. Something had just clicked. He'd felt it that morning.

He stood upright, as tall as a pine tree, like the day he'd stood with her at the bridge over the River Kelvin with the twins when they were babies in their Silver Cross pram and they were going to the Botanic Gardens first for a walk and then on to Ruchill.

'My goodness, Cathie, we've a lot to catch up on,' he said, buttering her toast and pouring her tea. 'Sick for nearly twelve years?' He shook his head. He whistled long and low. He looked handsome. 'But I don't think we have a lot of time.'

'What do you mean?' my mother asked.

'Well, I can't stay out of the chair for too long. My legs are still sore. I can hardly stand. My voice is weak. I've only got a short while and then I'll have to go back . . .'

'You can't leave me again, John. Please.'

'I'm not leaving you, Cathie. I'm staying. Of course I am. But my head is still sore. I can't overdo it, you know what I mean?'

She nodded and leaned upwards and kissed my father on his cheek and he leaned down and dried her tears with his fingers that were thin and stiff from the past. For a while they were stuck to each other, tighter now than old layers of paint. They'd never been closer their whole lives. He held her up as they walked together into the living room and all the while my mother said that she didn't know what this was all about, and how could it be happening? But my father just smiled and shrugged and said, who knows, Cathie? Who knows?

'Do you want some music on?'

My father said, 'Aye, that would be nice.' He wanted 'The Water Is Wide', sung by Liam Clancy. 'I haven't heard it for a while,' he said. He laughed. 'You keep putting Daniel O'Donnell on, Cathie, and, to be honest, it's driving me daft! But I couldn't say anything. "The Water Is Wide" makes me think of you. There's a nice line in it about boats. Remember I was going to build a boat out of the van?'

'You and your nonsense . . .' She laughed.

'I could have done it. Easy. People just need to believe, that's all.'

'A boat? You haven't changed a bit, John Tierney.'

He laughed along with her.

'It's a good song. I like to hear the guitar-picking. You remember my guitar, Cathie? I think I've got a few of his old records up in the loft. I'll check for them later.'

My mother smiled. She smiled at his memory of everything. 'Don't worry, John. They're safe. The guitar too.'

'Don't let anyone up there,' he said, but there was no anger or suspicion in his tone. His new voice had left all of that behind. He was happy to leave certain things in the past, he said. You had to, he said. That's what growing means. His voice sounded crystalline. Like a cold fountain. 'Keep your eye on Maureen and Michael, you know what they're like . . . I don't want all my stuff going missing. I've laid traps for them!'

She shook her head. 'You're a scoundrel, John Tierney . . .'

They sat on the couch. My mother leaned into his shoulder, like they were teenagers at the pictures sharing a first kiss. She asked him where they should begin, and my father said that it wasn't an interrogation and was she just a wee polis or something?

They rocked backwards and forwards for a minute or two, like a boat rocking on the rainy Barra tide. They could see Castlebay and Kisimul Castle in the mist, and the croft and the burn running past like a dream. When he thought of Barra he began to smile. When he thought of Ireland he saw the bodies of the dead and mourning. The images continued in front of them, like the whole thing was being played out on a projector screen. The silence continued. My father's wound, he said, was never his stroke. It was his inability to hold my mother every day.

My mother took another sip of her black tea.

'You're talking, John. You're actually talking.'

And my father replied, 'You didn't know? I could always talk, Cathie, it's just that no one could *hear* me. Sometimes people just didn't *listen*.' He sighed loudly.

'Was it really difficult?'

'It's been tough, Cathie. Just sitting there and not moving and not speaking. I wanted to speak out loud for so long. I said the words in my head but nothing came out. And I could see you all looking at me. That's why I just kept looking away. I just felt embarrassed that no one could understand me.'

'Remember when you shouted after the Celtic game?' she said, laughing.

It was warm in the room. He sat back and closed his eyes. 'Of course I do. Mark called me from America. It was the Rangers game. We beat them, didn't we? One–nil, I think. It was Chris Sutton who scored. I liked the way he played. He never gave up, did he? And I just wanted you all to know that I was *there*. I hate it when people talk to me as if I'm dead. They talk to me as if I'm deaf as well, and a child. Cathie, I feel like I've been drowning for years and years in a huge, black ocean.'

'I know, John. But you're back. I knew you'd be fine. We all did. The girls and the boys too.'

She touched his cheek. My father was trying to catch a breath. His breathing was hard. Shackled. Newborn.

'We used to sit in the other room,' he said, 'before we got the good room fixed up. Watching all the matches on the telly.'

'I remember, John. The girls too.'

'All of us. Eleven in one room. Settees and couches and dinner chairs. We all crowded round them. Remember? Watching films. Watching the football. The Scottish Cup finals, and the refs used to *give* the games to Rangers. Practically hand them on a plate. And you told the boys to stop shouting at the telly, and they were not to call the referee names because he was only doing a job. And Iain said they must have paid that ref a golden dinosaur egg for some of those decisions and you just looked at me and shook your head.'

'The twins said not to get too excited, boys, because it was only a game of football, and then when Rangers scored they shouted louder than the boys. I remember it all, dear. The children do too.'

My father could not have had a small family. It would have been impossible.

My mother exhaled.

'I've missed you so much, dear. All those years.'

'I've missed you too, Cathie. Remember when we drove the

358

Norton through the town and you were holding on to me? And you said to slow down a bit. Everything was going by too fast, you said.'

'I remember, of course I do.'

'I drove too fast and you were shouting and laughing too?'

'We were so young then.'

'I know.'

His eyes turned red. He shook the redness away.

'And the girls? They're all fine? It's great when they come back in the summer. I remember years ago when Lorraine just had Sean and she had to go back to Abu Dhabi with him and it broke my heart to see the two of them facing it all by themselves. It reminded me of my mother. I waved her away and I hated it because I couldn't do anything. God, I wish I could have it all back again.'

'She hated leaving too, John. But Sean's a big man now. He's almost nineteen. We sent him a Celtic strip to Abu Dhabi every year.'

My father shook his head back and forth. The years flashed past. Tarnished motorway signs that would never be seen again.

'Nineteen? He was just seven when all this happened to me. My God. My God, Cathie.'

My father touched his head and felt the tufts of hair that protruded over his missing skull bone. He looked up at the ceiling. 'I wouldn't have wished it on anyone. But I'm fine, Cathie, you know? Fine. But I *missed* talking. It's been hard. It's sore as well, you know, not talking. I never thought it would be so hard not to talk. It takes a lot of effort *not* to speak for almost twelve years. People think it's easy to sit here.'

'I know, John,' said my mother. 'It's not been easy. None of it has. Not for a minute. But you're here now. With me. Don't dwell on the bad things.'

'I know, Cathie, you're right. Remember when we all used to go to Barra? Remember all the children running around and old John used to drown the kittens in the sack and it scared the life out of them every time he did? Remember old John cut the front out of his new slippers and then made holes to put shoelaces through them when he was in hospital? What a man he was.'

My mother smiled. 'Remember the outside toilet and everyone took turns pouring the bucket of mess in the burn. The kids would go crazy if it was their turn.'

'Oh, it was stinking. Terrible. Flippin' awful. Rotten. Dead rotten.'

'And I would sit at the window with Morag and my tea and wait for the boat.'

'And remember we went to Stevenston too, in Ayrshire. The seagulls attacked us and then we all got soaked along the pier when that huge wave came crashing over? And we laughed and dried each other with blankets from the van and the children shivered in the wet and the sun.'

'And Fiona cut her head open on the door. She's still got her scar.'

After a while my mother got up and brought over a set of photographs that had been taken throughout the years that he'd lost. We were all there, with our own children. My mother pointed everyone out. Lorraine had her son Sean; and Maureen had John Martin and Michael; and Kathleen and I had Mahoney, Gabriel and Aidan-Joe; and Iain had Quinn, Aaron and Calum; and Fiona had Cian, Catherine and Ava; and Mark had Iain, Alisa and Betti; and Catherine had Eve, Lauren and Noah; and Vincent had Rhea and Amelia; and Claire had Christie, Joseph and Tess . . .

'Look at Quinn,' he said. 'He's grown too. I remember being with him in New York outside that bar in Woodside, what was it called?'

'I don't remember. Look at you in that one.'

'The Fenian, that was it. What a name for a bar.' He shook his head. 'I look old, Cathie. I look so different. What on earth happened to me?'

My mother touched his arm. 'You're still my handsome John.'

He grinned. 'We can spend the day together. Would you like that?'

'Of course.'

'But I have to go back later, you know? I can only stay and talk for a few hours.'

My mother shook her head. Her voice rang like a church bell with the sound of all her sadness. Sad as eyes behind a shroud. 'I don't understand this. How can you speak today? What happened?'

'I don't know, Cathie. But I feel good today. I felt great this morning.'

They spent the rest of the morning looking at photographs and laughing and talking about my father's stroke and my mother told him that, years ago, the doctors said that they might have to switch off his life-support system. But she wouldn't agree. She couldn't. And he clasped her hands together, like a preacher offering up good words, and said, 'I know, Cathie. I heard them. Maybe they thought it was only going to get worse . . .'

'That doesn't sound like you, dear. You've been in that chair too long. I thought you'd have called them for everything and then some?'

He smiled. 'You're right, Cathie. I have been in that chair too long. You get a chance to . . . *think*. I've been thinking a lot these past few years. Did I do everything OK?'

'Of course you did, dear. Of course.'

'I should have taken that job. You know the one? The one where I was supposed to write the letter accepting it. But I'd shaken the man's hand and that was enough for me. We shook on it. It didn't need a letter.'

'That's gone now, John. It's in the past.'

'I should have written back . . . It was hard for you without proper money coming in.'

'Never mind, John. It's fine. That's the past.'

'It feels like there are two of me. Me back then and me now. I should never have let it happen. Pride can be a curse.'

'It was no one's fault. I wouldn't have swapped you.'

'I don't know what I was thinking, Cathie . . .'

'Never mind,' she said, and that was the gospel truth. She never minded at all. And then she leaned forward. 'Michael's writing a book about you. He's told you about it. But, you know . . .'

The sun dappled through the window. His face was clear. 'I know.

Says it's about me and my father and Ireland and Celtic and the rest of us too. And my people. *God save Ireland, said the heroes!* That was written for the Manchester Martyrs. We used to sing it years ago. They're still my people. Always will be. That's who I am. I am them. And they're me. But it's not for everyone . . . I see that now.'

'Stop your Irish nonsense. We've not heard that for a while!' She grinned and laughed and gave a shrug. 'I've still got your *Ireland's Eye* magazines somewhere. I'll get them for you later. You and Ireland.' She shook her head. 'You never stopped.'

My father sighed loudly. 'I wasn't always right. But I wasn't always wrong either.' His words froze her.

'I still miss my mother,' he said. He paused briefly. If my father had worn a hat he'd have taken it off. 'She was a wonderful woman. I miss them all. Granny Quinn, oh, what a woman she was. Fierce old soul. And Peter. And Lena. And the rest. Francis as well. I miss my father especially. I wish I'd got the chance to see him. Just the once. But France was good. With the boys. But I do miss him. It must have been hard to die over there in that bloody tank. Sometimes I feel like *his* father, not the other way round.'

My mother nodded. For all the sadness in his voice she loved to hear him talking now. She could listen to the sadness all day. She'd have given anything, she used to say, to have a conversation with him again. Just once. And my father heard her saying this, nearly every evening when they were together watching the television.

'John, how is this happening?' she said. 'It's not a miracle, is it?' She said her words softly, gently, so as not to scare my father away.

'I'm not sure, Cathie. I woke up this morning and I thought I should get up. Make you some tea.' My father paused. 'And I just got up. My legs felt fine. Really fine. A bit stiff. My arms were a bit sore. But I knew I could get up. I just knew. I still feel like a battered old boat, but I feel good too. I just worry that everything went past so quickly. I can't remember a lot of things.'

'You didn't waste anything.'

'I just wanted to do the right thing for the children. And you. You know that, don't you?'

'Of course, John. And you did.'

She said something in Gaelic and he smiled. He loved to hear her speaking in the tongue of her own people. 'Let me hear it again, Cathie.'

For a long time, they were both quiet. Then they held each other again and rocked gently back and forth in each other's arms, the way they did when my father asked her to marry him in the café, or when they were dancing at a ceilidh. She remembered that he was *so* young. He was tall and slim and the only man she'd ever loved.

She whispered to him again in Gaelic and he smiled and although he didn't understand the words, he knew exactly what she meant.

He asked if he could see the garden and if he could look towards the Campsies, where we'd played and where we sang our way from summer to winter. They walked to the kitchen together and he looked out of the windows and shook his head a little, and breathed deeply. A lot of his trees were gone, and in their place was a vast expanse of empty grass for the grandchildren when they came to visit.

'It's OK,' he said. 'I understand.'

He looked at the garden for a little longer. 'Do you still have it?'

'Of course. It's somewhere safe. The boys plan to get it fixed and they'll ride it to Crinan and Oban and Barra . . .'

'That's good. Great.'

He closed his eyes. He could hear the rumble of his bike and the heat from the pipes beneath him and the cold rain as it lashed them and the sun as it burned them. 'They're still in here,' he said, tapping his head. 'My head might look like an old leather football but it still works. Don't think for a minute it doesn't.'

'I know.'

'I'll build you that boat, Cathie. I promise you. Out of the old van. I've been building it every day, in my head. Just like I always said I would. No one believed me. I could have built it if you'd let me. I wanted to build it. You know I did. I need a bit of welding gear and some metal, that's about it.'

'Leave it, please, John. It's fine.'

'We would have sailed away, Cathie. We still can.'

'You're still away with the fairies, John. I don't need to go anywhere. I'm fine here. You're fine here.'

'No, Cathie. I'll need to go somewhere soon. I need to build the boat. You know I do. I need to get it ready . . . It'll be a fine, fine boat. I'll sail away and get the island ready. We'll have a place we can rest together. How about that?'

My mother started to cry. 'Stop it, John, stop it!'

He squeezed her hands. He wiped her tears away.

'Is there anyone coming round today?' he said. 'The boys or the girls? Who's home?'

'Catherine has moved to a place round the corner. Claire will be home soon. Fiona is back from Hong Kong. Lorraine and Maureen are in Abu Dhabi and Al Ain. Vincent is in Azerbaijan. Mark is still in New York. Iain is in Belfast. Michael might be round later. The carers will come in after dinner. They don't know you can walk yet. No one does.'

'When are they coming home?'

'Who?'

'All of them . . .' He shifted in his chair. 'Home for good. I'd like to take the children to Hogganfield Loch, on Cumbernauld Road. The old kettle pond. We used to take them there and row the wee boats around the water, past the rhubarb patch. You know that there's gas underneath the clay there and when it escapes that's what causes the foggy haze over the water. Let's take them again, eh? I'll clean out the van.'

'I'm not sure, John. The carers will be round soon to put you back into bed.'

My father shrugged.

'I hate that hoist. By God I always used to sit there and think that they could have my voice but give me my legs. The flippin' thing is so . . . undignified.' He paused. 'How *old* am I now, Cathie?'

'Och, it doesn't matter.'

'How old? I forget my bloomin' birthdays the minute I have one.'

364

'You're . . . seventy.'

'Seventy? Good Lord, Cathie. What happened? It's taken years away from me. What happened to me? We're not long married. What about Partick? St Peter's Primary. What's happened to us? Where did it go?' My father began to get a little agitated. My mother laid a hand across his knees to calm him.

She lowered her head as she talked. 'I'm so sorry, John. I'm sorry.'

'It's OK, Cathie. It's not your fault. Don't think for a minute it is. It's just hard to think about it like that. We should go to Crinan, eh? Go to the pictures. That would be good.' He raised his eyebrows. 'Everything seems such a long time ago, Cathie, when I was a younger man. Remember I was young?'

My mother cried on his forearms. She used to tell us that my father was so young and strong that he could lift the sky.

But it's fine, he said.

He kissed her on the head, the way he used to when he left the house at night to go to Quins. He knew we'd all be watching so he did it softly and quickly. And sometimes we'd clap and make him embarrassed, and he'd turn and call us eedjits and laugh and tell us to get to bed or he'd shoot the boots off us.

My father asked about Francis and my mother told him that he hadn't been up for some time, but she thought that he was fine. But he was getting older too. He looked out of the window and then asked about some of the men from Quins: Michael, Frank, George . . .

Michael was dead. Frank was dead. George was fine and called sometimes. But he was getting on and she thought that he might be spending some of his time in Ireland, standing beside the sea. My father smiled at the thought of it.

'Michael is going to take you back to Celtic Park with Iain, you remember he mentioned it?'

'Yes, that's right,' he said. 'Michael told me. I'll see how I feel. I don't like going out in that wheelchair. But it would be good to go to a match. My God, it feels like for ever. Thirty years ago? They were just boys. I wish we'd had some more money in those days and been able to take the children out more.'

365

'They didn't bother at all, John. Don't worry.'

'I know. But we tried, didn't we? I tried as much as I could. It was just, you know . . . ach, some things are just in you. I should have done things differently.'

'No one thinks that, John. No one. Not the twins. Or the other girls. Or the boys. None of them wish it was different.'

'Maybe if I hadn't been so stubborn about things, it might have been easier . . . Might have had a bit more money. The boys might have seen a few more matches. The girls too.'

'If you hadn't been so stubborn about things, John, none of them would have turned out the way they did. It was *because* you were so hardheaded! They're happy the way you raised them.'

'You think so?'

'Yes.'

He sat back on the sofa and closed his eyes. Then he got up and stood in front of her. He rose up like barley from his Irish fields.

They talked for hours and it seemed like it would never end. Only their own laughter and tears and thoughts from the past ever interrupted them.

They only talked about their love.

The house was no longer broken.

The van was no longer outside.

The children were all grown.

They said they would rest together.

My father and mother were in the foothills of old age. But they didn't care. They listened to each other intently as all their lives spilled around them, quietly and peacefully as a whistling bird. For a while they danced together at weddings, sherry for my mother and whisky and beer for my father, and they stood solemnly at funerals, offering Mass cards to the quietly bereaved. My father played in the garden with the children and repaired the house and my mother made his dinner and they shared another glass of beer at home and the sherry was back on some nights too.

She threw her head back in laughter at something funny my father had said. They kissed.

Do you remember we went to Spain, she said. Calella. Costa del Maresme. Their very first time abroad. My mother's sister Katie looked after the children. My father called home constantly, checking and rechecking that things were fine and asking what the weather was like at home and the exact time in Scotland, as if the time difference somehow rendered their trip all the more exotic. And it did.

My mother talked and talked.

They walked down Byres Road to the University Café where they shared an ice cream and dreamed of getting married. They held hands and laughed as Elvis Presley or Buddy Holly sang out, while the café owner looked on, pretending not to see their stolen kisses. Small-town, bread-and-butter conservative Glasgow, where the Highlands met Ireland, especially on Sundays. It was perfect then for them. It was all they ever really wanted in their lives.

My mother was living proof that her vows meant something. And sitting there, as they spoke with each other and held each other, my father knew it too. Once late at night after Quins, he told me that he might not always have got things right, but if he had got *one* thing right it was loving Catherine Tierney.

My father got up to change the music. My mother tapped her feet.

'I'll put your dinner on in a minute, John.'

'Is that the time already?'

'We've been here all day.'

He was a little more tired now, what with all the exertions of the day and, if it was OK with her, would she mind if he went back into his chair? She said it was fine. They'd talk again after dinner. She said it was amazing to talk again. It was a miracle. The world worked in mysterious ways, she said. The Lord too. Could you believe it all? She choked back her tears. She said she'd make him some stew and potatoes and he smiled because my mother knew exactly how to make my father's dinner.

'I need to sit down now and close my eyes, Cathie, if that's OK?'

He sat down again in his chair.

And he disappeared inside it. It swallowed him whole.

He heard her voice from the kitchen some time later.

'Dinner won't be long, John. I've not had a minute. Are you OK? Sorry I'm late. I've been out at the shops but I'll sit with you shortly.'

He tried to look towards the kitchen, but his head would barely move. He could feel his body growing more tired. Gravity was taking him over, pulling him deeper and deeper into the chair. He was sinking. My mother could hear his sounds from the kitchen.

'Ddnnaa mmnnaa.'

'Just a minute, please, John. I'm putting on the dinner. Won't be long. I met Rosemary down there. She says hello. Martin's doing well.'

He shouted again at my mother but she could not understand him. Not a word. The sounds were so familiar but that's all they were. Sounds. He repeated himself, a little louder that time.

'Ddnnaa mmnnaa.'

From the chair he could see her, through the open doors into the dining room and the kitchen. She was dressed neatly as always, and her grey hair fell over her face. She looked beautiful. He reached out to touch her but he couldn't. And then it hit him. So suddenly and so harshly that his heart almost broke in two.

She could not understand him. Not a single word.

He'd been dreaming again that they were together, as he'd dreamed it every day for the past twelve years. He'd been dreaming of Barra and Stevenston and the boats at Hogganfield Loch and Crinan and the children and my mother sitting talking to him. He'd dreamed all of it. The dancing too.

My father started to cry. He held his head in his trembling hand.

Ten minutes passed. Dinner came once again on a tray. Tea in his mug. Tablets to be taken when he was finished with his food. My mother smiled.

Can't we sit again, Cathie?

'I'm sorry, John. I don't know what you're saying. I can't

understand. Poor Dad. I'm sorry.' She fixed his napkin around his neck. 'Michael called. He said he'd be round tomorrow for the match. The big game tomorrow, John. It's exciting, isn't it?'

My father tried to reach out to her once more.

Can't we sit again, Cathie? It doesn't have to be long . . .

But she still didn't understand him. He shouted this time. Louder and louder. That they didn't have much time left before the carers came. He stared at the blankness of the wall and the blankness of the couch that had been filled only hours earlier.

I can't take it much more . . .

My mother clasped his thin and varicose-veined hands. She leaned in towards his neck and began to whisper in his ear. And she kept talking, gently and softly, whispering in the same voice he'd heard years ago when they met. Reassuring him that everything would be fine. She was there. She talked in the Gaelic voice of the pretty girl from Barra who turned heads everywhere she went but who had eyes only for my father.

My father nodded. He held her tightly. Squeezed her arms. He touched her face with his wavering left hand. She kissed his cheek. He looked through the window. The tall trees that once stood outside were gone.

We'll go, Cathie, of course we will. To the running river on your mother's croft, where the children played by the bridge. We can sit there with the children and watch the boys play football in the long grass, and the girls play tig. Old Uncle John will come up from Castlebay for some tea. But, whatever you do, don't tell the children he's drowned those kittens. I'll take the children over to Eoligarry to see your uncle Neilly or over by Tangusdale. We can walk, of course we can. I'll leave the van there. It's a lovely day. I'll bring some sun cream, sandwiches and juice, but they'll be fine in the sun, of course they will. Just like me. Iain's going to run round the island tomorrow in the big race. Don't worry, he'll be fine. He's fast as a whippet.

My father closed his eyes.

He lay back in the long grass of Garrygall and watched the dark insects crawl over his hands. The children played around him.

Lorraine, Maureen, Michael, Iain, Fiona, Mark, Catherine, Vincent and Claire. He could see the gulls in their rookeries, white as candles, amid the moss-laden rocks. He could see El, holding a large, gnarled stick like the root of an apple tree, and Jane walking on the croft together, across the peat that belonged to El and also God.

He saw my grandfathers, Uilleam and Michael, talking about the merchant navy and the war. One was young and the other was old. He could see the boats drifting on the water like shimmering cities. He could see Uncle John, in his blue cap and accompanied by his dog, Whisky, sitting around telling stories that were as important to him as Sundays.

My father was happy.

He just lay back on the grass, wearing his sunglasses: he was tanned and handsome, with sunburned arms.

My God, children . . . this is the life. Who wants a game of football? Come on, I'll beat the lot of you! Nine against one. Come on. Big Celtic against wee Celtic!

And we all ran to his arms on Barra.

He breathed in deeply in the chair. His dinner was nearly finished. He hadn't even noticed he'd eaten.

'Take your tablets now, John.'

Then he lowered his head.

The doorbell rang. It was the carers. They'd come to hoist him away silently to his room. When they'd left my mother went into his room as he lay asleep and kissed him on the cheek. She said goodnight and went softly up the stairs to her bed.

She lit the candles in the hallway.

They were beautiful.

Chapter Sixteen

My Father, My Father

Sometimes we went for a walk in the woods near the school, my father, my brothers and I, with the two air rifles. We wandered past the tall trees, and hid in the bushes and pretended to be hunters, shooting at the bark and the branches and the fences. We walked for hours. My father pinned black and white paper targets to trees and we took turns shooting, seeing who could get closest to the heart.

He drove us down in the van and we parked it off the street. The road into the woods looked pretty, with an abundance of leaves, but frightening too. We felt like we were being watched and sometimes we were. We went on Sunday afternoons after Mass and my mother made up sandwiches and packed us crisps and juice, and we'd forget to eat them because the woods were filled with so many things to shoot at that it was impossible to think of anything else.

The woods were near the houses on St Mary's Road. The houses were well tended and the grass always cut and the fences and garages painted every summer, and the people who lived in them believed that life was pretty good and it was. There was a golf club nearby. There were boys in Celtic strips and others wearing Rangers tops. Birds soared across the sky and children played in the streets and it was safe. We walked along the track taking turns holding the rifles. My father made sure they were always pointed down at the ground until it was time for him, Iain, Mark or me to shoot. Vincent was too young to shoot but came along anyway. The girls didn't want to so they stayed with my mother while we were out.

When the sky was blue you could see everything, but when it grew darker the woods held you close and you couldn't see past the vegetation no matter how hard you tried. So we walked close together, with my father at the front. In the early afternoon the sounds of the birds in the trees echoed loudly. They were calling out to each other. There was a magpie and a crow. They could see us. They could see the rifles and hear the sounds of shooting and they knew.

The branches and the leaves crunched underfoot, giving us away to anyone who might be there in the woods with us. Out there, by the dried mud tracks and the fallen trees and the upright trees and the wide expanse of land, everything seemed remote. You could shoot a tree or a target and whoop with delight and no one would hear you. You could shoot a bird too or a small rabbit and no one would know. But he said there would be none of that. We wouldn't be shooting anything that was real because we would just want to do it more and more, and who knew when it might stop. Besides, the sky would run out of birds and where would we be then?

And the girls at home would hate us if we shot at the birds and the small animals. The twins would get upset and the younger ones would get upset and cry into their pillows and they'd call us names. They'd call us bullies. They hated the sight of blood. They'd say it wasn't fair to kill a small defenceless animal or a bird that flew around the open skies and never harmed a thing.

Iain and Mark walked ahead. Despite wearing glasses Iain was a good shot. It came naturally. He'd lift the rifle and the snap of his shot would find the target. Mark swung the rifle from his shoulder trying to hit a moving target but my father shouted that it was enough and if he ever wanted to come back he'd have to listen closely to what he was saying. Leave the birds well alone. My father shot at the dirt and the trees and the telephone poles in the distance.

The path rolled down towards an embankment and you couldn't see what was beyond and over it. My father had been behind me and then he caught up. We talked about nothing much. In between our talking we shot at the targets that he'd placed in the trees. He knew where they were so we could find them easily.

What was the difference between shooting at the trees and the birds in the sky? There were millions of birds. One or two wouldn't be missed.

Ask the dead birds what the difference is. A dead thing was a dead thing. You couldn't undo it.

'Did you shoot at the birds, Dad?'

A brief silence.

'Nope. And what about you?'

A longer silence.

'No, Dad, I didn't.'

'Good. Now, what is it you really want to talk about?' He took aim and fired at one of the targets. Just outside the centre.

'Nothing, really. I was just wondering if my grandfather had ever killed anyone in the war.'

He just kept walking, pretending not to hear. But he'd heard me. He lifted the rifle and aimed again but he missed the target this time. We carried on.

'Well, I imagine he probably did.'

He continued walking. The sky was thinning. It was getting colder. We caught up with Iain and Mark. My father set up a paper target on a tall, faraway tree. The light was going, the blue sky was becoming cloudy. We had two rifles and we each took a shot at the target, including my father. We peppered the tree with pellets. The sound was just loud enough to feel it. The tree looked like an unmarked grave. We could see that the paper was torn. Its centre was now gone and its edges looked like the edges of a mushroom. The tree filled up with our pellets. It was a lead-filled tree now, poisoned with each shot.

We all smiled. The rifles made us feel tall.

At the foot of the tree there was a bird lying on the ground. It was a blackbird, with a yellow beak and eyes. There was a small trickle of blood. The blood looked oily.

'Who shot that bird?' said my father. 'I told you not to shoot anything. Just the targets.' His face was angry. Furious. He snapped his teeth. Our heads were already bowed as he spoke. We said nothing. It seemed like an eternity that we stood there. He just shook his head and muttered.

Our eyes shifted. I looked at Mark and Iain and they looked at me. It was one of us, for sure. Or maybe it was my father. We couldn't figure it out. Either way he'd hung it on us like a fifty-pound sandbag. My father lifted up the bird. It was still warm, he said. He said we should all hold it before it died and we did, and we let the warm blood spill over our hands. I remember staring at my father and then at the bird and the trees. I could see a rabbit out of the corner of my eye. It was looking over. And then another. It felt like the whole wood was filled with eyes.

The leaves above us began to close in. They began to mesh together, blocking out the light. The earth seemed to move beneath our feet.

The bird stopped breathing in my father's hands.

It was an act of kindness.

He dug a hole in the ground with the heel of his shoe and then he bent down on one knee and began to dig a little more with his hands, deeper and deeper. We watched as the dirt got under his nails. He placed the bird in the ground and covered it up with the displaced dirt.

There was something noble about it. It looked precious.

My father nodded.

Then he said to us that it was time to go. We all walked back to the van. When we got home he took the rifles and put them back in their boxes and took them up to the loft. That night I told him it was me who'd shot the bird. He nodded quietly. He closed his eyes.

We never went out with the rifles again.

The rifle felt lighter now.

The wood stock was more comfortable in my hand. It had been heavy once. Everything was back then. So much heavier than it was now. It was heavy when I stood in the loft peering through the window with my father and shooting at the quarry boys, and when I walked in the woods with him and my brothers and shot the bird.

But now it was light.

I sat in the loft, on top of a box of tools, peering at the old rifle. It smelled a little of oil. I think that my father took us through the woods not because he liked to walk, but because he just wanted to see what it *felt* like. He wanted to understand the quietness of the walk and what it was like to hold a weapon, even though it was just an air rifle. He wanted to experience a little of what my grandfather felt, even if it was in the smallest way. He wanted to know what the quiet sounded like before a shot was fired or how monotonous the sky looked or how the darkness fell quickly and how everything changed and how it must have felt to think about something dying.

It was a rifle.

You couldn't say it was heavy.

But he carried it around like a coffin.

It was the morning of the match. The second of November 2013, wet and cold and sharp and bitter. Celtic were playing Dundee United.

I had planned a big European night for my father, like the one we'd gone to against Sporting Lisbon, but my mother said he'd never make it past seven in the evening and she was right. I'd hoped more than anything that his body might make an exception but it wasn't possible. I picked the first match in November. It fell exactly thirty years to the day since our memorable visit to Celtic Park with George and Iain. Thirty years had passed. How was that possible? It felt as close as yesterday and the day before that.

So much time had passed.

So much football had come and gone too. I had friends who attended every match without fail, home and away, taking up all their time. Taking up their life. I'd gone to games sporadically over the past few years. I became like my father. The radio and television suited me. It was a reflection of our times, I supposed. Too many distractions. Too many trips away. I used to go much more often in my twenties but that was such a long, long time ago that I didn't even know that person any more. I might walk right past him on the street.

But the strand of Celtic, the threads of the same cloth, was still weaving its way through our lives. The memory was still warm from the first time. All the things he'd ever spoken about had made their mark, in one way or another. The pond had rippled. Celtic had come to represent many of the things he held dear. Togetherness. A community.

Revealing yourself as a Celtic fan said something about who you intrinsically were or, at least, who you thought you were and who you wanted the rest of the world to see you as. It was *never* about being better than anyone. It was about being equal. To everyone. It was all he ever wanted to feel. None of us was better, he said. *Remember that.* But not a man or woman of us was worse because of what we were born into. He said that life wasn't a social-research paper filled with data either. You followed your nose and your heart to the truth.

Football was changing. Celtic and Rangers were changing.

Then came the biggest change of all.

Rangers were no longer even playing in the same division as Celtic. In early 2012 they were placed in administration and later that year went into liquidation. Business assets were purchased by new parties. The new Rangers entity sought entry into the Third Division of Scottish football. Speculators rolled dice. Briefly the new company became Sevco Scotland Ltd before voting to change its name to The Rangers Football Club Ltd. They would, remarked some Celtic fans, now need a compass to find their way around Scotland's lower leagues.

Arguments spewed with emotion. Were they the same club or not? Would the new entity also go into administration? Would the new Rangers ever get back to the Premiership to play Celtic? Would they in fact be playing Celtic for the first time if they were a new club? Or would they just be continuing from where they'd left off?

Maybe, just maybe, the Old Firm was dead?

Or maybe not.

Rangers fans were adamant. They still held on to their own history. No one could take it away. It had been part of their life, their childhood too. The story of Rangers belonged to their fathers and their fathers before them. It was part of their DNA. They had bits of Rangers growing inside them, like red, white and blue strands. Everyone knew that. They were Rangers to the core. They had Rangers in their bones.

They had a past that they could recognize, and that they would surely cling on to. They would *fight* for their name. They'd tell great stories of the past and talk themselves back into existence. They'd circle the wagons. That's what people did when they thought something was being taken away from them, wasn't it?

It all sounded very familiar.

History was always such a hard thing to fight over because people always ended up fighting over identity and tribalism and wondering where things started and where things ended, and were they ever that important in the first place? It was always Celtic who were accused of putting too much store by history. How things *had* changed.

Maybe now they understood how we felt?

My father was downstairs in his bed. The carers would come soon to change and dress him and we'd sit together for a while. Iain had arrived from Belfast. He always brought a smile to my father's face. The big polis now, eh, Dad?

I raised the rifle up and peered through the scope and pointed the barrel at the loft's brick wall. No one would hear me. Pull the trigger, just this once. Squeeze it gently. The trigger clicked. Empty. The pellets were in a tin in the cardboard box that stored the rifle. I picked them up and they rolled inside the tin like dull marbles, echoing around the loft. They were made of soft lead. There was no horror to them. They weren't like the Colt .45 bullets that Iain had asked me about that night. They were gone now. Long gone. I still didn't know where they'd come from and I didn't want to know.

377

Two new windows had replaced the old skylight. I opened one and rested the rifle barrel on the ledge. The new windows let in so much more light and they kept out a lot of the cold and rain too. For a while I just looked out into the expansive garden. How on earth had he managed to get us this house? He didn't *want* the house, he always said. He *needed* it. There was a difference. The quarry boys were gone and in their place were new houses, with cars in the drive and trees planted neatly in rows.

I watched two figures through the rifle scope. They lived over the back from where we used to play. They stood in their garden in the rain. I followed them with one open eye, my arms slightly bent. I could see them talking. The pad of my finger on the trigger. Then I put the rifle down and carefully replaced it in the box.

I sat down on a broken chair.

His *Ireland Eye* magazines were still there, unread for years. The dollar bill was still pinned to a wooden beam, next to the photograph of my grandmother with Iain. She was smiling. Iain was too. It was funny, I thought, how, in a simple photograph, someone could protect another for years. For eternity. Just by standing beside them. Iain had stayed beside my grandmother for years. Unmoving. A protective sentinel. That was what she needed. Proximity. It was all my father could give her too. And love.

The war must have felt unending for all of them.

My grandmother would have missed her husband. My father was too young to miss him at the time but, as he grew older, he would have missed him more and more. He would have made him up, his dead-soldier father. It would have helped, I imagined, to make him real again.

It would have been hard in the tank for my grandfather, sitting for hours on end and then days on end as the explosions went on around him. Even though the country was pretty and there were fields that looked like a picture and the orchards gave off summer apples, they would have been too hot and scared to think about anything apart from dying. He was thirty when he died. It was a hard age to be a soldier. It was hard because it was an age when a man could ask questions of others. And of himself. You could be impertinent. You could ask questions and not really worry about the reply or the consequences. What were they going to do? Shoot you?

He was in a war, for Christ's sake. He was old enough to be able to *think*. That didn't make for a compliant soldier.

The Jagdpanthers, with their heavy guns as long and thin as telegraph poles, worried them. They'd destroyed a number of Churchills and of Michael's fellow soldiers as they pushed forward. The Panzers carried extra-long 88mm guns and ammunition that was enough, literally, to destroy a tank, blow it to smithereens, blow it to kingdom come, to blow it all to hell, when fired at close range. But the men shrugged off the losses. Michael would have shrugged them off too. He was trying to get home and the hard part was over. They'd lost a lot of Churchills but he was fine and other soldiers were too. They would regroup. He'd got through the worst part. Men had been maimed and scorched. He could hear their voices screaming over the radios. But he couldn't worry about those that were dead. He needed to get home to Jane, Francis and my father.

The earphones of the wireless operator gave out a barrage of instructions and directions twenty-four hours a day. The smell of cordite didn't leave the men. It stuck to them fast. When the tanks rose up over the *bocage* they stopped momentarily, trying to ease more than forty tonnes of steel through the hedges, banks and fields without killing the soldiers inside. The gunner never took his eye off the telescope. He aimed at trees and haystacks and sheds and fields and men. It didn't matter who got in the way, as long as they crashed forward and broke the lines. Birds flew. Apples fell.

That was how they would get home. Keep pushing forward.

And then they were ordered to rest. Just for a brief time, when they would clean their guns and repair the tanks and restock with ammunition and eat. He might have heard the shelling. But the direction of it would have confused him. It was from the wrong direction. He'd probably have known what was happening. Already it would have been too late.

Someone shouted for me from downstairs.

'OK, I'll be down in a minute.'

My mother was in the kitchen. Food was being prepared and Iain was drinking tea. He looked well as always, my younger brother from the loft. We'd shared a few beers the other day and sat up talking about the past. About the loft, about America, about Ireland, about Celtic, about the match, about mortgages and about how we planned to change our lives before it all ran out but knew that we never would. It still bothered him that he'd been unable to get home to see my father when he'd had his stroke because he was working in America and didn't have the right papers.

But everything had its flip side. My father had loved staying with Iain and Natalie and Quinn at their home in Woodside near the Copper Kettle, where they ate steaks the size of breezeblocks, and he'd have wanted him to stay, even when he was ill, to see how things worked out.

They'd returned to Northern Ireland in 2003, to Bangor, where Natalie's family was from. They might have been opposites over there, the green and the blue, but Natalie was good for him and that was all that ever mattered with anything. There weren't many opportunities for him in construction the way there'd been in America, and he needed to provide for his family. A surname could help you in one place but not in another, and it didn't take a Rhodes Scholar to work that one out.

I remembered when he'd called me up.

'Do you think I should do it?' Iain said, after outlining his idea. 'How do you think Dad would feel?'

I paused for a few seconds. I probably laughed a bit too.

'Absolutely. Go for it. Try it,' I replied. 'You need to. As for Dad . . . you want the honest truth?'

'Yes . . .'

'Secretly he'd be delighted. You know what he's like. He always said you have to fight them all from within. Just don't mention . . .'

'I won't . . .'

We were a long way from childhood now. Iain, like my other two brothers, had grown up into a very decent man. He was still the only one to sing at parties and could tell jokes better than most. He was good with people. He was gregarious. He fitted in. It all meant it could have been only Iain out of all of us who did what he did next. In 2005 Iain became an officer in the Police Service of Northern Ireland, the successor to the Royal Ulster Constabulary, who'd once simply been known to men like my father as the dreaded RUC. To my father, they were the most potent symbol of British rule. He knew some people who'd been badly affected. But that was then. The past was the past.

'Remember the times in the bars in New York,' I said to Iain, 'and that time in Central Park and the homeless guys you shared your beer with, and when the cops pulled you over and . . . well, maybe we'd better not.'

A few months after Iain's passing-out parade, he visited my father in Bishopbriggs and he brought his green uniform with him and went upstairs to put it on. He looked incredible and my father cried and laughed at the sight of him because he looked the spit of my grandfather, standing tall and square.

'Keeping the Queen's peace now, Dad, eh?'

Although my father couldn't talk we knew that he was so proud. He smiled the biggest smile. As wide as the River Clyde. He could see his father standing in front of him, in uniform once again. He kept smiling. The years had passed quickly. Our admiration never did.

The house was filled with bustle now. My father's wheelchair was in the hallway, his hoist in the bedroom. My mother had given him breakfast and then cleared the plates away. The carers started their daily task of washing and dressing him and helping him into his wheelchair. The routine was often gruelling. To be lifted daily from his bed and then dispatched to the living room for the day and then returned from there at night just to be put back in pyjamas was not the life he wanted. But it was the life he had.

Today was different and he knew it.

He was looking forward to the match, and to the taxi journey through Springburn and into town and along London Road. It had been thirty years since he'd taken us along that road in the van and sometimes it seemed as far away as the silver moon but it didn't seem that way now. Sometimes, when he was feeling well, he tried to have a conversation with the carers. They laughed along with him. They knew him now and all his sounds more than most. They understood his ways. Even the new ones could tell there was something about my father. There was just *something* about him. Always. They knew it was hard to go through what he did but he just soaked it up and any bitterness that was there disappeared like the Friday-night cakes of our youth.

A stroke? You'll need to do a lot better than that, lads . . .

We'd all hoped that one day they'd turn up at the house and my mother would say that she didn't need them now, that John was fine and that he was walking and talking by himself. They'd have liked that, they said. They'd have liked *not* visiting the house, because it would have meant he was better. But they knew it would never happen. We knew it would never happen. He'd only get worse. He was older now, his body a kind of death mask. They'd keep needing to come back.

They liked my father's silent company. His non-talking. They knew his moods by heart now, like we all did. They were part of his life, whether they wanted to be or not.

But they only knew *part* of him. How could they know anything else? It wasn't their fault that they didn't know he spent every day talking to my mother. Actually talking to her, his wife, Cathie, from morning till night. And that was why he was so damn tired all the time.

The carers went into his bedroom every morning for over a decade. They lifted and moved him and they talked ten to the dozen and they chirped away to keep the silence at bay as my father woke up from his sleep. He looked up and saw them and smiled. He could remember them all, even the new ones. He could distinguish between them. He gave them his smiles but he kept other things to himself.

They didn't know that he'd been talking to me about a book I was writing. They didn't think it was possible. But it was. We spoke every day for nearly twelve years. They couldn't know because they first would have had to believe that it was possible. They had to have a little faith that we could talk. That was all they needed. Then they'd understand that it was possible.

They didn't know that my father talked to my sisters every single day. About the small things in their lives, and some of the bigger things too. They didn't think that was possible either. They didn't know that he spoke to my brothers. He sat with Mark in the Bronx and Harlem and White Plains, and even in Grand Central Station, and Mark showed him the brickwork and the tiles and my father said he'd done a fine job. My father looked with Vincent at the pipeline in Kuwait, and the project in Azerbaijan, and said that was a fine job too.

Even the doctors didn't know. They didn't know it because they didn't *ask*. And if they had they'd have been amazed.

They didn't know that he looked outside every day and thought how beautiful the sun was when it shone through his window at eleven o'clock in the morning. And how the birds always sat at the same spot on the tree in the driveway and watched him through the window, and how the sounds of children in the street carried over the rooftops and the sounds were the same as the ones he'd heard when we were children too. He thought about them all the time.

They couldn't see that he travelled the world from his chair and that sometimes he visited his father in France when the weather was warm and golden in August and they sat and talked in the turret of a tank, just talked, and he shared an apple with my grandfather from the nearby orchard where he died and my grandfather said, thank you, son. And my father said, why? And he replied, for looking after my wife.

And they couldn't see that my father shook his father's hand and said, you're welcome, Dad.

They were all in the war together.

It wasn't anyone's fault. They just didn't *get* it. They'd forgotten to listen. They didn't know that the first game with my father wasn't a Celtic match. How could they? They couldn't know because it took me a while to understand it too. But I'd watched my father dying and watched him recovering and watched him trying to walk out of the hospital. And I saw my mother sleeping with his jumper, and I saw my father naked, and he'd been sitting in a *chair* for almost twelve years, unmoving and unspeaking, and I knew that when he was lost in his world and almost dead in mine, then that football match – *their* football match – just wasn't nearly as important as his.

My father's life was just a pair of Sunday shoes. That was all he'd ever needed. It was all he ever wanted.

They didn't know any of these things. And he laughed about it. It tickled him that they never knew. It meant he was still alive. And that we were too. He pulled me up by invisible wires. He pulled us all up. His wife and nine children. Even a man who couldn't talk had secrets.

If they'd asked him he would have told them the truth. Not the facts. Just the truth.

The carers put my father in the hoist, and brought him into the living room. He looked well but older too and his body hung on him now like an ancient, unwanted overcoat. It was time for a wee drink before the match. He deserved it, everyone said, and no one had any reason to disagree.

Mark, my brother-in-law, arrived with a few beers. He was going to the match with us along with my daughter, Mahoney, who was wearing my old Celtic scarf, the one I'd had from childhood and taken to Seville. It was a totem. I always wanted to believe that it kept him alive. As long as I had that scarf he'd be safe. It was ridiculous, of course. The scarf was made of wool. And I had lost it a hundred times. It did nothing for my father's survival. Still, that's what faith was. Believing in something so utterly preposterous that it must be true.

My mother wrapped him up against the cold. He took a sip of beer.

Mahoney was eager to go to the match. Amazing how things changed. My daughter liked football more than my sons. Gabriel boxed up at Robroyston, amongst the quarry boys, and was sharp and quick. He was rarely seen in a Celtic jersey. He wanted to make films. Aidan-Joe took after his mother's line. Her father was a gypsy and had driven horses to Morecambe and fought in the booths and had once, he said, caught a whale. At the very least he'd stood in the monstrous mouth of the thing . . .

There were always things that fathers told you and you gave them a squinty look but why spoil life with facts when some tales were better? Aidan-Joe inherited his mother's looks and sense of drama. He preferred the stage to the pitch. He wanted to be an actor. He couldn't tell a football from a peashooter. That's the way I liked it. All things get broken. All things should. It was how they were fixed that counted.

My father tapped his feet in the wheelchair along to the Irish music in the background as my mother strapped him in. She kissed his cheek for the umpteenth time. Love endured. Love was a totem too.

It had been a while since I'd really listened to the music we'd both listened to for years. In truth, I loved the songs and I always would. They touched a part of me deeply. But they were never truly mine. Ireland had left me in the no-man's-land of his past. I certainly had never felt British, whatever that was supposed to feel like, or even truly Scottish, but I didn't feel Irish either. And neither did I want to. I remained somewhere outside of all of it. Like a boat, perhaps, on the peaked sea heading to Barra. Navigating between Kerrera, the Sound of Mull and the Ardnamurchan Peninsula, between island and mainland. Part of something, but separate too. Maybe we all were.

My mother steadied my father's half-glass of beer.

'You didn't have a clue about offside, Dad. Did you?'

He smiled and shook his head and reached his hand out and it trembled softly. I got up from the sofa and clasped his fingers.

'Mmnnn dddhhh.'

'It's fine, Dad. It's fine. There's nothing to worry about. *Nothing.*' He nodded. 'Look. We're all still here. All of us.'

We all kept returning and we always would.

'Thirty years, Dad,' said Iain. 'Incredible.'

'Ggdddd nnnaa.'

I hadn't seen George for some years now though I knew he still lived beween Bishopbriggs and Gweedore. He'd have been getting older too, like my father, and moving in an unseen and unspoken direction. The denouement of this story was supposed to resolve all of this.

But it couldn't. It was not a fairy tale. George could have gone to the match if I'd asked him but I didn't. I wanted my daughter there instead. I wanted a new chapter to begin. The past was all just tired threads and strands, fluttering like a torn flag in the rain. Too much past could kill you. The memories. They were just there. Some of them we were sure about, and others less so. And that's what made them real. Life was arbitrary and much of what we remembered in it was mostly untrue. Because that's what our lives were. Mostly made up. A sense of what it should be. And what we wanted it to be.

The taxi pulled out of the street.

I still lived in Bishopbriggs, and they still called it Spam Valley. I still shopped in Morrisons and drank in the Crow and bought ice cream from the café. I still found it hard to go into Quins without seeing the ghost of my father's tall shadow against the window. I rarely went in now at all. The village hadn't changed much. There was a middle-class ordinariness about it. It was safe. But ordinary life and ordinary families could be interesting too.

The taxi drove past my street. I could see that the light was on in my house. Kathleen would be with the boys and the dogs. We drove slowly through Springburn and my father, with a wavering finger, pointed to the site where the old Public Halls had been torn down earlier in the year. All those years ago he used to photograph them and now they were gone. The photographs were somewhere in the loft. He could see the Union Jack fluttering over the Orange Hall in Springburn, as it had done for years, but he only gave it a cursory glance.

It struck me that he no longer really cared for these things. And that might have been good or bad. It was hard to tell now that he'd grown so much older. Regardless, we all hid the fear of him dying. It was inevitable, but inevitability never made things easier. It just made things a little clearer. There really were times when I truly believed it would have been easier on him if he'd died earlier, to save him from the hardship and the indignity of being old and unable to walk or talk. But as I watched him in the taxi, wrapped up like an old man against the cold and the rain, I wanted him to stay alive for ever.

Maybe the match would keep him alive. Maybe not. Maybe that was just me dreaming.

It was just a football match, after all, wasn't it? A team with players I sometimes knew the names of and at other times forgot. They were mostly good, rarely incredible, but they brought together a lot of the things that my father had spoken to me about. They weren't always perfect. But they were our team. They allowed us all to meet somewhere in the middle.

Remember when I went to Liverpool, Dad?

Decades had passed since the 1980–81 season. Westpark Boys' Club travelled to Merseyside for a tournament against some English teams. I knew that he had very little money. The more I sat on the loft stairs listening to him and my mother, the more I understood.

But he gave me a fiver. He couldn't stretch to ten. Five one-pound notes for the trip. They'd been scrunched up in his pocket and he flattened them out and gave me them. A postcard too, please, he said. It's just for a few days, Dad. I would try.

During the trip we were given a tour of the Anfield ground, then home to the greatest footballer in Europe: Kenny. Derek, one of the boys in the group, found some tickets that had been lost in the stadium. They belonged to David Fairclough, at the time a regular on the Liverpool bench. Derek handed the tickets in and was later introduced to Fairclough, and while that was taking place the rest of our team spotted Kenny.

'There he is, there's Kenny!'

He chatted to us briefly, asking what we were down for. He seemed to enjoy hearing familiar accents from home. We were talking to *Kenny*. There he was, dressed as we'd never seen him before. In the clothing of mortals. We like to think he tousled our hair and offered some sage advice before telling us we'd be playing alongside him sometime soon. And then we left him to prepare for Saturday's game, while we all dreamed about scoring a goal like Kenny. Regardless of what happened, thinking of him always allowed us to pull on a jersey and be a kid again. That's what football did. You didn't need to *make* it as a footballer. But it let you dream.

No matter how many times I thought of him he *always* wore a Celtic jersey. Even now, when I closed my eyes. And he always would.

My father had found five pounds to allow me to look through the crystal prism of football. I didn't need to *go* to matches with him. I just held the crystal to the light and watched as it turned, slowly and quietly, more perfect and intricate. I went to the matches *every* day. I played in his garden *every single day*.

Kenny and my father both remained part of a deep and abiding sense of time and place. They were childhood longings and the growing pains and the skinned knees and the football that existed in our past. They were the football dream in all of us. My father's brain told me that. He *showed* me that. Small things were simply worth remembering. About memory and about childhood. And about time, and place.

Whatever else there hadn't been in our football life there'd always been, always would be, Kenny. There'd always be my father. There'd always be Celtic. Kenny was always more Glasgow than Celtic, but still more Celtic than *he* ever imagined. My father was always more Ireland than Celtic, but more Celtic than he ever imagined too.

The taxi drew us nearer and nearer.

He was smiling now, at the lights and the streets and the fans walking with their scarves and the vans selling chips and pies and hot dogs. Mahoney fixed his scarf for him. He was still handsome and always would be. Handsome is as handsome does. It made sense now. Cars were trying to find places to park. Fans walked in twos and threes and fours. It was good to be around them again with my father. Memories flashed back in a torrent. It felt good. We pulled over and got out at Kerrydale Street in the bright daylight. It was different from before, when we'd watched the Sporting match in the evening dark. But that was then. The past again. You shouldn't just dig it up like a hidden treasure and hope that it looked exactly as you'd left it. It wouldn't. It couldn't.

The area around Celtic Park had changed. It took him a while to take it all in. He stared at the velodrome that had been built beside the stadium in time for the Commonwealth Games. The building was shiny and new and he pointed it out. It looked like a spaceship had landed quietly and stayed, and changed the area beyond recognition. His face recoiled in wonder more than anything. I think he saw the death of something. Change was necessary. Though he believed it left a scar on the heart.

The man at the entrance to the disabled access area opened the large, vaulted gate. We pushed my father through the entrance and then stopped to take some photographs. Here he was, smiling in his wheelchair, wrapped up against the cold. We took turns having our photograph taken and he smiled in each of them and looked amazed when he heard the noise inside the ground.

All those years ago, standing on the terraces of Celtic Park, I had no idea at the time that it might be the only football match we'd ever attend together. Back then it felt like a miracle. The only thing that mattered to me was football. The only thing that really mattered to me was Celtic. I could recite all the players as if recalling the ten-times table. I could barely remember them now. They'd faded, once more, like a song.

He always said it was never about how often you went to watch football, it was about what you brought when you did.

The singing grew louder and louder. 'The Fields of Athenry' was sung with gusto and we joined in with the rest of the crowd. I could feel myself getting a little emotional and tried to bury it in my throat. It wasn't the song. It was my father sitting in his chair, with a hood covering his head against the rain. He was freezing. He tried to fix the hood but his hands didn't work as fast as the rain did. He wouldn't let me fix it. He got soaked.

Yet, even in his chair, he still had poise.

The players were on the pitch, running and jumping and stretching. He wasn't looking at them. He was looking at the fans and the sky and he was listening to the shouts and the sounds as they drifted out of the stadium.

The Dundee United fans, over to our left, sang their songs. But the few hundred fans that they had didn't make much of a dent in the noise coming from the Celtic fans. There were pockets of empty stadium but the seats were filled with cheering. They always would be. That would never change.

I kneeled down beside him.

I still wasn't sure if I should say anything.

The details were sketchy. When it came to war they always were. Who really knew? The man at the Scots Guards Association said he was sure. That he'd checked. I'd talked to him recently on the phone and we'd met once more. He'd checked and it made sense. He'd go over it again. It wasn't a long story, he said. And there was nothing that could redeem it really. But it had happened. That was war.

The Battalion assembled. They readied each other for what would come next. They fixed their weapons and welded metal plates to the tanks to protect them against the Panzers. They probably drank cider and wine. Perhaps they had their first taste of Camembert. The men would have joked about it. They'd have spoken some words in French, trying to copy the locals.

The ridges of Caumont lay ahead.

The men slept little during the two days of battle between the 28th and the evening of 30 July. They ran into mortar shells and machine-gun fire and progress was impossible. They moved from hedge to hedge. S Squadron moved forward. The Panzers appeared with their 88mm guns. They left in their wake the blazing hulks of Churchills. Twenty-one men were killed and eighteen were wounded. S Squadron had suffered terrible losses on the ridge.

The man had already told me that my grandfather had survived the onslaught that befell the Churchills. He'd avoided the minefield diversions and sniper fire. The Battalion was allowed to rest following the battle. They would *rest*. They'd take it easy, perhaps for a few brief hours. Then the man paused. I'd heard the term before. It hit me like a storm.

Blue on blue.

A shell from one of our own, he said, killed my grandfather. That was his information. A shell from one of my grandfather's own side. Three guardsmen died from that shell. My grandfather, he thought, was the eldest. It was a mistake, of course. It was war. He died of his wounds. Not long after he'd been shelled. I remembered his Soldier's Service and Pay Book. *Died of Wounds*. The Guards sent my father their best wishes for his father's sacrifice. I thanked them for everything too.

It was summer. The weather was fine. Michael had acclimatized to the stench of war.

There were cider orchards and farmhouses. The rest would have been welcome. Along with his mates he'd have stopped for a drink and food and a smoke and maybe even a wash in the mobile shower unit. There'd have been some laughter too before getting back into the tank and before starting another round of killing and dying. The apples would have masked the stench. They would have smelled incredible. He might even have drunk some local Calvados during the lull. I hoped that he had.

They rested.

Six days you shall labour, but on the seventh day you shall rest.

I hoped that before the shell landed he was looking into a blue sky over France, drinking brandy, and thinking of Jane and his sons. I hoped that he'd thought of my father because I knew that his son always thought of him.

And then there was the sound of the shell.

The match still hadn't kicked off.

The players were warming up, stravaiging around the pitch. The fans were in full voice. The two sides stood opposite each other.

Shouting and screaming. The rain was soaking us through. It didn't matter at all. Mahoney smiled in the rain. The waters flowed past us. I loved that she was there with her grandfather. Mark brought over teas, pies and some chips. I stood with my father. He rubbed his skull and felt the missing bone again. His eyes were wet from the rain. Mahoney held his hand for a minute or two.

The truth was, I'd always suspected that he knew something of his father's fate. I couldn't say for sure but it made sense. At least to me. He knew that Michael was dead. That was a fact. But the truth was something different. It *felt* different.

He looked right at me.

I couldn't tell him. I wanted to, but I just couldn't. It was impossible.

So I told him a lie instead.

I told him that the man from the Scots Guards had been on again. He said that he'd looked into my grandfather's death and had some good news for us amid all the sadness. He said it was written down somewhere, in a book or a diary, a place where they kept notes of things like valour and honour. He said that Michael had died heroically. He'd died saving the lives of others, the men alongside him in the tank.

It was partly true, of course. His tank had crashed over a hill, he said, and they advanced through the minefields. They avoided the snipers in the trees and high up in the barns. They fought as well as they could, he said. But there was just too many around him. There were mines and snipers and grenades and enemy tanks. The odds were always against him anyway. There was nothing they could do. Sometimes a man was just outnumbered. That was life. None of them could do anything. They tried but it was fate.

They found him later, with his cigarette case and his gold ring and his Rules of Communion and his prayer case. And he was holding a photograph of his sons.

I whispered it in his ear.

He nodded.

He held my hand. Squeezed it hard.

The match kicked off.

The players started attacking. The ball moved from left to right. From the back of the stadium stands to the trenches the fans chanted and screamed. Shoot, they shouted. *Shoot*.

There was less urgency than ever before. Celtic were ahead in the League. But it all felt so different now. Premiership football in Scotland was a new landscape without Rangers. Perhaps it was one filled with new possibilities. Who knew? Who really knew? There hadn't been a Celtic and Rangers match since Sunday, 29 April 2012, when Celtic's 3–0 defeat of their ancient rivals was comprehensive.

There was mischief in there as well.

The death knell sounded on Rangers' spectacular demise, and it echoed around Celtic Park, via the Tannoy system.

'When Will I See You Again', by The Three Degrees.

Not everything could be true. And maybe it never was.

A boy stood in front of a house wanting his father to lift him up, higher and higher and higher, and his father held the house like Atlas holding the celestial sphere. It might have happened. It might not. It might have been winter. I'm sure it was. And it would be winter again, at some point. But it felt real. And, therefore, it was true for me.

My grandfather died. A shell from his own side killed him. He had made it past the worst part of the fighting, past all the death in the blazing hulks of Churchills, and he might have made it home to see his wife and his sons. It didn't really matter how he died, I suppose, by accident or with what's sometimes known as valour. He was still dead. And even though my father was just an infant when it all happened a little part of him died too. So he invented his father. And he invented some of his father's people too.

We all did. We all *do*.

When I was in the woods with my father and my brothers and the blackbird died I told my father later that night that it was me who'd done the shooting. But I lied then too. It was my father who'd shot the blackbird. I'd watched him take aim. And I'd watched the blackbird fall. And I'd watched his face when it did. He just wanted to know what it *felt* like.

We all did.

My father spent most of his life searching for his father who'd died in the war. Years after he'd had his stroke I began to believe with all my heart that it had to happen, and that his illness released him from his search. He realized then, as he sat in his chair staring out of the windows at the birds and trees, and listening to the sounds in the street, that all he ever really wanted was to live. No matter how hard it would be. He just wanted to *live*. And that the past didn't matter so much any more. And that Ireland didn't matter so much either. It was just a place. His real story was here, at home, with my mother. At home with his children.

The stroke saved my father.

It saved all of us.

I know, of course, that my father will die. No matter how hard I try there is nothing that can be done to save him. Nothing. It is an utterly devastating truth. I can do *nothing* to save his life. He could do nothing to save his father's too.

Perhaps these memories may soften that inevitable blow.

Whatever happens now I will always remember his beautiful, chaotic loft and the snow outside our house and the garden and the quarry boys and his rifle and the van with the paraffin heater and my brothers and sisters, all of them.

I will remember Celtic and the tapes he sent to me in America and I will always know the reason why he did. I will remember the food that was supposed to go to the priests and the trip to his father's graveyard in France and all his saints and a few of his sins as well. I will remember the boat he promised to build. And now, as I sit with him, I know it is finished. I will always remember his towering strength, as strong as Kisimul Castle, that held him through more than a decade of silence and I will always remember my mother sleeping with his jumper and a look that just spoke of love. *Only* of love.

I will remember the remembering too.

But most of all, when his music is finished and his songs have finally been sung, more than anything, much more than anything, I will always remember the first game with my father.

My father, my father.

Acknowledgements

This book could not have happened without my father, my mother and my three brothers and five sisters. I am lucky to have them and I hope that they will be happy with the end result.

I'm also so grateful to my beautiful wife, Kathleen, for her support over the years (Katie . . . it's never too late. *Just do it*.) This book is also for my amazing children, Mahoney, Gabriel and Aidan. The past year was hard and your support has been magical. Thanks for loaning me your time. Mahoney, I love your sense of humour. Keep it. Gabriel, I love your decency. Nurture it. Aidan, my beautiful wee boy, I love that you believe everything will come true . . . It will. Dream it.

To all my nieces and nephews, thanks for being kind to Granda. This book is so that you will all get to know him a lot more than you do now.

Big thanks to Mark *the Vegas Years* Healy and Marc *the Milton Mob* Hamill, my brothers-in-law, for the regular beer, wine and the fish. Big thanks also to Martin *the Coogster* Coogan, my other brother-in-law, for Room 414, in Al Ain. And the Speakeasy . . .

I have to mention my uncles and aunts for their visits and prayers for my father, especially in the early days. Donnie and Gerard – capturing back Mingulay is one of our priorities.

There have been so many carers and members of the medical profession and hospital staff who have had a hand in my father being here today, and you have my apologies that I cannot name you individually. Perhaps collectively as the NHS might work. Thank you so much for giving us our father for the past twelve years.

A major thank you to Mark *Stan* Stanton, my literary agent (Jenny Brown Associates) who saw the real potential in my father's story and made sure it was published. Thanks to my editor, Giles Elliot, at Transworld Publishers who picked up on all the important details at the end. Thanks to Elisabeth Merriman for her meticulous copy-editing and Vivien Thompson, who manages the editorial production side. Thanks also to our delightful publicist Alison Barrow and everyone else at Transworld Publishers who helped bring it together.

A few random thanks too:

James, who died, but was on hand with biscuits for my father. Elaine Livingstone and Gordon Darroch for when things were tough with you know who … See you in the brilliant Chinaski's. Cheers to Fergus, and his staff there, who have been damn fine people over the past few years.

My grandfather, and the men who died with him in the Scots Guards. I hope you all ate well and drank well before you were gone. The Scots Guards Association who filled in some important gaps. All the teachers who taught me at Turnbull High School and St Matthew's.

Andy Dodds, for always asking after my father, and telling me I was good. I flattered to deceive. And here's to football, whoever you support. Thanks to the Quins mob and also the lads in the Crow.

John Brash. Friend, creative partner and Rangers fan. Helluva cross to carry. Big thanks for all the support. James Reilly and Janice Green. Thanks for helping out back then . . . Davy McAllister. I've never known Davy to say no to anyone who asked for help.

James, aka Tiger, and Stevie, at Robroyston Amateur Boxing Association where Gabriel and I train, and all the boys there who have dreams of their own. Jean, John and the gypsy mob. Anyone I have known in Bishopbriggs over the past umpteen years.

George, of course, for all the Celtic programmes and the Sporting

Lisbon match. Derek Proudfoot (proof that it *is* possible to know absolutely everything about your team).

To all the quarry boys out there too.

And Brian Savage. Cheers, mate. For everything. Imagine if we could start over? We'd be millionaires instead of dreamers! And we *would* have gone in that taxi . . .

Any mistakes here are all mine. Unless there is a lawyer involved. In that case Brian is happy to take the blame.

I've written a book. I haven't put a hand *inside* a man's head and stopped him from dying. I haven't mined coal, like some of the men in our past. I haven't gone to war and I haven't nursed the sick in hospital. And the last decent goal I scored was almost thirty years ago. But I have tried to make this book the best I could under the circumstances. I tried to find my father. And I tried to find myself too. I hope that you enjoy it.

Finally, again, Mahoney, Gabriel and Aidan. You have no idea how much you mean to me. If this book, somewhere in the future, is no more than a letter from your father you don't even have to read it. Just know that it was written.

'Anything to add, Dad?'

Yes.

'What?'

Eedjits . . .